UNIQUELY HUMAN:
THE BASIS OF HUMAN RIGHTS

UNIQUELY HUMAN:
THE BASIS OF HUMAN RIGHTS

Gabriel Moran

Library of Congress Control Number:		2013914802
ISBN:	Hardcover	978-1-4836-8566-3
	Softcover	978-1-4836-8565-6
	Ebook	978-1-4836-8567-0

This book was printed in the United States of America.

Rev. date: 08/19/2013

CONTENTS

INTRODUCTION: RIGHTS, UNIQUENESS, TRADITION, DIGNITY

This book is an exploration of whether anything deserving of the name *international ethics* exists. For many people who work at international relations, there is no international ethics. They believe that ethics (or morality) applies to individuals but is irrelevant for nation-states. Nations act from their self-interest; any other motive than national interest is claimed to be a cover-up of the simple truth.

International law, in contrast to international ethics, does have standing. When all or nearly all nations accept an agreement about proper behavior in the international arena, another law is added to the body of international law that has existed from the eighteenth century. The question of ethics does not necessarily arise in such discussions. But even when people say that law can be separated from ethics/morality, the question of moral right or wrong continues to hover in the background. When an international incident causes horror and revulsion, the popular response is not to complain about a violation of international law. Instead, people assume that there is some ethical/moral standard that has been violated. Is this assumption naive? Are there any standards of ethics in international affairs?

For raising the question of international ethics, human rights has become the main currency. Government officials everywhere praise human rights. It is a card that is difficult to trump. Despite criticisms of his administration for allowing the torture of prisoners, George W. Bush said in an interview: "No president has done more for human rights than I have."[1] At the conclusion of their 2010 meeting in Libya, the twenty-two Arab League members said that the need is "to support the principles of fraternity, tolerance, and respect for human values that emphasize human rights."[2] Were they aware of what this proposal might entail?

What everyone seems to agree upon might actually be empty rhetoric to avoid doing something about urgent problems. From the earliest uses of *human rights* there has been a danger that the phrase would be used either as a political tool or else as an unrealistic hope that morality could replace politics. Jacques Maritain, who headed a UNESCO survey of philosophers concerning human rights, concluded that "we agree upon the rights but on condition that no one asks us why."[3] That attitude is not adequate today. The need is to deepen and strengthen the idea while also acknowledging its limitations. In the hundreds of books on human rights, it is surprising how little sustained reflection there is on the basis of human rights.

This book is for people who are interested in asking what we are talking about when we refer to *human rights*. If that question is legitimate, then the way to answer it is to trace where the term came from and how it has evolved during its history. The main story line is simple, but there are complications along the way. The argument depends not on scientific proof or legal precedents but on an accumulation of various kinds of evidence about human life and its relation to the nonhuman world. The quest is not for a *definition* of human rights—an overrated idea when any complex term is at issue. The aim is to find language that is consistent with the texture of past meanings of *rights* and makes theoretical and practical sense today.

This introduction has four sections: First is a consideration of the idea and historical background of rights. The second consideration is the specifically human meaning of uniqueness that situates human rights in human history and the natural world. The third section considers the meaning of tradition and a paradoxical claim that there is a *human* tradition. The fourth section examines the meaning of dignity, which can be best grasped in the context of human uniqueness and human tradition.

Rights

Presupposed in a discussion of human rights are assumptions about the term *right*.[4] The most obvious ambiguity of the word *right* is hardly ever mentioned perhaps because it is so obvious. *Right*, meaning that an action is appropriate, correct, or good, is an adjective of long-standing. Eventually the adjective led to the noun *right*, referring to something that a person has. We speak of someone having a right to do something or to possess something. The adjective *right* obviously has not disappeared. This distinction within the meaning of *right* may seem a minor point of language. Actually, it opens the door to understanding the eighteenth-century's strengths and weaknesses when the "natural" rights of man were proclaimed.

The idea of rights is overburdened if it is forced to carry the whole weight of ethics. The category of rights is an invaluable element but only one element in a pattern of ethical language. For example, *responsibility* is a more comprehensive term than *right*; responsibility can include duties or obligations along with rights. Although it has become almost a cliché to say we need rights and responsibilities, that use of *responsibility* is misleading.[5] The correlative to a right is a duty or an obligation. When someone affirms rights and responsibilities, heads nod in agreement, but usually nothing happens. In contrast, responsibility as a listening to what has to be done to secure rights is a challenge that can be placed before persons, communities, and nation-states. Rights can be a central category around which a pattern of ethical language can be developed, but ethics cannot be deduced from or exclusively built upon rights. International ethics cannot be based exclusively on human rights.

There is a tendency today to speak as if human rights are a product of international law. There is a difference between referring to "international law of human rights" and "international human rights law."[6] In the first case, *international law* can be understood as a protector of human rights. In the second case, use of the adjective *international* as a modifier of *human rights* is either redundant or unduly limiting. That is, *international human rights* either redundantly specifies that these rights apply internationally, or else limits these rights to international agreements.

The relation between international law and human rights has always been problematic. The term *international* was coined at the end of the eighteenth century by Jeremy Bentham to specify a law between nations.[7] It is perhaps more than coincidental that Bentham was also the most severe critic of the "natural or imprescriptible" rights, which are claimed in the Declaration of Independence and the French Declaration of the Rights of Man and of the Citizen.[8] International law was not concerned with the rights that were claimed for "man" or "all men."

Until World War II, international law consisted of laws governing the relations between nation-states. The *right* in this context was whatever the treaties between nation-states decided was right. Piracy was outlawed, but colonial exploitation was not. The category of human rights did not fit within the framework of international law. The focus of human rights is the person not the nation-state. Human rights, if they exist, would have to be "trans-national," not international, in origin.

International law, starting with the Convention on the Prevention and Punishment of Genocide in 1949, began a transformation that has not yet been completed. The change in the character of international law did not gain much momentum until the 1980s. One of the most significant signs of change was in 1998 when Augusto Pinochet was held to be responsible for his actions as Chilean dictator from 1973 to 1990.[9] Unfortunately, international law that protects the rights of persons suffered a setback during the U.S. presidency of George W. Bush. The United States has always been a reluctant participant in international treaties. But its disregard of both the Geneva Conventions for the protection of war victims and the 1984 Convention against Torture of prisoners was stunning.[10]

The effort to enforce international laws for the protection of vulnerable populations is admirable. The twenty-first century cannot get along without better international laws. Human rights can inspire the creation of international laws; human rights are not the child of international law. International law can and should protect human rights; international law cannot establish human rights. But if that is true, there is an obvious question about the origin and basis of human rights.

When someone first used the term *human rights*, a reader or listener would surely have had some questions. Why would someone put the adjective *human* before *rights*? Is the intended contrast between the rights of human beings and the rights of nonhuman beings? Logically that makes sense, but historically that is not the way it happened. Until the term *animal rights* was coined a few decades ago, *human* before *rights* might have seemed redundant. If the aim is not to contrast human and nonhuman rights, what is the point?

Jeremy Bentham rejected the idea "that there are such things as rights anterior to the establishment of governments: for natural, as applied to rights, if it means anything, it means to stand in opposition to *legal*."[11] It is true that there are no rights chronologically prior to governments; but such rights need not be in opposition to the legal. The idea of *human* rights (a term that did not exist in the eighteenth century) is compatible with and needs the support of legal rights.

Logically, the term *human rights* could include any right that a human being has. Or *human rights* could mean only those rights that pertain to every human being. This ambiguity has been a reason for the rhetorical attractiveness of human rights. Unfortunately, what makes *human rights* an attractive term for rhetorical purposes threatens its effectiveness. In this book, I argue that it is important that human rights are those rights that both extend to *all* human beings and refer *only* to those rights that apply to all human beings.

The evolution of language is not entirely logical. A different way of referring to these rights might have evolved. For example, one could refer to *basic moral rights* for addressing this question. However, that phrase would still be ambiguous. It would leave unclear the universality of the rights that is intended by the term human rights.[12]

For many years, I have been teaching a course on human rights. At least that is the way the director of the international education program referred to the course. I preferred to call it the course on international ethics. I have never felt comfortable with *human rights* as the name of the course. While the advocacy of human rights or the preaching of human rights made sense to me, an academic course did not. So as to avoid becoming a preacher in the classroom, my strategy was to approach the course mainly as history. But even the history of human rights left me with the feeling that there were some big unanswered questions about the nature and the existence of human rights.

A book by Samuel Moyn, *The Last Utopia: Human Rights in History*,[13] helped me to identify my problem with human rights. It suggested to me a path to follow that is not the same as the author's. Moyn's provocative thesis is that a human rights movement did not begin until 1977, the first year of Jimmy Carter's presidency.[14] There had been scattered uses of the term *human rights* early in the twentieth century, and the idea was promulgated by the United Nations in 1948. The term *human rights* began to gain momentum in the late 1950s, but it was not until the 1970s that *human rights* became commonly used by readers of the daily newspaper as well as by lawyers, politicians, and international aid workers.[15]

Many histories of human rights go back two centuries, some two millennia, in tracing the idea of human rights.[16] Scholars often dismiss the importance of when a term was first used and when it came into common use. While some authors acknowledge that Stoic philosophy, the Magna Carta, or the Declaration of Independence did not use the term *human rights*, they assume that human rights was the idea that was meant. If one pays attention to language, which is the focus of this book, then there is no history of human rights before the second half of the twentieth century. There is a history of natural rights that goes back at least several centuries; and the history of natural rights may make a contribution to the understanding of human rights. However, simply to equate natural rights and human rights blocks the path to an understanding of the distinctive character of human rights.

In 1948 the United Nations published a document called the Universal Declaration of Human Rights. Although it is now revered as a monumental achievement, it did not attract much attention at the time of its adoption.[17] Its potential effect was quickly overwhelmed by the conflict and propaganda of the Cold War. One problem with the document is its title in which the term *universal* seems to be misplaced. The Declaration itself clearly was not universal; it received a stamp of approval by forty-eight nation-states (eight others abstained).

When the proposed document was first being discussed, it was called An International Bill of Rights. That was an unrealistic hope, and *declaration* was substituted for a legally binding bill. A further change was made just before the declaration's approval. *Universal* was substituted for *international* on the supposition that *universal* would strengthen its claims. The logical change would have been to make *universal* a modifier of *human rights* although that wording could be construed as redundant. Unfortunately, the document's focus was on a long list of supposed rights, an approach that undercut a realistic claim that some few rights are indispensable for every human being, that is, they are universal. An accurate and realistic name for the document might have been An International Declaration of Human Rights.

The term *rights* has been in common use since the seventeenth century. But even in 1971 when John Rawls published his major study of rights, *A Theory of Justice,* he had nothing to say about human rights.[18] The same is true of Ronald Dworkin in *Taking Rights Seriously*, published in 1976.[19] Moyn's explanation for why human rights emerged in the late 1970s is that it was a response to the failed political utopias of the 1960s. In this context, he calls the movement for human rights the "last utopia," a moral substitute for the failed political utopias. According to Moyn, human rights has acquired a political program that is at odds with its original meaning. If he is correct, human rights would be the last utopia in the sense of most recent, but not the last in the sense of final because it is destined to be replaced by another utopian idea.

A different way to view the 1960s and 1970s is as the time of a worldwide collapse of authority.[20] Human rights in this view would be a fragile attempt to rebuild political and moral authority on a basis different from the past. In the 1960s, it was as if a secret was let out that nobody is in charge. Individual institutions found it difficult to sustain the criticism that was launched against them. In the United States, the presidencies of Lyndon Johnson and Richard Nixon undermined the authority of the national government; the effects have lingered on. The Roman Catholic Church, one of the world's oldest and seemingly most stable institutions, revealed to its members in the debates at the Second Vatican Council that church authority is fallible and political.

University students from Tokyo to Paris to New York led the way in challenging every claim to authority. The attitude was captured in a scene from Jean-Luc Godard's film *Weekend*. A professor and a student are talking. The student says, "First, we must burn down the Sorbonne." The professor asks, "What then?" The student replies, "I don't know, but first we must burn down the Sorbonne." It seems safe to say that the student did not have a realistic plan for rebuilding a worldwide sense of authority. For that to happen, human beings would have to agree that some activities are unacceptable in every society, nation, and culture.

Human rights is the idea that there are three or four or some small number of legitimate claims that every member of the human community can make upon the rest. In relation to the nation-state, the claim is sometimes for the nation-state to help a person exercise the rights. At other times, the claim is a protest against a nation-state to stop violating those rights. In this latter case, the hope is that if a nation-state is, for example, torturing or starving its people, exposure of that fact will bring pressure from the rest of the world to change such practices. There is no guarantee that such an approach will work. But human rights has become an international way of appealing to feelings of shame, decency, or empathy that characterize human beings.

Authors often defend the universality of human rights by taking a minimalist approach. That phrase is often understood, especially in the United States, to mean securing "political" rights while leaving "economic" rights until later. The division of human rights into political rights as opposed to economic rights was embodied in two United Nations covenants in 1966. The division had arisen during the creation of the Universal Declaration of Human Rights. The language was a response to the standoff between the United States and the Soviet Union. The UN Committee saw the question as whether to add welfare rights to liberty rights.[21] This disastrous dichotomy has outlasted the Soviet Union.

An example of a fruitful minimalist approach to human rights is Henry Shue's *Basic Rights*.[22] He describes basic rights—physical security for one's person, the means of subsistence, and liberty of participation and movement—as justified demands upon the human community for those rights that are an intrinsic element of all other rights.[23] These rights cannot be classified as either political or economic; instead, each of them includes a political and an economic element.[24]

The basic duty of the human community in its various embodiments is to care for each human individual in the relations that constitute his or her life.[25] The idea of human rights is especially tested at the beginning and at the end of life when it is apparent that each human being depends upon the kindness, assistance, and skill of others.

While human rights belong to an individual person, the correlative duty may belong to an institution, including the government of a nation-state. Shue distinguishes three kinds of duties in relation to basic rights: not to deprive, to protect, and to aid in the recovery of rights.[26] The first applies to all persons. Every individual person has a duty not to deprive another person of his or her human rights. The second and third kinds of duties usually require institutional activities.

Beyond the duty of not depriving citizens of their human rights, governments have a duty to work with nongovernmental organizations to protect human rights and to aid in realizing their exercise. The duty is not always best served by a direct grant. For example, if people are starving, the immediate duty is to supply food, but the further duty may be to institute changes to the conditions that are causing starvation. Obviously, that can be a complicated problem, and many people share in the duty to improve the system.[27]

Human rights, if they are to be effective, have to be seen as the moral grounding of politics, not as an alternative to politics.[28] Human rights are not a matter of choosing "values over interests," as some authors put it.[29] Human rights have to be part of the discussion of what constitutes the genuine interests of persons, communities, and nations. That is why the political cannot be separated from the economic, cultural, and social as if politics were an isolated area with its own rules. That is also why ethics or morality cannot be thought of as rules that can be imposed on individual behavior but which are irrelevant for the way a nation-state behaves. The ethical/moral question is what human activities serve the good of persons, communities, and nations. Human rights, while few in number, have to be the support of the political, economic, cultural, and social life of the human community.

Human Uniqueness

One of the keys to understanding a human claim to rights is the uniqueness of human beings. If one understands the meaning of *uniquely human*, then terms such as *life*, *liberty*, and *equality* represent rightly cherished ideals. If in contrast, one misunderstands human uniqueness, then life, liberty, and equality are dangerous claims and can have destructive effects within the human race and for all living beings.

The term *unique*, like many words in the English language, has two nearly opposite meanings. Endless arguments occur between people when they are using nearly opposite meanings of the same word.[30] Such words usually have a root meaning that has split into two directions. The root meaning of *unique* is to be different from all others. It is sometimes pointed out that a thing cannot truly be unique because it at least shares the note of being the same kind of thing with other things in its class or at least that it shares thingness with things generally.[31] That fact does not stop people from using the word *unique* and sensing that it points to a special quality or set of qualities.

It is also said that a thing's claim to be unique means that it cannot be compared to anything else, but in fact the use of *unique* is *always* comparative. Grammar teachers have insisted that an adjective, such as *very*, or *more*, cannot be put in front of *unique*, but people almost always do just that. When people say that something is "very unique," they sense that while nothing may be (completely) unique, nevertheless it makes sense to say that something is (very nearly) unique. "Something that is very unique" means that it approaches being different from all others.

Difference from all others can be imagined as going in two opposite directions: the process can be one of increasing exclusiveness or one of increasing inclusiveness. Note that the two meanings cannot simply be described as exclusiveness and inclusiveness because in both cases there is movement toward an imagined conclusion that is never reached. In one process, a very unique thing can be seen to share fewer and fewer notes that are in common with other things. An atom is more unique than a molecule, that is, it is very unique or more nearly unique, but if there are subatomic particles, an atom is not the most unique thing. In the sequence *abcdef, abcde, abcd, abc,* the fourth element is (the most nearly) unique because it is different from all others by an increasing exclusiveness. It is not entirely unique because one can imagine another element, say, *ab*.

In the opposite direction, uniqueness can increase as a being is open to others by its nature and by its activities. We recognize this openness in the world of the living and most especially in humans. A being is more unique to the degree of its difference by inclusiveness. In the sequence *A, AB, ABC, ABCD,* the fourth element is (the most nearly) unique by a movement of inclusiveness; it is unlike any other element because it is like each of them. It is more unique or very unique, but because one can imagine *ABCDE*, it is not fully unique. No historical reality is unique in this way because history has not finished.

Both meanings of *uniqueness* apply to human beings. They occupy one place on earth and no other; they are born at one moment of history and cannot step back to the past or jump ahead to the future. The individual human being is itself, and not another; it has the uniqueness of every physical entity. Because the human being wishes to differentiate itself from other human beings, it may set out to exclude all similarities to others. The quest to be unlike anybody else is a tragic misunderstanding of the specifically human form of uniqueness. A critic of Western individualism writes that it "has promoted a culture that so celebrates uniqueness that people are driven mad trying to prove themselves unique."[32] The problem is not a celebration of uniqueness but the assumption that human uniqueness is attained by becoming more eccentric rather than by listening and responding to one's community and its history.

The specifically human meaning of *unique* may seem an unusual usage, but people regularly imply it in describing human events and works of art. Time passes at the rate of sixty minutes an hour, but some human events contain greater meaning than other events. An event that is loaded with meaning may be described by a date (July 4, 1776; Sept. 11, 2001), but the very unique meaning of the event is not restricted to a day, a year, or even a century. Historical events can vary in their degree of uniqueness, and the meaning of an event can become more unique over time. It has sometimes been said that a crucial event in history (the Holocaust, or the French Revolution) is a *caesura*, that is, a radical break from the past. But continuity-versus-discontinuity is not the way to understand humans and their history. Radical change happens within the continuity of historical events that are unique to varying degrees.

A work of art is often described as unique. In one sense, each work of art is obviously different by excluding all others. But citing a work as (very) unique is meant to be praise. The work while being very particular to its time and place somehow manages to transcend those limits. Great works of art are (very) unique because they can be appreciated across human divisions such as gender, class, or century. Their uniqueness can increase over time.

The human being is the most nearly unique reality we know of. It is the "workshop of creation," which by its nature and its powers is open to all others. Every human being is born (very) unique with a vocation to become more unique. Does that make human beings superior to all others? In most physical aspects, such as size or speed, the humans are nowhere near number one. In one respect, however, the humans are superior; they are the uniquely responsible animals. They can and they should listen to all the other animals and to the process of life itself. From this responsibility to listen, they can and they must exercise worldwide care for the planet. This responsibility and a consistent language of responsibility form the context for human rights.

The human being has a unique relation to all other beings. A human right to life is dependent on the human relation to other living beings. The uniqueness of human life is a culmination of every living being's uniqueness. A human right to liberty has to be clearly distinguished from the attempt to separate human existence from its participation in the world of animals. *Liberation* is an ideal only when liberation from some specific oppression is identified. Similarly, *equality* is a desirable ideal for certain specified goods. But in some environmental literature of recent decades, the claim is made for an equality of all species. That claim is a call for humans to abandon their responsibility.

Human rights depend upon listening to all humans in their uniqueness, that is, listening not to individuals as abstractions but to humans in their living actuality. The community that encompasses a human being is all human beings, the animal world, and all that is earthly. Human rights have to be uniquely human in recognizing the right to exist of other natural beings. The irony of the eighteenth century's claim of *natural* rights was that they were assertions against the nonhuman natural world in the name of an abstract humanity.

Human Tradition

The argument in this book is that human rights have to be based on human tradition. Only to the extent that a human tradition exists do human rights have a basis in reality. Human rights have in fact come into existence as human tradition has achieved some degree of actuality. Human tradition presupposes the existence of many traditions. The convergence of these traditions is the way in which a human tradition has been formed.

Tradition, like uniqueness, can be seriously misunderstood, resulting in some unfortunate consequences. No other animals rely on tradition although we recognize that (nonhuman) animals transmit a pattern of living across the generations. What distinguishes the humans in their tradition is the rich body of knowledge that they can store from the past, which in turn makes great novelty possible. No innovation can be entirely new, but humans are dazzling in their imaginative possibilities and, alas, in their power to destroy each other as well as other kinds.

The term *tradition* is of religious origin; it was a brilliant invention of the pharisaic reform in ancient Israel. Instead of attacking the priestly control and interpretation of the sacred texts, the Pharisees proposed that there was a second source of authority. In addition to written tablets given to Moses, there were oral truths that Moses received and which have been passed down by word of mouth. The adjective *oral* would have been redundant as a modifier of tradition until such time as the oral source was itself put into writing.[33]

Inherent to the original meaning of *tradition* was room for debate as to whether the writing and the tradition were entirely separate sources, or whether the tradition was the context for the meaning of the texts. A debate about the relation between biblical text and tradition has been present in the Christian religion from its beginning and continues today. Christianity itself has been interpreted either as a rejection of the Jewish tradition out of which it emerged or as a radical reformation of that tradition. The Christian church incorporated the Hebrew texts into its own Bible while recasting the interpretation of their meaning. For interpretive keys to those texts, the church fathers could not get along without a claim to tradition, that is, a context for their New Testament writings.[34]

The image captured in the term *tradition* is a "handing over." In a preliterate culture, the idea of tradition could be said to encompass everything known from the past. The term *tradition*, however, surfaced at that important moment of transition when writing began to assert an authority over the past. In that light, the pharisaic invention of a second source can be seen as a conservative return to an authority before there were texts on which political and religious leaders based their power. The invention of *tradition* was thus a reassertion of a fullness of life that can never be captured in writing.

Plato feared that the spread of literacy would undermine human memory.[35] The fear was justified because writing had such attractive qualities that it quickly took control of the memory of the race. Writing provides for accuracy, permanence, and the wide dissemination of important human matters. Such was the power of writing that tradition itself came to be written down although the whole tradition could never be captured that way.

Although *traditions* could be put in writing and in fact they were, *tradition* retained its power as the context for all writing. Put another way, while *tradition* as a verb is the act of handing on both written and unwritten material from the past, *traditions* is a noun referring to what is produced by and remains from the process of tradition. H. G. Gadamer, who has written extensively on tradition, states the paradox that "tradition exists only as it becomes other than itself."[36] The human race is in a constant process of reinterpreting the past or, rather, reinterpreting as much of the past that is remembered. The various movements described in this book, which have contributed to a human tradition, are rebellions against the limits of particular traditions, but they are not rejections of tradition.

Many people unfortunately have an image of history as a line that situates us at a present point between points that have disappeared called the past and points that are yet to come called the future. We are constantly encouraged to forget the past and to look forward. Tradition is a resistance to that linear image, a reminder that the past is never wholly past and that the future is not here for the taking. Tradition's image is one of human practices that have drawn commentary and then commentary upon the commentary. Tradition piles up the past; any attempt to create a new world finds a stubborn obstacle in tradition. On the other hand, anyone who wishes to engage in a radical transformation of what exists will find tradition to be an indispensable source of content, inspiration, and caution. "The new does not emerge through the rejection or annihilation of the old but through its metamorphosis or reshaping."[37]

The modern temptation to think that time can be mastered by escaping the past and creating the future was mocked in the twentieth-century plays of Samuel Beckett. The character Winnie in *Happy Days* keeps singing of a bright future even as the ground comes up to meet her, covered to her waist in the first act, covered to her neck in the second. The character in *The Unnamable* points out that "time doesn't pass, don't pass from you, why it piles up all about you; instant on instant, on all sides, deeper and deeper, thicker and thicker . . . . It buries you grain by grain . . . buried under the seconds, saying any old thing, your mouth full of sand." In *Endgame*, Clov asks Hamm, "Do you believe in the life to come?" Hamm answers, "Mine was always that . . . Moment upon moment, pattering down, like the millet grains . . . and all life long you wait for that to mount up to a life."[38] If time is imagined as a series of points, the uniquely human has no place on earth.

The traditions that have been generated by tradition are not necessarily good. In fact, many of the particular traditions of the human race are nightmarish. Some developments have enriched a human tradition, but other developments have proved to be, or will prove to be, terrible distortions. Only a wide and deep knowledge of the tradition enables someone to judge whether an item is consistent or inconsistent with the whole tradition. "Everything figures by comparison not with what stands next to it but with the whole."[39]

Traditions regularly have people who are elected or appointed to play the role of watchdog for maintaining the integrity of the tradition. It might seem that a *human* tradition would need a world government for humanity, but if that were even desirable, its possibility is in the distant future. For the present interpreting of human tradition, no individual or group or nation can be wholly trusted for the task. In developing guidelines for a human tradition, innumerable communities and networks of information have to be developed with the help of modern technology.

Passionate debates within a living tradition have never been excluded. A human tradition does not mean that the human race agrees on everything. Alasdair MacIntyre notes that "traditions, when vital, embody continuities of conflict."[40] In that context, premature agreements are one of tradition's dangers. The leader's task is to keep open a running debate. Many conflicts are between people who are superficially conservative and people who are deeply conservative. The person who is holding on to something "traditional" from the nineteenth century may be unaware that it is a distortion of a richer vein in the tradition from centuries previous. Within a "women's movement," there was an intense debate about how to improve women's lives. Within an African American tradition, there continue to be debates that echo the different strategies of Booker T. Washington and W. E. B. Dubois who were striving to attain a similar end.[41]

The term *tradition* usually has at least a shadow of its religious origins, but it has been adopted by many groups for tracing an historical set of beliefs and practices proper to the group. Thus, there is a British tradition, a medical tradition, a liberal tradition, a baseball tradition, a jazz tradition, and innumerable other traditions. If you are in the tradition, you know things that are not written down, and you engage in practices that are shaped by a history whether or not you consciously attend to that history. The way to be educated in a tradition is to practice it and gradually pick up the interpretation of the practices.[42]

From the beginning of the race, there has been an inchoate human tradition, but the richness of what the human includes has never been available. An ancient Chinese thinker, a Roman philosopher, or the author of the Book of Genesis could conceive of "humanity" but could not fill out the variety of beliefs and practices of people everywhere. Eighteenth-century philosophers knew more about human history, but they were still very limited in their knowledge of all peoples in every part of the world.[43] Today we know a lot more, but we must nevertheless remember how limited we still are. If an ancient or early modern thinker could be shown the Internet, the reaction would probably be one of envy at the material so easily available but also doubt that human wisdom is achieved by an avalanche of data that no human being can assimilate. Google cannot give shape to human history and human tradition.

Whether we are morally better than our predecessors is very doubtful. In the most advanced countries, the split between the rich and the poor is obscenely large and has continued to worsen during the last few decades. At some point, there has to be a major overhaul in how the world's goods are distributed. That revolution is needed before the rights that are human can be effectively recognized for all. Perhaps today's uprisings in several regions of the world herald such a change, but there is nothing inevitable about the success of revolutions.

Where progress of a sort has been made is that diverse parts of the human race now have a voice that was previously lacking to them. We do not have a unique human tradition, but it is more nearly unique than in the past. Not everyone gets heard, but there is now an opportunity to oppose the assumption that some human beings are less than human and, therefore, are not to be included in the idea of human rights. Aristotle held the view that some human beings are born to be slaves; that view would not find much support today.[44]

Many human beings are still trapped in inhuman conditions, but responsible members of the human race no longer attribute that fact to their being an inferior specimen of the human. It is now widely accepted that women, gays, and blacks should have all the rights of human beings. In countries where this equality in rights is now affirmed, it is shocking to realize that it was not clear just a few decades ago. And of course, it is still not clear in many places, but at least this issue is bubbling up from under the surface almost everywhere.

It is true that the idealistic hopes of political transformation in the 1960s failed to be realized. However, the decade was more about cultural change than politics conceived of as government actions. Many of those cultural changes have continued and gone further. Modern communication and travel, along with interlocking economic systems, unite the peoples of the world whether or not they are ready for it. Today's context for economic, environmental, and political questions is the unique human race in both its unity and diversity. People are often oblivious of this context, but they regularly get reminders from another part of the world that a single killing or someone's offhand remark or a damaged nuclear reactor can reverberate in their own lives.

The idea of tradition is often assumed to be an obstacle to universality, but it is actually the basis for movement toward universality. Alasdair MacIntyre has written extensively on the need to root moral judgments in a tradition, and he is therefore skeptical of human rights.[45] Chris Brown notes that "if it is the tradition itself that is the justification for a particular practice, the potential for universalist claims goes by the board, or at least is severely damaged."[46] The alternative possibility is one of global communication to find human commonality as embodied in many traditions.

For rights to be effective, they need to be embedded in a tradition that is supportive of the idea of rights. If political rights require a political tradition, it would follow that human rights have to be based on a human tradition. Only in the second half of the twentieth century did a human tradition take practical shape. This human tradition obviously includes politics, but it is not reducible to politics. A human tradition is continuing to develop, but it has been especially enriched in recent times by many political and nonpolitical movements. These movements have not always viewed each other as allies, but they can be seen to converge toward a tradition of supporting human life in all its diversity.

A series of these movements achieved prominence in the second half of the twentieth century. Each of these movements deserves consideration for its contribution to the meaning of *human rights*. A worldwide movement of black liberation has been visible since the 1950s. A gay rights movement that surfaced in the 1960s is an important recognition of the full range of the human. A children's rights movement is a crucial piece of thinking about the meaning of both rights and human. The women's movement that started in the nineteenth century reached a kind of culmination in the 1970s. Many religions in the 1970s broke out of their modern isolation as private affairs and entered the arena of public debate. The environmental movement emerged in the 1970s, and it is the great challenge to the idea of human rights. These movements and others are part of a dramatic shift in communication among the particular traditions and diverse cultures of the world.[47]

Dignity and Human Rights

The term *dignity* is closely associated with the uniquely human claim to rights. In his speech before the United Nations on September 22, 2010, President Barack Obama asserted that "dignity is a human right." That is not the most helpful way to use the word. Dignity can be better thought of as the premise of human rights.[48] As is true of human rights, almost no politician attacks the idea of human dignity. The problem is that *dignity* has a more complicated history and ambiguous meaning than are usually recognized.

Dignity is a word of Latin origin (*dignitas*). In Roman times, it referred to the respect that a gentleman was due from the lower classes. Some people possessed dignity while other people were forced to recognize dignity by accepting the role of inferior.[49] The slow movement toward a more democratic world was signaled by the spread of dignity to a wider population. As R. W. Southern shows, the prevalence of dignity after the twelfth century was an expression of confidence in the nobility of the natural order.[50] Mystics, such as Meister Eckhart, affirmed that every human being possesses dignity simply by the fact of being human. "Every man a nobleman," was one of Eckhart's sayings, an insistence that all humans possess greatness as creatures before an all-powerful and all-caring creator.[51]

Dignity made the leap from medieval language to the modern era but at a cost. The dignity of the human was identified with the individual's capacity to think rationally and act independently.[52] This was not good news for any earthling that is not human and for those human beings whose rationality and agency are severely limited. Man was said to have dignity; the only opponent was thought to be nature, and she would eventually be conquered. The power of man over nature turned out to be a power that some men had over other men as well as over women, children, and animals.[53] Despite some shaking up of the language of *man* and *nature* in the twentieth century, the idea of dignity has not shifted much from the individual's ability to control his (and now her) life.[54]

The inherent problem with the idea of dignity has always been that it seems to imply a servitude of some kind. An upper class of gentlemen cannot exist without a lower class to serve, honor, and respect them. The spread of dignity to all of mankind still involved servitude, explicitly for the other animals and implicitly for women, children, and vulnerable people such as infants and the sick. Anyone who lacks independent agency is thought to lack dignity. It is not an accident of language that the phrase "dying with dignity" was coined to refer to suicide. One's last scrap of dignity, it is thought, is the rational control of killing oneself. In a hospice, one hears a different use of "dying with dignity." It means the responsibility to provide the best care possible to a dying person.[55]

These contrasting uses of "dying with dignity" reveal the fundamental ambiguity in the meaning of dignity. Like a great many words, dignity has two almost opposite meanings. It can refer to what an individual possesses, or it can refer to the respect due to someone. In a world of isolated individuals, dignity is up for grabs; those who have the power to demand respect will claim it for themselves. In that world, dignity is a quality of superiority that only some people can possess. Michael Ignatieff offers that "on occasion, men and women behave with inspiring dignity. But that is not the same thing as saying that all human beings have an innate dignity or even a capacity to display it."[56]

In a world of mutual relations, the two meanings of dignity can be seen as opposite ends of a single relation; that is, there is something proper to a person that generates respect in a community of persons.[57] Someone who is doing the caring today might be the one who needs care tomorrow. An assumption that dignity is equivalent to rational control of oneself makes it impossible to cover all humans in human rights. In fact, the humans who are most in need of human rights are among the first ones who are excluded. We need a comprehensive meaning of dignity that refers to the physical and mental integrity of a person, an integrity which is affirmed by oneself as aided by others.

A violation of someone's dignity may involve interference with individual autonomy. But more fundamentally, it is treating a person as something other than human. Torture not only causes pain, but it is intended to humiliate the person by disrespecting the person's integrity. Humiliation unmakes the person's world so that even after the humiliation ceases the person cannot return to what he or she was.[58] The torture and humiliation of any human being is an attack on the very idea of human dignity. Avishai Margalit examines the ultimate basis of what he calls a decent society and concludes, "We have a simple formula which claims that a society is a decent one if it punishes its criminals—even the worst of them—without humiliating them."[59]

Steven Pinker, in an essay entitled "The Stupidity of Dignity," gives examples of what he says are "indignities;" these include a security search, a pelvic or rectal exam, and a colonoscopy. He concludes that since we agree to those things, "Dignity is a trivial value, well worth trading off for life, health and safety."[60] He misses the point entirely. A pelvic exam or a colonoscopy may be unpleasant, but far from violating human dignity, they express care by a competent physician for the person's bodily integrity. Pinker's one example that may be a genuine violation of a person's dignity—"putting a wand up your crotch"—is such a violation when the practice is no real protection of anyone's security and is performed with no regard for personal privacy. In any case, human dignity is not "a trivial value," and it is never worth "trading off."

The most basic philosophical problem in this context is seldom discussed, namely, why should humans as opposed to other animals have dignity and rights? The claim that humans are superior because they are in rational control of the world has always been an illusion that is finally catching up with us humans. What is needed for human rights to be appropriate language is a dignity of all living beings and a human interconnection with the whole earthly environment. Human dignity is the culmination of the dignity of all living beings. The uniqueness of the human resides not in its separation from the rest of life but, on the contrary, in its relatedness to everything. Respect for a living being is shown by care that its degree of independent activity is affirmed while at the same time it is given whatever support and aid are needed for the enjoyment of its life.

The term *dignity* in that it is derived from Latin is by that fact culturally biased. However, it is less of a problem in contributing to a universal claim about humanity than is the term *right*. The committee that composed the UN declaration could have profitably spent more time on developing the idea of dignity in relation to ideas that converge with dignity from other cultures. They could have searched in Asian and African languages for terms that indicate a respect for each person.[61] Then the declaration could have more realistically made a case for a few rights that deserve to be called universal or human. In addition to the claim of universal rights, the UN document could have provided ideas and examples to encourage nations to provide political and economic rights to their citizens.

A Look Ahead

The first part of this book is mainly historical, but it is not a history of human rights. Human rights, I am arguing, is a twentieth-century concept. Books that routinely assume that *human rights* is simply another name for *natural rights* fail to uncover why the term *natural rights* was and is inadequate.

The first and second chapters trace the evolution of the Latin phrase "*ius naturale.*" When the eighteenth century invoked *natural rights*, it relied on a traditional language, but one that could not support the grandiose claims of the Declaration of Independence and the Declaration of the Rights of Man and of the Citizen. Nineteenth-century reformers generally dismissed the idea of natural rights as having no basis. World War II awakened the world to a need for protecting vulnerable people beyond what many nation-states provide. But on what basis was that to be done?

The third chapter recounts some developments in legal and ethical theories that focused on a new idea, human rights. The United Nations Charter while mentioning human rights in its preamble was almost entirely concerned with nation-states. After a few years, the UN did produce a document on the idea of human rights. The document was a great achievement in 1948, but it was among the first words on human rights, not the last on the subject. Books on human rights that treat the Universal Declaration of Human Rights as akin to sacred scripture do a disservice to the document and fail to trace how the idea of human rights has been in formation since the middle of the twentieth century.

The second part of this study describes how human rights have emerged in the second half of the twentieth century and in the first decade of the twenty-first century. There are innumerable traditions that can contribute to a human tradition. Chapters 4 to 8 follow movements by groups of people that have insisted that they too are fully human. These five chapters are linked by the theme of a dialectic of same and different within each movement. These movements contribute to human rights in diverse ways.

Chapter 4 traces two different women's movements, both of which are concerned with the full humanity of women's lives. The fifth chapter on age, with emphasis on infants and the very old, is a rethinking of human rights as based not on individual agency, but on the integrity of persons in community. The sixth chapter on religion distinguishes between an intended universality found in the world's major religions and the failure to achieve universality in the historical evolution of religions up to now. However, communication between religions and even some convergence of their themes is a characteristic of recent times. The seventh chapter on the relation of humans and their environment is crucial for understanding human rights as a help, not a hindrance, to dealing with the environmental problems that confront the human race. The eighth chapter on culture and cultures suggests ways that cross-cultural exchanges can provide support for human rights. Cultures, like traditions, are numerous and particular, but they can point in the direction of universality.

I do not claim to provide more than a sketch of these movements. However, there is enough material to support my thesis that a human tradition and human rights gained practical meaning only as an inclusive language emerged, one that includes dialogues between adults and children, Europeans and Asians, whites and blacks, women and men, gays and straights, rich and poor, Christians and Muslims, healthy and sick, artists and nonartists, humans and nonhumans. The reader is invited to add important dialogues that I may have failed to include.

CHAPTER 1

The Historical Origin of Natural Rights

This chapter begins the examination of possible sources of human rights. In much of human rights literature, *human rights* are assumed to be simply another name for what in earlier centuries were called natural rights. While I reject that assumption, I acknowledge that the idea of natural rights played an important role in the twentieth-century idea of human rights and that we have much to learn from the history of natural rights. The evolution of the idea of natural rights took many centuries. Most of that history is embodied in the shifting meaning of the Latin *ius naturale* from Roman times to the seventeenth century. The eighteenth-century assertion of natural right in the British American revolution and *le droit naturel* in the French Revolution drew upon the long history of *ius naturale*. Before I trace the history of *ius naturale*, it is necessary to set a context of contemporary views on the basis of human rights.

Discussing the Basis of Human Rights

The inquiry into the basis of human rights involves several academic areas. Legal scholars, philosophers, and historians have their distinctive ways of looking at a question. The approach I am taking is open to contributions from all areas. Eclecticism has its dangers but so does a single way of approaching human rights. My claim that a human tradition is the basis of human rights attempts to synthesize the two main approaches to human rights. The first approach analyzes a legal or philosophical concept of rights in which *human* rights can seem to be a shaky extension of the meaning of rights. The second approach is an historical one of tracing how human rights discourse has arisen as a useful rhetoric of protest against the inhuman treatment of human beings.

It is frequently claimed that there are three possible bases for human rights: God (or religion), human nature (or natural law), and some variation on historical experience.[1] The first two of these possible sources are usually dispatched without much argument other than the assertion that each of them is unpersuasive to most people today. That leaves the third source as the only one left standing and, therefore, the answer. Since this answer—whether under the rubric of empirical evidence, pragmatism, history, experience, or consensus—has its own problems, it might be useful to explore what the past has to offer under the headings of God, religion, human nature, and natural law. At the least, it seems unnecessary to immediately dismiss all claims for God, religion, human nature, and natural law in order to explore history and human experience.

Discussions of God or nature as the basis of human rights often blur together. A chief reason for this close link is the prominent role that eighteenth-century declarations play in this discussion. The revolutions in France and North America were heirs of the medieval meanings of nature even as they were distancing themselves from the Christian church and medieval thought. The Declaration of Independence made appeal to "nature and nature's God" for the rights of all men. The French declaration traced the origin of the rights of man to an all-embracing nature.

At least three different meanings of *nature* were mixed together in the eighteenth century. The idea of natural rights in British and British American writing mainly drew upon the medieval meaning of nature as *what* a thing is and especially what a man is. That meaning of nature was related to the assumption of a law that follows and governs human nature. In a reversal of our usual way of thinking, it was thought that we first have duties imposed by this natural law; the duties in turn implied rights.[2]

In the seventeenth century, however, the primary meaning of *nature* had undergone a radical shift. Nature was now the object that confronted man, and the choice was to submit to nature or to conquer her. Leaders of the revolutions in North America and France did not directly advert to that meaning of nature, but they were inevitably on the side of man against nature. There was a third meaning of *nature*, which was in tension with this second meaning. An ancient myth of nature as the mother of us all provided some resistance to thinking of nature as an object for conquest. French *philosophes*, the German philosopher, Immanuel Kant, and poets of nature drew upon this ancient myth of Mother Nature. Nature is the encompassing source of all our human benefits.[3]

Jeremy Bentham is famous for describing natural rights as "nonsense upon stilts."[4] However, earlier in that essay, Bentham had hold of a brilliant idea but seemed not to notice its significance. He writes, "It is in England, rather than France, that the discovery of the *rights of man* ought naturally to have taken its rise: it is we—we English—that have the better right to it."[5] He bases that claim on the fact that *right* in the English language is both an adjective and a noun; French had no such word. In the English language, the long tradition of the adjective *right*, meaning "acting in accord with our nature" (doing the right thing), could evolve into *right* as a noun, meaning "some power that a person has that is in accord with human nature."

Bentham pokes fun at his own insight, calling right a magical word. He then says, "The French language is fortunate enough not to possess this mischievous abundance." That sentence must be ironic because his next sentence is "But a Frenchman will not be kept back from his purpose by a want of words: the want of an adjective composed of the same letters as the substantive *right*, is no loss to him." But surely the point of Bentham's essay is that it is a terrible loss. A transition in English from *right* as descriptive of an element within traditional law to right as an affirming of the person who is a subject within law could not happen in French. Instead, the French Revolution announced the existence of rights (*les droits*) that were the beginning of a new ethic, one without historical roots.

The historical result of this difference was paradoxical. British authors since the eighteenth century have been skeptical of natural rights even though British tradition rooted the idea of rights in an historical understanding of what is natural to human beings. In contrast, the term *natural rights* became almost totally identified with the French Revolution and its aftermath even though French thinking rejected rights based on human nature and attempted to restart history from the natural rights of man.

To the extent that authors continue to interchange *human rights* and *natural rights*, they tend to assume that human rights are without any philosophical basis. Alasdair MacIntyre, in his 1981 book, *After Virtue*, while equating natural rights and human rights, asserts, "The truth is plain: there are no such rights, and belief in them is one with belief in witches and unicorns."[6] A more apt metaphor that MacIntyre might have chosen would be belief in a fairy godmother. That myth fits in with his noting that for eighteenth-century writers, "nature is conceived as an actively benevolent agent; nature is a legislator for our good."[7] That meaning of nature is particularly true of the French declaration. The Declaration of Independence refers to "nature and nature's god" while the French philosophers simply made nature and god equivalent. The characteristics that Christianity attributes to God, the benevolent creator, were now attributed to nature. It seems safe to say that human rights cannot be based on an eighteenth-century meaning of nature as a benevolent mother.[8]

As for a more traditional image of God, which the eighteenth-century writers were trying to replace, there is not much to say. For the existence of human rights, the God of Jewish, Christian, or Muslim traditions is not in competition with other possible sources. A Jew, Christian, or Muslim attributes the source of human rights to God for the simple reason that God is said to be the creator of everything. The significant question is *how* God is the source. The relation between divine creativity and human action in a particular religion is a crucial question for how human rights might find support. Is human creativity, including the gathering of empirical evidence, encouraged by divine creativity, or is it in opposition to divine control of the world?[9] The relevant issue is not God as the source, but the claim that one religion or another is the basis of human rights.

I think history shows rather clearly that no one religion is the source of human rights. But it is also clear that movements for human liberation have often been religiously inspired. Religions can divide people, but an important element within human tradition is an appeal to God that supports struggle against authoritarian regimes. I think that secular writers who aggressively exclude all references to God and religion may neglect help for human rights. Human rights are not likely to be put into practice unless they are at least compatible with religious traditions.[10] In chapter six, I explore how the plurality of religions and the conversation between religions might be helpful to the cause of human rights.

While religion's frequent violence "in the name of God" makes a suspicion of religion understandable, the dismissal of human nature and (moral) laws of nature is more difficult to understand. Human nature seems to be practically indispensable for rights. One can try to find other phrases to indicate that a human being differs in kind from other things. For example, one can refer to *humanity, human characteristics*, or the *human condition*.[11] Ordinary language refuses to give up references to human nature.

The boundaries of human nature remain as contestable as ever—perhaps more than ever—but the great majority of people presume that the term has some meaning. I agree with Michael Ignatieff that "a prudential—and historical—justification for human rights need not make appeal to any *particular* idea of human nature."[12] A similar claim is made by Martha

Nussbaum for her approach to justifying human rights "independent of any particular metaphysical or religious view."[13]

The alternative to one *particular* view of human nature, as Kwame Appiah has argued, is that human rights have to be based on a convergence of many particular ideas of human nature.[14] An idea of human nature that has proved to be too narrowly conceived is not grounds for abandoning human nature and those laws that follow from the nature of human beings. "If there is indeed such a thing as human nature, we might very well never come to agree on what it essentially consists in, as the philosophical record to date would strongly intimate."[15] There is no need to claim knowledge of a "metaphysical essence" but only that agreement might be possible about some needs, interests, or capacities of human beings.

I would grant that, in contrast to *human nature*, the term *natural law* is more difficult to salvage. In human rights literature today, the frequent supposition is that the meaning of *natural law* is obvious and that the idea has long since been discredited. All that I would say here is that the term at least deserves historical investigation before it is dismissed. Because *nature* is itself an ambiguous term, then a law called natural is bound to be highly ambiguous.

If *nature* refers to differences in kind, then a law or laws would describe the rules that are followed by each of these kinds. This meaning of natural law would be clear, but it would be useful only if it summarized how each kind of thing acts (that is, laws of *natures*). Most kinds do seem to act in predictable ways. In this sense of nature and of law, modern science has been an attempt to discover the laws of natures in the uniform, predictable things of what is called the natural world.

Where some degree of variability and unpredictability becomes evident is in the world of the living, especially among animals. Nonhuman animals have a range of malleability and unpredictability. For animals that have been close associates of the humans, the malleability was used to limit the unpredictability. Plato compared his guardian class to watchdogs that could be trained to be gentle with friends and fierce with enemies.[16] A dog, however, cannot be trained to act like an elephant or a fish. Its law is dogness or a canine nature.

The humans have a wider range of malleability and unpredictability than their animal kin. At least that appears to be the case to the humans themselves. There have been thinkers throughout history who have claimed that the surface perception is a delusion. Not many thinkers have claimed that humans have no freedom at all (for one thing, the status of the denial would itself be left unclear). However, numerous thinkers have concluded that the claim "I can do anything I want" is a delusion; the range of human freedom is much narrower than the belief by many individuals about their own choices. The basis of whatever human freedom there is lies below the surface of consciousness in a complex interplay of forces that can only be indirectly controlled.

If there is some meaning to human freedom, a law of human nature would have to have some strange characteristics. The meanings of *law* as well as *nature* would have to differ from their use to describe a world of things. What can one say with certainty of a strange animal that can reflect on its own actions, make promises about the future, imagine a different world, and contemplate its own death? There might be a few rules or laws that would set boundaries for human nature's survival, but a legal code to cover all activity seems impossible.

For example, to kill oneself or another human being is destructive of human nature. It is therefore opposed to the law of its nature and is unacceptable—unless a human being is convinced that under some circumstances the alternative might be worse. This element of human nature—its power to conceive of exceptions to lawful order—is a strength but also a danger. It allows for humans to grasp that in certain circumstances the right thing would be human compassion beyond the rules. Unfortunately, a lot of terribly destructive actions have also snuck in under the cover of special conditions. ("Yes, killing people is against the law of human nature, but this particular war is justified by the circumstances").

For many people, law for human conduct is something written. That could not have been the case before there was writing. An understanding of what law demands would have been passed down from one generation to the next. The eventual writing of a legal code was helpful for instructing the young and pointing out to everyone in a community the boundaries of acceptable behavior.[17] A society needs rules particular to its time, place, and other circumstances.

The law based on human nature has often been thought to be unchangeable. Other laws had to be added as circumstances required. These conventional laws did not logically follow from the law of human nature, but it was thought that they should not contradict that nature. Philosophers at least since Plato's time assumed that a human nature would have a law of human nature. Religions presumed to supply the content of such a (moral) law, but if the details of a law applying to all human beings were convincing only to members of one religious group, the result could be to undermine the idea of a natural law.

It will be helpful to consider a few examples of what authors put in place of human nature and natural law as a basis for human rights. Michael Ignatieff is cited above as saying human rights do not require any particular idea of human nature. Although he seems to be saying that we need no meaning for what is naturally human, he regularly refers to natural propensities, natural tendencies, and natural attributes. Ignatieff says that the United Nations set out to "re-establish human rights at the moment when they had been shown to have no foundation whatever in natural attributes."[18] Human rights, he says, are "an attempt to correct the natural tendencies we discovered in ourselves as human beings."[19]

Not only is there a meaning of human nature implied here, but the meaning is also so negative as to make human rights seem a hopeless venture. Throughout the centuries, most philosophies and religions have viewed human nature as the source of both good and bad tendencies.[20] For example, James Madison, in explaining the basis of republican government, wrote, "As there is a degree of depravity in humankind which requires a certain degree of circumspection and distrust, so there are other qualities in human nature which justify a certain portion of esteem and confidence."[21] That attitude is assumed in communities that have tried to counteract bad tendencies by appealing to good tendencies. Rituals and rules have supported the good tendencies and restrained the bad. If human rights have "no foundation whatever in natural attributes," it is difficult to see what they are supporting.[22]

Some writers on human rights seem to assume that if something is historical, then it is not natural. It would make more sense to say that it is the nature of human beings to be historical. An argument that human rights have to be based on history need not be a denial that there is a human nature, the extent of which is still being revealed in and by history. David Boucher writes that "the rights we have are historical and contingent rather than 'natural.'"[23] His context is the praise of British idealists of the nineteenth century. A separation of nature and history was a distinctive tendency of those nineteenth-century writers, and that separation still has residual effects today

Richard Rorty writes about "a growing willingness to give up asking 'What is our nature?' and substitute 'What can we make of ourselves?'" The result, according to Rorty, is that "we have come to see that the only lesson of either history or anthropology is our extraordinary malleability. We are coming to think of ourselves as the flexible, protean, self-shaping animal rather than as the rational animal or the cruel animal." Rorty's main claim is "that nothing relevant to moral choice separates human beings from animals except historically contingent facts of the world, cultural facts."[24] It would seem, nonetheless, that the description of a "flexible, protean, self-shaping animal" who produces cultural facts rather than being a rational animal is still answering the question of what is the nature of the human.

William Schulz insists that human rights are grounded not on God or natural law but on "pragmatism."[25] Schulz describes his third way as "the capacity for human empathy or solidarity."[26] One can readily agree that empathy or solidarity is an important trait if human rights are to have any chance of succeeding. A question remains that if empathy is a trait that is naturally human, are there other human traits that history shows to be in tension with empathy? And does the solidarity of a small group generate conflict with strangers, something that would undermine the extension of rights to all humans?

Schulz does not seem interested in exploring the mixture of attributes in human nature. He insists on human rights as "the rights of humans, something they possess or claim but not necessarily derived from the nature of the claimant."[27] If his point is that human rights cannot be logically deduced from an abstraction called human nature, he is surely correct. It is not clear, however, that meaningful human rights can be supported without appeal to the nature of the claimant and its attributes.

Thomas Haskell, in an insightful essay, tried to find a way between the assumption of a timeless and universal human nature and the historicist assumption that there are only the relativities of historical events. His answer to this conflict is conventions, which, he says, "must be rooted deeply enough in the human condition to win the loyalty of more than a few generations (and ideally, more than a few cultures). Conventions possess the requisite durability."[28] The parenthesis in that statement is worrisome; *human* rights require more than his qualification "ideally, more than a few cultures." Even more worrisome is his statement that "every attempt to apply them beyond the boundaries of one's own culture will carry grave risks of injustice through the unwitting effects of parochialism and ethnocentrism."[29] That qualification all but excludes human rights as conventions.

I am sympathetic to Haskell's overall argument. I just do not think that the term *convention*, given its long history, can bear the weight of what is deeply rooted in the human condition. Haskell refers to the "classic polar opposition between nature and convention" and goes with the latter.[30] But as I have pointed out above, nature is highly ambiguous; a choice between (one meaning of) nature and convention is unnecessary. Instead, human nature has interests, needs, and capacities that include conventions. Human rights can be supported by historical and empirical evidence together with a diversity of ideas about the nature of the human.

My use of *human tradition* is intended to be a comprehensive category that does not have to begin by excluding God, religion, nature, natural law, history, experience, consensus, pragmatism, or empirical data. In addition, human tradition does not have to set reason and emotion in opposition to one another. Such comprehensiveness for the meaning of *tradition* does come at a price. It implies that there is no factor *x* that is the logical basis of human rights. Human tradition does not *cause* human rights in the scientific sense of cause and effect. Human rights are based on human tradition in the sense that a lawyer bases a case for a defendant by amassing and interpreting all the evidence. The case for human rights can begin by examining what the ancient and medieval worlds conceived to be the moral order of a world of natures.

History of *Ius Naturale*

A tradition of natural rights needs to be explored for what it may directly or indirectly contribute to the human tradition and the meaning of *human rights*. Up to the seventeenth century, Latin was used for scientific, philosophical, and theological writing. Depending on the century and the context of its use, the Latin *ius* can be translated into English either by "law" or "right." In addition, the Latin *naturale* is obviously translated into English with the word *natural*. But the term *natural* was extremely complex in the seventeenth and eighteenth centuries, and it is no less so in the twenty-first century. Any comments on the relation between human rights and what is natural need to take account of the complex meaning of the term *natural*.

I am exploring here an important strand of how human beings in their history understood their relation to nature. The story is not the standard one of the triumph of modern rights, but neither is it a story of decline and failure. The rise of the early modern idea of right is entangled with individualism, rationalism, and sexism. That conclusion suggests we owe a debt of gratitude to earlier history for the idea of rights, but it also suggests the deficiency of rights as they were first conceived.

Early history. The first few centuries of the Common Era are the setting for the origin of *ius naturale*. There are two main parts to this early history:

Stoic philosophy and Christian writing. Today we might categorize the approaches as secular and religious. At that time, however, philosophy was a way of life, and the Christian way of life would have been understood to be one such guide.[31]

Christians borrowed or simply absorbed much of the language of Stoicism, including the word *religion*. However, rather than the Christian movement basing itself on Stoic philosophy, the two movements were competitors for providing a worldview and a set of practices for people in every walk of life.[32] The Christians were noted for attracting the urban poor, but converts came from all social classes.[33] Something similar can be said of Stoicism. One of Stoicism's most prominent authors was Marcus Aurelius, a Roman emperor, while another was Epictetus, a slave. Stoicism, like the church, had wide appeal.

The Stoic meaning of *ius naturale* corresponds to what many people assume is the meaning of "natural law," that is, a fixed law of the universe to which humans must humbly submit. The Stoics provided this worldview in the first centuries of the Common Era before the Christian Church came to dominate the West. When the Christian Church fragmented in the sixteenth century, a variation on Stoicism resurfaced. And today's environmental movement has once again revived a Stoic outlook.

Although early Christian writers admired many Stoic virtues and adapted them within the Christian philosophy of life, the cosmic framework of Stoicism was incompatible with the Christian story of creation, fall, and redemption. The fundamental conflict between Stoic and Christian philosophies was where nature fits. For the Stoics, nature was ultimate, the mother of us all. For Christians, nature or natures were the creation of our father in heaven. Both groups could use the phrase *ius naturale* but differently; for Christians, obedience was to God; nature was only one element in creation. To be sure, nature—or more exactly, nature understood by reason—was for Christians a guide planted in human beings by God and not to be violated.

Stoics. The Stoic movement began in Greece; together with Epicureanism, it provided what today might be called psychological answers. The grand schemes of Plato and Aristotle did not directly wrestle with problems of human emotion, what to do about pleasure and pain, and how to make sense of death.[34] Despite Plato's portrait of a heroic Socrates facing death and Aristotle's writings that were later invoked in support of human dignity, the two great theorists did not offer much in the way of personal advice.

The early Stoic thinkers in Greece concentrated on the plight of the human individual. The later Roman Stoics had a different emphasis. They were aware that, in Cicero's words, "we are born for the company of others and the social fellowship of the whole human race."[35] The Romans were engaged in spreading their empire to the whole known world. The Stoics taught an attitude that might be characterized as benevolence toward all of humanity.

Some writers today trace the origin of human rights to the Stoics.[36] That would seem to be an anachronistic reading of *ius naturale*. A more plausible attribution is a Stoic origin for dignity and self-respect.[37] The Stoics assumed a fixed cosmos that does not yield to human wishes. The human vocation is to accept that fate with wisdom and courage. The human choice is to say yes or no to nature. The wise man is aware that saying no to nature is to resist in vain what will be. The Stoics addressed their views to "the city of the wise."[38]

Cicero is not given much attention in histories of philosophy. Although he wrote beautiful treatises on topics such as friendship and old age, he is not credited with being a profound thinker. However, he had a great influence in providing the vocabulary of later philosophy, especially political and moral philosophy. For many centuries in the West, when Greek was a lost language, Cicero's Latin words that were used to translate Greek philosophy shaped the thinking of writers. For example, there are no treatises on ethics in the Middle Ages, but there are numerous works on morals, or more precisely, moral theology.

Cicero did not speculate about nature in a metaphysical way; instead, he was concerned with the human's place within nature as expressed by law. He was directly concerned with written laws, but he was aware of the need to ground a written code in the reality of the cosmos. "Law is right reason in agreement with nature, universal, unwavering, and everlasting."[39] Justice is the point of laws, and law has to be "in accordance with nature, the most ancient and primary principle."[40]

Cicero did not seem to think there was a great tension between levels of fellowship. A love of one's family flows over into a love of nation and then to a love of all people.[41] He argued that we should not attack or do injury to any human being. However, his Stoic belief that material things are not important led him to think that people of a rich nation are not, in justice, required to help people in a poorer country.[42] Referring to levels of fellowship, Cicero wrote, "None is more serious and none dearer than that of each of us with the republic."[43] At the height of empire, men have tended to identify loyalty to the nation with love of humanity.

Cicero is well known for his threefold division of law: *ius naturale, ius gentium*, and *ius civile*. The first and third of these categories are fairly clear: the law of the cosmos in the first case, and in the third case, codes produced by political bodies that establish civil laws. The second law, the law of nations or the law of peoples, has generated much debate throughout the centuries. The ambiguity allowed for a variety of applications of the idea.

What Cicero was pointing to by *ius gentium* is that there were commonly accepted precepts of right and wrong. Some of these rules were written; others were just an acceptance of the ways things have always been. They were laws because they were the way people were supposed to act. What was unclear was how Cicero related his "natural law" and this "law of peoples." It would be too much to say that he equated the two kinds of law. On the other hand, he was identifying laws that went beyond the "civil" laws that are based on arbitrary choices of lawmakers.

If a custom or a rule is found everywhere, then one might suppose that it is based on the nature of things. However, given the difficulty of proving the universality of any practice, a commonly accepted practice may be general, but it is not always the case. Nonetheless, *ius gentium* as some kind of transition between natural and civil laws has had a useful place in political history. For example, in the seventeenth century when the attempt was made to codify laws that apply to all nations, the appeal was to customs and rules that transcend national boundaries. The available term was *ius gentium*, which Hugo Grotius made use of in laying out the laws regulating the interaction of nations.[44]

Stoicism is best known for advocating a calm acceptance of what most people perceive as human tragedy. Epictetus wrote that "men are not disturbed by the things that happen, but by the opinion about things; for example, death is nothing terrible, for if it were, it would have seemed so to Socrates; for the opinion about death, that it is terrible, is the terrible thing."[45] Epictetus warned that it was a bad idea to speak of "my wife" or "my child" because when they died, we would be torn by grief. Better to think that "a woman died" or "a child died." Each human being is to play the part as the scriptwriter wrote it. A prayer by an early Stoic, Cleanthes, is cited by Epictetus: "Lead me Zeus . . . for I shall follow without hesitating. But if I am unwilling, becoming wicked, I shall follow nonetheless."[46]

Probably the most famous and most admired Stoic is Marcus Aurelius. His reflections on human nature and the law of nature have been a comfort to innumerable people throughout the centuries. Aurelius was the supremely rational man, one who is not distracted by passing fashions and unsettling emotions. Like Cicero, his loyalty to Rome was understood to be a commitment to the whole human race. "My nature is rational and social; and my city and country, so far as I am Antonius, is Rome, but so far as I am a man, it is the world."[47] The Roman poet Terence had expressed the idea most succinctly: "I am a man and nothing human is foreign to me."[48]

A great challenge for accepting nature is one's own dying. Aurelius's outlook was similar to that of Epictetus, but he does not sound so cold blooded in accepting death. Death is a release from "twitchings of appetite" and "service to the flesh." Marcus Aurelius's attitude is thanksgiving for the time that nature has allotted him. To protest against dying or try to flee from it would be unmanly and ungrateful. "Spend, therefore, those fleeting moments on earth as Nature would have you spend them, and then go to your rest with a good grace, as an olive falls in its season, with a blessing for the earth that bore it and a thanksgiving to the tree that gave it life."[49] If nature rules human life, it would be difficult to argue with Marcus Aurelius's attitude.

Early Christian Thinking. The Christian Church arose at a time of great philosophical and religious upheaval. It arose in a place that was a main crossroad of the world. The languages of Greek, Hebrew, Aramaic, and Latin swirled about its beginning. Jewish religion was a distinct tradition but nonetheless had recently been influenced by other religious currents, particularly an apocalyptic strain from Persia. The Jesus movement did not conceive itself to be one more philosophical school. It placed its founder, Jesus of Nazareth, in the line of Jewish prophets, bringing to fulfillment the hopes of the Jewish people though not in the way that most Jews had expected. Its leader was proclaimed king of the universe, not a king in any political sense.

When the followers of Jesus tried to put together a coherent doctrine, they used the language at hand while stretching its boundaries. Church writers took over many religious terms from the Romans, such as *piety*, *virtue, reverence, sacrament*, and *religion*. Stoicism was an obvious source of Christian language although it was only one influence on early Christianity. A strand of Plato's thought, known as Neoplatonism, was thought to be particularly compatible with the Christian narrative. Aristotle's influence would come later.

Paul, in his Epistles, occasionally refers to what is natural and also to what is unnatural. He uses *unnatural* to describe sex between males (Rom

1:26) and long hair on men (1 Cor 11:14), without elaborating a systematic framework of nature. He was intent on telling the tale of the human race from its misdirection at the very beginning of the story to its second chance to put things right. The key was the one whom Paul calls Christ Jesus, whose death/resurrection overcomes sin and death.

In the Christian story, death is natural but human death is not; it is a sign of human failure. In fact, much of what humans do is not right, including their animosity toward other humans, their uncontrollable emotions, and their killing of nonhuman animals.[50] What was implied in Paul's story of creation, fall, and redemption was that there was a more perfect world that preceded history's tale of hatred, bloodshed, and death. Similar myths of a lost golden age run from Greek and Roman literature to modern theories of the origin of society.[51] The sixteenth and seventeenth centuries would call this prehistorical condition the state of nature.

Paul was amazingly successful in carrying the Christian message around the Mediterranean world. The flourishing of the movement in North Africa and Europe quickly resulted in a transcending of its Jewish roots, opening it to greater philosophical influence. The universalistic implications of Christianity were developed with both good and bad effects.

The first four centuries of the church included constant and confusing debate about Jesus's relation to God. The controversies were carried on in Greek and Latin. What emerged in Latin and subsequent languages in the West was a distinction between *nature* and *person*. The words were employed in almost opposite ways to speak of God (one nature, three persons) and the Christ (one person, two natures). To anyone not a Christian, this theology is likely to seem only an exercise in torturous logic. However, histories of human rights or natural law seldom acknowledge the Christian transformation of the term *nature*.

Theological controversies honed out a helpful philosophical distinction between who a human is (person) and what a human is (nature). Person is a theatrical metaphor: the mask that an actor wears. A person is one who speaks; but a person is also someone partially hidden even while speaking. In the language developed in the early church, a person acts with his or her nature. It is immoral to act against one's nature, but morality is not based on submitting to an impersonal nature or a set of rules called natural law.

Although Christian writers took over *ius naturale* from Stoicism, its meaning was bound to be different. That was not always clear to writers of the time. Even today when church spokesmen rely on Cicero or Aristotle for their moral framework, including a meaning of natural law, they often seem unaware of their own heritage.

Almost all of Western church doctrine was funneled through one person: Augustine of Hippo. He is one of history's great geniuses, but his power over subsequent teachings was bound to cause some serious limitations. His personal idiosyncrasies and his social situation have affected Protestant and Roman Catholic teaching to this day. He even has had a profound influence on United States foreign policy, an influence that continues.[52] Augustine wrote at a time when the world was collapsing around him; the mighty Roman Empire was in its last days. Augustine did not know Greek, but he was aware of many Greek philosophers. An Augustine scholar notes that as a young man, Augustine read Cicero, Virgil, Plotinus, Porphyry, and many others; his successors read only him.[53] After Augustine, the Latin Church produced little innovative thinking until the twelfth century.

Peter Brown writes that "the somber preoccupation of Augustine with the manner in which a man could imprison himself in a 'second nature' by his past actions makes the *Confessions* a very modern book."[54] Brown's reference to a second nature, throws light on an idea that is widely understood today but was a new perspective with Augustine. Human nature is not static; the person's actions and habits are like a second nature that develops personality but also limits what a person can do. Every person is free to develop a second nature. Whereas for Stoics the choice was between yes and no to nature, for Augustine, the choice was *a*, *b*, or *c* in deciding what kind of second nature one would have and, as a result, what kind of person one would be.

There is some irony in the fact that Augustine is well known for the doctrine of original sin.[55] It is commonly assumed that Augustine messed up human freedom with the myth of a sin passed down from Adam and Eve. Actually, it was Augustine who articulated a doctrine of free will and human choice, but in addition, he was realistic about the interior and exterior factors that affect freedom of choice.

Original sin has been a badly understood doctrine even by Christians. It was an attempt to describe the nearly universal experience of a lost innocence and the feeling that we are not always in control of our own actions. As far back as we can go in history, the human race has been acting badly. Bad choices lead to further bad choices and to bad examples for the next generation. Yet there seems nothing in human nature that necessitates hatred, violence, and war.

In addition to a doctrine of continuous failure, Augustine developed a corresponding doctrine of grace (gift), which was the needed help for human transformation. Augustine disagreed with Cicero's orienting of morality to justice. For Augustine, the agreement at the base of human community has to be "the things we love." The primacy of the will means the choice to love rather than simply the conforming to a just order.

Augustine's own life was an embodiment of conflicting philosophies. He started from a Manichean split between good and evil. But he came to resist a radical view of history wherein the world would soon come to an end in apocalyptic fury. He had great admiration for Cicero and quoted him often. He was familiar with Neoplatonism through Porphyry's translation of Plotinus. Augustine shows the influence of Neoplatonic thought, especially in the tension of finding God either within or above his person.

Plato had referred to a One beyond being, who is the source of all being and intelligibility.[56] Plotinus began from this Platonic vision and professed to go beyond where vision goes. He elaborated a complex system in which the One or the Good overflows to create finite beings. The things of our experience participate in nature that is created by the One.[57] Some Christian thinkers saw the possibility of identifying the One with the creator God. A big problem was that diverse beings "emanated" from the One necessarily, whereas Christian and Jewish thinkers insisted that God freely created the world "because there was no envy in him."[58]

In Neoplatonism each level of being participates in what is greater than itself. In turn each being shares what it has been given. A morally good act is one that is receptive to the good and shares the good with others. The good is what is "diffusive of itself." This imagery and language held out interesting possibilities for the development of a personal and communal ethic. Arthur Lovejoy traced the Neoplatonic framework of Western philosophy through more than ten centuries of history. The influence on all aspects of society was profound. Still, as Lovejoy suggests, the medieval church for the most part settled into a more mundane sense of the good as what can be attained by following the rules.[59]

The early church perhaps succeeded too well. Millions of converts were given answers to profound questions before they could understand the questions. Moral guidance was available in rules known through reason or by opening the Bible. Only the mystics sensed the transforming possibilities of a godhead beyond god, of the good as receptiveness to life, of the material world not as something negative but simply the limits of the spirit. The mystics kept alive the sense of something profound that was obscured by the formulas of a mundane institution. A few great thinkers preserved a sense of deeper realities until a revival could begin in the twelfth century.

Developments in the Early Middle Ages

The story in this section is the beginning of the idea of natural right in the twelfth and thirteenth centuries. The section has two main parts: a legal side to the story and a philosophical contribution. Both parts are about tradition. The legal tradition has its start with the publication of a book by Gratian in 1140 CE. The philosophical tradition begins with scientific and technological thinking in the twelfth century that accompanied translations of Greek philosophy. The legal tradition included a specialized development within English history. The philosophical tradition included mysticism at its outer edge.

The two traditions represented contrasting approaches to perceiving an intellectual order in the universe. Some individuals were conversant with both traditions. Thomas Aquinas, the central figure on the philosophical side, absorbed some of the legal distinctions. In turn, Aquinas's philosophy had repercussions in the world of jurisprudence.[60] The philosophical tradition produced *ideas* that gave support to the early modern notion of natural rights. The legal tradition supplied the *words* for a gradual emergence of "natural rights."

Legal Tradition. One of Western history's most important books is by a twelfth-century author, Gratian. The name of the book is *Harmony of Discordant Canons*; it is nearly always referred to as the *Decretum*.[61] Probably only canon lawyers and Christian theologians are familiar with the book; it is not easy reading even for them. The book was not intended to be an innovation. Gratian tried to gather into one place church laws, theological opinions, and pieces of classical learning. In addition, as the book's title promised, he wished to show the harmony of all this material. But like Peter Abelard's *Sic et Non,* which was published about twenty years earlier, Gratian could achieve only a harmony of dialectical contrasts. The greatest contribution of the *Decretum* is not its content but the fact that it set off centuries of commentary. Already by 1160, the published text was surrounded by commentary in the book's margins, which is called the ordinary gloss.

Gratian took over the language of *ius naturale* that went back as far as Cicero. The change of meaning that was implied in Gratian's use was not evident at the time. But by the end of the medieval period, the canonists who taught and commented upon the *Decretum* had found what became known as natural right.

Gratian begins the *Decretum* by distinguishing two kinds of law. The human race is ruled by natural law and "usages."[62] The *ius naturale* is of divine origin and is found in the law and the gospel. *Usages* refers to humanly devised codes that vary from place to place, time to time. Gratian reduces the divinely given natural law to the so-called golden rule: each person is commanded to do to another what he wishes done to himself; each is forbidden to do what he would not have done to him. This summary of *ius naturale* is unusual although not original to Gratian. The full meaning of *ius naturale* referred to a system of "objective laws." Natural law was complemented by many other kinds of law: customary, civil, military, and public.

By the twelfth century, the term *ius* was commonly used in a way that we would recognize as a right. Persons were said to have various rights, such as a right to own property and a right to defend one's life. In the course of time, this popular meaning of *ius* infiltrated the descriptions of *ius naturale*. By the beginning of the thirteenth century, *ius naturale* referred to commands and prohibitions; it could also refer to a neutral sphere where humans were free to choose. Gratian acknowledged a right of ownership even though he believed that originally all things were held in common. Commentators dealt with this discrepancy by saying that there was more than one meaning to *ius naturale*.

One of the early commentators on the *Decretum* was Rufinus. He picked up on the popular meaning of *ius* as a right and carried this meaning into *ius naturale* as a force instilled in every person. Rufinus described *ius naturale* as including commands, prohibitions and "demonstrations," referring to areas where choices are "licit but not required." Rufinus and another key commentator, Huguccio, developed this idea of an area of free choice from Paul's Letter to the Corinthians regarding meat sacrificed to idols. For Paul, the Christian was free from the prescriptions of Jewish law; that is what he called liberty from the law. A right of nature was permitted by the law of nature.[63] A distinction gradually grew between *lex*, meaning a body of laws, and *ius*, which included the person and his powers.

The Great Charter of Liberties. As I noted above, writers in the British tradition have often been skeptical of natural rights. These writers are supportive of rights, but they rely on history rather than metaphysics for the basis of any rights. Alan Ryan writes that "common law's root principle is tradition rather than nature; when it appeals to nature it is to natural law rather than individual human rights."[64] However, as Ryan admits here, tradition and a meaning of nature need not be competitors; they can be allies in support of rights.

The document of 1215 called Magna Carta is at least symbolically the origin of a common law tradition that guaranteed the rights of every Englishman. The Magna Carta was actually a ratification of earlier agreements such as a charter of liberties in 1100 accepted by King Henry I. The charter of 1215 between King John and his barons was only one step in a process of revisions that continued throughout the century, and it was several centuries later before Magna Carta became enshrined as the great fount of political rights.

The significance of the Magna Carta was established by Edward Coke in the fight against King James I. "Thus it was an anachronistic, biased interpretation of a thirteenth century document by seventeenth century politicians that became the cornerstone of liberty for the English-speaking world."[65] When the British American colonies were gathering their ideas to justify resistance to Britain, one of their spokesmen wrote, "Magna Carta itself is in substance but a constrained declaration or proclamation in the name of King, Lords, and Commons of the sense the latter had of their original, inherent, indefeasible, natural rights."[66]

When a copy of the Magna Carta found a home in the new British Museum in 2007, an accompanying note of explanation read, "The Magna Carta is a disappointing document. It contains none of the sweeping principles of the Declaration of Independence." The seeming deprecation is ironic. The British value their long political tradition without which there would have been no Declaration of Independence. As I will describe in the following chapter, the Declaration of Independence, beyond its opening paragraphs about all men and all governments, was in the tradition of English charters in its listing of specific grievances against a particular king.

The *Magna Carta Libertatum*, as its full title indicates, was a document spelling out liberties. The word *right* is used only seven times in the sixty-three paragraphs; two of those uses are in the first paragraph in reference to the church. The document's main concern was the protection of individual liberties, that is, freedom from encroachment on the individual by the king's power. It was quite specific, for example, in excluding imprisonment without a trial. It established a twenty-five-person committee, including the mayor of London and the archbishop, as a check on the king's power.

It was not until the end of the thirteenth century that Parliament could be said to fully exist. King Edward I established it as a consulting body to strengthen his own powers. But as happens when political bodies grow in urban environments, Parliament became a force to be reckoned with. By the end of the fourteenth century, there were three parts to Parliament: the clergy, the king with his barons, and the knights of shires and burghers. The last group was condescendingly called the commons, but it became the base of political power. In 1376 the Commons refused money to King Edward III. They did not send petitions—they made demands. One of their actions was to send away the king's mistress. Their action was called, in the Norman French of the time, *ampeschement*, which means "embarrassment." It was the first but not the last time that a king or president would be impeached.

Eventually the word *right* was added to *liberty* in describing the concerns of the document. Or perhaps it would be more accurate to say that *right* became understood as liberty in the Anglo-Saxon tradition. There remains today, especially in the United States, a widespread conviction that the only defensible meaning of a human right is political liberty, the freedom of the individual from government intrusion.

Insofar as the long tradition of a common law has guarded the liberty of individuals, it is an indispensable contribution to today's human tradition in support of human rights. It is, however, only one tradition that needs complementing by other particular traditions and other movements of people for whom other kinds of rights may be needed. A charter of liberties, as Michael Oakeshott points out, is not a bill of rights. The charter recognized rights as liberties, privileges accorded to a feudal class.[67] A bill of rights was considered by the British to be an abstract way of trying to protect individuals. Such rights would be realistic claims only when accompanied by a political and judicial system that is ready to enforce them.

Philosophical Tradition. In the twelfth century, a Christian tendency to bypass the world of the senses in explaining natural phenomena was reined in by the budding science, art, and commerce of the time. One historian of the period writes of a "technological revolution," which is an anachronistic use of the term *technological* but a pointer to the beginning of modern science and technology.[68] Before the twelfth century supranatural explanations were regularly invoked. The distinction between the natural and supernatural did not come about by adding an upper storey to nature but rather by establishing the integrity of the natural within a supernatural or graced world.[69]

The mark of the twelfth century was a growing confidence in the human capacity to understand and to regulate the natural elements of the world. The rise of the university signaled a world of vigorous intellectual debate and a tradition of learning. Gratian initiated the canonists' dialogue on *ius naturale* from the law school of the University of Bologna. One of the faculty members at the University of Paris in the thirteenth century was Thomas Aquinas who dominates the philosophical tradition.

Like Gratian, Thomas tried to encompass all that had gone before him, including the Bible, the writings of the fathers of the church, opinions of theologians, and church practice. Even more ambitiously, he tried to put all of the material into a philosophical unity. As is well known, he freely used the newly available material from Aristotle, whom he calls the philosopher. Thomas's adoption of Aristotle (as translated by Arab Muslims) was highly suspect within the church. It helped to get him condemned by the archbishop of Paris three years after his death.

Thomas, however, was not simply a follower of Aristotle. What was not fully recognized until the twentieth century was his strong reliance on Neoplatonic philosophy. Thomas used material from Aristotle but situated it within a Neoplatonic framework. Second only to his quoting of Aristotle, Thomas quotes Dionysius, his chief source of Neoplatonic philosophy. Thomas's questions were less about Aristotelian "matter and form" than about "to be" and "not to be." Both the Aristotelian and Neoplatonic elements in his philosophy have a bearing, if only implicitly, on the evolution of rights.

Thomas's tone is unemotional, and his conclusions are pronounced with certainty. The format of asking a question and producing an answer was vulnerable to being turned into a catechism, which did indeed happen later. Catechisms skip the importance of the dialectical process within each question in which Thomas lets both sides of an issue be placed on the table before he draws his own conclusion. The conclusion in any article is only one step in a continuing dialectic of question to question, article to article.

Thomas states that in matters of science, the use of authority is the weakest argument.[70] He regularly quotes other writers, not only Aristotle and church fathers, but Muslim and Jewish writers as well. These were not so much "authorities" as interlocutors in a search for the truth that goes beyond any individual thinker. Only rarely does he attack opinions of the people he disagrees with. That is especially true of Augustine, the most respected source of theological opinion. Thomas avoids contradicting Augustine even though he has a quite different worldview.

An example of his blurring the difference between himself and Augustine can be found in his treatise *Truth*. He asks, "Can a man or only God teach?" Both Augustine and Thomas assume that God is the great teacher; from there they go in opposite directions. Augustine thinks that if God is the teacher, then no one else can be. For Thomas's philosophy of participation, it is because God is teacher that every creature can have a share in the activity of teaching. Thomas lists eighteen objections to his view, half of them having some reference to Augustine. At no point does Thomas say that Augustine is wrong. He covers their differences by leaving open possible distinctions that Augustine did not actually make, such as that Augustine is only referring to interior teaching.

The question of who and what can be a teacher is revealing of Thomas's attitude to the natural world of persons and things. Thomas joins the Neoplatonic doctrine of participation in a metaphysical framework with an Aristotelian affirmation of the physical world. Wherever there is a human (or other animal) open to learning, everyone and everything is a potential teacher. Thomas agrees with Aristotle that teaching-learning is a single relation. We learn because we are taught: by parents as well as school teachers, by writing as well as orally, by child as well as adult, by nonhuman animals as well as people.

The underlying principle here is a respect for each being and its distinctive powers. The term *theology*, which Thomas seldom uses, can suggest that God is available for rational explanation without attending to the material beings of our immediate experience. The opinion, Thomas says, "that it is a matter of complete indifference what one thinks about creation provided one has a true interpretation of God . . . is obviously false."[71] Any truth about God or the world can only be appropriated by plunging deeply into the complex world of natures.

Thomas's project in the *Summa Theologiae* may appear to be a detailed description of God and everything in the universe. However, the most startling line in the book appears at the very beginning where Thomas says, "Since we cannot know what God is but only what God is not, let us proceed to investigate the ways that God does not exist."[72] The whole work is one of negatives, which links Thomas to the mystics.[73] The names of God tell us what he is not. When Thomas asks what it means to say that God is living, his answer, in agreement with the Jewish writer, Maimonides, is that God is not dead.[74] That tells us little about God and throws us back to the study of the living.

For Thomas, being is intelligible, but human intelligence is blinded by what is most knowable. He quotes Aristotle that "as the eyes of the bat are dazzled by sunlight, so it is with human intelligence when face to face with what is by nature most obvious." While agreeing with Aristotle, Thomas slyly adds, "Though the eyes of the bat do not avail to behold the sun, it is seen by the eye of the eagle."[75] He is suggesting that humans should not assume that they possess the greatest intelligence. Humans have to use all of their powers to understand natural beings while never forgetting to acknowledge how little they know.

By linking Aristotle to the Neoplatonic tradition, Thomas pushed Aristotle's philosophy beyond the physical and biological. Conversely, by an Aristotelian grounding of the Neoplatonic inclination to the mystical, Thomas made sure that affirmations of unity respected the diversity of the natural world. The result was a sane outlook on the world and especially in regard to human nature with its own inclinations, desires, and possibilities. "God is only offended by us," he writes, "when we act against our own well-being."[76]

That principle is a simple basis for a morality of not doing violence to human nature. It is not a simple principle to carry out in practice because humans are often mistaken about what is good and what is bad for their own well-being. What is good or bad for human nature has to be determined from careful analysis by "practical reason" applied to human experience. A moral law directing actions to human well-being can involve disciplining one power for the good of the whole. Morality is not about being a killjoy. "It is against reason to be burdensome to others, showing no amusement and acting as a grouch."[77]

On some matters Thomas had the right principle but some disastrously wrong facts or opinions in applying his principles. His sexual views were based on medieval biology and the limitations of his own experience. The narrowness of his opinions lives on in some quarters. He thought that all sexual activity other than a husband and wife trying to conceive a child is immoral. Other sexual activities could be graded by their degree of unnaturalness.[78] Thomas's wrong-headed opinions in an area that he did not understand should not obscure his principle that morality is about a healthy disciplining of the body for the purpose of transforming natural possibilities into unified personal activities. The will is not a faculty alien to understanding; the person acts as a psycho-physical unity.

Thomas is often cited as the main advocate of a natural law morality. Given the stereotyped meaning usually assumed for natural law, the description is misleading. What he stood for might be called a personalized morality. Like other medieval writers, Thomas assumed the existence of *ius naturale*. This law is found by humans in their embodied personhood. Humans should not act counter to their own nature. What exactly they should do has to be discovered through reason guided by faith. "In moral matters," wrote Thomas, "general statements are of minimal utility because actions are particular."[79] Jacques Maritain, a leading neothomist of the twentieth century, summed up Thomas's "unwritten law or natural law" this way: "The human will must act in order to attune itself to the necessary ends of the human being."[80]

For the eventual rise of *human rights*, Thomas does have a contribution to make. Human rights depend on a convergence of traditions that support a respect for the human person. In Thomas's philosophy, "person signifies what is noblest in the whole of nature."[81] A person is one who listens and responds to others. Some people can exercise their own claims to basic human goods; other people permanently or temporarily have to rely on a community for help to act. Thomas's philosophy of personhood can provide helpful support for a philosophy of human rights.

Developments in the Later Middle Ages

The story of the fourteenth and fifteenth centuries is about a clearer split of *ius naturale* into law or right. For Thomas Aquinas the meaning of *ius naturale* is clearly natural law. What seems mysterious to modern readers is how *ius naturale* could shift from an objective meaning (law) to a subjective meaning (right). That way of asking the question gets in the way of understanding that there could be and was a gradual change in emphasis that made more explicit and more important the meaning of right as natural to humans.

Some comments are first needed on how our meanings of subjective and objective differ from the late medieval world. Modern science created as the ideal of truth a machinelike description of the world in mathematical terms. Objectivity required eliminating subjective elements as far as possible. An objective description is an accurate report on the external world. Saying that someone has been objective in judgment is to praise the person as sticking to the facts. In contrast, someone being subjective is thought to have his or her mind clouded by emotion.

In the late nineteenth century, there began to be serious questioning of whether an objective attitude was always the sure way to truth. Objectivity does not come first nor is it the pristine way of seeing. An objective view is a withdrawal from the natural human state of knowing. That "natural" human state of knowing is engagement with a physical world that is shared with others. An objective view can be appropriate for objects. For persons as subjects, an objective view is reductive of the person to an object. To understand a person's subjective elements, one has to bring into play one's own subjective life and try to get inside the skin of another. Empathy is intrinsic to the understanding of a person.

For the medieval world, the objective and the subjective were distinct but not separate. They were the reciprocal poles of a single relation. If that fact is kept in mind, then a movement from objective (law) to subjective (right) over several centuries can make sense. The move was a shift of emphasis that did not require a denial of the objective to affirm the subjective.

A developing tension between objective and subjective poles and the eventual breaking apart of relational language were not the work of one writer. Gradual changes in science, art, philosophy, and politics were the conditions for an evolution in the meanings of nature, rights, and natural rights. The result was great progress in the mathematical sciences and technology. That progress had its down side in that the person was often treated like an object, nature became objectified, and the idea of a natural right lost its moorings.

It should be noted that in addition to the shifting meanings of nature, right, and subjective, the term *reason* also underwent change by moving to the subjective side. In medieval language, *reason* was a relational term that could include the order of the universe as well as a human power. In the medieval context, humans had a share in the reason that ordered the world. *Ius naturale* was described as a "force of right in man." To a modern reader that phrase may seem to assign *ius* to the human interior. But at the time, the phrase was expressive of the link between a right that a man has and the order of the universe.

The fourteenth century is sometimes portrayed as a hotbed of voluntarism in which law was wholly dependent on the will, human or divine. However, even the most famous philosopher of that century, William of Ockham, still spoke of *ius* as "consonant with right reason."[82] Ockham does represent progress in the direction of *ius naturale* as denoting a power, habit, or activity of the individual.

As *reason* shifted toward the subjective side of the relation, *nature* shifted toward a more objective meaning. Nature understood as an object of aesthetic contemplation is sometimes given a precise date. Petrarch describes an experience that he had in 1336 at the top of Mt. Ventoux. Nature is contemplated as a means for man's self-expression.[83] The danger in turning nature or Nature into an object of contemplation was that the human became separated from nature.

A century and a half after Petrarch's contemplative experience, Giovanni Pico della Mirandola describes man not as a fixed part of the universe but as sharing with God in the subjectivity that should rise above nature. Man is free to be whatever he chooses to be. Pico identifies this sentiment with the instructions that God gave to Adam. Pico probably assumed that he was articulating Christian doctrine, but his separating man from nature was a breaking away from Christian tradition.[84]

Over the centuries, distinctions had been introduced that had the effect if not the intent of differentiating between *ius* as a law or guide and *ius* as a power or faculty of the human subject. In a further development, Marsilius of Padua (1275-1342) was one of the first authors to consistently use *lex* for "law." He uses *ius* as a power, habit, or activity that should conform to *lex*; that is, *ius* as law had shifted into the background, and *ius* as a right came to the fore.

Natural law had always allowed for more than divine commands and prohibitions. To the extent that *ius naturale* absorbed all or some of *ius gentium*, changeability was included in natural law. William of Ockham wrote of "natural law by supposition," by which he meant a relative response to contingent events. For Christian writers, natural law after the fall of Adam was necessarily different from natural law before it was affected by human failings. For example, there was now ownership of property; and if a person can own property, then he can be said to have a right to the property. Thus, a right of ownership (*dominium*) became included in the meaning of *ius naturale*. Similarly, if one man can have an obligation to pay a debt, another man has a right to be paid.

A further distinction in the emergence of *ius* as right was between rights that could be "alienated" (waived) and rights that are inalienable. The man who has a right to payment of a debt could waive his right to be paid. Similarly, a man who has a right to defend himself when attacked can choose not to do so. In contrast, there are inalienable rights that cannot be renounced because they pertain to the nature of the human. A person has a duty to preserve his life; he does not have a right to renounce his life. And "as by nature, no man may abuse, torment or afflict himself, so by nature, no man may give that power to another, seeing he may not do it himself."[85] By implication, a man would have a right in extreme circumstances to take what is necessary for his survival.

Another important distinction was between a right to do something and a right to receive something, a difference between active and passive rights. The latter category did not mean a mere openness to receive. Aquinas had made regular use of "active potency" in contrast to emptiness. His favorite metaphor, which still works well, is that medicine can only heal by drawing on the active potency of the body. A "right of recipience" is important for the meaning of natural rights; a right is not only the power to do certain things but the power to receive help from a community.

Jean Gerson (1363-1429) was concerned with *ius* as "an immediate faculty or power pertaining to anyone according to the dictate of right reason."[86] He saw no conflict between a freedom for personal activity and a right to receive whatever help is required for a fully human life.

Culmination: Sixteenth and Early Seventeenth Centuries

The use of *natural rights* in the sixteenth and early seventeenth centuries is found in the writings of a group of Spanish Jesuits and in the beginnings of international law by the great Dutch scholar, Hugo Grotius (1583-1645). After a long period of decline, scholastic philosophy had a second spring in sixteenth-century Spain. The attachment to Aristotle in the late medieval period had been disastrous for scholastic philosophy's confrontation with the new mathematical sciences. Aristotle acquired a blemish on his reputation, but he surely would not have agreed with the "Aristotelians" in their unwillingness to see a new world both microscopically and macroscopically.

Instead of just quoting Aristotle and Aquinas, a group of Spanish scholars did their own thinking while being inspired by Aquinas. Foremost among these scholars were Francisco de Vitoria (1483-1546) and Francisco Suarez (1548-1617). In Vitoria's time, what sparked a vigorous debate in Spain was the case of the American native. The "discovery of a new world" was filled with alluring possibilities; it was also a crisis in the Christian belief that the human race is descended from Adam and redeemed by Christ. America, as a German map maker called this new world, took on images both of paradise and of the end-time.

The native peoples, lumped together under the term *Indian*, did not fit into the European picture of the world. They were declared to be barbarians, a term that had been used since ancient Greece. The question was whether traits associated with barbarians, especially a lack of reason and good will, applied to the Indians. The Spanish warriors were mightily impressed by the city of Tenochtitlan, the center of Aztec culture, but were shocked by the Aztec practice of human sacrifice.[87]

The Spanish conquerors were accompanied by missionaries, some of whom were severely critical of Spanish policies. The most famous of these churchmen was Bartolomé de Las Casas who was called Defender of the Indians. Much of what is known about the harsh treatment of the Indians by the Spanish is from the histories written by Las Casas.[88]

The pressing concern of whether the Indians had souls was settled by an affirmative ruling in Spain, thereby qualifying the Indians for conversion to Christianity. Concern for their immortal souls did not necessarily translate into respect for their persons and their right to ownership. Las Casas employed the doctrine of natural rights, citing Aristotle, Aquinas and the canonists' tradition. In the world after Adam's sin, the land that originally belonged to all men in common could now be owned by way of occupancy. Once the land was occupied, no one else had a right to dispossess people of their homes. The Indians, who had no such theories in their use of the land, were prey to European charades of entering into contracts for purchase of the land. The promises were regularly broken.

Las Casas was not a scholar. He lived in the midst of the problem he was describing. His writings have many inconsistencies, and his attitude to the Indians was paternalistic. He was not opposed to the Spanish mission to convert the Indians. He simply argued that violence was not the way in which the Indians would be persuaded to become Christians.

Back in Spain, the scholar Francisco de la Vitoria gave support to the defense of Indian rights and to criticism of the military conquest of Indian lands. Vitoria, in agreement with previous tradition, held that dominion, an element within *ius naturale*, meant the right to choose a ruler and to own lands. The Indians had their own leaders, and they occupied the land. The Christian invaders did not have a right to land that was occupied by the "heathens" or a right to determine the Indians' political arrangements. Vitoria cited Aristotle and Aquinas in support of respecting personal rights; his view was also consistent with the tradition of the canonists.

Like other medieval writers, Vitoria did not see a conflict between the political community and the person as a bearer of rights. The state has a divinely established right that follows from the nature of the human being. Although Vitoria originally defended a divine right of monarchy (in his writings at the beginning of the Reformation), he moved away from that position. Distinctions about the right of citizens to establish the form of government they wish and a right to overthrow tyrannical forms of governance were left to future writers.

Although Vitoria gave prominent place to the state, he also emphasized that every human being is a unique bearer of rights. In arguing against the supposed lack of reason shown by the Indians, he noted that children are bearers of rights. That point is noteworthy for today's human rights, inclusive of children and others who are limited in the exercise of reason. On the other hand, Vitoria denied any sort of rights for animals, a position that also needs discussion in the context of today's rights.

The most heralded debate on the Spanish treatment of the Indians was held in Valladolid in 1548. Unfortunately, Vitoria had died just previous to the debate. Bartolomé de Las Casas was left to carry forth the argument against a noted scholar, Juan Ginés de Sepulveda. Sepulveda argued, citing Aristotle, that the Indians were slaves by nature. Las Casas also called on Aristotle for a theory of rights and for respect based on human nature. The debate was declared to have ended in a draw. However, since Las Casas held his own against the great scholar, many people thought he deserved to be given the edge as the winner of the debate.

The greatest of the Christian writers in the Spanish second spring of scholasticism was Francisco Suarez. Like Vitoria, he was a disciple of Thomas Aquinas. He was perhaps out of touch with the Neoplatonic metaphysics of Aquinas, and he read into Aquinas a doctrine of rights that was not there. On the whole, however, he developed ideas of government, law, and rights that were compatible with Aquinas and also spoke to the emerging modern world.

Unlike Vitoria, Suarez strongly opposed the divine right of kings. The state comes about through a power inherent to persons. In the "concessive" part of natural law, citizens are allowed to transfer their power to rulers. The power is not just delegated to the ruler but is given over to the ruler so that once government is established the power cannot be withdrawn. Citizens do retain the rights to life and liberty, something that can justify rebellion against tyrannical forms of government.

In describing *ius naturale*, Suarez begins with justice (*iusticia*) from which he believed the term *ius* was derived. He cites Aquinas as saying that *ius* is what is just or fair. He then continues on a path that Aquinas did not go, contrasting what *ius* customarily means to what it strictly means. This second meaning, a faculty of the person, refers to a "right in a thing" or a "right to a thing." The first is exemplified in the right to property; the second can be seen in a worker's right to his wages. The rights inherent to a person are not in conflict with the political community because of the natural sociability of man. Rights are personal, but persons are communal and social beings.

Suarez was at the edge of the modern idea of right; Hugo Grotius crossed that line. Although Grotius remained a loyal Protestant Christian, his writings were more accessible to the secular reader of his time and today. Whether or not he was trying to hide his continuity with five centuries of writing on natural law/rights, he usually cited classical sources for his views.

Grotius is most famous as the founder of international law. Although the term *international* did not exist, he attempted to establish a code of behavior for modern states. He wrote in the midst of the European slaughter known as the The Thirty Years War. The title of his major work, *On the Law of War and Peace*, indicates his passionate concern with the violence and destructiveness of war. European nations failed to follow his rules for what constitutes a just war. He criticized Erasmus for going too far in opposing war, but perhaps an opposition to all war was a case worth making.[89]

Hugo Grotius's language was ambiguous enough that he can be read as modern even though many of his assumptions about laws of nature are rooted in the Middle Ages. His two most basic laws of nature are human sociability and human solidarity.[90] Law is not arbitrary; human nature is the "mother of natural laws." Like his immediate predecessors, Grotius takes *ius* to mean what is just. That meaning implies *ius* is a moral quality that enables one to act justly. As a human faculty, it includes the power over oneself (liberty) and power over others.

Grotius's assertion of self-love as the basis of law is sometimes taken to be a novel development. In later centuries, it would become almost a truism that everyone acts out of self-interest. Apparent exceptions to that rule were considered delusionary. In the twentieth century, personal sociability received a new life, but not especially in the field of international relations. What still dominates thinking about the relations between nation-states is that they act from self-interest; nothing else needs to be considered.

The modern world posited a choice between self-interest and altruism, a term that means acting for the good of another. It was firmly believed that while an individual might act altruistically, a nation-state always acts out of self-interest. For many writers, morality and altruism are interchangeable terms.[91] In contrast to that opposition, Grotius drew upon a tradition going from the Bible, through Augustine, Gratian, Aquinas, Suarez, and innumerable others in which the interests of the self are not necessarily opposed to morality. Morality is based on love of self, neighbor, and God as a single package. The love of oneself in Jewish and Christian views of morality is not only allowed but is a duty. The interest of the self, starting with self-preservation, is a "dictate of right reason." The self's interests are in a world where others have interests too.

What is true of a person's self-interests applies to nation-states although the interests of a nation-state are immeasurably more difficult to ascertain than the interests of a person. Like persons, a nation-state has a right to self-preservation; other nations do not have a right to cross its borders and take over its life. That fact is only a first step to setting up a body of laws that applies to nations. Grotius opposed the Machiavellian principle of *raison d'état*, which justifies any action that a state takes on the basis of its own interest. He argued that "one does not do violence to his own interest if he consults the advantage of others." He also pointed out that "there is no state so powerful that it may not sometimes need the help of others outside itself."[92] Cicero's *ius gentium*, a law of peoples, indicates that we can learn from the experience of people in the past. And what is fair and just in the mutual relations of modern states has to be worked out by careful attention to detail and with a willingness to seek a ground of common interests.

Grotius sounds thoroughly modern when he writes at the beginning of *On the Law of War and Peace*: "By mutual consent it has become possible that certain laws should originate between states, or a good many states."[93] Despite Grotius sounding voluntaristic here and endorsing the principle that the right thing is whatever we agree is right, he never severed his connection to the dictates of reason. *Ius*, meaning "law," refers to a rule of action that obliges us to do what is right. Grotius argued, for example, that a right of property did not extend to the sea; no one can claim to occupy the sea.[94] The pope had no business dividing up the ocean in 1493 between Spain and Portugal. Maritime laws have to be worked out with the mutual consent of all states or "a good many states."

Grotius accepted a world of free sovereign states not subject to any external superior. Catholic writers generally viewed this situation as chaotic, one that would lead to violent conflicts. Three years after Grotius died, the arrangement known as the Peace of Westphalia established the modern pattern of nation-states. Grotius would not have been happy with the results of that accord from the midseventeenth to the midtwentieth centuries. "War made the state, and the state made war."[95] Grotius's dedication to laws between nations cannot be blamed for the subsequent developments—or lack of development—in international law.

Grotius was writing at the time that the "new sciences" were taking shape, as reflected in the writing of Francis Bacon. "Man" was now to confront "Nature." In a famous image of Bacon's, man was "to put nature to the rack to compel her to answer our questions." That image is somewhat misleading in that Bacon did not advocate violence against nature; his favorite metaphor for the relation is the marriage bed. Man has to woo nature, listening to and obeying her, even as he gets on top and gets her to submit.[96] This image of a gentle partnership of lovers was supplied by Bacon's Christian belief that man and nature will eventually be fully united. Bacon's successors left behind the restraint of that belief and instead wished to conquer nature and discover the laws of nature.

The seventeenth century thus broke with the meaning of natural law/ right from the previous centuries. The change was not from an objective to a subjective meaning of *ius*. It was from a law of natures based on moral imperatives in human nature to laws of nature that are discovered in the world outside man. From the beginning, it was clear which side would win the contest between the medieval law of natures and the modern laws of nature. The laws of nature that could be discovered by the senses, be described in mathematical terms, and be applied for the progress of the human race made previous speculation on the laws of nature seem like child's play.

The idea of *ius naturale* continued into the eighteenth century, but the tradition in which the idea was embedded no longer existed. The political revolutions in North America and France used the term *natural rights* because that was the language they had inherited. However, the context for asserting such rights was no longer evident, especially in the French Revolution. The rights would simply be declared to exist, but the preaching of natural rights did not establish their basis.

Claims of rights are too easily dismissed unless they are backed by a tradition that has a long history, a present community, and effective education. The task in the twenty-first century is not to reappropriate the natural rights of the eighteenth century but to understand how those rights were limited, most blatantly by racism and sexism. Beyond what the eighteenth century meant by natural rights, the need today is to cultivate settings in which human rights apply to every human being. The basis of those rights is not Nature but the nature of human beings in their historical movement toward a community that is responsible for the most vulnerable natures.

CHAPTER 2

Revolutions and Men's Rights

This chapter picks up the story of natural and other rights from the middle of the seventeenth century to the end of the eighteenth century. This period brought about several revolutions that proclaimed the rights of man. The fact that neither women nor slaves were included in the natural rights of man raises a serious objection to any claimed universality of such rights.

Before examining some of this history, it will be helpful to reflect on the meanings of *liberty* and *freedom* and their relation to revolution. A tension between liberty and freedom is a theme that runs throughout the eighteenth-century revolutions in France and British America. An argument over the meaning of *liberty* dominated the pre-Civil War period in the United States.[1] And today's failure to differentiate between liberty and freedom could threaten the existence of the country.

Liberty and Freedom

For distinguishing between liberty and freedom, one has to look at the origin of the words, their evolution, and their meanings in use today. As is often the case in the English language, the words *liberty* and *freedom* might seem to have the same meaning. And indeed in both the distant past and in the present, the two words are often used interchangeably.[2] In all such cases, however, each term has its own history and accumulated connotations. Subtle differences can show up in the actual use of the terms even though it is impossible to draw a firm line between meanings of the two terms.[3]

Both words have long histories going back at least to the fourteenth century. *Liberty* was often used in the plural especially in a political context. The document known as the *Magna Carta Libertatum* was an attempt to guarantee a set of liberties or protections from government interference. *Freedom* could be used for similar political purposes, but it had a more comprehensive philosophical meaning; liberty as "freedom from" was complemented by a "freedom for."

A cry for liberty or liberation most often means resistance to an oppressor. Freedom comes later when the oppression ceases. When Sarah Grimké in the nineteenth century said, "All that I ask of our brethren is that they will take their feet from off our necks," she was not describing the freedom of women but an indispensable step of liberation before women could explore their own freedom.[4]

In the British American and French Revolutions, *liberty* rather than *freedom* was used to refer to one of the natural rights of men. The focus was on the overthrowing of oppressive governments in the name of an expanded human freedom. Article 4 of the French Declaration says that "liberty consists in the freedom to do everything which injures no one else." So defined, liberty becomes highly desirable for most people, but the place of government is left unclear.

The ideal of political power residing in "the people" has come down to us from the eighteenth century. On both the political right and political left, government is regularly viewed as the main obstacle to the people's liberty. When the choice is between the intrusions of government and individual liberty, there are few defenders of government. Dick Armey in his Tea Party manifesto, *Give Us Liberty*, puts the matter succinctly: "Less government and lower taxes equals freedom."[5]

Freedom has a positive meaning almost everywhere. The most authoritarian governments do not admit to being opposed to freedom. Freedom cannot be delivered by politics, but without effective government, freedom can be overwhelmed by outside forces, especially by large concentrations of money. Freedom for the very young, the very old, the sick and the poor is vulnerable to forces beyond the individual's control. Freedom implies more than liberation from government. In John Milton's words, "To be free is precisely the same thing as to be pious, wise, just and temperate, careful of one's own, abstinent from what is another's, and then, in fine, magnanimous and brave." *Freedom* in the period since Milton's seventeenth-century meaning has shed many of those qualities, but freedom continues to be one of the most positive words in the language.[6]

The idea of liberty as a freedom from government restrictions was enthusiastically embraced in the United States. If one could count the uses of *freedom* and *liberty* in the history of the United States, *liberty* would be the sure winner. The revolution was fought in the name of the "sacred cause of liberty." The Bill of Rights to the United States Constitution includes a series of rights as liberties.[7] One of the chief symbols of the United States is a French gift, which came to be called the Statue of Liberty.

Revolution

In the last few decades, there has been an attempt to return to a nonviolent meaning of *revolution*.[8] Many people would dismiss the idea as nearly a contradiction in terms. The British American revolution followed by the more violent French Revolution set the meaning of revolution as an overthrow of a government by violent means. The nineteenth and most of the twentieth centuries seemed to confirm that meaning. It was assumed that an exceptional case such as Gandhi's could not be replicated under other conditions.

The current discussion of nonviolent revolution was helped by Gene Sharp's *From Dictatorship to Democracy: A Conceptual Framework for Liberation*, first published in 1993, and still being republished.[9] Sharp's book, which was translated into forty languages, is a manual of nonviolent tactics that has had worldwide influence. George Lawson, in his book *Negotiated Revolutions*, offers case studies of the Czech Republic, South Africa, and Chile as nonviolent revolutions.[10] Neither Lawson nor others who speak today of nonviolent revolution would deny that there are likely to be violent incidents that occur within popular uprisings. Nonetheless, guerilla warfare is not the essential means for getting rid of a tyrannical government. Aided by the "technological revolution" in communication, political revolutions by peaceful means now have some hope (but no guarantee) of succeeding.

After the French Revolution, the word *revolution* carried connotations not only of violence but of rejection of the past in favor of a new beginning. This attitude was symbolized by the French attempt to create a new calendar in which the year one began with the birth of the republic on Sept. 22, 1792. The attempt to wipe clean the slate of the past was bound to fail but not before a sea of violence and bloodshed confirmed that fact.

Neither the etymology of *revolution* nor its history before the second half of the eighteenth century connoted a violent rejection of the past. On the contrary, "to revolve" carries an image of circular movement.

A revolution would be a turning back to the beginning. The first prominent use of *revolution* in the English language was to translate the fifteenth-century work of Copernicus, entitled *De Revolutionibus Orbium Coelestium*. Copernicus used *revolution* to describe the regular, lawful, orbital movements of heavenly bodies. Neither in Latin nor in English did the word imply newness or violence.[11]

The war for independence (or liberty) by the British colonies in North America that lasted from 1775 to 1781 is usually called the American Revolution. From one perspective, the war was a *consequence* of the revolution that had occurred in the 1760s. In another respect, the war was a first step to the completion of the United States's revolution in the 1780s. The first of these two perspectives was expressed by John Adams in an 1818 letter to Hezekiah Niles: "The revolution was effected before the war commenced. The Revolution was in the minds and hearts of the people . . . . This radical change in the principles, opinions, sentiments and affections of the people, was the real American Revolution."[12]

Adams was accurate in pointing to the change in minds and hearts that swept across the colonies in the 1760s and early 1770s. But in political terms, a more important point was made in 1787 by Benjamin Rush: "The American war is over; but this is far from being the case with the American Revolution. On the contrary, nothing but the first act of the great drama is closed. It remains yet to establish and perfect our new forms of government."[13] The new form of government was developed by looking back to classical models and to what was called the Glorious Revolution in England at the end of the seventeenth century.

The English reform of 1689 was to *restore* the monarchy and rights that had been lost or suppressed. The revolution looked to the Magna Carta and the rights of Englishmen guaranteed by the unwritten constitution of four centuries. In 1775, the British American colonists appealed to the British people, acting as "descendants of Britons" and acting in defense of "the glorious privileges" for which their ancestors fought.[14] The British American revolution thus retained some of the older meaning of revolution even as it fed into the more violent meaning that the word came to connote.

While every political revolution invokes a right to liberty, the individual person's liberty needs a context of some new form of government. In British America, the Declaration of Independence proclaimed a right to liberty; the Constitution was intended to secure freedom. The French Revolution's *liberté* was in tension with equality (fraternity came later), and both needed the context of a stable constitution.

The Individual and Society

What led up to the eighteenth-century's declarations of the rights of the individual was a reconstituting of the question of how the human being is related to other human beings and to the human environment. Hugo Grotius had enough continuity with the ages before him that he could speak of the rights of individuals as grounded in reason or nature. The theorists who followed him—Hobbes, Locke, Rousseau, Hume and others—had to start with a different set of assumptions because the world had changed in so many ways.[15]

A favorite metaphor in this period was the "state of nature." It is the state from which man emerged to form society by consenting to the rights, privileges, and obligation of civilized men. Not everyone accepted this image. David Hume is the most prominent philosopher who rejected the exercise of imagining a state of nature. Edmund Burke, although accepting a form of contract across the generations, was also skeptical of social contract theories.

The idea that there was a "state of nature" preceding the world as we know it has echoes of the Christian belief that there was a prelapsarian world. None of the modern theorists, however, imagined the state of nature as a paradise from which man and woman were banished. Rather, thinkers of the seventeenth and eighteenth centuries imagined a not very desirable condition of man in the state of nature.

Whatever deals and compromises men made in passing from the state of nature to civilization, they acquired duties and rights in relation to other human beings. Rights were henceforth to be based on human agreements. The obligations of each man were to his fellow men; his rights were legal claims on the basis of agreed upon laws. The rights in society could be described as social rights. It was especially in the seventeenth and eighteenth centuries that *society* came to be a grand category that can encompass all things human—although not the nonhuman.

The idea of "natural rights" had an uneasy relation to political rights in civil society. The term *natural* here could refer to the state of nature and therefore be opposed to the political and social. That could be a way of asserting that natural rights are superior to any political rights, but it could also make the idea of natural rights part of a mythical world that was imagined to precede any human society. Did man give up his natural rights when he entered society? Does man leave nature to enter society? The only way to work through the maze of meanings for *natural* and *natural rights* is to attend to individual authors within different traditions.

Thomas Hobbes. The seventeenth-century writer who set the direction for much of what followed was Thomas Hobbes (1588-1679). His book, *Leviathan*, was a new kind of theoretical imagining under the claim to be science. Hobbes's name is often associated with Grotius, and there are definite connections. But while Grotius's relation to the centuries before him remains somewhat ambiguous, Hobbes asserted a radical break. Except for retaining the medieval language of *ius naturale*, his political philosophy was thoroughly modern. Hobbes interprets "right of nature," as meaning "the liberty each man hath, to use his own power, as he will himselfe, for the preservation of his own Nature; that is to say, of his own Life; and consequently of doing anything which in his own Judgment, and Reason, hee shall conceive to be the aptest means thereto."[16]

Hobbes does not speak of natural rights but of the "right of nature." There is only one right, that of self-preservation. Anything that the individual deems to be the "aptest means" to preserving his life follows upon the right of nature. Because every man is intent on defending his life against every other man, the state of nature is also called the state of war, which in Hobbes's famous description of man's life is "solitary, poor, nasty, brutish and short."[17] To stay in this state is to court death.

The only way out is that men give up their ineffective liberty in the state of nature and agree to give over power to a single head of a society. The state so formed would then protect each individual's life and liberty. The modern individual and the modern state were conceived together. One can imagine the state as a project of individualism, or conversely, one can view the individual as formed on the model of the state. Each is bound only by "self interest."[18] *Leviathan* was written during the civil war in England; Hobbes's theory justified a powerful state that would use whatever force is necessary to keep the peace.

John Locke (1632-1704). Another important English theorist, John Locke, was writing at the time of the restoration of constitutional monarchy. What Parliament had done, Locke justifies on paper. His *Second Treatise of Civil Government* was generally understood in the American colonies and during the French Revolution as a statement of abstract principles to be put into practice. "But so far from being a preface, it has the marks of a postscript, and its power to guide derived from its roots in actual political experience."[19]

In the history of rights theory, Locke is famous for the trio of "life, liberty, and property."[20] Locke has often been harshly criticized for saying that the chief end of government for men "is the preservation of their property, to which in the state of nature there are many things wanting." But in the paragraph immediately before that statement, he defined property as "their lives, liberties and estates."[21] Thus, one could say that for Locke the fundamental right is property which includes life and liberty.

Locke drew upon one strand of tradition in invoking a right to property. In most medieval writing, private property arose after the sin of Adam. It was a right but, unlike life and liberty, one that could be "alienated." Locke, by including life and liberty within property, made a right to property inalienable. He was not, however, endorsing the private wealth of millionaires. He was interested in property as *proprium*, that is, the security of a person's physical integrity and the immediate extension of the self in the stewardship of goods. Jefferson would draw on a different tradition going back to Grotius by way of Jean Jacques Burlamaqui that property is not included in inalienable rights. Around this point, significant differences would arise between British American and French Revolutions

The context of Locke's political writing was the Glorious Revolution of 1689, which established or reestablished the rights guaranteed to the men of England. King James II, on ascending the throne, agreed to a document that limited the crown's power. Only with the consent of Parliament could the king engage in most of the activities of governing. The document outlaws cruel and unusual punishment; it likewise forbids excessive fines. It guarantees free speech and a trial by jury. (It also guaranteed that "the subjects which are protestants may have arms for their defense suitable to their conditions.") Most important, with reference to the whole document, the members of Parliament "do claim, demand and insist upon all and singular the premises, as their undoubted rights and liberties."[22]

David Hume (1711-1776). In the eighteenth century, a distinct school of philosophy emerged in Scotland. The group included Adam Smith whose *Theory of Moral Sentiments* provided the basis for a group of Scottish theorists of morality.[23] Smith's economic theory in *The Wealth of Nations* was lifted from its context of a philosophy of human sympathy. "All the members of human society stand in need of each other's assistance . . . . Where the necessary assistance is reciprocally afforded from love, from gratitude, from friendship and esteem, the society flourishes and is happy."[24]

The most famous philosopher in this group of theorists was David Hume who became a chief critic of contract theories of society. He is especially critical of the rationalist philosophies of his day, which assumed that the will can be moved by "reason alone." Modern ethics to this day is in large part an attempt to answer Hume's contention that reason is the slave of passion and that no abstract principle is capable of overriding the emotions.[25]

Hume rejected the theories of Hobbes and Locke on the origin of society and natural rights. Moral life begins with the affective life of the family. Morality is not sustained by abstract reasoning but by custom and prejudices, a positive term that refers to the judgments of tradition. Education has to help the individual to sort out which prejudices can be justified and which cannot. While the contract theories posit adult males setting up the world, Hume realistically begins with unequals, that is, women and children as well as those men who have a variety of incapacities.[26]

Human beings are not born as selfish and egotistical. Hume writes that "it is requisite that there be an original propensity of some kind in order to be a basis to self-love, by giving a relish to the objects of its pursuit; and none more fit for this purpose than benevolence or humanity."[27] While Rousseau later used pity as the main feeling we are born with, Hume's basic sentiment is sympathy, a capacity to feel with the other, to put oneself in the place of another.

David Hume was an opponent of *natural* rights, but he could be an important resource in understanding *human* rights. Unlike many of his contemporaries, Hume was clear and consistent in his meanings of *nature* and *natural*. He contrasts nature and artifice but not as opposites; the artificial can be what is thoughtfully contrived and designed. "Justice is artificial but not arbitrary."[28] Unlike Hobbes's ethical problem of every man at war with every other man, Hume sees the problem as my family and friends in conflict with someone else's family and friends. His "laws of nature" are a cumulative attempt to work out peaceful and just relations dependent on promises and on adjustments that deal with inequalities.

Hume's metaphor describing reason as the "slave" of passion overstates his case. That image can interfere with what Hume is concerned with, namely, a way to overcome dichotomies of reason and emotion, thinking and willing. Ironically, his most often quoted line is "you cannot derive an ought from an is."[29] Often the line is glibly announced as if it ends any argument about the source of morality. Statements of morality are then detached from any connection to the "real world," the world of facts. Morality is sent to the shady world of values that are based solely on choice.

If one considers Hume's work as a whole, it is clear that his intention was not to affirm a world separated into facts and values. What he denied was that statements of obligation can be *derived* or *deduced* from statements that attempt to describe the world. That is the beginning not the end of the story. What is needed are terms that embody our moral stance and include our experiential knowing. Hume uses the term *sympathy* in this way. Annette Baier, a contemporary scholar of Hume, takes *trust* to be the fundamental moral category.[30] One could also begin from care, love, responsibility or many other terms that can be used as anchored in reality while taking a moral position. *Human rights* is not such a term, that is, a starting point of ethics. Hume would probably be skeptical of the idea of human rights, but his concern with justice and sympathy for all persons could be a contribution to the meaning of human rights.

English Colonists and Liberty

John Adams said that the British American colonists began declaring independence "upon taking ship in European ports to find a land of their own in America."[31] They left their homes to make a precarious trip to a "wilderness," which was thousands of miles away. Why would any seventeenth-century European do that? Individual motives are not always easy to ascertain. However, the people who wrote accounts of colonial life consistently cited two reasons for the colonization, namely, economics and religion.

The Virginia charter of 1606 states that the purpose of the plantation is "the propagating of Christian religion to such people, as yet in darkness and miserable ignorance of the true knowledge and worship of God."[32] There is no reason to think that this ostensible purpose of converting the natives was fraudulent. An intention to spread the Christian gospel was a regular part of the invitation to migrate to America. However, the economic motive that is usually stated as secondary was no doubt the primary reason for many individuals.

Later history books in the United States tell the story of Virginia from the perspective of the European settlers. America represented freedom, that is, liberation from the old world and old ways. Unfortunately, one man's liberty can be another man's oppression. In the case of Virginia, the white man's liberty was at the expense of American natives and imported Africans.

The arrival of Africans in 1619 probably seemed at the time a minor event. Laborers were needed to work the tobacco crop. However, a recent writer puts the event in proper perspective: "The flag she flew was Dutch; her crew a motley. Her port of call, an English settlement, Jamestown, in the colony of Virginia. She came, she traded, and shortly afterwards was gone. Probably no ship in modern history has carried a more portentous freight. Her cargo? Twenty slaves."[33] Technically, these first Africans were not slaves, but their condition of servitude in these alien surroundings began the terrible practice of slavery that nearly ended the union of the states. The plight of African Americans remained the shame of the country long after slavery had ended.

As for the native people, they could not be subdued for work in the same way as the Africans could. They could be bargained with, as occasionally happened, or they could be subdued with firepower. The Europeans looked on the Indians as savages, ignorant of civilization. If the Indians could not be converted, they would have to be eliminated.

The myth that envelops the United States's origin is centered on the 1620 settlement at Plymouth. For most U.S. Americans, the Puritans fled the religious oppression of Europe and founded America (United States) as the land of freedom. Since they were beyond where the patent of the Virginia Company applied, the group on board were required "to Covenant and Combine ourselves into a Civil Body Politic." The one-paragraph document known as the Mayflower Compact has been highlighted in the myth that the Puritans were founding the United States and its government. This covenant, the first of many in New England, does deserve credit for its contribution to evolving notions of government.[34]

As in Virginia, the Indians were the other side of the story of God leading his people across the sea to conquer a wilderness. Commentators who were otherwise humane seemed oblivious of the native peoples' having a right to defend their homes and their way of life. If God was on the side of the settlers, then their enemy was the enemy of God. In a war with the Pequot in 1637, William Bradford describes the killing of four hundred Indians: "It was a fearful sight to see them frying in the fire and the streams of blood quenching the same, and horrible was the stink and scent therof." These horrible sights, sounds, and stench do not generate sympathy for the Indians' loss of life. On the contrary, Bradford continues that "the victory seemed a sweet sacrifice [referring to Leviticus 2:1-2] and they gave praise thereof to God who had wrought wonderfully for them to enclose their enemies in their hands and give them so speedy a victory over so proud and insulting an enemy."[35]

A voyage in 1630 that established Massachusetts was tied to political changes at home. King and Parliament were at a standoff. When the king dissolved Parliament and could not raise taxes, England's war with France came to a quick end. Ships became available for a westward voyage, and the company obtained the *Arbella*. The passengers on the *Arbella* did not sign a covenant before disembarking, but they were admonished by their leader, John Winthrop, to "knit together" as a community. In his speech, "A Model of Christian Charity," Winthrop said, "We must delight in each other, make others' concerns our own, rejoice together, mourn together, labor and suffer together."[36] He warned that getting rich could not be the aim of the settlers.

A less often quoted part of Winthrop's sermon reminded people that they should know their place and stay in it. "God almighty in his holy and wise providence hath so disposed the condition of mankind as in all times some must be rich, some poor, some high and eminent in power and duty, others mean in subjection." It may be that there will always be rich people and poor people, but even God-fearing Calvinists did not necessarily accept that the present arrangement of the rich and the poor was God's disposition.

Liberty, Civil and Religious

German Arciniegas notes that independence was not something that sprang up in Philadelphia in the year 1776. "The experience of three centuries was needed to define it. America had emerged as the continent of European liberation at the moment when the first immigrants occupied it. The Spanish, Portuguese, Englishmen, and Frenchmen discovered a land to which they went in search of their own emancipation."[37] The English settlers gave their own distinctive twist to the theme of liberty.

The eighteenth-century British Americans devised an interpretation of the previous century in which liberty—religious and civil—became the one central concern.[38] Children in the United States would later read the history of seventeenth-century New England through the myths elaborated in the eighteenth century. The colonists saw as united two kinds of liberty, civil and religious. The overarching idea that held together the two ideas of liberty was *America*. For many Americans both then and now, *America* is another name for liberty. Both the Christian Church and the United States government are taken to be legitimate insofar as they are instruments of liberty.

The increasing emphasis on political liberty was influenced by an antimony of power and liberty. Thomas Hobbes provided a distrust of power, understood as a lust for dominating others. Hobbes's solution for the danger and destructiveness of power was an authoritarian system, a sovereign power to restrain individuals.[39] The British American colonists influenced by Hobbes and by English radicals believed that (political) power is the opposite of liberty. But with help from theories elaborated by Montesquieu, they came up with a solution different from Hobbes's. The British American solution involved interacting powers and individuals who are educated to use liberty with virtuous restraint.[40]

Bernard Bailyn traced the history of the eighteenth-century meaning of *faction* as an index of political change.[41] At the beginning of the eighteenth century, *faction* was negative in meaning, a disruption by minorities who had only their own interests at heart. At the end of the eighteenth century, James Madison in the *Federalist Papers* was still distrustful of faction or party, but his question was not how to eliminate factions but how to put them to use.[42] "The concept of a republic turned from one that can find the common good through representative assembly to one in which a shifting sea of interest groups can be constrained to observe the minimal rules of procedural justice."[43]

Bailyn identified a shift in *faction* starting in 1733 with the recognition that "a free government cannot but be subject to parties, cabals and intrigues."[44] The widespread involvement of the population was bound to include conflicts of interest. Voting and other political participation in the colonies were limited to white men who owned property. Today that seems a severe restriction, but the availability of land spread the franchise more widely than in Europe.[45] On the eve of the revolution, two-thirds of the white males were voters compared to one out of six in England.

In the early eighteenth century, the colonists were still convinced that England was the world's leading example of liberty. The constitutional monarchy established at the end of the seventeenth century guaranteed the rights of Englishmen. During England's French and Indian War, there was little doubt in the colonies that liberty was on the side of the English. At the same time, however, egalitarianism and the rebelliousness of competing factions in the colonies were growing. Pamphlets and newspapers spread political ideas; the existence of a lively press was itself a sign of rebelliousness in the name of liberty. A pamphlet by Jonathan Mayhew in 1750, *A Discourse Concerning Unlimited Submission*, was the opening of a new stage of rebellion.[46]

The corner was perhaps turned in 1753 when it was suggested that the Crown itself could be "factious."[47] Instead of the king presiding as a paternal presence over political order, politics came to be seen as a search for order out of competing factions that included the king. The colonists had to struggle to separate the king from his paternal role. As late as 1774, they addressed the king as "our dear father."[48] One of the things that Thomas Paine's 1776 tract, *Common Sense*, did was to sever the bond of a parent-child relation between king and colonies.[49] In the Declaration of Independence, Thomas Jefferson would make a list of twenty-eight accusations that were directed at the king.

The year 1763 represented a dramatic change in the colonial perception of who is the enemy of liberty. The war between France and England was over; the colonists had sided with England as the seat of liberty; the forces of liberty had triumphed. The end of the war meant the opening of new lands and the development of new instruments of local government. Uneasy with the colonists going their own way, the British tried to rein in the colonies, starting with the Stamp Act in 1765 and culminating in four laws in 1774 known in the colonies as the Coercive Acts. The policy proved to be a disastrous strategy for controlling the increasing rebelliousness of the colonies. The colonists suddenly saw themselves as Carthage being assaulted by Rome; the king was Nero, the vilest of the Caesars.[50] By 1765 civil and religious liberty were joined in the understanding that "the stamping and episcopizing of our colonies were . . . only different branches of the same plan of power."[51]

By 1770, parliament had become a "foreign jurisdiction" and a "pretended power." The colonists were not represented in parliament, so they claimed that the imposition of taxes was tyrannical. Several British statesmen, most prominently Edmund Burke, warned that repression was the wrong policy for distant colonies that had become accustomed to self-rule and where the literacy rate was higher than in England. In a 1775 speech before parliament, Burke listed six ingredients of American liberty, including the fact that the Americans had emigrated from England. "They are therefore not only devoted to liberty, but to liberty according to English ideas and on English principles."[52]

Declaration of Independence

The declaring of independence on July 2, 1776 brought to a close that phase of revolution seeking to restore the rights of English citizens. The political revolution, however, was just beginning. Unlike so many attempted revolutions during the last two centuries, the British American revolution was based on local constitutions and functioning governments.

The existence of thirteen self-governing colonies was a blessing but also a challenge to creating any kind of united front.

The document declaring independence was signed by representatives of twelve colonies on July 4, 1776 (New York came in a week later). There are innumerable points of debate concerning the sources and the interpretation of the text. The standard reading for many years was Carl Becker's 1932 book, *The Declaration of Independence*. In 1978, Garry Wills's interpretation in *Inventing America* drew immediate praise but also considerable criticism.[53] Critics complained that Wills had imposed his own liberal ideology on the text although most critics seemed to bring their own ideology.

Wills played down the influence of John Locke's political philosophy on Jefferson and emphasized Scottish thinkers. The change of interpretation was from an individualism in which government is primarily for the protection of private property to a communal orientation in which moral "sentiments" are the ground of reason. Wills introduced many helpful concerns but perhaps overplayed his hand. There are many interesting points of interpretation that I will not pursue. For my purposes, there is one overriding concern that the Declaration raised, which is the relation between liberty and freedom.

The Continental Congress was intent on achieving cooperative action by the thirteen separate colonies. The Declaration's heading reads, "The Unanimous Declaration of the thirteen united States of America." In the text itself, the last paragraph says, "We therefore, the Representatives of the united States of America, in General Congress assembled . . . do in the name of these *colonies* [Jefferson's draft had used *states*], solemnly publish and declare, that these united colonies are and of right ought to be free and independent states." They speak as colonies but declare themselves to be states. In the Declaration both uses of *united* are in the lowercase.

There was a near contradiction between declaring that there are thirteen free and independent states and implying that there is a single entity named the "united States of America." The authors did not innocently or carelessly use *state*. They precisely list the powers of a state as "to levy war, conclude peace, contract alliances, establish commerce and do all other acts and things which independent states may of right do." If each state could do these things, how can there be one state made up of thirteen states? When the Articles of Confederation were approved, they included in Article II that "each state retains its sovereignty, freedom and independence." A United States of America, it seems, existed in name only.[54]

These independent states immediately began setting up constitutions for governing the people of their respective states. A federation of these states was feasible for the purpose of a war defending the independence of the states. But the Declaration of Independence did not establish a government of the United States. Even when the British abandoned the fight and recognized the independence of the states, the future was not promising for a United States.

It seems clear that the Declaration of Independence's immediate purpose was to do what its title stated—a declaring of independence or separation from England and the British Empire. Its main concern was political liberty rather than human freedom. The heart of the document is the series of accusations leveled against King George III that made "necessary" a separation. That is the way the document was received domestically. Consequent upon this claim to "separate and equal status" among the other powers of the earth, this group of states could negotiate for help with other international players.

The move was most successful in gaining military aid from France. Such a realignment of former enemies in a mere two decades was astounding. France entered the war on the colonists' side out of rivalry with England, not from philosophical agreement about universal rights. As Pauline Maier points out, a declaration of universal rights would not have received enthusiastic embrace from King Louis XVI.[55]

Jefferson's preamble on self-evident truths, starting with the claim that "all men are created equal," did have a later influence on French political thinking.[56] And after the War of 1812, the Declaration shifted from a document that asserted liberty from England to being understood as a theory of human freedom. Jefferson himself at the end of his life encouraged this interpretation of the document.[57]

Thomas Jefferson, while influenced by John Locke on many points, differed on what Jefferson had originally called "sacred and undeniable rights." As noted above, in Locke's trio of life, liberty, and property, Locke's meaning of *property* was that "every man has 'property' in his own 'person.' This nobody has a right to but himself."[58] Jefferson substituted for a right to property a right to "the pursuit of happiness." Jefferson probably sensed that Locke's meaning of *property*—life, liberty, estate—although having some historical justification, would quickly be obscured by the powerful and wealthy. For the tradition that Jefferson was relying upon, property could be called natural, in one of the several meanings of natural; it deserves the protection of civil law, but it is not on the same plane as life and liberty.[59]

Unlike the French Declaration, the Declaration of Independence has no right to property, but it does support a right to revolution. Although a right to property is implied in the Declaration, a right to "the pursuit of happiness" for everyone implies restriction on the acquisition of wealth by a few.[60]

In the United States of today, especially among people called conservative, the Declaration of Independence is referred to as if it provides the legal structure of the United States and a model of government for the world. People often think they are quoting the Constitution when they are actually citing the Declaration. John Boehner, Speaker of the House of Representatives, while holding up a copy of the Constitution, declared he was standing with the Founding Fathers who wrote, "We hold these truths to be self-evident."[61]

The Declaration of the first republic in America was linked to revolutions in other parts of America. Herbert Bolton refers to the American Revolution as "lasting half a century—from 1776 to 1826—and it witnessed the political separation of most of America from Europe."[62] The second American republic was Haiti in 1804. The United States, with Thomas Jefferson as president, scandalously refused to recognize Haiti because it emerged from a rebellion of slaves against France. The United States feared it would encourage rebellion of its own slaves. Even the French recognized Haiti in 1825, but the United States did not do so until 1862 when Abraham Lincoln was president.[63] The Haitian revolution, which was in response to the French Declaration of Rights, did not get much notice at least in U.S. and European textbooks. As a protest of slaves in the name of humanity, its importance as a forerunner of the claim to human rights deserves recognition.

The glaring failure of the first American republic's attempt to be a lesson to the world was its retention of slavery. An objection to slavery was frequently made in the years leading up to the Revolution, but the usual referent for slavery was the colonies' relation to England. Some authors did acknowledge that their slaveholding contradicted their apotheosis of liberty, but the practice nonetheless continued.

The Declaration of Independence in its final form made no effort to address this contradiction of liberty. Jefferson in his draft of the Declaration did take on the question of slavery with breathtaking arrogance. Among Jefferson's accusations against the king was the statement that "he has waged cruel war against human nature itself, violating its most sacred rights of life and liberty in the person of a distant people." And Jefferson expressed disdain at this "warfare of the *Christian* king of Great Britain, determined to keep open a market where men should be bought and sold."[64] The delegates, showing a modicum of discretion, excised the whole paragraph (Jefferson's notes say it was done "in complaisance to South Carolina and Georgia"). They replaced the paragraph with an accusation that the king has "excited domestic insurrections."

The Declaration was thus spared even greater mockery by British critics who focused on the contradiction between the right to liberty and the actual practice of slave-holding by Jefferson and other signers of the Declaration. As Thomas Day, an English abolitionist, expressed it, "they signed the resolution of independence with one hand, the whip over slaves with the other."[65] Jeremy Bentham, in his "Short Review of the Declaration (1776)," provided the most extensive criticism of what the Declaration says about universal rights.[66] In that context, Bentham notes, "Rather surprising it must certainly appear that they should advance maxims so incompatible with their own present conduct."[67]

This painful disparity was not just a topic for philosophical debate. The slaves had the most accurate and long-suffering view of the hypocrisy in the Declaration's philosophical claims. Frederick Douglass reminded the white majority of the slave's view in his oration "What to the Slave is the Fourth of July?" Douglass responds to that question: "I answer, a day that reveals to him, more than all other days in the year, the gross injustice and cruelty to which he is the constant victim."[68] Slavery in the United States was not just a failure to extend rights far enough; it is the evidence that "human" rights were not yet the question. It is perhaps not an accident that in 1850, Douglass makes one of the earliest uses of the term *human rights* in protesting slavery's "outrageous violations of *human* rights."[69]

Slavery was a key issue as to whether *united* States constituted a United States after the Declaration and even after the compromises of the U.S. Constitution. Economic considerations pushed together a group of Southern states to defend slavery. The cry of "states' rights" would have surfaced without slavery, but slavery became the leading edge in controversies over the rights of states and the power of the federal government. States' rights were often a cover story for the defense of slavery.

A first problem with the Declaration of Independence was that "united states" seemed impossible. The logical alternatives were either *united provinces* or *separate states*. A second related problem was what followed *united States* in the Declaration. The words *of America* were inaccurate. The former colonies were a part of the continent of America, which suggests that the country should have had the name United States of *something* or United States *in* America. The name *America* was already taken; it was the name of a continent that contained French, Spanish, and Portuguese colonies.

America from its origin in the sixteenth century also had a religious or quasireligious meaning; it referred to the end-time when the original paradise will be reestablished. America became the idea, ideal or dream that held the states together; it was also a way to avoid the issue of whether there was a United States of New York, Virginia, South Carolina, Massachusetts, and the rest. The United States Constitution did not resolve this problem.

Constitution of Freedom

The term *declaration* has a double meaning: the act of declaring and the document that records the declaring. The first declaration of independence was on July 2, 1776; the second declaration was on July 4, 1776. Aside from raising a question of whether the holiday in celebration of liberty should perhaps be on July 2, the ambiguity does not create serious problems.

The same is not true of the double meaning of *constitution*. In the 1780s, the people's agreement was the constitution of a government; the constitution as a legal code was then set up by the government. "The people should endow the government with a constitution not vice versa."[70] As the case of Great Britain shows, the second constitution is not necessary for the existence of the first. The constitution of the United States government by the people was to establish freedom; the power over that constitution was to remain with the people. The written constitution was the product of a particular time that distributed the powers of government for the protection of freedom.

The fact that the U.S. Constitution was the work of one group of gentlemen meeting in Philadelphia in 1787 does not imply that it should be discarded for something more up to date. William Gladstone referred to the U. S. Constitution as "the most wonderful work ever struck off at a given time from the brain and purposes of man."[71] Nevertheless, a constitution written in the eighteenth century cannot by itself give answers to twenty-first century questions that were unimaginable in the 1780s. The effort to discover the minds of the founders as expressed by the text is a valuable exercise for understanding what they wrote. But a claim that even a perfect reconstruction of their intentions can resolve contemporary debates is a strange assumption.

The strength of the federal constitution was that it emerged from and built upon the local constitutions of villages, townships, and states. The Declaration of Independence had not thrown the colonists into "the state of nature" because they had previously developed self-governing bodies that had their own constitutions.[72] However, out of a distrust of executive power, most of the state constitutions made the government practically equivalent to capricious popular assemblies. At least that is the way many of the leaders of government thought.[73]

The task of the Constitutional Convention, therefore, was not to invent a constitution but to draw upon local constitutions and at same time recognize sovereignty not in the government but with the people. The federal government would establish a unity of interests among the several states while being itself regulated by a complicated set of interactions. The result was a "harmonious system of mutual frustration."[74]

The writers of the Constitution did not base their hopes for government on virtue. They did not have an exalted notion of human nature; they produced a government for ordinary people. However, the idea of a republic, in contrast to a democracy, had some strict conditions: "The well-being of the Republic required promotion of learning and intellect, infused with a spirit of public service in order to develop an expanding class of responsible social leaders."[75] A class of hereditary privilege was to be excluded; a class of disinterested gentlemen was to be cultivated.

For some people, the Constitution is opposed to the Declaration, a pulling back from equality, universal rights, and the sacred cause of liberty. That negative attitude was already present in the anti-Federalist rhetoric of the 1790s and is very much alive today. According to Hannah Arendt, "The basic misunderstanding lies in the failure to distinguish between liberation and freedom; there is nothing more futile than rebellion and liberation unless they are followed by the constitution of the newly won freedom."[76] True, the Constitution makes no reference to universal rights; it is written in sober legal prose. But the Constitution was intended to protect freedom not only from the oppression of rulers but also against the tyranny of majorities. It was Madison's insight that one part of society can oppress another. The Constitution was to save "the rights of the individuals or of the minority . . . from interested combinations of the majority."[77]

Within a few decades, the country had moved toward a more democratic form of government: "one man, one vote." It retained, however, many of the checks and balances to prevent one branch of government from acquiring dictatorial powers and to protect the rights of unpopular minorities. Whether some of those mechanisms, such as the Electoral College, should now be jettisoned is an issue worthy of debate. The Electoral College is at the root of the crazy pattern of presidential campaigns that are never-ending. Whether a country of fifty states and three hundred million people is governable as a democracy remains an open question.

The Constitution would probably not have been ratified except for a "bill of rights" that was immediately attached to it. Most of those ten amendments to the Constitution were in the tradition of the liberties in English law. For many people, these rights are more important than anything in the Constitution itself. Practically everyone in the country cherishes some of these rights, such as that government agents cannot enter someone's home without due cause or that a person accused of a crime has a right to face his or her accusers. Some of the guaranteed rights are subject to conflicting interpretations, such as the Second Amendment's right to bear arms because "a well regulated militia" is necessary for the security of a free state.

The First Amendment, with its five basic freedoms, is the most often invoked amendment, and it keeps an army of lawyers employed in the interpretation of the text and the defense of its stated freedoms. A freedom of speech is probably the most cherished of all the liberties. The United States takes great pride in the lack of restrictions on the right to express one's opinion, even extending such a right to corporations contributing unrestricted amounts of money to political campaigns. Many other countries consider the United States to be unrealistic in thinking that speech can go unregulated. Speech that is important might be overwhelmed simply by the amount of trivial speech. The United States trusts that truth will win out in the "free market of ideas," which some people fear means that money is the final arbiter.

The other rights in the First Amendment, which include freedom of assembly, freedom of the press, and freedom to petition the government for redress of grievances, are valued by nearly all groups although inevitable practical restrictions are regularly challenged. If a million people descend on a city to protest, there have to be some agreements on where the people assemble and how necessities of life are taken care of. The two clauses referring to religion are probably the most confusing statement of a right.

The most important amendment of the Bill of Rights is the tenth which, though not much discussed, underlies the political conflict in the country. It is usually summarized by saying that the powers not assigned to the federal government remain with the states; but that is not what the Tenth

Amendment says. The Constitutional Convention had originally met "for the sole and explicit purpose of revising the Articles of Confederation." The Tenth Amendment of the Bill of Rights was an adaptation of what had been the Second Article of the Articles of Confederation. That article stated, "Each state retains its sovereignty, freedom and independence, and every Power, Jurisdiction and right, which is not by this confederation expressly delegated to the United States in Congress assembled."

The Tenth Amendment adaptation of that article states, "The powers not delegated to the United States by the Constitution, nor prohibited by it to the states, are reserved to the states respectively, or to the people." The authors of the amendment wisely left out "sovereignty, freedom and independence," as a description of the states. They also left out *expressly* before the word *delegated*, which led to later developments of power for the federal government. But strangely they also left out "in Congress assembled," which results in the amendment stating a contrast between the *states* and the *United States* rather than between state and federal governments. One might dismiss the significance of this use of *United States* as legal shorthand, but it suggests confusion as to whether what existed was the United States or an assemblage of united states.

Although the Articles of Confederation had referred to *United States*, what existed at that time was a confederation of states united for certain purposes. James Madison pointed out at the convention that under the Articles of Confederation, "the Union was a federal one among sovereign states." The Constitution should give the United States "a national government."[78] But people such as Madison who believed in a strong national government became known as the federalists. The name was sealed with the publication of influential essays by Madison and Alexander Hamilton under the title of *The Federalist Papers*.

The federalists called their opponents the antifederalists, which was not accurate. The opponents of the new constitution, organized by the New York Republican Committee, said that antifederalist really meant "one who is for preserving the Confederation."[79] That is, the believers in the supremacy of states' rights were defending the idea of a federation of states rather than one nation called the United States. This problem, which was not resolved in 1791, continues to this day. The French were more logical in using "federalist revolt" to describe a 1793 movement opposing the central authority of a national government. In today's United States, one of the conservative opponents of strong national government is logically called the Federalist Society.[80]

The eleventh amendment in 1795 refers illogically to "one of the United States." Until the Civil War, *United States* commonly took a plural verb. South Carolina seceded from the Union by declaring that she had "resumed her separate and equal place among nations." The United States's Civil War appeared to be a triumph of union over confederacy. But union mainly triumphed under the rubric of *America*, a term of religious or continental meaning. The reliance upon the claim to *America* for uniting the states continually increased until the end of the twentieth century. And since 2001, *America* has almost overwhelmed the United States.[81]

German Arciniegas writes that when the constitutional convention met, "they did not think of giving the new state a name of its own, and thus the United States is the only country in the world that does not have one. To say United States is like saying federation, republic or monarchy."[82] That is not quite accurate. The Constitutional Convention took over the Declaration's "united States of America" and capitalized the first word. The "United States of America" became the name by which the country is known throughout the world. Admittedly, it was an illogical name and a dangerous name in what it implied.

Arciniegas is also inaccurate to say that the founders did not consider other names. He acknowledges that at one point they planned to call the country Columbia. Another possibility was Freedonia, derived from the Greek word for *liberty*, which would have been a logical name but not one with popular appeal. In the end, they let "United States of America" stand or stand in for a proper name.

This linguistic equivalence between the new republic and the continent of America indicated political aspirations that even preceded the Declaration of Independence. The British American colonists in the 1770s seem to have had affection for the term *continental*. The meeting of delegates in a conference of 1774 was called the First Continental Congress; the Declaration of Independence was issued by the Second Continental Conference. When the defense of the colonies was called for, they raised a continental army. And the currency they created was called the continental.

One could say that both of these problematic claims—that the states were united and that the states were continental America—represented the intention and hope of the new nation rather than hard fact. That may be true, but while the aspiration to be united was their own business to be solved by domestic efforts, the aspiration to be America was tied to illusions at home and violence for anyone else in America who stood in the way.

If the republic had been called the United States *in* America, the tendency to identify itself with the quasireligious meaning of *America* would have been restrained. And instead of implicitly laying claim to the continent, the United States *in* America might have entered bilateral covenants with others *in* America. The claim *to be* America might not have seemed a major problem in the eighteenth century, but the problem grew in importance throughout the nineteenth and twentieth centuries. Other American countries, including the United States of Brazil, the United States of Venezuela, the United States of Mexico, and the United Provinces of the Rio de la Plata (Argentina) are hindered from finding linguistic, economic, and political space by the claim that there is a United States of America.

The native peoples in the northern part of America were keenly aware that continental America was a direct threat to their existence. The glory of westward expansion by the United States of America meant a brutal and relentless war on the people who had been on the land for centuries or millennia. Jefferson, Adams, and other founders thought it was inevitable that the United States of America would fulfill its name and spread across America.[83]

The United States of America remains an experiment of humanity in uniting disparate peoples and in using various forms of governing. *America* has undoubtedly been an idea carrying the hopes of many oppressed people in the world. Domestically, the country could not have survived its early days and its greatest crises without belief in America, which includes the conviction that the future is brighter than the past. But *America* throughout U.S. history has also been a blinder to the need for effective government at home and to the danger of misguided ventures abroad in the name of liberty.

The Rights of Man and of the Citizen

The French Revolution is a more complicated story than the American Revolution, and its influence was much greater during the two centuries that followed. There is not even agreement among historians about which years the term *French Revolution* should refer to.[84] I will not attempt to cover the whole story with all of its effects. I am mainly interested in the Declaration of the Rights of Man and of the Citizen in 1789 and its repercussions.

In 1989 French President François Mitterrand threw a party to celebrate the bicentennial of the Declaration of the Rights of Man and of the Citizen.

That document was held to be the quasisacred source of democratic freedom in the modern world. The only discordant note at the celebration came from Margaret Thatcher of Great Britain who asserted that British freedoms owed nothing to the French. She referred to the Magna Carta as the chief source of British rights and that the idea of rights originated with the "ancient Greeks" (later clarified by her office as a reference to the Stoics).[85]

Thatcher was renewing the argument voiced by Edmund Burke in a speech before Parliament on Nov. 4, 1789. Burke was responding to a sermon by Richard Price who contended that France had overtaken Great Britain in the pursuit of liberty. Burke had no use for a movement that began by despising the past. As for learning about rights, said Burke, "we are as unwilling to learn these lessons from France, as we are sure that we never taught them to that nation."[86]

Whatever valid points Burke raised about the conflicted nature of the revolution, the French Declaration has had a powerful worldwide effect. Just a few weeks before the French celebration in 1989, Chinese students had rallied under the banner of liberty while singing the "Marseillaise." On the other side of the ledger, the Soviet Union, which claimed inspiration from the French Revolution, had just collapsed.

So it has been for more than two hundred years: the hope and promise of liberty for all has been offset by movements that turned violent and suppressed the rights to life and liberty. The ten years that followed the Declaration of the Rights of Man and of the Citizen contained in miniature this conflict between the liberty of the individual and the oppression of political structures. In response to Edmund Burke's attack on the revolution in France, Tom Paine produced *The Rights of Man.* After his visit to Paris in 1789, Paine was unstinting in praise of what he had seen: "From what we now see nothing of reform in the political world ought to be held improbable. It is an age of Revolutions, in which everything may be looked for."[87] Paine was accurate in ways he could not foresee, given the violent years that followed as the Revolution tried to stabilize itself.

Philosophes. It is customary to refer to the eighteenth-century French writers with the word *philosophes* rather than with the obvious English translation of philosophers. The reason seems to be that they were literary men first, philosophers second. Nonetheless, starting with Voltaire (1694-1778), a group of writers in France put forth philosophic positions about nature, human nature, religion, society, liberty, natural rights, and political rights. More than in most periods of history and for most historical events, philosophers had direct influence, for good and ill. Their celebration of human reason would raise the discussion of natural rights to a claim for the universality of rights. Unfortunately, their assumption that philosophical ideas could easily be implemented politically was a reason for the havoc of violence that quickly emerged after 1789.

The philosophical writers were ready for revolution before 1789, but the minds and hearts of the people were not well prepared for what suddenly made its appearance in the middle of an economic crisis. The *philosophes* were a force behind the movement toward revolution, but they were not in a position to develop the political institutions needed for a reformed society. Before the revolution, the king possessed all power, the people none. The revolution was to turn things upside down. "The Revolution replaced the conflict of interests for power with a competition of discourses for the appropriation of legitimacy. Its leaders' job was not to act; they were to interpret action."[88]

The people were now the power, but that equation depended on public opinion, one of the lasting effects of the French Revolution. Previously, *opinion* was used in contrast to knowledge; subsequent to the French Revolution, political survival depended on opinion. Voltaire had shown his skill in mobilizing public opinion in defense of an unjustly accused man, Calas. "Opinion governs the world," Voltaire presciently said but added naively that "in the end philosophers govern men's opinions."[89] One thing that seems certain about the last two centuries is that philosophers have not been in charge of public opinion.

The idea of nature took on a new significance in the eighteenth century.[90] The *philosophes* who dismissed the past as the work of barbarians or animals were remarkably naïve about the complexity of nature. They spoke with certainty of nature, human nature, and natural law despite the ambiguities of the concepts; the conflicts in their own usage went unnoticed. Natural rights were asserted as self-evident, presumed to be obvious to any reasonable man.

Seventeenth-century writers had wished to avoid a conflict of science and religion. By leaving *nature* ambiguous in meaning, scientists could speak about empirical laws of nature. In contrast, *natural law* could still be used for the moral order of the universe, embodied in the human being. The scientist could profess belief in a god of nature without that belief interfering in his study of nature. Christian theologians were willing to accept the deal that God was still necessary as the creator, the one who was needed to give the universe an original fillip. Isaac Newton believed that his scientific theories would strengthen belief in the need for a creator god.[91]

Whereas seventeenth-century thinkers were sure that matter needed an original mover, French thinkers after Voltaire simply attributed to nature what had previously been reserved for "nature's god."[92] For many people, the god of theism/deism was judged to be superfluous. *Nature*, however, had to take on new meaning. For Baron d'Holbach (1723-1789), a leader of the French enlightenment, "man is the work of Nature; he exists in Nature: he is submitted to her laws; he cannot deliver himself from them; nor can he step beyond them even in thought." [93] This renewed Stoicism—Nature as all—is understandable as a consequence of atheism, but it raises questions about liberty as a natural right of man.

The most prominent of the French thinkers of this period was Denis Diderot (1713-1784) who like Holbach substituted *Nature* for God. Diderot was the man behind the grand project called the *Encyclopedia*. In that work, Diderot contributed the 1755 essay on natural right. "In every individual the general will is a pure act of understanding that reasons in the silence of the passions about what man can demand of his fellow man and about what his fellow man has the right to demand of him." Thus, Diderot says, "You have the most sacred natural right to everything that is not disputed by the rest of the species."[94]

The one writer of the time who seemed to sense the complexity of *nature* and *natural* was Jean-Jacques Rousseau. What comes with Rousseau's complexity is a diversity of meanings for *nature* and seeming inconsistencies in his writing. Histories of philosophy have difficulty classifying Rousseau; his work and his life embody all the conflicts and contradictions of modern times. "Rousseau may well have been the most far-sighted genius ever to appear in intellectual history for he invented, or sensed, so many of the problems that were to obsess the nineteenth and twentieth centuries."[95] Early in his life, Rousseau was a friend of Diderot and a collaborator with him. But in Rousseau's first important essay, he argued that science and art corrupt the human. With that thesis, he placed himself in opposition to the assumption on which the Enlightenment was built.[96]

Despite Rousseau's being out of synch with his age, he became the prophet and patron saint of the Revolution. At least some version of his thought was invoked in support of what happened. "He unwittingly assembled the cultural materials that went into revolutionary consciousness and practice."[97] The "general will" and the "sovereignty of the people" became key phrases of the revolution but without the safeguards that Rousseau thought necessary if democracy was to be a practical possibility.

Robespierre thought that "happily, virtue is natural to the people," a principle that Rousseau would not have accepted.[98]

It is easy to misread the conflict that Rousseau posits at the beginning of *Emile*, a conflict between man and nature. It is not the challenge that Francis Bacon had described, that is, of man who is called to subdue (nonhuman) nature. The *nature* that Rousseau refers to is human nature or the life of the individual. In contrast to individual nature, man is the society that the individual has to live in. Thus, the conflict is between individual (human) nature and society as (collective) man. The natural right of the individual has to be relinquished, traded in for civil rights. For Rousseau, the conflict of individual and institutions can never be fully resolved; however, the perfect education of the student Emile allows him to possess an inner freedom and to live in society with equanimity.

The Declaration of 1789

Significant reform in France was stirring from 1787 onward. King Louis XVI had already lost much of his authority before he accepted a reform package in the summer of 1789. Fiscal reform was promised along with guarantees of free speech, no imprisonment without a trial, no taxes without the consent of representatives.[99] The demands came from a body that called itself the National Assembly, which the King said was "only a phrase," though his advisers knew better. Arthur Young, an English observer, commented in June 1789 that "the whole business now seems over and the revolution complete."[100] Young's announcement that the revolution was over was the first of numerous similar judgments that proved to be premature.

On August 26, 1789, the newly named National Assembly of France approved a brief document entitled Declaration of the Rights of Man and of the Citizen. The British historian Lord Acton said of the Declaration that "it was a single confused page . . . that outweighed libraries and was stronger than all the armies of Napoleon."[101] In histories of human rights, the Declaration of the Rights of Man and of the Citizen is sometimes cited as the first proclamation of *human* rights. The document is most often referred to as the Declaration of the Rights of Man. That truncated title leaves out the tricky relation between the (universal) man and the (French) citizen. One can read the title in at least two ways. It may refer to two sets of rights, one set that is universal and another that depends on citizenship. It might also mean that the rights that belong to all men are actually available only to citizens. The repetition of the word *of* before citizen (that is, "*de* l'Homme et *du* Citoyen) seems to tip toward the first meaning.

The document itself does not comment directly on the relation between nation and universality although it posits the nation as the source of authority. The first article asserts that "men are born and remain free and equal in rights." This refrain, which would be used in many subsequent documents—"men are born free"—is difficult to pin down even without the addition of the phrase "and remain free."[102] It seems only in an imagined state of nature are all men born free. "Equal in rights" is clearer although the rights seem to require a political body to recognize and guarantee rights.

The second article, similar to the claim of the Declaration of Independence, says that the aim of all political association is the preservation of "natural and imprescriptible rights." That might be philosophically arguable, but it is not historically accurate; political associations throughout history have not been organized to preserve natural or other kinds of rights.

According to the French Declaration, the natural rights are liberty, property, security, and resistance to oppression. It is interesting that the first right in Jefferson's version, namely, "a right to life" is not listed though it is obviously implied in the four that are named. Given the river of blood during the Terror, perhaps the right to life should have been stated. Property is put second only to liberty; it is a right to own whatever is needed for the protection of one's liberty and security.

The third article locates all authority as coming directly from the nation. One might think of a nation as a limiting principle, but here the nation is a protection of the individual and his rights. Abbé Sieyes explained that there are natural rights for developing society and political rights by which society maintains itself.[103] The laws that the nation enacts have to be an "expression of the general will," (Article 6), which never conflicts with the true will of the individual. How to determine the "general will" was not at all clear. What the concept excluded was parties or factions that would act for their own interest in competition with other parties.

The fourth article is revealing of what a natural right is: "Liberty consists in the freedom to do everything which injures no one else." The only limit is another person's enjoyment of the same right. The final part of the article—that these limits can only be determined by law—leaves considerable room for limiting those rights even with the assurance that "law can only prohibit such actions as are hurtful to society" (Article 5).

Most of the remaining articles are about political rights or alternately about the legal protections of natural rights. These rights, for example, free communication of ideas, no imprisonment without due cause, and the presumption of innocence until proven guilty, are marks of a just society in the modern world. A right to assembly was strangely omitted, but that was corrected with the Introduction to the Constitution of 1791, affirming "the liberty of citizens to assemble peacefully, unarmed, and in conformity with police regulations." Those regulations at the height of the Revolution outlawed most meetings of societies, clubs, and associations of citizens.[104]

Article 10 was fated to be a central problem: "No one shall be disquieted on account of his opinions, including his religious views, provided their manifestation does not disturb the public order established by law." Since the time when Cicero coined the term *religion*, it has referred to *manifestation* in the form of outward displays that others may find offensive. Trying to reconcile the right to express one's religion and the right not to be offended by someone else's religious expressions has remained a central problem.

The French Revolution's suppression of the Roman Catholic Church was a cardinal error. Reform of religion was indeed desperately needed. A wealthy church that was intimately tied to the monarchy was a terrible arrangement even for the church's own good. The National Assembly confronted the issue by passing the Civil Constitution of the Clergy in 1791 that made the priests and bishops into civil servants. Rome resisted and so did about half of the clergy. What was intended to clear away an obstacle to rule by the people succeeded in creating a severe division within the society. The convention backed away from the Civil Constitution in February 1795 when it proclaimed freedom of religion, but that did not entirely correct the problem.[105]

The Declaration of 1789 had been proclaimed "in the presence and under the auspices of the Supreme Being." Several of the revolution's leaders, most notably Robespierre, thought that a cult of "the Supreme Being" could and would substitute for Christian belief and practice. Only someone with little or no understanding of religion could have imagined that such a substitution would work.[106] The problem festered for a decade until Bonaparte signed a concordat with Pope Pius VII in July, 1801.[107] The Church lost its privileges, but it was more recognizably a religious body.

The preamble of the declaration says that one of its purposes is to "remind them [the people] continually of their rights and duties." In some early drafts, there was an attempt to list duties as well as rights.[108] The final draft retained only one fleeting reference to duties. The declaration does of course imply duties, such as paying of taxes (Article 14). Nonetheless, the relation between a person's right and someone or some group having a duty relative to that right is a central question for the very meaning of rights.

In 1793, a revision of the declaration was made. The revision was twice as long as the original, but it did not leave much trace in history. Its Article 21, however, has this remarkable statement about duties: "Public relief is a sacred debt. Society owes maintenance to unfortunate citizens, either procuring work for them or in providing the means of existence for those who are unable to labor." If universal rights to life, liberty, and security are to be actually achieved, some such provision of this "sacred debt" of society is needed in whatever way a society might fulfill its obligation.

The two terms most associated with the Declaration of the Rights of Man and of the Citizen are equality and liberty. Only the second is proclaimed to be a right. Equality is stated as a presupposition (although in the 1793 revision it replaced resistance to oppression as a right). The position is one similar to the Declaration of Independence's statement that "all men are created equal." In the French declaration, the equality is immediately joined to rights; Jefferson, in a follow-up sentence, specifies that the equality is in reference to a certain group of rights. Obviously humans are not born equal in many respects such as size, talents, or sex.

Slavery was still very much an issue at the time of the French declaration. To their credit, the French moved soon afterward to condemn slavery while the United States perpetuated this clear violation of an equality of rights. The French did fail to confront the issue of equal rights for women. The word *man* in the title of the declaration was not an assumption that the word could include women; women were explicitly excluded. The only prominent male writer who took on the issue was Jean Condorcet who posed the obvious question about the authors of the declaration: "Have they not all violated the principle of equality of rights by quietly depriving half of mankind of the right to participate in the formation of laws, by excluding women from the rights of citizenship?"[109]

Condorcet's advocacy of rights for women was met with derision. That was not so bad a fate as was met by Olympe de Gouges who produced a Declaration of the Rights of Women in 1791. She went to the guillotine in 1793, condemned as a counterrevolutionary and denounced as an "unnatural" woman.[110] Pierre Gaspard Chaumette said before the General Council of the City Government of Paris in 1793: "It is shocking, it is contrary to all the laws of nature for a woman to make herself a man."[111] That would indeed be shocking if that were what women were trying to do. What they seemed to be trying to do was to play an important part in the revolution in roles that were equal to those of men.

After Louis Prudhomme set forth the "natural domesticity" of women, he still demanded that they "rally from door to door and march toward city hall." His explanation for this inconsistency was "once the country is purged of all these hired brigands . . . we will see you return to your dwellings to take up once again the accustomed yoke of domestic duties."[112] Nature's laws could apparently be suspended while women were needed at the front.

These writers and others believed without doubt that nature or natural law was obvious when it came to the differences between men and women. Rousseau was mistaken in the fixed characteristics he assigned to womanhood, but at least he did something interesting with the *relation* between the sexes instead of just saying women are inferior.[113] In the following chapter, I trace Rousseau's influence on the *woman's* movement of the nineteenth century.

In the Wake of 1789

William Stuntz asserts that the French declaration was the mirror image of the U.S. Bill of Rights. In comparing the two, he finds that the Bill of Rights was at fault because it is concerned only with procedure. "In the [French] Declaration, procedure is governed lightly, and more wisely than in Madison's document. Substantive law is seriously contained—or would be, had the Declaration been given binding effect."[114] His last phrase is obviously crucial: the difficulty of translating the Declaration to a constitution that could guarantee that liberty would not lead to chaos.

The French Declaration was followed by one attempt after another to establish a working constitution. The Declaration of the Rights of Man and of the Citizen was made a preamble to the Constitution of 1791, but it is mostly the preamble that is remembered. While the Constitution of 1793 was not given a chance to work, the Constitution of 1795 did restore order after the bloodiest period of the revolution.[115]

An indispensable element for the success of a constitution is improvement in education. At the beginning of the revolution, only half of the population spoke French; the urban center did not have the support of the outlying provinces. The twenty-second article of the Constitution of 1793 contained the remarkable assertion: "Education is needed by all. Society ought to favor with all its power the advancement of the public reason and to put education at the door of every citizen." Unfortunately, that grand project was hampered by the dislocations of violence. In 1789 there were fifty thousand students in colleges; in 1799 there were no more than fourteen thousand. Basic literacy that was 37 percent at the beginning of the revolution fell to 30 percent by 1815.[116]

Despite the pronouncements of equality, then, not all citizens were equal in relation to the law. The Constitution of 1791 divided the citizenry into active and passive citizens. Active citizens were defined as men over twenty-five who could pay the equivalent of three days labor in taxes; they chose electors who were then voted for by men who could pay a tax that was equivalent to ten days labor. The legislature was thus elected by only a small fraction of the population. In introducing the Constitution of 1795, Boisy d'Anglas said, "A country governed by non-proprietors is in a state of nature."[117]

The propertied class controlled the electoral process but could not control the waves of the revolution. When the Jacobins set up an "insurrectionary commune" in August of 1792, they declared that "when the people place themselves in a state of insurrection, they withdraw all power from other authorities and assume it themselves."[118] It is difficult to fathom the savagery that took one leader after another to his execution.

The guillotine was introduced as a humane form of killing, guaranteed to make heads "fly off in the twinkling of an eye." In the Terror of 1793, as many as seventeen thousand went to their deaths because the Committee on Public Safety found those executions necessary.[119] The guillotine produced a stream of blood in the middle of Paris, a development that did not deter thousands of citizens regularly gathering to view what J. A. B. Amar called the "red Mass" performed on the "great altar" of the "holy guillotine."[120]

There was no head of government. There was a relentless attack by each man on his opponents before they could attack him. "Every leader and every group took the risk of extending the Revolution in order to eliminate all competitors instead of uniting with them to build new national institutions."[121] The attempt to eliminate all intermediaries between power and the sovereignty of the people produced an obsession with eliminating a feudal order but also blindness to what the past could teach.

Edmund Burke's criticism in 1790 proved to have some validity as the French Revolution unfolded. Burke had warned that if the present is completely unmoored from the past, disorder would be the result. The partnership of society, he argued, is "a partnership not only between those who are living but between those who are living, those who are dead, and those who are to be born."[122] The English Declaration of Rights in 1689, according to Burke, was "an act for declaring the rights and liberties of the subject, and for *settling* the *succession* of the crown." There was no suggestion "to choose our own governors." Burke has an extended praise of prejudice, which he says "engages the mind in a steady course of wisdom and virtue."[123] Burke's defense of *prejudice* as meaning a respect for the judgments of the past would not triumph.[124] But a need for a partnership between the unborn, the living, and the dead is still worth pondering.

Conclusion

Histories of human rights often take the Declaration of the Rights of Man and of the Citizen as the touchstone for the idea of human rights despite the fact that eighteenth-century writers and speakers referred to natural rights. Many contemporary writers seem to accept natural rights even while they resist the idea that such rights are based on (human) nature or natural law. It is possible that human nature and natural law have meanings that are worth considering not as *the basis* of human rights but as a contribution to human tradition on which to base human rights. One need not embrace natural law as one's own in order to recognize that it may be a helpful way for some people at some time to find a basis for human rights.

The case is even clearer for religion as an unavoidable part of human tradition. Long before the Declaration and the Revolution, leaders of the Enlightenment had launched an attack on the Roman Catholic Church as the enemy of progress. The Roman Catholic Church may have deserved most of the criticism, but religion is not equivalent to French clerics of the eighteenth century and to a foreign head of state called the pope. The *philosophes* were forced to try to invent a new religion, but it was a more difficult task than they had realized. A festival of the Supreme Being found few supporters, and installing the Goddess of Reason in the Cathedral of Notre Dame fooled no one. Eventually, the leaders of the revolution had to admit that religious tradition could not be either eliminated or invented by decree.

If human rights are distinguished from natural rights, then one is not forced either to attack religion as an enemy of human rights or to accept religion as the basis of human rights. Religions are a fact of history. A human tradition requires not a religion but a plurality of religions. The way to avoid the excesses of any one religion is through a convergence of traditional religions. A dialogue among religions will not lead to agreement on all points, but a mark of human tradition is a continuing debate over what constitutes the nature of the human and what is the proper relation between human nature and nonhuman natures.

CHAPTER 3

The Twentieth Century and Human Rights

The focus of this chapter is the decade of the 1940s, the time in which the term *human rights* was given a stamp that is still with us. The 1940s contain a series of extraordinary events that had the effect of giving meaning to *human rights*; they also placed restrictions on that meaning. The period under consideration starts with a modest document called the Atlantic Charter and finishes with the beginning of the Cold War. In between was the major event called World War II.

An understanding of the events of this decade requires some looking back to earlier talk about rights as well as what happened in the decades after the 1940s. The history of rights before 1940 is subject to very diverse interpretations, but there is a rich set of data leading to the relevant events of that decade. The events since 1950 are definite but open-ended. It is possible that the world is still at an early stage of finding the proper nature of and effective means for achieving human rights.

The authors of the Universal Declaration of Human Rights began their reflection on rights from their understanding of the eighteenth-century meaning of natural rights, a meaning which had been narrowed during the nineteenth century. The eighteenth-century authors might have been dismayed that their idea of rights became associated with one economic system. In that system, the purpose of government was to guarantee unfettered economic activity. The rights of man were interpreted as political in contrast to economic although rights to life, liberty, security, or the pursuit of happiness would seem to have an economic dimension as well as a political meaning.

Throughout most of the nineteenth century, liberalism meant the protection of individual rights and a suspicion of governmental power.[1] It was not until late in the nineteenth century that liberal thinkers began to recognize that the powerful business corporations might be a bigger threat to personal freedom than government was. Liberal reformers had to reverse field and call upon government to protect the well-being of vulnerable individuals. The term *social* came to the United States from Europe and became the watchword of progressive reform. The energies of the progressive movement were largely spent by 1918 although Franklin Roosevelt would provide a brief revival.[2]

The progressive reformers did not invoke the natural rights of man as the basis of social reform. Rights language, preeminently the right to property, was seized on by their opponents.[3] Business and government leaders could quote John Locke that "the great and chief end of men's uniting in commonwealths and putting themselves under government is the preservation of their property."[4] Talk of natural rights had almost disappeared in the nineteenth century, and individuals looked to positive laws of society for protection. Society as the source of rights was the nineteenth century's replacement for nature. However, there was a danger of society submerging the individual in what is "useful" to society.

Even John Stuart Mill, champion of liberty and the sovereignty of the individual, qualified the affirmation of liberty as applying only to human beings in "the maturity of their faculties" and in "advanced societies."[5] Consistent with these restrictions on liberty, Mill rejected the idea of natural rights. The individual was free to pursue the good of society. "Utility," wrote Mill, "is the ultimate appeal on all ethical questions; but it must be utility in the largest sense, grounded in the permanent interests of man as a progressive being."[6] There has been debate whether in this quotation Mill wrote *man* or *a man*, a difference that is considerable. The "interests of a man" would have a more individualistic meaning and be supportive of individual rights. The "interests of man" would give precedence to society over the individual. Most likely a printer's error added the letter *a*; early editions in England and the United States have *man*.[7] The interests of society take precedence.

Mill worked assiduously to reconcile the individual and the interests of man. He tried to formulate a principle of utility that would do justice to the liberty of the individual. He disagreed with Herbert Spenser about deducing ethics from "the laws of life and conditions of existence."[8] He opposed the idea of natural rights. However, he recognized "the claim we have on our fellow creatures to join in making safe for us the very groundwork of our existence" and says the claim "assumes the character of absoluteness, apparent infinity, incommensurability with all other considerations."[9] Based on what Mill calls the consilience of human nature and empirical evidence, he might have supported human rights, at least at such time when, as he says, we have stigmatized as unjust "the aristocracies of colour, race and sex."[10]

Karl Marx also rejected the idea of natural rights, which he thought to be a cover-up of the clash between the rich and the poor. While Marx was critical of the French Revolution, he called for the completion of the revolution that would abolish private property and religion.[11] The Declaration of the Rights of Man and of the Citizen had located property on the side of (universal) man rather than under the control of citizens in the political community.

In Marx's view, the rights of man were an endorsement of the isolated individual and the protection of his property. The rights of the citizen were reduced to a mere means in support of the propertied class. The course of the French Revolution made the rights of man vulnerable to Marx's criticism on behalf of flesh and blood citizens. Marx did not call for adding "welfare rights to liberty rights" but for economic revolution.

The United States, in its Declaration of Independence, had given less prominence to a right of property and did not have a wide split between the propertied class and everyone else. Or at least it was assumed that by hard work anyone could acquire property. *Political rights* were interpreted to mean procedures to limit government's interference in the individual's life while the individual pursued his happiness through the acquiring of property. But already by the 1790s *liberty* had taken on the meaning of a right to accumulate property.[12]

The idea of a *human* right would have to include political and economic concerns by being an intrinsic element of all rights. Instead of the rights of the citizen being a means to support the rights of man, the concept of human rights nearly reverses the relation. Human rights are the support of the rights of the citizen who is a political, economic, social, religious being. The political community of the nation should in turn protect human rights and provide help for their realization where and when appropriate.

Marx included the economic and political within the category of the social, and trusted in a "social revolution." That continues to be a common way of describing the worldwide struggle against the oppression of the vulnerable, especially the poor. Given the long history of *social* and especially its prominence in the nineteenth century as the opposite of individual, it is unlikely that *social* can escape being part of the unhelpful dichotomies that it is employed to overcome.[13]

Marxism became known as *socialism*, a religious, philosophical, moral, and political movement under the umbrella of a complicated economic theory. Marx succeeded in getting both friend and foe to call his theory scientific socialism in contrast to all the other socialisms of the nineteenth century, which he dismissed or ridiculed.[14] The corruption and finally the collapse of the Soviet empire severely damaged the hope for a revolution that would get at the roots of the gaping inequalities between nations and within nations.

In the United States, the brandishing of the term *socialistic* is enough to block even minor economic reforms. Ironically, however, the right wing in the United States stole the word *social* from the left in the 1980s and gave concrete meaning to the word. The common examples now of social issues in the United States are abortion, homosexuality, and prayer in the public school. The left wing does not seem much aware of the fact that its treasured term has been stolen.

Not surprisingly, Karl Marx was caught up in some of the problem from which he was trying to extricate the human race. Similar to Sigmund Freud, Marx was determined to provide a scientific account of history instead of being content with his criticism of the rights of man and with shedding some light on the next steps toward human emancipation. The eighteenth-century declarations of freedom and equality for all men were deficient, but the hope that every human being should have some fundamental rights needed to be cultivated in the nineteenth century and still needs to be encouraged in the twenty-first century.[15]

A contemporary author writes that "one could argue that Marx was critical of human rights because they were not human enough and their entitlements were not equally shared."[16] The author's helpful point would be clearer if he distinguished between natural rights and human rights. Marx was not critical of *human* rights but of the "rights of man," which he thought applied to an abstraction. Those rights were not human enough for some of the reasons that Marx identified and for other reasons that we are still identifying.

The Emergence of "Human Rights"

The decade of the 1940s is the period in which *human rights* took on definition. The decade was dominated by World War II, and it is often assumed that the United Nations's Declaration of Human Rights was a direct response to the war (or more specifically to the Holocaust), but its prescriptions are only indirectly related to the war.

The coining of the term *human rights* represented an attempt to address universal problems with a universal instrument. The first prominent use of the term *human rights* was by two Human Rights Leagues in 1933. Subsequently, Herbert Hoover criticized Roosevelt's New Deal for interfering with human rights. From the opposite end of the political spectrum, socialists criticized Roosevelt for trampling on the human rights of workers.[17] The United States Supreme Court used the term *human rights* in six of its decisions during the 1940s; the uses more than doubled in each of the three decades that followed.[18]

From the many events and forces that led up to the Universal Declaration of Human Rights in 1948, I will comment on three: the Atlantic Charter, the Nuremberg Trials, and the Charter of the United Nations. I will also describe the process that led up to the UN Charter, including discussion of a preliminary draft of the Charter at Dumbarton Oaks in 1944, the criticism of that document, and finally the approval of the Charter at San Francisco in 1945.

Atlantic Charter. A brief document—actually a telegram—has the imposing name of the Atlantic Charter. It was the product of a meeting between Franklin Roosevelt and Winston Churchill in August, 1941. From Churchill's side, the meeting was an effort to get United States support for England's conflict with Germany. Churchill actually left before the document was complete so that Roosevelt signed for both of them. From the president's perspective, the charter was a universalizing of the theme in his 1941 State of the Union Address. Roosevelt's New Deal for the World was the proclamation of the four freedoms that every human being should have. The four freedoms listed in Roosevelt's address were freedom of speech and freedom of religion, freedom from fear and freedom from want.[19]

The freedom from fear and the freedom from want were part of what Roosevelt would call a second or economic bill of rights. "We have come to a clear realization of the fact that individual freedom cannot exist without economic security and independence . . . . We have accepted, so to speak, a second Bill of Rights under which a new basis of security and prosperity can be established for all."[20] The proclamation of a freedom from want was rhetorically powerful, but it is not clear how governments can guarantee such a right. The words *desire* and *want* have historically different meanings, but they tend to blur together so that people say, "I want something" (I lack) when they mean "I desire something" (I wish to have it). A government is responsible for its people not lacking in the necessities of life, that is, their basic wants.[21] That obligation would be complicated enough without its being confused with the limitless desires of people. Similarly, governments are responsible for seeing that people have a basic security of their person, but governments are not able to guarantee an absence of all fears.[22]

The statement in the Atlantic Charter that drew the most attention was the affirmation of a peace "which will afford assurance that all the men in all lands may live their lives in freedom from fear and want."[23] The phrase "all the men in all lands" was a late revision, perhaps mainly for its poetic sense. But the assertion had explosive implications, especially for the British Empire. Churchill was understandably wary of an implied promise to grant political freedom to all of the colonies still under British control. Churchill said of the Charter: "it is not a law—it is a star."[24]

As for Roosevelt, the phrase was part of his attempt to get U.S. people to think globally. There was little doubt that the United States was inescapably tied to international happenings even though Republicans in Congress were adamant in rejecting any international agreements. Churchill, at the meeting with Roosevelt, wished to announce a plan to set up an "effective international organization." Roosevelt, although already envisioning a world organization, resisted such a declaration as premature. He eventually agreed to the Atlantic Charter's somewhat vague call for all nations to abandon the use of force "pending the establishment of a wider and permanent system of general security."

Nuremberg Trials. The trials held immediately after the war in what was left of the city of Nuremberg are usually cited as a step in the direction of the Declaration of Human Rights. Although the judges did not invoke human rights as the basis of their judgments, they were obviously in search of some kind of law or principles on which to base a condemnation of Nazi war criminals. All things considered, the court did an admirable job of trying to administer justice beyond the kind of victor's justice that is typical of war and its aftermath.

World War II was, of course, not just the ordinary war. It was an unprecedented outpouring of violence on every side that killed tens of millions of people. Hitler and the Nazis had obviously gone beyond all the rules of war. And it is arguable that Stalin's killing machine was as bad or worse. The United States allied itself with one war criminal to stop another.

In the course of the war, the United States itself engaged in acts that were morally indefensible. The documentary film on Robert McNamara, *The Fog of War*, is mainly about McNamara's part in the Vietnam War. The movie includes a discussion of a minor role that McNamara had in World War II when fresh out of college he became an advisor to General Curtis Lemay. Starting in early 1945, Lemay's strategy for winning the war was the firebombing of Japanese cities. He believed that the indiscriminate killing of Japanese civilians would bring a halt to the war. The carpet-bombing of sixty-seven cities culminated in the atomic bombings of Hiroshima and Nagasaki. McNamara recounts a conversation with Lemay in which the general says to the college graduate, "You know if we lose the war we will be tried as war criminals." McNamara rightly wondered whether winning the war would prove he was not a war criminal. By a strange and ironic coincidence, the Nuremberg Charter was signed on the same day as the bombing of Nagasaki.

An obvious problem with the Nuremberg Trials was the selective character of the people who were charged with war crimes.[25] A few of Hitler's closest associates were fairly easy to target. Beyond that, drawing the line of culpability was bound to be arbitrary. Stalin at one point suggested taking out fifty to a hundred thousand German officials and shooting them. Churchill said he was appalled at the suggestion, but he too at first preferred summary executions to the attempt at fair trials.[26] Eventually at Yalta, the United States, U.K. and U.S.S.R. agreed on the need for some kind of a judicial process. The United States clearly took the lead so that the production of the trials was almost entirely a U.S. show.

Supreme Court Justice Robert Jackson opened the trials with a stirring speech in which he acknowledged the tenuous position of the court. Nonetheless, he pointed out that the victors were attempting to transcend the usual victor's justice: "That four great nations, flushed with victory and stung with injury stay the hand of vengeance and voluntarily submit their captive enemies to the judgment of the law is one of the most significant tributes that power has ever paid to reason."[27] The difficulty with Jackson's idealism was to find the law on which the court would base its judgment. Jackson's reference to reason as winning out over power might carry the day rhetorically but not legally or morally.

What the Nazi leaders had done was beyond all reason, but so is all war. Since the early Middle Ages, numerous attempts had been made to keep war within some boundaries although the phrase "just war" strikes a preposterous note. Carl von Clausewitz's classic treatise, *On War*, is often criticized for describing war as an extension of national policy, but Clausewitz's intention was to keep war within bounds. He feared that after Napoleon's escapades the rules of war had been destroyed. If war could not be kept within the rational limits of a nation's policy, there would be no limit to war's destructiveness. His 1815 book was a warning of what would happen in the 1940s and the problem that confronted the Nuremberg judges.[28]

It is sometimes said that the Nuremberg judges tried to reinstate some version of natural law. They did not actually use that term, nor did they talk about human rights. They admitted that it was an unusual case to judge the leaders of another nation according to some version of law applied retroactively from outside the nation. The judges did not appeal to a law of nature or to a basis in human reason. Their judgments were based on behavior that was unacceptable within the rules of war. Nazi Germany had waged a war of aggression and committed atrocities within that context. The court avoided consideration of what Germany had done during peacetime, including the persecution of the Jews in the 1930s.

The Nuremberg Trials were thus not about the Holocaust, a term that was not available in 1945. The word *genocide* had been coined in 1944 by Raphael Lemkin.[29] Like the term "crimes against humanity," genocide's primary referent was the Turkish killing of Armenians in 1915.[30] The 1948 Convention on the Prevention and Punishment of the Crime of Genocide was a remedy for Nuremberg's limiting itself to wartime.[31] Genocide whether in peace or war was made a crime under international law. There is a continuing debate whether use of the term *genocide* has had much practical effect. When terrible slaughters have occurred, the word *genocide* is usually avoided, which allows international bodies not to do anything to stop the slaughter.[32]

The Nuremberg Court delivered the expected guilty judgments though the judges did try to discriminate among the defendants. Seventeen of the convicted were executed, which may have seemed the appropriate punishment to most people. From the standpoint of human rights however, the state execution of prisoners seems to violate the first human right, the right to life. The question always is not whether a criminal deserves to die but whether the state has the right to kill him. Of course if there was little moral protest over the incineration of the people of Dresden, Tokyo, Hiroshima, and Nagasaki, the lack of moral questioning at that time over killing a few Nazis is not surprising.[33]

Whatever shortcomings can be attributed to the Nuremberg Trials, the fact that they were held at all and administered swift justice is amazing.

The judges did the best they could under difficult circumstances. It seems unlikely that anything similar could be achieved today. In 2011, the United States government, after numerous delays, conceded that a civilian trial of Khalid Sheikh Mohammed was impossible. He was accused of involvement in the 2001 bombing of the World Trade Center. The proposed trial in lower Manhattan near the scene of the crime was judged to be prohibitive in both cost and the disruption of people's lives. Only a military court in hidden surroundings was deemed possible.

Many people in the 1940s hoped that Nuremberg would serve as a groundbreaking precedent. Looking back from today, one could argue that it has.[34] However, it found no immediate successor during the four decades that followed. Only after the end of the Cold War was it a practical possibility to establish an international court to try people accused of war crimes. Even then, the United States of America refused to be a participant in that undertaking. From being the leader of a search for justice in 1945, the United States opted out of the International Criminal Court in 2002 because of a fear that it might indict U.S. citizens.

Whether the International Court will be a great success remains to be shown. What was clearly the lasting effect of the Nuremberg Trials is that it highlighted the question of a law beyond national laws. The lawyers have not provided an answer other than international treaties that depend on the consent of the states that are a party to any treaty. The world's resistance to atrocities is unlikely to be secured by written or positive laws although laws are worth writing so that at least there is pressure on offending nations.

The larger point was made by Geoffrey Robertson, a distinguished jurist involved in recent trials for crimes against humanity: "Nazi offenses were crimes that the world could not suffer to take place anywhere, at any time, because they shamed everyone."[35] His view coincided with Justice Robert Jackson's opening speech, which said that these wrongs were "so calculated, so malignant and so devastating that civilization cannot tolerate their being ignored because it cannot survive their being repeated."[36]

The Charter of the United Nations. Although the League of Nations after the First World War did not prove up to its task, it was evident during World War II that a new attempt at an international organization would be needed. Foremost among the believers was Franklin Roosevelt, the president of the United States. Roosevelt's State Department began laying the groundwork for an international organization as early as 1939. In January, 1942, a meeting of twenty-six nations in Washington issued a "United Nations Declaration" to conquer the Axis powers.[37] By February,

1942, Roosevelt was already thinking of "United Nations" as the name for the planned organization.

The name was not quite accurate. The members of the organization are states, so that logically it should have been called the United States, but that obviously was not feasible. It could have been called the Uniting States to indicate that the creation of an effective interstate organization is still in the making (the initials *U.S.* would have doomed that idea). The point is more than a fussy concern for linguistic accuracy. In the decades that have followed the founding of the United Nations, a central issue has been the rebellion within states in the name of a people or a nation.

The conference in 1945 that established the United Nations was preceded by at least four meetings of the "great powers" and several regional and international gatherings starting in 1943. One international conference dealing with economics was held at Breton Woods, New Hampshire, in July, 1944. Forty-four nations met to create a world monetary system. The United States and Great Britain were in the lead and their representatives, Harry Dexter White and John Maynard Keynes, seem to have done their best to create a genuinely cooperative international system that got the world through the next few decades. Henry Morgenthau, the U.S. Secretary of the Treasury, said of the meeting: "None of us found any incompatibility between devotion to our countries and joint action. Indeed, we have found on the contrary that the only genuine safeguard for our national interests lies in international cooperation."[38] Some of that feeling of solidarity was fostered by the war; fortunately a cooperative attitude survived for the meetings that followed at Dumbarton Oaks and San Francisco.

The meeting at Dumbarton Oaks in Washington D. C. lasted from August to October in 1944. A first draft of a United Nations Charter had been hammered out over a long period of time. The United States had the benefit of a brilliant and tireless Leo Paslovsky who had worked at this project in the U.S. State Department since 1940. His draft of the charter was "the basic frame of reference for building a plan of world organization."[39] The search was for an organization more effective than its predecessor, the League of Nations. Roosevelt had long believed that the four great powers—the United States, United Kingdom, Soviet Union, and China—had to act as the world's policeman and maintain a balance of international power. At a February 1944 meeting, Paslovsky persuaded Roosevelt to accept an eleven-member Security Council (instead of just the four great powers). Issues of security would be decided by the council rather than by the whole assembly as was provided in the League of Nations.[40]

The Security Council's power was restricted by the veto power of any member, a provision that had a paralyzing effect on the UN during the Cold War. The General Assembly was not given a prominent role, but in time, with the addition of dozens of new states, the General Assembly took control of the rhetorical power of the organization.

Regional associations of power, which had been a topic in the charter discussions, sometimes filled a power vacuum when the United Nations would not or could not act. A meeting in Mexico City in February 1945, had proposed a regional security organization. The United States did not agree to that, but a negotiated settlement specified that an attack on one American country would be considered an attack on all and would demand immediate consultation.[41]

In the preparation for the meeting at Dumbarton Oaks, there is no record of a diplomatic discussion of human rights.[42] At the meeting itself the United States did bring up the issue, but Great Britain and the Soviet Union rejected the inclusion of human rights as a main purpose of the United Nations. The preliminary draft of the charter was widely circulated and submitted to detailed criticism. The draft was severely criticized by the respected black leader W. E. B. Dubois for its failure to attend to issues of justice, including individual rights.[43]

The fact that the United Nations is composed of states creates difficulties in its being a defender of human rights. The state is often the institution that suppresses those rights. The United Nations was not founded as a human rights organization. Over the decades, its rhetoric and its mission have shifted in that direction. When the Charter of the United Nations was drawn up, *human rights* was not a common term. In the original draft of the charter, there was no mention of human rights. After advocacy by several groups, *human rights* found a place in the charter's preamble and in Articles 1 and 55.[44]

In Article 1, the third paragraph, which refers to the promotion of human rights, follows a paragraph that proposes "to achieve international cooperation in solving international problems of economic, social, cultural or humanitarian character." The relation between these two sets of concerns is left unclear. Are human rights separate from economic, social, cultural, or humanitarian problems? Or are human rights intrinsically related to the solution of economic, social, cultural, humanitarian problems?

Article 55 is on International Economic and Social Cooperation. Instead of clarifying human rights and indicating what might be done to promote them, the article does little more than repeat what is in Article 1.

After saying that the UN will promote "solutions to international social, health and related problems; and cultural and educational cooperation," the article concludes that the UN will promote "universal respect for, and observance of human rights and fundamental freedoms for all without distinction as to race, sex, language or religion." Whether human rights are especially concerned with solutions to economic and social problems or whether human rights are in addition to the solutions of those problems is left unclear. The question would surface immediately at the United Nations, and the problem has bedeviled the idea of human rights ever since.

At least the United Nations Charter did give a push to the idea of human rights while leaving the articulation of the idea until later. One should acknowledge that the founding of the United Nations was an extraordinary achievement. The United States government, and especially Franklin Roosevelt, provided not only intellectual leadership but also the logistics for all of the countries of the world to meet and come to an agreement. It is a sad fact that Roosevelt died thirteen days before he planned to speak at the opening of the conference, but it was fortunate that a totally inexperienced President Harry Truman was determined that the conference would be held.

The fact that would have saddened Roosevelt is that his own country has been so stubbornly resistant to the United Nations, which has its home location in the United States. The United States Senate approved the UN Charter by a vote of 89 to 2. However, when President Dwight Eisenhower succeeded Truman in 1953, one of the first acts of his administration was to announce that it would not sign any treaty or covenant on human rights.[45] Secretary of State John Foster Dulles opposed any references to international law and praised those people "who voiced concern that treaties might impose 'socialistic conceptions'" on the country.[46] Up to the present, any U.S. cooperation with the United Nations involves a struggle with right-wing forces that are dismissive, suspicious, or contemptuous of the United Nations.

Much of the credit for success at the San Francisco conference goes to Leo Paslovsky's work on the charter and to Edward Stettinius who, although considered by some people in Washington to be an intellectual lightweight, proved to be skillful in handling the organization of the conference and the details of its meetings.[47] Soviet insistence on a right to an "absolute veto" had threatened the existence of the organization. Eventually, Stalin gave in to an agreement that none of the permanent members of the Security Council could veto either the discussion of a topic or a peaceful settlement of a problem involving that individual state. Stettinius noted later that "if Stalin had adamantly supported Molotov [his representative at the conference], there would have been no United Nations formed at San Francisco."[48]

The Charter of the United Nations accepted and affirmed the sovereignty of each nation-state. There would be no intervention in domestic matters. Article 2 did indicate that the United Nations would act to maintain international peace. The seventh chapter then spelled out in detail what steps would be taken, including military force, when peace is threatened. Article 51 allows for a state or a regional association of states to act in necessary self-defense and report their action to the Security Council. That provision allowed the United States, often as the leader of NATO, to use its massive military force when it has wished to use it.

The system of nation-states, which went back three centuries, was thus left in place by the United Nations Charter. In fact, what seemed desirable was a strengthening of the system. Many people see a contradiction between the sovereignty of each state and a rhetoric of human rights. Who will defend human rights against the state itself? One answer that developed over time was the NGO, the hundreds of nongovernmental organizations that have often led the fight for human rights. There is a plaque in the Garden Room of the Fairmount Hotel in San Francisco commemorating the contribution of NGOs to the UN Charter. Charles Malik said that the NGOs were "unofficial advisors to the various delegations, supplying them with streams of ideas and suggestions."[49] However, the plaque is more a signal about the future than the actual contribution to the charter in 1945.[50]

Paslovsky had persuaded Stalin to accept an Economic and Social Council to deal with the causes of war, such as poverty and famine.[51] In the charter discussion, the Australian delegate, Herbert Evatt, led the support for an Economic and Social Council as a principle organ of the UN. The intent was to relieve the Security Council of its burdens although keeping those concerns separate had questionable implications. The Economic and Social Council established a Human Right Commission; it was the single exception that the United States made in its opposition to special commissions in the charter. Stettinius announced at the San Francisco conference that this Human Rights Commission would prepare an International Bill of Rights and in May, 1946, the commission was told to proceed with the writing of such a document.

In President Truman's speech at the signing of the United Nations Charter on June 26, 1945, he said that he looked forward to the framing of an International Bill of Rights. He was picking up a theme that President Roosevelt had used in calling for a second bill of rights. When the United Nations talked of an international bill of rights, it was promising something that was very ambitious, namely, to produce a legally binding set of rights that the United Nations would enforce. Although the phrase "bill of rights" was soon replaced, the idea of two kinds of human rights, political and economic, persisted, especially given the conflict between the United States and the Soviet Union.

Statements of Human Rights

A brief excursion into the difficulty of stating human rights will be helpful for understanding what the authors of the Universal Declaration of Human Rights struggled with. In June 1947, the Executive Board of the American Anthropological Association sent a letter to the Human Rights Commission. The anthropologists opposed "a statement of rights conceived only in terms of the values prevalent in the countries of Western Europe and America." They argued that the discussion must "take into account the individual as a member of the social group of which he is a part."[52] Their concern was well-founded. Coincidentally, in that same month the writing committee had changed the name of its document from "international declaration" to "universal declaration."

The anthropologists had identified the problem, but they did not offer much help toward solving the problem. It was all but inevitable that the authors of the universal declaration would begin with rights as understood in Western Europe and North America. They then tried to reach universality by a process of addition. That route could not succeed. The anthropologists in their urging to take account of the social group as well as the individual did not provide a sufficient rethinking of the basic concepts. Ever since the 1940s, it has been difficult to try a new approach to universality.[53]

The first thing that has to be acknowledged is that it is impossible to have a *universal statement*. Every statement in every language is particular not universal. Possibly the human race will some day have a single language. A realization of that possibility is a long way off, and if it ever occurred, the human race would probably be the poorer. There have been many attempts to create a universal language especially since the seventeenth century. The attempts are often the work of young mathematicians who believe that they have figured out the problem of human communication.[54] "Who speaks a universal language?" asks Mary Midgley, "the sad little joke has it—Nobody."[55]

This stubborn fact about human existence does not kill the search for universal rights, but it should generate some humility on the part of anyone making pronouncements about universal rights.[56] The term *human rights* originated in the English language of the nineteenth and twentieth centuries. For most users of the term in Europe and North America, it has simply been another name for what they were already familiar with. One of the first books on human rights opens with this sentence: "Human rights is a twentieth-century name for what has been traditionally known as Natural Rights or, in a more exhilarating phrase, the Rights of Man."[57] That assumption has not often been challenged over the last half century. When it is said that the eighteenth-century rights are political, there is a call to add economic rights. Similarly, if the eighteenth-century rights are thought to be too individualistic, there is a call for collective, group, or people's rights.

It is unlikely that a single word can convey a human right. For example, *equality* has often been a flag under which oppressed people have marched. But the word is too abstract and too ambiguous in meaning to be a human right. The word *equality* immediately cries out for an answer to the question "equality in respect to what?" I think Peter Westen overstates his case in "The Empty Idea of Equality," in which he refers to equality as "entirely circular," "an empty vessel," and "superfluous."[58] Equality has a definite meaning when the choice is between equal and unequal quantities. Westen is right that most political and legal matters do not fit within such measurements. But as Henry Shue notes, "There are types of inequality that are morally unacceptable, namely, inequalities that are degrading."[59] Equality can be a useful word but not as the name of a human right.

Similarly, liberty has a rich history in movements of human emancipation, but the connotations of *liberty* differ according to the political context. The meaning of *liberty* is stamped in English and French. An exact equivalent in many languages is highly problematic. Even in English and French, the term *liberty/liberté* carries different historical connotations. There are even differences within the English language; liberty has different connotations in the United States and U.K; or even differences in England and Scotland. Like equality, liberty is an abstract ideal.

I am not denying the values that are historically associated with equality and liberty; it is just that liberty and equality cannot function as the names of human rights. Nor is any single word likely to succeed.

A contrast commonly made is between negative rights and positive rights. As with other contrasts, there is something important at stake, but the language is confusing. The idea of negative rights, (for example, freedom of speech) can refer to the nonintervention by the government in the life of the citizen. Positive rights (for example, unemployment insurance) would mean a government obligation to intervene so as to provide a needed good for individuals. However, a test of rights that are *human* would be that they imply both negative and positive aspects.[60] For example, a "right to be secure in one's person" (one formula pointing toward universality) involves both the negating of unwanted invasions and positive actions by oneself and others.

The Declaration by the United Nations

The Human Rights Commission had its orders to write a document that was at first referred to as an international bill of rights. Amid the details of the final document, it is important not to lose sight of the overall nature of the document and the assumptions on which it was based. Some of those assumptions were altered during debates over the document but the ideas of the main players—the persons and the states—remained largely intact.

The Human Rights Commission was an arm of what was called the third committee, the Economic and Social Council. The slightly disparaging implication in the name *third committee* indicates that it was not to be the main show of the UN's work. Eleanor Roosevelt, a delegate from the United States and the widow of President Roosevelt, was assigned to this committee on the assumption she would not cause any problems there. Eleanor Roosevelt was not the typical first lady, having kept her independence and expressed her own views—sometimes in opposition to Franklin's—during the more than twelve years of the Roosevelt presidency. Her main desire was to see that her husband's legacy be continued and completed.

The shepherding of the Declaration of Human Rights from its inception to its approval turned out to be a personal achievement for Eleanor Roosevelt. At the start of the United Nations, her appointment as a delegate was opposed by many officials of the U.S. government. In her own diary, she acknowledged that she was doubtful about her ability to serve her country in this undertaking. But by the time that the declaration was signed on December 10, 1948, the praise of her was almost universal. A Mexican delegate put it succinctly: "Never before have I seen naiveté and cunning so graciously blended."[61]

Like the United Nations Charter, the creation of the Universal Declaration of Human Rights was an extraordinary achievement, especially given the circumstances of its origin. In 1945 the UN Charter's creation was dependent on the feeling of solidarity among the allies of the war that was nearing its conclusion. But already by 1946, the world was splitting apart, a sense that was captured in Winston Churchill's speech in March of that year on the falling of an "iron curtain." Eleanor Roosevelt managed to keep things going through the year of 1948 when there was one big crisis after another from Berlin to Israel, to Greece, to India.

Roosevelt constantly tussled with the Soviet representative, Vladimir Koretsky, without alienating him. The fact that the Soviet bloc abstained from the final vote on the declaration rather than voted against it was a victory of sorts. Charles Malik, one of the declaration's main contributors, said in 1952: "The proclamation of the Declaration in 1948 was really something of a miracle, so that if it was not proclaimed then, possibly we would still be working on it now."[62] By 1952, it was evident that there was to be no smooth path to the covenant on human rights that had been promised to follow the declaration.

The first meeting of the Human Rights Commission was held in May 1946. Eleanor Roosevelt was elected chairman. The first of its tasks was to submit to the General Assembly an international bill of rights. The United Kingdom at once drafted what it understood "bill of rights" to mean, that is, a list of rights that could be legally enforced. The Australian delegate, Will Hodgson, logically proposed an international court of human rights as a necessary part of such enforcement; the proposal was not accepted.

A committee was assigned to do the writing; Roosevelt chaired the meetings. A proposal to have the commission composed of independent experts rather than state representatives had been turned down. That decision guaranteed that any document from the commission was not going to seriously challenge state sovereignty. Only states, not individuals, could submit petitions to the Human Rights Commission. Nevertheless, the drafting committee set out to accomplish its task and was dedicated to producing an effective document on what the members understood human rights to be.

From the beginning of the work, the United States and the Soviet Union were in agreement about the nature of the document while they disagreed about what should be the contents of the document. That is, both countries wished to have a declaration, but their views on the subject of rights were different. The United States and the United Kingdom were

in agreement about the nature of rights, but they disagreed about the kind
of document that was desirable. The United Kingdom (together with many
of the smaller countries) wanted to have a bill of rights; the United States
did not. Roosevelt had been told by her State Department advisor to use as
an analogy the Declaration of Independence rather than the Bill of Rights
to the U.S. Constitution. Although the term "bill of rights" had originally
been used by the committee, what the United States and USSR wanted
inevitably carried the day.

The chief architects of the declaration were John Humphrey, a Canadian
law professor; P.C. Chang, a Chinese Buddhist; Charles Malik, a Lebanese
philosopher; René Cassin, a wartime advisor to Charles de Gaulle. Two
other significant contributors were Carlos Romulo from the Philippines
and Hernan Santa Cruz from Chile. When the members are described this
way, the creation of the declaration seems to be impressively multicultural,
multireligious, and multiregional in its origin.

Realistically, however, the document was from the beginning strongly
influenced by Anglo-American assumptions. Even Chang and Malik,
who provided the most intellectual heft, had studied at U.S. universities.
Chang was influenced by John Dewey at Columbia University, Malik by
Alfred North Whitehead at Harvard University. Cassin objected at the
first draft being written in English and regularly attempted to bring in
another tradition.[63] For most of the world, however, the English and
French traditions were not so different. At the time and ever since then, the
charge has been made that the document is based on Western assumptions.
Despite the best efforts of the contributors to speak to the whole world, the
English and French languages gave their stamp to what the document says
and how rights are addressed.

From within the writing subcommittee, John Humphrey was assigned
the task of writing a first draft. He produced a document that was double
the length of what would eventually be approved. Malik's notes from the
meeting say that the draft "included every conceivable right which the
Drafting Committee might want to discuss."[64] One could surmise that
listing all possible rights was not the best way to begin. The focus became
the number of rights to include instead of a lengthier discussion on the
meaning of *human rights*, a relatively new term.

The Human Rights Commission accepted a compromise that divided
its work into three parts: a declaration of human rights, a covenant of
human rights, and measures for implementing human rights. When
Roosevelt reported to the third committee in the fall of 1947, she assured

them that the covenant and the implementation were still being worked on. She was not being disingenuous, but by then only a declaration had a realistic chance of completion. Eventually, the idea of a covenant fell victim to the committee's internal division between the United States and USSR, which led finally to two covenants decades later. The measures of implementation remained cloudy.

The Text of the Universal Declaration

The declaration's writing committee and the other members of the Human Rights Commission spent a great deal of their time on the first article of the declaration. That was appropriate because they were attempting to state in this article not one of many rights but the basis and the meaning of human rights. The final form of article one is "All human beings are born free and equal in dignity and rights. They are endowed with reason and conscience and should act toward one another in a spirit of brotherhood."

The Road to Article 1: In the Humphrey draft, the first article said, "Everyone owes a duty of loyalty to his State and to the United Nations. He must accept his just share of such common sacrifices as may contribute to the common good." The second article adds that "in this exercise of his rights everyone is limited by the rights of others and by the just requirements of the State and the United Nations." Only after stating these restrictions on rights does the draft introduce actual rights: a right to life (with exception for a state's death penalty), a right not to be tortured, and a right to personal liberty.

Humphrey's draft document proceeds through forty-six articles covering a great variety of rights, including "a right to education," "a right to medical care," and "a right to good food and housing and to live in surroundings that are pleasant and healthy." One article asserts a *state's* right to grant asylum, which is surprising to find in a list of rights attributed to "everyone."

The last article of the document says that "the provisions of this International Bill of Rights shall be deemed fundamental principles of international law of each of the Member States of the United Nations. Their observance is therefore a matter of international concern and it shall be within the jurisdiction of the United Nations to discuss any violations thereof." In a bill of rights, the provision that their violation will be a "concern" and that the United Nations has the jurisdiction "to discuss" is a long way from legal enforcement.

In response to this Humphrey outline, René Cassin proposed a draft in which there was a more extensive preamble and a shift in emphasis for the opening articles. He summed up his overall philosophy of rights in two principles: "Every human being has a right to be treated like every other human being" and "the concept of solidarity and fraternity among men."[65] His first article therefore was "All men, being members of one family are free, possess equal dignity and rights, and shall regard each other as brothers."

The third article of Cassin's draft explains further the claim of family and brotherhood: "As human beings cannot live and achieve their objects without the help and support of society, each man owes to society fundamental duties which are obedience to law, exercise of a useful activity, acceptance of the burdens and sacrifices demanded for the common good." Cassin argued passionately for inclusion of this article at the beginning of the document as the context for all the rights that follow. In the final version however, his concern with duties, community, and the common good was relegated to the twenty-ninth and next to last article which simply says, "Everyone has duties to the community in which alone the free and full development of his personality is possible."

Cassin's first article became the basis of lengthy debate and numerous revisions. The draft in June 1947 added the words "All men are brothers." More significant was the debate about an addition after the word *reason* to indicate what makes the human being deserve rights. For Cassin, the tradition of eighteenth-century enlightenment provided the answer: man is endowed by reason. Several committee members did not think that reason by itself was sufficient.

The main objection to reason as the distinguishing element of man came from P. C. Chang who was drawing upon a different tradition. He suggested the addition of what the Chinese letter *ren* means: "two-man-mindedness." That translation could not be used in English or French. The closest term in English would seem to be *sympathy* (or its Latin-derived equivalent *compassion*). *Sympathy* is a capacity to feel with other persons, especially to be moved by their wants and suffering. It is unclear why *sympathy* or *compassion* was turned down except that words carry connotations that differ from person to person. The eventual choice was to include *conscience*, but that term fails to convey the passion and compassion that Chang was trying to include. Chang later lost interest in retaining *conscience*, but Malik argued successfully for it to stay.

The question of whether human rights are based on reason or on some other characteristic or set of characteristics remains an issue to this day. For example, Richard Rorty is famous for his dismissal of reason as the basis of human rights. The one thing important, according to Rorty, is that we can imaginatively put ourselves in the place of a stranger or a person who is suffering. Borrowing from the eighteenth-century philosopher, David Hume, Rorty used the word *sentiment* to describe the driving force of human action.[66]

Obviously, *sentiment* was a word that is rich in positive connotations for Rorty. There is a question, however, of whether the word carries as much weight in the twenty-first century as it seems to have carried in the eighteenth. Particularly, there would seem a problem when Rorty describes efforts to apply human rights as "a sentimental education." Perhaps it did not bother him that this phrase could sound mawkish and superficial. In any case, *sentiment, sentimental,* and *sentimentality* have their problems when one is trying to speak universally. But then again, it has to be admitted that so do all words.

One issue that is by no means irrelevant to this point is that the authors began with "All men are brothers." To today's reader, it seems obvious that while they were asserting the rights of all humans, they were leaving out half of the human race. Actually, it is surprising that the issue did get raised, and more surprising that it was the Soviet delegate, Koretsky, who raised it. He called it an historical atavism to refer in this context to "men" who constitute only one-half of the human species.

Roosevelt replied to Koretsky that "when we say 'all men are brothers' we mean all human beings are brothers, and we are not differentiating between men and women." She went on to say that "while I have always considered myself a feminist," she was willing to abide by the committee.[67] Eventually *men* did disappear, but no one seems to have had a problem with *brother* or the eventual wording of "a spirit of brotherhood." A critique of language on the basis of gender exclusivity was more than two decades in the future. It was therefore an accomplishment that the first article of the Universal Declaration of Human Rights begins by affirming that it is "all human beings" who are "born free and equal in dignity and rights."

In the end, Article 1 was kept simple despite the pleas of individual delegates for what each saw as necessary. In one instance, the South African delegate, Te Water, argued for removing the term *dignity* because it is not a right. Roosevelt explained that Article 1 was meant to affirm why there are human rights.[68] That being the case, Water could say his point was that dignity should be in the preamble rather than the list of rights. Dignity was and is central to almost all discussions of human rights and perhaps deserved more attention than the simple statement that all human beings are "born free and equal in dignity and rights." In that formula, dignity functions not as a right or as a basis of rights but as something parallel to rights.

The other advocacies for change in Article 1 were for additions of a reference to nature or God. At one point, "endowed by nature" was included in the article. Malik, along with a Brazilian delegate, proposed that "endowed by their Creator" be substituted. Cassin objected to that change, and Chang also thought a reference to God was not helpful. In the end, the declaration says that all human beings are endowed with reason and conscience but does not speculate as to who or what does the endowing. Roosevelt was left with the task of explaining to her U.S. audience why it was preferable to leave the issue open to a diversity of beliefs rather than assert that rights come from God.

Article 2: The first paragraph of article two reads, "Everyone is entitled to all the rights and freedoms set forth in this Declaration, without distinctions of any kind, such as race, colour, sex, language, religion, political or other opinion, national or social origin, property, birth or other status." The second paragraph in article two says that no distinctions should be based on political jurisdiction. Like the first article, this second article does not list particular rights but rather tries to get at the basis of human rights. It asserts that a human right is based on a person's status as a human being and nothing else. The listed distinctions are given as examples so that in time other possible distinctions could be and have been added. Sex, for example, is ambiguous. Today the list might instead name *gender*, a term not available at that time, and "sexual orientation," also coined since then.

The term *distinction* seems to be inaccurate. The authors probably meant *discrimination*.[69] Either they were unaware of the difference in connotation between the two words, or else they were proposing something that is not desirable and perhaps not possible. *Distinction* and *discrimination* would originally have been very close in meaning but were different in connotation by 1948. And the space between their meanings has considerably widened since then. The term *discrimination* has taken on a meaning that is almost always negative. When people use *discrimination* this way, they are using shorthand for "discriminate against." (One can still praise a person's discriminating taste).[70] The term *distinction* has remained positive or neutral in meaning. Distinctions are what the human mind makes; without distinctions, one cannot think at all.

Once again, it may seem picky to complain about the use of one word. However, what is at stake here is whether human rights belong to an abstraction (humanity) without human characteristics or whether the subject of these rights is a personal-communal being, one who can be distinguished by race, gender, age, nationality, and so on. The authors were against a particular characteristic, such as race, being used as the basis for disregarding or violating someone's human rights. However, as Justice Harry Blackmun said in a difficult case concerning race, "in order to get beyond racism, we must first take account of race."[71] In order to make no distinctions of race, one has to try to be color blind, which is to abstract a person from his or her actual, historical, communal existence. Richard Rorty is accurate in saying that this approach considers kinship and custom morally irrelevant details and assumes that obligations can be imposed simply by recognition of membership in the human species.[72]

One important characteristic that is conspicuously absent from the Declaration's list of distinctions is age. As I will argue in chapter five, it is important to include young children for the meaning of human rights, but it is just as important to distinguish between a two-year-old and a thirty-year-old in considering how to formulate human rights.

Article 3: "Everyone has the right to life, liberty and security of person." A test of the meaning of this article is how far the *everyone* extends. Delegates from Chile and Lebanon wished to include a specific reference to "the unborn." How a right to life applies to the unborn, starting with how to ask the question, was contentious then and remains so. The Chilean proposal was to add, "Unborn children and incurables, mentally defectives and lunatics, shall have the right to life." The Lebanese proposal referred only to the unborn saying that everyone has a right to life "from the moment of conception." The committee chose not to engage the issue.

Quite a different issue in this article is the state execution of prisoners, euphemistically called the death penalty or capital punishment. The call for a ban on such executions came, interestingly enough, from the Soviet delegate. The Soviet Union had passed such a ban in 1947. The Soviet bloc received support for such a prohibition from several Latin American countries.[73] There was little inclination to make a general condemnation of the practice, certainly not from the United States. It is difficult to understand the logic of asserting that the first inalienable right is to life and then giving the state the right to take the life. In the 1950s and 1960s, simple logic had seemed to win out in the United States, but then the killing of prisoners recommenced. Today, the movement in state by state to end the killings is slowly making its way across the country, but state executions enjoy considerable popular support.

Articles 4 to 28: The Division of Rights. More attention might have been given to the meanings of *life, liberty,* and *security* if there had been only a few human or universal rights asserted. The Humphrey draft had forty-eight articles; Cassin's had forty-six. The final document reduced the number to thirty articles. The number of rights was still too many, but that was not the main problem. The question of how many rights to include became entangled in the debate whether rights that were assumed to be well established as rights should be supplemented by "new" rights, especially economic rights.

The Soviet Union was not the only champion of the economic and social rights that were described as new rights. Chang and Santa Cruz were also promoters, but the cause of economic rights became especially identified with the Soviet Union. Delegates in the Anglo-American tradition saw a sharp dichotomy between political rights that have a long history and economic and social rights that were something new. Jeane Kirkpatrick once described a report of the Human Rights Commission, which was mainly on nutrition, as "a letter to Santa Claus."[74]

What the committee at the time could not see was that there were no human rights that had been established. It was their job to decide what counts as a *human* right in contrast to a political or an economic right. Roosevelt attempted to be evenhanded in saying that there was never a doubt about adding new rights to the old rights. Her formula has remained the standard liberal defense of human rights. But that defense has been vulnerable to endless sniping from people on the political right wing who assert that paid holidays or social security may be desirable aspirations, but it makes no sense to call such things human rights.

The fundamental criticism of the Universal Declaration of Human Rights has not varied much since Maurice Cranston asserted, "What vitiates the Universal Declaration of Human Rights is precisely that it does not distinguish between rights and ideals, or, rather that it attempts to be a statement of both at the same time." He refers to "secondary and hypothetical rights" such as a holiday with pay.[75] Cranston is right that a weakness of the Declaration is that it does not distinguish between rights and ideals, but ironically he has the two groups almost reversed.

Many of the stated rights in the early articles are in reality political ideals such as equality and liberty. In contrast, "a paid holiday" names an actual right. It is not a human or universal right because it depends on particular conditions, but it can be clearly stated as a right in a contract between an employer and an employee. The main ambiguity in the Universal Declaration is between (nearly) universal rights and rights that are contracted by states or other arms of society.

For example, freedom of speech is too abstract a formula to name a universal human right. One can get closer to universality by saying that human beings cannot live humanly without communicating with others. A person who is kept in solitary confinement indefinitely would have his or her human rights violated. States should be criticized for repressive policies that prevent almost any flow of ideas among its citizens.

There can be regulations of speech within a country that do not violate a human right. In the debate on the declaration, the Soviet delegate wished to qualify freedom of speech with the phrase "except to fascist and anti-democratic elements." The disingenuousness of the Soviet Union on this point does not invalidate a concern that every nation has. The 1949 Basic Law in Germany allows restrictions if speech is used "in order to combat the free democratic basic order."[76]

The United States takes great pride in the government not preventing its citizens from expressing their views, even views that are repugnant to the majority. One can admire this commitment while still recognizing that in the United States there are political, social, and economic conditions that shape what freedom of speech actually means. People in other countries are not necessarily lacking in an appreciation of free speech when they place the practice of speech in a context. Justice Holmes's famous metaphor, that one does not have the freedom to falsely shout "fire" in a crowded theater, is regularly noted in the United States, but it is only a start to thinking about how speech functions in a complicated world.[77]

What is true of a right to freedom of speech applies to many of the rights in the declaration. I will comment in chapter six on the complicated idea of freedom of religion, which is not reducible to any simple formula. After intense discussions between Chang and Malik on the subject of religion, Roosevelt played down the topic of religion except for a brief comment. That may have been necessary to get the document written and approved, but the United Nations has had to constantly deal with the claims of religion and with religious conflicts.[78]

The Saudis abstained from the vote on the declaration; they did so in part on religious grounds; but other predominantly Muslim countries did not object to the document. There was also objection to a right to marry whomever you wish without regard to the particular culture and religion.[79]

The right to emigrate seems to have been the main objection by the Soviet bloc. South Africa's objection on racial grounds was the least defensible.

In his speech presenting the declaration for the General Assembly's approval on December 9, 1948, Charles Malik described it as "a composite synthesis" of all existing rights traditions and much of Asian and Latin American wisdom. "This is the first time the principles of human rights and fundamental freedoms are spelled out authoritatively and in precise detail."[80] Malik certainly deserves much of the credit for creating this synthesis of traditions. It was not the fault of Malik or the other contributors that they could not completely transcend the biases of the time and the circumstances under which they worked to get an international agreement. If there is a fault, it is the limited progress since 1948 in understanding "the principles of human rights."

The last word on the formation of the document belongs to Eleanor Roosevelt. In one of her final speeches at the United Nations in March 1953, she made a low key but insightful and elegant plea for understanding human rights. "Where, after all, do universal human rights begin? In small places, close to home—so close and so small they cannot be seen on any map of the world. Yet they *are* the world of the individual persons; the neighborhood he lives in, the school or college he attends, the factory, farm or office where he works."[81] She was describing both the personal-communal being who is the subject of human rights as well as the process by which rights move toward more (nearly) universal recognition.

After the Declaration

It would be encouraging if one could report that the Universal Declaration of Human Rights triumphed and that the road from there to here is a story of unswerving progress. Some histories of human rights tend in that direction, but a triumphalistic attitude is not helpful to the cause of human rights. Like the Nuremberg Trials, the UN Declaration of Human Rights was affected by Cold War rhetoric. Human rights were seized upon as a banner in the West for the defense of capitalism. The Soviet Union sometimes gave support to the economic and social provisions of the declaration, especially when they were being appealed to by anticolonial movements. The fact that the Soviet bloc of nations had not voted for the declaration made suspect any later Soviet appeals to it.

The story of human rights in the second half of the twentieth century includes these elements: the approval of two covenants of human rights, the anticolonial rhetoric of a people's rights, the United Nations continuing to add "conventions" to the international laws of human rights, the development of regional bodies to support human rights, and the steady rise of NGOs as advocates of human rights.

The Two Covenants of Human Rights. As I have discussed above, a split in the meaning of *human rights* surfaced immediately during preparation of the declaration. The split made it obvious that the United Nations was not ready in 1948 to publish an International Bill of Rights. Many nations, including the United States, would not have consented to a legally binding document. Eleanor Roosevelt, aware of that fact, opted for the best that could be achieved, namely, a declaration. Over time, the declaration has increased in the moral pressure that it can bring to bear on nation-states.

The Human Rights Commission in 1948 promised that a Covenant on Human Rights would be forthcoming. Within a few years, it was obvious that no covenant would soon be agreed upon. By 1952, it was decided that there would be two covenants. The idea was that a covenant on political and civil rights could be quickly agreed upon while a covenant on social, cultural, and economic rights would require more extended debate. This practical decision, however, undermined the idea of a covenant on human rights. The practical efficiency also proved questionable. Both covenants appeared eighteen years later. The two covenants were approved by the General Assembly in 1966 and took effect ten years later. The United States, with its reluctance to sign any international covenants, finally approved (with reservations) the Covenant on Political and Civil Rights in 1992. It remained skeptical of the idea of rights that are included in the Covenant on Economic, Social and Cultural Rights.

The covenants do attempt to be more specific about many of the rights that are listed in the declaration. For example, both covenants specify that parents have a right to determine the moral and religious education of their children. "Religious education" is a twentieth-century term that is still not widely used or agreed upon. Parents in several countries have appealed to that provision in objecting to the topic of homosexuality in the curriculum of a state school.

The logic is not clear for the duplication of the first article in the two covenants: The first article in each covenant is (1) "All peoples have the right of self-determination. By virtue of that right they freely determine their political status and freely pursue their economic, social and cultural development. (2) All people may, for their own needs, freely dispose of their natural wealth and resources without prejudice to any obligations arising out of international economic co-operation, based upon the principle of mutual benefit, and international law. In no case may a people be deprived of its own means of subsistence. (3) The States Parties to the present Covenant, including those having responsibility for the administration of Non-Self-Governing and Trust Territories, shall promote the realization of the right of self-determination, and shall respect the right, in conformity with the provisions of the Charter of the United Nations."

Two comments on this duplicated article are relevant. First, it does not seem logical that if there is a need for two covenants that each one would start with the same article. If the contents of the article were a unified context in which to assert disparate rights in the two documents, the repetition might be understandable. But starting with the first sentence, the article is not about context, but it is instead an assertion of rights.

The second comment is that the asserted rights are a dramatic departure from what the Human Rights Commission discussed and approved in 1948. The covenants are not so much the application of the declaration as an attempt at a new beginning for the discourse of human rights. The starting place of the covenants is shaped by the particular context of their origin in the fight against colonialism. The formulation of Article 1 in both covenants is more a protest against European imperialist and colonial policies than a statement of universal rights.

The two covenants are strikingly different in form. The Covenant on Civil and Political Rights, after the first five articles, asserts the rights of persons. The Covenant on Economic, Social and Cultural Rights asserts throughout the document the obligations of "the States Parties to the present Covenant."

One could provocatively argue that the first covenant, the Covenant on Civil and Political Rights, comes close to meriting the name Covenant of Human Rights (not to be killed, not to be tortured, not to be enslaved). A better name for the second covenant on Economic, Social and Cultural rights would be Covenant of Civil Rights, that is, rights that can and should be guaranteed by each of the "states parties." However, the first covenant contains both too little and too much to be called the Covenant of Human Rights. It contains some rights that should be called civil rights rather than human rights (right to join labor unions, right to equality in marriage), and it does not bring out the economic dimension of human rights.

The two covenants unfortunately perpetuated a split in the meaning of human rights. They also confusedly added "collective" rights to what were said to be individual rights. The 1948 declaration was criticized as too individualistic although it should be noted that the declaration did not typically refer to the "individual" as the possessor of rights. It usually refers to "everyone," occasionally to the "person."[82] The two covenants, by opening with the statement that "all peoples have the right of self-determination," was intended to correct an individualistic bias. Unfortunately, neither covenant proceeds to work out the complex relation between a person and a people.

The cry for a people's self-determination is understandable. The struggle to achieve that status often draws the admiration of most of the world. There are no good reasons for denying that a people should be free. The problem during the last century has been how human rights and other rights fit in with groups that overthrow governments in the name of "the people." Alain Finkelkraut points out that the "cultural identity," which has been the means of resistance under colonial rule, can quickly become an instrument of oppression once the Europeans have left. "We won" means a loss of the right to free expression except in the first person plural.[83]

The question is not whether a people should be free, but what in actual conditions is a "people." At the end of World War I, there was a call for national self-determination. President Woodrow Wilson was foremost among the advocates. However, in testimony before the Senate Foreign Relations Committee, he confessed, "When I gave utterance to those words [that all nations had a right to self-determination], I said them without the knowledge that nationalities existed which are coming to us day after day . . . . You do not know and cannot appreciate the anxieties I have experienced as the result of many millions of people having their hopes raised by what I said."[84] The problem that Wilson suddenly discovered remains to this day. It is unlikely that the issue will ever be completely resolved. However, a degree of progress has been made by the removal of some of the arbitrary lines that colonial powers drew without understanding ethnic, religious, or tribal loyalties.

In this complicated issue of what a people is, human rights should be a help though it cannot be the main instrument for a solution. At the least, one would hope that human rights would not be used as an ideological tool. The rights of a person always involve his or her relatives: family, tribe, neighbors, fellow religionists, and nation. There are inevitable tensions in the relation between person and community. The problem is to work out the tensions between the human rights of persons and the rights of dozens of groups that a person is related to. Those groups vary, starting from the family, a group that goes to the core of the person's identity. At the other extreme, is one's membership in a club to which one can stop paying dues if one is dissatisfied. In between those cases are neighborhood, tribal, religious, ethnic, or professional relations from which it may be difficult for a particular person to exit.

Across the range of such groups a right to the protection of law varies. The family most clearly has a right to be protected from forces that can seriously damage it. Religious or ethnic minorities in a nation have a right not to be oppressed. The support or the restriction of such minorities can appropriately vary according to time and place. A nation has a right to be protected by international law, assuming that it is recognized as a nation and tries to abide by international agreements. The citizens of the nation have *human* rights; the nation has international rights which other nations have a duty to respect. As I noted in the "Introduction," the use of the phrase "international human rights" confuses the distinction between human rights and other rights whose existence is based on international agreements.

The assumption that human rights have been conceived as too individualistic may be true. But to add collective rights worsens the problem by adding one abstraction to another. Human beings have human rights not as individuals but as persons who are constituted by their relations to families, communities, organizations, societies, genders, and cultures. Neil Stammers complains that "many proponents of human rights see collective rights as being of dubious provenance, if not entirely anomalous." No doubt many proponents of human rights do resist the idea that *human* rights belong to collectivities; they are not denying that groups can have rights.

Stammers uses as an example that "workers' struggles in the western industrializing countries demonstrate how understanding of collective rights have been a persistent and fundamental way in which human rights claims have been formulated and developed."[85] Stammers's examination of social movements, especially the struggle for economic justice as a key element in the recognition of human rights, is very helpful. But to attribute human rights to a labor union is not a help to labor unions and confuses the meaning of human rights. The collective bargaining rights of workers' unions need protection in many countries, including the United States. Those rights need to be secured by national and international laws. Otherwise, the human rights of the workers are likely to suffer.[86]

A right to development has been debated since its inclusion in the 1972 African Charter on "Human and People's Rights." In 1986 the UN

General Assembly passed a Declaration on the Right to Development. This move to claim development as a right has its roots in the 1960s movements to take seriously the economic, social, and cultural rights of a people. The demand was for recognition by the developed world that developing or underdeveloped countries have a right to a fair share of the world's wealth. The demand is understandable. In a country of desperate poverty, most talk about human rights cannot be heard. Grappling with the outrageous disparity in material wealth between developed countries and everyone else should be at the top of the world's agenda.

It should be noted, however, that development is an intrinsic characteristic of the person in community. Human beings develop and human rights are a protection of that development. While *economic* development is indispensable, development is not an exclusively economic issue. There are, for example, libraries of books on psychological development. The literatures of psychology and economics, each of which tends to assume ownership of development, seldom meet. Psychology and economics could each use a strong dose of the other. And both should be reminded that neither psychology nor economics owns the meaning of *human* development.

A nation has a right to develop within a system of nations. That includes not being invaded, not being economically exploited, and being given at least a minimum of respect by other nations. Those rights should be what international law specifies. But saying that a nation, a people, or other collectivities have human rights undermines a consistent and effective meaning for human rights.

Other United Nations Instruments. Since the 1966 covenants, the United Nations has continued to search for ways to strengthen the commitment to human rights. The form that this has most often taken is conventions, that is, international treaties in defense of the rights of particular populations. Thus, there have been conventions on the rights of women, the rights of children, the rights of indigenous peoples, and the rights of persons with disabilities. Other conventions specifically outlaw practices that violate human rights, for example, the 1984 Convention against Torture and Other Cruel, Inhuman or Degrading Treatment or Punishment.

The various treaties which come from the United Nations issue from one of the committees or other bodies that make up the UN. Most of these bodies have human rights as part of their agenda. One important advance in 1993 was the creation of an Office of the United Nations High Commissioner for Human Rights. The idea for such a position goes back as far as the discussion of the declaration in 1948. René Cassin's proposal for such an office was dismissed as unworkable. Over the years, however, it became evident that human rights could be promoted by an office coordinating all the efforts of the UN.

The final push for such an office came from a UN World Conference on Human Rights in Vienna in 1993. Six months after a declaration of 171 countries at that conference, the Office of High Commissioner for Human Rights was established. Its mandate is to deal with "the most pressing human rights violations, chronic and acute," focusing on "at risk" and "vulnerable populations." This office has proved to be one of the most visible and effective arms of the United Nations.[87]

The Human Rights Committee of the UN was replaced in 2006 with a Human Rights Council, which is drawn from forty-seven member states. The Human Rights Committee had often been criticized for its biased selection of the countries that received criticism. The new council was to sit for longer periods and do a universal periodic review, that is, look at all rights in all 193 member states. It also was given an advisory committee to act as a think tank for the group.[88] The result is an improvement in the instrument, but the inherent problem of national biases will never be entirely overcome.

A special note should be taken of a 2001 report that was endorsed by the General Assembly and the Security Council in 2005 on the "responsibility to protect." Although this decision was not formulated as a human rights convention, it is central to the United Nations's relation to human rights. The criticism from the beginning of the UN has been that by accepting state sovereignty as absolute it allowed states to violate human rights with impunity. As one commentator described the situation, "The government-operated international human rights law is the best illustration of the poacher turned gamekeeper."[89]

The principle adopted in 2005 is that the international community has a responsibility to intervene in order to protect people from mass atrocities by their own government. It remains to be seen if this resolution will be effective. As with any community, interventions in the life of one member are always a struggle. If this resolution is taken seriously, it would not be just one more statement by the United Nations but a fundamental reorientation of that organization.

Regional Bodies. When the United Nations has been unable to represent the international community in stopping domestic slaughter, the job has often fallen to regional bodies. The idea of regional associations was a central issue in discussions of the United Nations Charter. Franklin Roosevelt wanted a more centralized power in an organization composed only of nation-states.

The charter did allow for regional groups but without granting them any power. Regional bodies are not an obstacle to claims for universality. Only if the human individual and human associations are thought to be opponents would regional groups be viewed as interfering with the establishment of human rights. Representatives of states who meet in New York or Geneva try to have a universal outlook on human rights. However, a stronger claim to (near) universality would be based on particular bodies in particular regions for which human rights are a primary concern.

The first and most important such group to develop was the Council of Europe in 1949. A year later it promulgated the European Convention for Protection of Human Rights and Fundamental Freedoms. The council established a European Commission for Human Rights and a European Court of Human Rights. Both of these bodies can receive petitions from individual persons as well as from states. These bodies took time to develop but have become important for international stability. In 1998, the Human Rights Act in the UK incorporated into common law the European Convention of Human Rights.

In more recent years, the still-developing African Union has held out intriguing possibilities. One of its founding principles is "the right of the Union to intervene in a member state pursuant to a decision of the Assembly in respect of grave circumstances, namely, war crimes, genocide and crimes against humanity."[90] The African Union needs help from beyond the continent, but its interventions are often more appropriate than having the United Nations or NATO engage in military action.

The Latin American countries, as noted earlier, tried to establish a regional organization in 1945 among American states. The United States objected but did agree to a common responsibility to respond if any one nation is attacked. The Organization of American States offers a form of regional association. But any organization with the name *American* is complicated by the United States's claim to own the term. It is difficult to have a partnership with one of the American states that assumes it is America.

For human rights policies to be effective, the establishing of an International Criminal Court was an important if only a single step in handling the worst offenses against international peace. Tribunals were established in the 1990s to deal with war in the former Yugoslavia and the massacre in Rwanda. One hundred and twenty nations met in Rome to create a charter for the International Court. Only seven nations opposed, one of them the United States of America. President Bill Clinton signed for the United States, but President George W. Bush "unsigned" the approval. The United States feared that its military personnel might be the target of unfair trials even though provision was made so that the International Court would not supersede the power of U.S. courts.[91]

NGOs. Of the many nongovernmental organizations that advocate human rights, the first and still the most prominent is Amnesty International. The organization was founded in 1961 to bring attention to "forgotten prisoners." The organization gradually widened its concerns to include both research and action for promoting human rights. It has tried to be fair in its assessment of different countries. Its reports are much more helpful than the self-reporting done by individual states at the United Nations.[92]

Amnesty International's reports on human rights' violations in the United States have drawn howls of protest in some quarters even though the reports are mainly statistical.[93] George W. Bush dismissed the 2005 report as coming from "people who hate America."[94] Amnesty International has been especially concerned with state executions as an obvious violation of human rights. It reported that in 2004 94 percent of the world's executions were in China, Iran, Saudi Arabia, and the United States of America.

The other well-known human rights organization is Human Rights Watch. It had its origin in 1976 as the "Helsinki Watch," referring to efforts led by Yuri Orlov in support of an international agreement called the Helsinki Accords. To many people, that agreement seemed not to be worth the paper it was written on. However, the agreement was the first time that the Soviet Union had signed a document that acknowledged the rights of all people to know their rights and act upon those rights. It was a pledge "to act in conformity with the purposes and principles of the Charter of the United Nation and with the Universal Declaration of Human Rights." The Soviet Union was probably trying to shore up its crumbling base but the Helsinki Accords became a step in the direction of the dissolution of the USSR. The group that had formed the Helsinki Watch widened its attention to a worldwide concern with human rights.

Human Rights Watch and Amnesty International have established their authority by the fairness, consistency, and integrity of their practices. The Soviet Union may not be the only state to have its authority weakened by the pressure that these and other human rights groups can bring to bear in the world. Gestures of protest can now be circulated around the globe instantaneously. Television was a big step in providing power to human rights groups; the Internet has now dwarfed that power. The Internet's possibilities still go beyond anyone's imagination. The future of human rights remains tenuous, but when the movement focuses on stopping the killing and torture of human beings, it has a power that every nation-state has to reckon with.

CHAPTER 4

Women, Men, and Human Rights

The focus of this chapter is the movement to recognize that human rights must include women. What might seem to be the simplest of logical issues has involved a long struggle throughout the last two centuries. Recognition of women as full human beings was a prerequisite for *human rights* to be a meaningful term. The particular controversies discussed here were not, until recently, about human rights but about political and economic rights. Nonetheless, the political and economic recognition of women was a main condition for a genuine language of human rights to develop in the second half of the twentieth century.

The theme of sameness and difference runs throughout this chapter and the four chapters that follow. The reason for exploring this theme is to make sure that both an emphasis on sameness and an emphasis on difference are included. In that way, a diverse population, not just an ideology about them, is included in the meaning of human rights.

The natural rights explored in the previous chapters were identified with adult white males. In the attempt to include other populations (in this case, women) it is crucial to notice their differences from the previous bearers of rights as well as their sameness. The category of human rights needs a meaning of the human in all its diversity. Women around the world are not just being admitted into the "rights club"; they challenge the built-in biases of the existing club members.

The same and the different that are the concern of this chapter are in the relations that have a sexual dimension. The focus is the relation between men and women, but the context is a full range of sexual relations, including homosexuality. The revolution that is now known as gay and lesbian (or

LGBT) deserves a study on its own that I do not attempt here. However, I do recognize that the full force of a women's movement in the 1970s and beyond could not have happened without the public acknowledgment of lesbians. On the side of men, the history of male homosexuality is long and mostly hidden from public view (the term *homosexual* was coined in the 1870s as the name of a disease or a crime).[1] The emergence of the term *sexual orientation* was helpful in freeing same-sex love from past opprobrium, but the term also applies to the straight population. Everyone has a sexual orientation, which is sometime very clear, sometimes confused.

The same and different that I explore in the history of the women's movement has a connection to a tension between same and different within each person. It seems likely that when men who glory in their masculinity react violently to women or gay men, it is because of unresolved issues of their own sexuality.

The refashioning of the term *gender*, as distinct from sex, has been a helpful step for understanding differences between men and women. Gender, referring to social roles, does not replace the physical-biological category of sex. Both *sex* and *gender* emphasize differences between men and women. It is usually assumed that social roles are easier to change than the biology of sex. While that may be true, there is no absolute separation between sex and gender as was suggested in such slogans as nature versus nurture.[2]

For emphasis on the sameness of men and women, it may sometimes be a helpful strategy to employ sexually neutral terms or terms that abstract from both sex and gender. But a sexless and genderless vocabulary would not describe the actual persons who have human rights. It would also cover up an important question of whether a particular difference is the basis of oppression or a source of rich variety in human life.

The sexual and gender relations that need exploring are between women and men, women and women, men and men. Mature people have friendships with people who are the same sex and with people who are a different sex. For intimate, passionate sexual expressions, people are (primarily?) oriented toward one sex or the other. Whatever a person's identity, an understanding of sexual/gender relations needs the full context of the relations of women-men, women-women, men-men. The even larger context of human-nonhuman relations will be discussed in chapter 7.

A temptation in trying to understand sexual/gender relations was to see a "woman question" based on assumed experts who weighed in with their views of the nature of womanhood. The fact that until recently those experts were usually men is a symptom of a deeper problem. A change in the conception of womanhood and a change in the place of women cannot happen without changes in men's lives and a change in the relations between women and men. Jean Baker Miller was not exaggerating when she wrote that "today, as women turn to the issue of their own development and enlargement, they are confronting society with *real* change, change in the very basis of everyone's existence and the way each person defines her or his self."[3]

Thus, the issue is as much a man problem as a woman problem. We have come a long way, nationally and internationally, in only a few decades, but there remain intractable problems in the relation between the sexes. The relation does not have to be a zero-sum game in which every gain for women would be a loss for men. Nonetheless, that is the way it is likely to be experienced unless one understands the logic of human uniqueness. That uniqueness includes a dialectic of sameness and difference within each person as well as between people. Women and men bring different *mixes* of sameness and difference to the meaning of the human. A change in the relation between the sexes can benefit both of them and the change has been indispensable to the full meaning of human rights.

Sexual Language

The language for describing the complexity of the relation between men and women does not exist. Probably in no other area is it true that every term is burdened with a bias from the past. There is no neutral vantage point from which to begin a dispassionate description of the sameness and difference in relations affecting men and women. One has to judge whether a particular term, though it may be tainted, is defensible or whether it needs to be avoided (*woman* is biased by its etymology, but it is not likely to be replaced any time soon). It is always helpful but not decisive to recognize a term's etymology; one also has to follow the history of the contexts in which it has been used. The possibility of a shift in a term's meaning is realistic if there is a latent strand of meaning supportive of the change and if there are current activities that support the shift.

Language is always changing and the revolution in "gender sensitive" language has not been completed. Better solutions in the English language are needed for such phrases as "he or she" (perhaps *they* has already begun to fill that gap), but the development of simple and accurate ways of including both genders when appropriate will take a while to evolve. Today's technology has speeded up linguistic change, especially in the direction of simplicity. The tricky part is to combine simplicity of speech with comprehensiveness and depth of thinking. Changes in ways of speaking reflect changes in social interaction which in turn bring on further linguistic change. The language of sexual/gender relations has changed and the whole world has changed with it.

If this history were an account of what woman has wanted and man has resisted, it would be a relatively simple story. But the history is not of woman and man but of women and men. The conflicts in the story are as much among women as between women and men. Individual women and groups of women have sought what seemed to be a better life for women. They have often found support among men in their struggles. They have also found resistance by many men and some women who for a variety of reasons have disagreed with what has been advocated as progress for women. There are groups of women who have sincerely believed that progress for some women has been a loss for woman's place in humanity.

One might speak of two movements by women that differed in what they thought should be emphasized about women's lives. Although the lines have sometimes blurred between the two opposing camps, there is nevertheless a value in recognizing a continuing argument about whether to emphasize the sameness of men and women or their differences. As an alternative to speaking of two movements, one could speak of one movement that has had two strands within it. That usage would soften the sharp edge of the disagreements among women but with the risk of not acknowledging the paradoxical position that women have had to argue from.

As an exercise in stripping sexual relations of language and conceiving the relations in mathematical terms, I offer the following possibilities. This exercise is a playful reduction but with a serious purpose. The history of sexual relations seems to offer only two possibilities:

$$1 + 1 = 2$$
$$\frac{1}{2} + \frac{1}{2} = 1$$

The first equation represents a movement that has usually marched under the banner of sexual equality. One man and one woman equal two people. Nothing could be simpler. Nearly all differences that do exist, therefore, are the result of oppression. As a matter of justice, all of these oppressive differences should be eliminated. Women and men would then have equal rights. The motto here is that "men and women are the same." Of course, there has to be an addendum to that claim, namely, "same except for a, b, and c."

The second equation starts from the opposite end. Its motto is that "men and women are different; each of them has to be completed by the other." A man or woman is half a human who is in search of his or her other half. This complementarity of men and women as being different also has to attach an addendum: "different except for x, y, and z."

This mythical belief in complementarity is not only common in ancient history; it seems to affect much of modern psychology and social science. There could be a kind of equality here, but in practice there has been imbalance. In the mythical world, there has been more talk of an "eternal feminine" completing man than an "eternal masculine" for women. And in the political and economic world, the unity that resulted from joining a masculine half and a feminine half was a man. The legal result was exclusively a man's world in which women had their place.[4]

Neither equation seems satisfactory. While there is a kind of equality in each case, women have found a lack of justice in the application of these principles. In each case, the afterthought of a, b, c to qualify sameness, and x, y, z to qualify difference either gets relegated to unimportance or else undermines the logic of the starting principle. Theoretically, the two groups could end with exactly the same understanding of the relation between men and women. Practically, however, the two positions—sameness with some difference or difference with some sameness—does not come to the same result. There are occasions, however, when they do find agreement on an issue. In the successful run up to the suffrage amendment in the United States, one group favored getting the vote because women brought something different to politics; the other group favored getting the vote because women should be the same as men in political representation.

After fifty years of studying this issue, I have reached a conclusion. The principle that women and men are the same except for a, b, c is correct. The principle that women and men are different except for x, y, z is correct. But for each principle to maintain its correctness, both principles have to be accepted. Each principle is correct but not sufficiently comprehensive. Depending on the situation, one or the other principle may be the more appropriate. As for what a, b, c, x, y, z are, no one in the human race knows for sure. A few things are obvious about the sexes; for example, both have feet and eyes; only one has a uterus. The difficult issues lie in everything beyond the obvious. Modern science has made great advances in understanding where men and women do differ, but sometimes what has been offered as scientific evidence has been balderdash.

As an alternative to starting with either sameness or difference, I wish to propose a logic of uniqueness. Sameness and difference are found within each person so that a relation between the sexes can produce a variety of mixes of sameness and difference within the unique union of the sexes. For a mathematical formula of sexual/gender relations, I suggest the following:

$$2 + 2 = 1 \text{ (inclusive of 3)}$$

The duality of sexual relations reflects a duality of sameness and difference within each person. Physically and intellectually, a person is in a constant movement that includes sameness amid the difference. One of the most important dualities in men and women is the relation between the active and the passive. A distinguishing mark of the human is its radical passiveness, that is, its capacity to take in the world, play imaginatively with what it has received, mull over its meaning, and connect it to future possibilities. A being that acted with no interior life of receptiveness and reflection would be less than human. Conversely, someone who did not react to what presses in upon him or her would be dehumanized by such passivity.

Every human being is a mixture of the active and passive. The active element is more obvious to external observation. We tend to think of power as activity that puts us in control of the world around us. The power to dominate others clearly links the human animal to other animals. Interestingly, however, the word *power* is etymologically related to *passive*. Humans have their greatest power in receptivity, the ability to take in the world as it is and reshape it to human advantage. In their most intelligent and responsible activities, humans are sensitive to the needs of other animals and try to act for the good of all creatures.

Throughout most of history, the structure of sexual relations has led to women being thought more passive than men. In the context of a proper relation between active and passive, to speak of someone having a strongly developed passive or receptive side can be offered as praise. But what is intended as praise can be received as insult; words carry a meaning that may not be intended. In this case, the term *passive* has too much baggage to be quickly embraced by many women. And the main need, if this analysis is correct, is not to praise the passive element in women's lives but to reeducate men to the human value of receptivity, interiority, reflection, and compassion. Women need not praise passivity, but they might well refrain from attacking it.

The duality of men joined with the duality of women holds the possibility of a marvelous human richness in the relations between women and men. Thus, the two dualities create a unity. Human love can be based on similarity; love can also be based on difference. Ideally, it includes a union of sameness and a union of differences to create a permanent bond that overflows in its effects. The one union includes a more unique man, a more unique woman and a third—a unique offspring of their love. That is the reason why the one union includes three elements.

Throughout human history, the offspring were biological and multiple. Simply to survive, the human race needed men and women to produce many children. Even in the late eighteenth century, Rousseau was insisting that each woman had to produce at least four children for the race to continue.[5] Since the early twentieth century, world population has been growing almost exponentially. It is imperative now that not all of the offspring of love should be biological. The love between men and women (and the love between men and the love between women) can overflow into care for the needs of other human beings and care for the physical world.

How to humanely control population growth is one of the most urgent problems facing humanity for which there are no simple answers at present. But it is well known that the rate of population growth is directly tied to economic well-being. Unless economic improvements can be made in the poorest sections of the world, the human race will soon face insuperable problems.

The relation between men and women has always included some recognition of sameness and difference that are the source of tension. History, art, literature, religion, and philosophy testify to the beauty, passion, joy, suffering, and tragedy that have swirled around the relation between the sexes. It is now imaginable that technology could eliminate all or practically all sexual differences. New human beings could be grown or produced outside of a woman's body. A few feminist authors have argued that women will not really be free until they are free from pregnancy.[6] Life would undoubtedly be calmer and likely less interesting. Whether or not that is a route that the human race will eventually follow, it is not the issue found in the past nor what immediately confronts us in the present.

Premodern Sexual Relations

It would be impossible in a single book, let alone a chapter of a book, to provide a coherent and detailed history of sexual relations. What follows are some representative figures and an analysis of some issues that embody the theme of how to reconcile sameness and difference. I draw a somewhat arbitrary line between premodern and modern in the late eighteenth century. It is at that point that the relation between the sexes becomes thematized as a problem and women's voices are heard in increasing numbers.

Women historians and anthropologists in recent decades have been digging at prehistoric evidence. It seems likely from what can be pieced together that women were in the ascendancy over men. "Only women could produce new life, and they were revered accordingly; all the power of nature, and over nature, was theirs."[7] The awe at women was no doubt mixed with fear, and to this day, men sense at some level of consciousness that women are in touch with the forces of life, a power that can frighten men.

For a long time, the role of men in the generating of a child was overlooked. Then history's most spectacular reversal occurred. Men discovered that they had a part in producing children. From that fact they used their "brute" strength to decree that women's part in the birth process is insignificant. The Greek dramatist Aeschylus (524-456 B.C.E) articulated the ideology that would take hold in the West. The "Judgment of Apollo" at the climax of *The Eumenides* is that "the mother is not the parent of that which is called her child: but only nurse of the newly planted seed that grows. The parent is he who mounts." [8]

Aristotle. (384-322 BCE) Despite his brilliance and insight as a scientist, Aristotle was sadly deficient in what he had to say about women. Some of it can be excused because he was working with the assumptions of his day, but one might expect a great scientist to transcend the common thought patterns of the time. He may have been the first, but he was by no means the last of scientific men whose views of women have turned out to be prejudices masquerading as science.

Aristotle's great breakthrough in philosophical theory was to explain physical change by a duality of components in each individual thing. When change occurs, it is the relation that changes; the material element remains but it now has a different form. He applied the theory of form and matter at several levels. A "substance" might remain even as there is "accidental" change. Most generally, the theory recognizes an active and a passive element in every being. Aristotle called the active element in animals, including humans, the soul.

In his study of animals, Aristotle concluded that the female was an infertile male, incapable of producing semen (the seed of life).[9] If one applies that to the human animal, the woman provided the matter; the man produced the soul that gives form to a human being. Carolyn Whitbeck calls this the "flower pot theory of pregnancy."[10] Even today, to mother a child means caring for an infant; to father a child mean to impregnate.[11] If something went wrong with the pregnancy, it was the woman's fault for not providing the proper receptacle. Aristotle was on the right track in positing an active and a passive element, but within the terms of his own philosophy, the active and the passive should not have been assigned to each sex separately.

In his *Politics*, Aristotle looks directly at human life, community, and forms of government. He declares that the fundamental form of community, the family, is constituted by three relations: master-slave, husband-wife, father-child. In his description that follows, the master-slave relation receives the most attention. What he says of human slaves is shocking to modern ears; it bears testimony to how even brilliant people can look at the world and see the current state of things as the ways things have always been and must be. Interestingly, his discussions of slavery and women do not overlap though there were women slaves as well as men slaves.[12] He does note that "the poor are obliged to employ their wives and children in servile offices for want of slaves."[13]

Aristotle's discussion of women and family is remarkably brief. He apparently thought that there is not much to explain. After commenting upon the taming of animals and the relation of slaves to their masters, he wraps up the relation of husband and wife in these words: "So it is naturally with the male and the female; the one is superior, the other inferior; the one governs, the other is governed; and the same rule must necessarily hold good with respect to all mankind."[14] What was evident to a man in the Athens of fourth century BCE is assumed to "necessarily hold good with respect to all mankind."

Plato (428-348 BCE). Alfred North Whitehead famously said that all of European philosophy consists of footnotes to Plato.[15] That is surely debatable, but no one doubts that Plato left an enduring mark in the history of human thought. Plato's views are expressed through dialogues, myths, and parables. What Plato himself thought cannot be directly lifted from the printed page.

The *Republic* is widely considered one of the greatest works in the history of philosophy. Plato offers a plan for an ideal society composed of three classes. The upper class, concerned with politics and military force, are called guardians. In stating the requirements to be a guardian, Plato poses the question of how men and women differ. He answers that question by offering that "the only difference apparent between them is that the female bears and the male begets."[16] Plato concludes that a woman's difference from a man should not disqualify her from the guardian class.

Plato never indicates whether the actual number of women guardians would be more than a token. He sometimes seems to forget his assumption that women will be guardians when he refers, for example, to the "guardians' wives" or to a "community of women and children." Was he playing with his own idea that women and men are essentially the same or did his radical thinking simply outstrip the language of his time?

The main problem with Plato as a proto-feminist is that while some women may be guardians the rest of the women, presumably the great majority, do not seem to have their lives improved. That is especially true of the nurses who are assigned the task of raising the next generations of guardians. Pregnancy in the guardian class is closely regulated by having only the best men mate with the best women. Abortion and infanticide seem to be implied as a quality control. Almost nothing is said about the education and living conditions of the women who have the important work of child-rearing.

While the *Republic* is read as emphasizing the sameness of men and women, Plato's *Symposium* tells a different story. In this dialogue, the myth of the androgyne is presented by Plato. It is recounted in the text by Aristophanes in these words: "Originally there were three sexes: man, woman, and the union of the two. The primeval man was round, one head with two faces looking in opposite ways . . . Terrible was their might and they made attack upon the gods. After a celestial council, Zeus said: 'Methinks I have a plan which will enfeeble their strength . . . I will cut them in two and they will be diminished in strength and increased in numbers.' Zeus cut them in two, like an apple which is halved for pickling or as you might divide an egg with a hair. Zeus turned their parts of generation round to the front . . . and they sowed their seed in one another . . . . Each of us when separated, having one side only like a flat fish, is but the tally-half of a man, and he is always looking for his other half . . . . When one of them meets his other half, the actual half of himself . . . the pair are lost in an amazement of love and friendship and intimacy."[17]

Plato was tapping into a nearly universal experience of duality, including the inability to control our own emotions. The androgynous myth speaks to anyone who has fallen in love. The feeling is that of finding what one was lacking, the completion of one's being. The two lovers are impelled to embrace and form a new unity. Because there were three original sexes, the story encompasses both gay and lesbian love as well as heterosexual relations. In recent history, Carl Jung made an explicit use of the androgynous myth in describing masculine and feminine principles within each person. Jungians defend the language, but it easily lends itself to a dualism of male and female, which is bad enough in psychology but disastrous for politics.[18]

Early Modern Writing on the Sexes

A woman's movement in the nineteenth century was ignited by two books in the late eighteenth century: *Emile* by Jean-Jacques Rousseau in 1762 and a direct rejoinder to Rousseau by Mary Wollstonecraft's *Vindication of the Rights of Woman* in 1794. The two works exemplify the contrasting strands of a woman's movement in the nineteenth century and the women's movement of the twentieth century.

Jean-Jacques Rousseau (1712-1778). Rousseau is often referred to as the first modern man; he embodies all the contradictions that are found in the modern era.[19] His writing is never free of an intense subjectivity that makes his philosophy reflect his personal life. Nowhere is that clearer than in his views of the relation between the sexes. He is often denounced as the main opponent of the rights of women, but in his own time he was heralded as "the birthplace of love."[20] He inspired the strand of the woman's movement that tried to strengthen the role of women as wives and mothers.

Far from hating women, Rousseau's problem was his awe of women. Starting in childhood and throughout his life, Rousseau was dependent on women. The dependency began with the sister of the Protestant minister he was sent to live with. He found the physical punishments that she imposed to be a mixture of pain and sexual stimulation.[21] Later he received economic help from several rich women. He looked to women as the moral power for guiding society. He was severely critical of the mothers of his day, in part because he held them to an impossibly high standard. In a letter to Toussaint-Pierre Lenieps, Rousseau wrote, "Everywhere men are what women make of them."[22] He never succeeded in having a healthy mutual relation of love with any woman. He treated badly his common law wife, Theresa, and he was hopeless as a father.

Rousseau's political and educational theories are found in separate books published in 1762: *Social Contract* and *Emile*. The education of Emile was to prepare him for life in a reformed society. A common misinterpretation of *Emile* is to read it as proposing an education that is directed by no one except the boy himself. In fact, the book has a nearly omniscient teacher who plans every step of the boy's education. The boy is prepared not to be a supreme individualist but to be a husband and father, and thereby a responsible citizen.

Early in the book, Rousseau praises Plato's *Republic* as "the most beautiful educational treatise ever written." That is actually faint praise because he adds that the public education Plato advocated no longer exists in that there is no longer a fatherland and citizens. Instead of public instruction, Rousseau's interest is private or domestic education.[23] By the end of the book, however, his total separation of public and private seems to be overcome in the form of the family and in Emile becoming both father and good citizen. Rousseau strongly condemns Plato for doing away with the family: "Having removed private families from his regime and no longer knowing what to do with women, he [Plato] found himself forced to make them men."[24]

The fifth and last book of *Emile* is a portrait of Sophie who is to be the perfect mate for Emile and the mother of his children. Some of today's schools of education omit reading this last book because women students' may find it offensive. This educational policy seems to assume that students should read only what they agree with. The problem is that *Emile* (originally entitled *Emilius and Sophie*) cannot be understood without the concluding book.[25] While far more space is given to Emile's education, Sophie's education is just as important to the success of family life. Rousseau assumed that Sophie's education is uncomplicated and is done by the mother in the ordinary course of the day while Emile has to be led every step of the way by the tutor.

Book 5, like the treatise as a whole, proceeds dialectically, starting with a total opposition of men and women. He says that "in the union of the sexes each contributes equally to the common aim, but not in the same way."[26] That sounds reasonable enough. But he immediately concludes from this principle that "one ought to be active and strong, the other passive and weak" That theme is developed for the next several pages: man is superior in strength and woman is made to please man. Along with this apparent swagger of the man taking charge, there is an underlying theme of women having secrets that men do not understand. Women, by way of their sexuality, can get men to do whatever women want. The tutor's genius was letting the student think he was doing whatever he wanted to do while in fact the tutor was getting him to do exactly as the tutor wished. At the end of the book, the tutor gives Emile over to Sophie who will henceforth be the teacher, the one who is in charge of the unsuspecting student.[27]

Emile has a vision of Sophie, the ideal woman, before he actually meets the girl whose name is Sophie, a word meaning wisdom. The joining of the qualities of manhood and womanhood creates an ideal marriage. Emile announces at the end of the book that he will be the tutor of his son. No mention is made of how their daughter will be educated. Presumably, Sophie as an exemplar of womanly wisdom, will pass on her attributes and virtues.

Rousseau seems to think that the complementarity of roles for Emile and Sophie solves the great paradox of sex; it is "one of the marvels of nature to have been able to construct two such similar beings who are constituted so differently."[28] Rousseau did leave an unfinished novel in which Emile and Sophie have a disastrous breakup of their marriage.[29] Perhaps Rousseau recognized the tenuous nature of his solution in which the active and passive in human life are dealt with by means of the passive woman manipulating the active man.

Mary Wollstonecraft (1759-1797). While Mary Wollstonecraft admits admiration for Rousseau's literary style, her aim in *Vindication of the Rights of Woman* is to refute his argument concerning the relation between women and men. Rousseau assumed an extreme difference between men and women; his search was for how to create a unity out of such difference. Wollstonecraft works from an opposite assumption, that in all the important aspects of humanity women and men are the same. She is rightly credited with beginning the modern struggle for the rights of women, that is, what is due to all women as their fair share of human goods.

What Wollstonecraft had to confront is the problem inherent in the cry for equal rights: Why is there now such a difference? Whatever the explanation, the tricky part is to avoid seemingly attacking women in their present state, in the name of woman as she should be. Wollstonecraft says, "that women at present are by ignorance rendered foolish and vicious is, I think, not to be disputed."[30] But surely some of her sisters whom she was fighting for would have disputed this description and taken umbrage at it. Is Wollstonecraft's statement one of self-hatred, or is it an arrogant claim that she alone has escaped the present condition of women?

Wollstonecraft laid the blame for women's condition on men's oppression. "It is vain to expect virtue from women till they are, in some degree, independent of men," and what women need is better education. But she is always perilously close to sounding like she is blaming the victim. "Whilst they are absolutely dependent on their husbands, they will be cunning, mean and selfish."[31] Writing in the years of the French Revolution, she chides the French to carry through their enlightenment by allowing women to share with men in the advantages of education and government. "See whether they will become better as they grow wiser and become free. They cannot be injured by the experiment; for it is not in the power of man to render them more insignificant than they are at present."[32]

As Wollstonecraft saw the problem, Rousseau had separated the sexes and divided the virtues of men and women. He had placed reason on the side of men, leaving to women emotion or sentiment. In any rebellion against oppression, there is a danger that the oppressed try to get what the oppressor has, instead of trying to overcome the dichotomy that has created the oppression. In the seventeenth and eighteenth centuries, reason was taken to be the supreme power of man, his ability to control women, children, nonhuman nature, and his own emotions. In the thinking of most (male) philosophers, women were lacking in reason, a deficiency that was compensated for by their virtues of care and compassion. Because human dignity and rights were regularly associated with reason, the unavoidable implication was that women quite properly lack rights.

Wollstonecraft insisted that all virtues are founded in reason and that there are not separate sets of virtues for men and women. Women need an equal share in reason. "Children cannot be taught too early to submit to reason . . . for to submit to reason is to submit to the nature of things, and to that God, who formed them, to promote our real interest."[33] The danger here is assuming that what men in the eighteenth century meant by the term reason was identical to the nature of things and what God had formed. If reason is split off from emotion, it might lack a human context for its calculations and control. Wollstonecraft advised a mother to "give true dignity to her daughters" by proceeding on a plan "diametrically opposed to that which Rousseau has recommended." But the opposite of Rousseau's plan might not escape from being limited by the terms Rousseau had used.

A trust in reason defined in opposition to emotion was inimical to qualities without which the human race cannot manage. Wollstonecraft wished to persuade women "to endeavor to acquire strength of mind and body." To do that she has "to convince them that the soft phrases, susceptibility of heart, delicacy of sentiment, and refinement of taste, are almost synonyms with epithets of weakness."[34] She is certainly right that the oppressive men she is opposing have made such phrases into signs of weakness, but those qualities can also be seen as invaluable aspects of a full humanity.[35] She is wary of Rousseau's advice to use weakness as a means of manipulating the strong. But if men as well as women shared in heart, sentiment, and taste, then men might be better husbands, women better wives, and together they might be better parents of the next generation.

Rousseau's starting point of male and female principles that are opposed to each other made it impossible for him to reach a mutuality of women and men. Wollstonecraft zeroed in on that vulnerability, but given the language and political situation of her time, there was no way to describe the mutuality that she sought. She is led to this ironic and tragic formulation of the problem: "Nor will the important task of education ever be properly begun till the person of a woman is no longer preferred to her mind." One can hope that choosing a woman's mind over her person is not the choice that women have.

An alternative approach in the 1790s was Judith Sargent Murray's *The Gleaner* that championed political equality for women while arguing that women were superior in feelings. Women's virtue derives from "sentiment at once sublime and pathetic."[36] Murray unfortunately had less influence on the nineteenth-century discussion than did Rousseau and Wollstonecraft. In more recent times, however, many women have found attractive this combination of political equality and a claim to the biological/cultural superiority of women.

The Nineteenth-Century Movements

Rousseau and Wollstonecraft set the direction for the nineteenth century in which the improvement of the lot of women was identified either with a strengthening of her role in the family or with her using her talents in roles besides those of wife and mother. The two directions do not necessarily contradict each other but advocates on both sides often perceived it that way. A new kind of tension between home and workplace began early in the nineteenth century and has continued to the present. The tension involves the relation between men and women, but the focus has usually been on the woman's family responsibility.

Man's World, Woman's Place. The late eighteenth century had begun the social and economic transformation that would lead to a radical change in the relation between men and women. That change is reflected in the language of separate spheres of activity. Actually, a separate sphere of woman's activity was not contrasted with a man's sphere but with the man's *world*. At the center of the transformation was a change in the nature of work as the modern industrial economy was born. The rhythm of human life became controlled by the machine and its needs. It seemed obvious to most people that the men would leave the home each day and go to the factories for production of goods while women would stay at home and take care of the children and the necessities of life.

Women were to provide a respite from the harsh realities of the work world while also having the key role of consumer in the new economy. "The two roles, saint and consumer, were interlocked and mutually dependent; the lady's function in a capitalist society was to appropriate and preserve both the values and commodities which her competitive husband, father and son had little time to honor or enjoy; she was to provide an antidote and a purpose for the labor."[37] The existence of two spheres would not logically be an unfair arrangement. Equality between the spheres was claimed, but individual women became uncomfortable at a place being assigned to them without their having had much choice.

The woman did have one big choice, that of a husband. She did not have a realistic choice to remain outside marriage and a family setting. Alexis de Tocqueville's classic study of the United States in the 1830s has positive things to say about the arrangement that was taking shape. He attributed the "singular prosperity and growing strength of that people to the superiority of their women." Care has been taken, he says, "to trace two clearly distinct lines of action for the two sexes, and to make them keep pace one with the other, but in two pathways which are always different."

Tocqueville favorably contrasts this arrangement in the United States with what was happening in Europe, which in attempting to make one sex equal to the other had degraded both: "From so preposterous a medley of the works of nature nothing could ever result but weak men and disorderly women." Tocqueville did recognize that in the United States "the independence of woman is irrevocably lost in the bonds of marriage." Nonetheless, "she has learned by the use of her independence to surrender it without a struggle and without a murmur when the time comes for making the sacrifice."[38] As was usual in this way of thinking, the talk was about woman and her nature rather than about women and their lives.

The word *home* took on a special meaning in American English. It does not just refer to being at my house or in one's country. *Home* is supercharged with emotional meaning, the repository of all that is good about America. It is where men return to discover their human qualities.

From early in the nineteenth century, home was equated with a retreat or an oasis in the desert. Home provided an escape for men while for women there was no escape. Woman's work was never done; even the maintenance of the physical plant was now part of her agenda in addition to taming the husband and rearing perfect children. As one author in the 1850s candidly stated, "A wife is almost a necessary part of a physician's professional equipment."[39]

The nineteenth century is especially noteworthy for the rise of the modern professions led by the medical profession. The world of science and technology needed experts in specialized areas. Among those areas was thought to be the woman's work in the home; thus arose a demand for the professionalization of motherhood. The foremost advocate of this profession was Catherine Beecher although the idea went back as far as Hannah More at the end of the eighteenth century.[40] Beecher's work, starting in the 1830s, articulated a theory of separate but equal spheres of influence and the need for the education of women to perform their tasks. She advised women to obtain "appropriate scientific training for her *profession* as housekeeper, nurse of infants and the sick, educator of childhood, trainer of servants and minister of charities."[41]

The idea of motherhood as a profession strikes most people today as just an attempt to imitate real professions such as medicine and law. Actually, the claim of motherhood to be a profession was closer to the older meaning of *professional* than was the proliferation of claims to professionalism by groups looking for higher status and more money. The idea of profession that goes back to the medieval monastery was a professing of belief in values beyond money, especially through serving the needs of a community. By the nineteenth century, the professing of service by a lawyer, physician, or minister was being overshadowed by the demands of "making a living" in an industrial society. The rhetoric of professional service continues to this day, but *profession* almost reversed its meaning: from service to control, from community to individual, from poverty to big money. It was women in the home who continued to exemplify service to a community without a paycheck.

Women were allowed into two professions, or at least two jobs, that have struggled for nearly two centuries to be respected as professions. Until the middle of the twentieth century, more than 90 percent of professional women were in either school teaching or nursing. School teaching was the first profession that was opened to women because it was thought to be an extension of motherhood. The educating of women to manage the home was intrinsically related to preparing them to be schoolteachers when school meant elementary schools. When high school and then university education became common, it was men who took those jobs that were higher in status and better paying.

Until the 1840s, schools were generally the workplace of schoolmasters. A rapid change then began in the personnel of school teaching. In Massachusetts 61 percent of school teachers in 1840 were men; by 1865, only 14 percent were men. Nationally, by the end of the century, 70 percent of schoolteachers were women, and the percentage was continuing to grow.[42] This professional breakthrough was a limited victory for women. The Boston School Committee in the 1840s expressed a preference for women teachers because they were "unambitious, frugal and filial." Similarly a New York legislator praised women as better teachers of children "because of their very weakness for they taught pupils whose intellectual faculties were less developed than their affections."[43]

The change that occurred in a profession of healing was even more crucial for solidifying the separation of man's world and woman's place. Until the 1840s, most healing took place by women at home and by some women who extended their healing arts beyond the home. It was not a job for making big money. An emerging male group called doctors (learned men, teachers) complained in the 1840s that "the merest pittance in the way of remuneration is scantily doled out even to the most industrious of our ranks." The problem, as the newly founded American Medical Association saw it, was "a long list of irregular practitioners who swarm like locusts in every part of the country." These "locusts" were the women who were using traditional means of health care.[44]

As men shaped a profession of medicine and eventually made it a well-paying job, the woman's role was reconceptualized as nurse. The doctor was the scientific expert who could prescribe medicine and practice surgery. The day-to-day care of the patient was work that required compassion and dedication but not intellectual learning. Until the second half of the twentieth century, most nurses did not receive a college education; it was thought they needed only on-the-job training. Like schoolteachers, they were paid poorly to do difficult and indispensable work. The separation of doctor and nurse was perfectly aligned with the idea of separate spheres that were supposedly equal. But like schoolteachers in relation to school administrators, nurses could act only in following orders of the doctor.

It should be noted that women did work beyond the home when it involved low-paying and unskilled labor. One of the most striking cases was the textile mills of New England that hired thousands of young immigrant girls and women. They started working at age fifteen and usually stayed until they found a husband in their twenties. Women who stayed beyond the marrying age became known as spinsters. The work was dirty, noisy, and boring; it was allowed to women because it was work that had previously been done at home, and women did not have to be paid much.

One good aspect of this woman's work was that it sometimes provided a sense of community and sisterhood along with the satisfaction of being paid. Later in life, some of the women looked back nostalgically: "It was just one big happy family." "The mills were our home. They were our whole life, and we were very happy there."[45]

Where a sense of community among women particularly developed was in female academies that often included evangelical religion. Wollstonecraft had objected to "many females being shut up together in nurseries, schools or convents."[46] Such institutions were in fact places of confinement, but they could also generate friendships and communal movements. Catherine Beecher, having founded Hartford Seminary for Females in 1823, became one of the leaders in women's education. Beecher was no advocate of women's rights. The aim was to train women in the profession of motherhood. However, once women were exposed to higher learning some of them began to question the hierarchy of men and women.

The problem for men on the issue of women's education had some similarity to the slaveholder's relation to slaves. After Nat Turner's rebellion, teaching a slave to read became illegal. The slave owner endorsed the obedience of slaves that Paul taught in the New Testament. There was fear that the slave who could read might find that the Book of Exodus was more relevant to the slave than to the slave owner.[47] But unlike the slaves, women could not be denied education; they needed it to be good wives and mothers. And yet when women discussed ideas with other women, they might start considering the arbitrariness of many social arrangements.

The Second Great Awakening during the early 1800s was led by men, but it was mainly populated by women. The official role of women was confined to teaching in Sunday School, but similar to female academies, the church was a place for women to gather and possibly to discover their strengths. Religion raised the issue of an authority based on a reality beyond men.[48] This strand of the woman's movement, whose premise that woman is different from man, had the unintended effect of mobilizing women for political advocacy. The goals of the "cult of domesticity" were dramatically different from the movement for women's rights, but it was possible for the former movement to lead into the latter.

Women's Rights. A demand for political and economic equality by women was the minority voice within the woman's movement in the nineteenth century. It emerged in part as a protest against separate spheres but also in part as a continuation of that movement. The issue of women's rights had been raised by only a few women and men at the time of the British American and French Revolutions. However, the blatant inconsistency of proclaiming universal rights in England, France, and the United States and then excluding half the population guaranteed that the issue would not disappear. The U.S. Constitution's one reference to women is to enslaved women. Women, slaves, and Indians formed the "other" against which the masculinity of "the American" was defined. Women could not be entirely silenced, however, and there was continuing protest against the contradiction between "liberty and justice for all" and the subordinate position assigned to women.[49]

The 1793 "Declaration of the Rights of Women" by Olympe de Gouges affirms that "if woman has the right to mount to the scaffold; she ought equally to have the right to mount to the tribune."[50] Her activities led de Gouges to the guillotine in 1794, but a half century later, her ideas sparked a demand for women rights. Harriet Martineau in 1837 asked the obvious question: Why aren't women included in rights within a democracy?[51] The answer that had been given by Rev. John Ogden in 1793 that "every woman is born with an equal right to be the wife of the most eminent man" could not forever hold up.[52]

The usual date for the beginning of the women's rights movement is 1848 with the convention at Seneca Falls, New York. The ideas had already been stirring with women who were working in the cause of the abolition of slavery. As would eerily be repeated in the civil rights movement of the 1960s, women began to wonder why the rights that they were fighting for did not apply to them as well. Angelina Grimké made the case to her abolitionist husband: "Can you not see that women could do, and would do, a hundred times more for the slave if she were not fettered?"[53]

The convention published a Declaration of Sentiments followed by a list of fifteen grievances and twelve resolutions. The Declaration of Sentiments follows in detail the Declaration of Independence, including the "self-evident truth" that "all men and women are created equal" and the right of a people to throw off a government that oppresses them: "Such has been the patient sufferance of the women under this government, and such is now the necessity which constrains them to demand the equal station to which they are entitled." In the document's recitation of grievances, men substitute for the role that the king played in the Declaration of Independence.

Like other arguments for women's rights, the Declaration of Sentiments was forced to paint an unflattering portrait of women as they are: "He has made her morally an irresponsible being." "He has made her, if married, in the eye of the law, civilly dead." "He has withheld from her rights which are given to the most ignorant and degraded men, both natives and foreigners." The need for rights required showing how infantile women are, which was a delicate argument when speakers were trying to get women behind the movement.

The only resolution in the Declaration of Sentiments that caused a lengthy debate was "that it is the duty of the women of this country to secure to themselves their sacred right to the elective franchise." Even Lucretia Mott, one of the organizers of the convention, thought that demanding the vote was too radical and would hurt their overall cause. Frederick Douglass spoke to the convention and encouraged the women to retain the call for suffrage. The right to vote became a cause, but it took seventy-five years for the cause to succeed.

At the time of Seneca Falls, Europe was in the middle of a great upheaval with political realignments and the publication of the *Communist Manifesto*. Marx and Engels took the side of women whom they portrayed as prisoners of the capitalist system. Whether they could offer a solution was questionable, but they zeroed in on many of the same issues that the Declaration of Sentiments had identified. In his work on the family, Engels argued that "the emancipation of women will only be possible when women can take part in production on a large social scale, and domestic work no longer claims anything but an insignificant amount of her time"[54] The socialist movement had few takers in the United States, but the accusation of socialism became an effective tool in rejecting proposals for economic justice.

If women were to make an economic and social breakthrough to the more valuable jobs in society, they first had to get admittance to the colleges and professional schools that were the gatekeepers of these jobs. Female academies provided a beginning, but they were not designed to prepare women for competition in the job market. When Vassar College opened in 1865, it advertised that it was neither a female academy nor a college in which "women were allowed in the side door."[55] Vassar and its sister successors intended to establish the woman's college as the intellectual equal of men's colleges. When women did get in the side door of men's colleges, they more than held their own. Some colleges had to impose a quota on the number of women accepted lest it appear that they could outrun the men as indeed they often did.[56]

The more difficult barrier to surmount was entrance to the professional schools. Women as lawyers, physicians, ministers, engineers, scientists, or university professors were almost unknown. In 1847 when Harriet Hunt applied to Harvard Medical School, the students threatened to riot. Three black men had come the year before, and now this? The board of admission reversed its decision to admit her. Nevertheless, when women did get admittance to medical schools, they came in large numbers; by the first decade of the twentieth century, they had begun to change the image of the physician. A medical school, such as Tufts, was 40 percent female in 1910.[57] But then those gains were almost completely lost by economic downturns, and it was not until the 1960s that the permanent change occurred. Women concentrated on the medical profession as the linchpin for professional advance; other professions, such as law, trailed behind.[58]

Early Twentieth Century

The two different strands of the women's movement were present at the beginning of the twentieth century, and the contrast was even more pronounced at the end of the century. The coining of the term *feminism* early in the century signaled a new aggressiveness in the push for social, political, and economic rights. Feminism became a rallying cry for the women (and some men) who demanded equality of the sexes. The women who were united under the banner of equality thought that their cause was clear, but equality could also be divisive of the women's movement. The 1910s were years in which the two parts of the women's movement joined forces, but by the late 1920s, the unity had been lost.

The Decade of the 1910s. Feminism in the first decades of the twentieth century was able to align itself with the aims of the Progressive Movement. The idea of the educated woman united what had previously seemed in conflict, namely, the duties of motherhood and the value of a college education. The two sides of the women's movement, their differences at least temporarily overcome, could agree that women should be able to vote. One side argued that women should have the right to vote because they are the same as men in every way that is relevant to voting. The other side argued that women should have the right to vote because they would bring a different perspective on issues where reform was needed.[59]

Feminism, as the name of a political ideology, was from the start a movement that emphasized the sameness of men and women. The feminists led the fight for women's suffrage without alienating proponents of separate spheres for men and women. Those women who believed in a sharp difference between the sexes could agree on the need to develop women's self-esteem, to free them from men's whims, and to advance educational opportunities for women.[60] The only blot on the suffrage movement was a racist suggestion by some people that giving the vote to women would strengthen white control.[61]

In general, progressives argued for both racial and sexual equality. In the late nineteenth century, a misapplication of evolutionary theory had led to the claim that both blacks and women were less developed than white men.[62] Progressives vigorously opposed this position. It is somewhat unfortunate that since the 1910s, arguments about race and sex (later, gender) have been joined without appropriate distinctions. That is, discriminations according to race are nearly always racist and indefensible. However, discriminations according to sex/gender, while often sexist, may sometimes be based on relevant sexual differences.

John Dewey was one of the foremost thinkers during the ascendancy of progressivism. Early in his career he had written an essay exploring whether advanced education was harmful to women. That concern was expressed by many male authors in the late nineteenth century.[63] By 1911, Dewey was writing in praise of coeducation as good for both boys and girls.[64] Speaking at Columbia University in 1912, Dewey said, "Women are shut out from the culmination and zeal for full citizenship, the outward and visible sign of the inward and spiritual grace which is liberty."[65] During his long subsequent career, which extended to 1950, Dewey seldom referred to girls and women, not out of neglect, but because he assumed the issue had been settled. What is educationally good is good for both men and women.[66]

The issue had not been settled in 1906 when a female physicist, challenged the rule that women academics were not allowed to marry. Professor Harriet Brooks wrote to the dean of Barnard College: "It is a duty I owe to my profession and to my sex to show that a woman has the right to the practices of her profession and cannot be condemned to abandon it merely because she marries." Dean Lauren Gill was not impressed by this argument. She wrote back: "A married woman was expected to dignify her homemaking into a profession, and not assume that she could carry on two full professions at once."[67]

Until World War II, married women were not hired as schoolteachers and were dismissed from the job if they married. They could also be dismissed for attending a minstrel show, for being a waitress who serves beer, or for dating a married man. The young woman might also have to pledge "to abstain from drinking, dancing and falling in love."[68]

The most creative thinker of the time, Charlotte Perkins Gilman, actually had some sympathy for the argument that housework and professional work are incompatible. Her solution to the conflict between these two "professions" was to socialize housecleaning, cooking, laundering, and childcare through the work of paid employees. Not many people were willing to follow her all the way. Public laundries did "socialize" the cleaning of clothes although the home washing machine largely reversed that trend.[69] The fast food restaurant eventually took much of the cooking out of the home, but McDonald's and Burger King are hardly what Perkins Gilman had envisioned. In the care of the home, upper-class women found their freedom by hiring housecleaners who were usually women. That, too, was hardly a victory for all of womankind.

The most problematic part of Perkins Gilman's plan was considering childcare to be one part of housework. It is quite common to refer to house work and child care in the same sentence. The upper class could deal with the care of children by hiring an *au pair* or nanny to allow the woman to work outside the home. As with Plato's solution in the *Republic*, trusting underpaid and untrained people (usually women) with caring for the next generation is not an ideal solution.

Perkins Gilman was consistent in her emphasis on women's need to develop the full range of human characteristics. She called herself a human feminist in contrast to other women that she called female feminists. The choice of names was unfair. The women she referred to as female feminists were not trying to remove women from the meaning of human; they were emphasizing the difference between men and women in the constitution of the human.

The message of sameness was carried the furthest by a literary group that started a new journal in 1919, announcing that "we're interested in people now—not in men and women." They declared that moral, social, economic, and political standards "should not have anything to do with sex." They declared themselves "post-feminist" in being "pro-woman without being anti-man."[70] The logic of that position is not clear. Can one be pro-woman if standards have nothing to do with sex? This is the conundrum that has run throughout the history of a woman's or a women's movement. One has to first distinguish the sexes in order to unite them in a better way. To argue for a better life for women, one has to emphasize what is wrong with women at present.

The movement of the 1910s finally succeeded in 1920 with the passing of the Nineteenth Amendment, which granted suffrage to women. It was the one thing that most women could agree upon. And by the time of ratification, most men had given up resistance to the simple principle of logic. Women should have representation as citizens and what seemed likely was that they would not vote as a bloc but would divide along political and class lines as men did. "The only cogent reason to be advanced for the technical 'enfranchisement' of women was that in all or most other respects they had already been enfranchised."[71]

1920s and Beyond. The year 1920 seemed to represent the triumph of feminism and its emphasis on women having the same rights as men. However, there were immediate signs in the 1920s that progress might not be as smooth as many women anticipated. A sign of what was to come is found in an article in the June 1920, *Ladies Home Journal*; that was the same month that the nineteenth amendment on suffrage was passed. The article proposed a "Credo for the New Woman."

In the following summary of that credo, the reference throughout is to *woman* not *women.* The credo expresses belief in four propositions: woman's rights, woman's suffrage, woman's brains, and woman's assertion of self. Next to each of these four beliefs is a *but*: belief in rights but also sacrifices; belief in suffrage but other things vastly more important; belief in brains but more her emotions; belief in assertion of self but her new freedom is to serve others.[72] The article was professing equality in the balancing of beliefs, but for feminists, it was a call to return to the nineteenth century.

Gaining the vote did not guarantee economic rights for women. Without economic independence, many women felt that they were still captives within the system. A National Woman's Party was organized to sweep away remaining discriminations against women. In 1923 a convention at Seneca Falls, commemorating the 1848 meeting, proposed an amendment to the U.S. Constitution. It simply read, "Men and women shall have equal rights throughout the United States and every place subject to its jurisdiction." For its advocates, the amendment may have seemed like an obvious principle of justice, but it signified a renewed split within a women's movement along class lines. The proposal was tabled in Congress where it sat for forty years.

In the 1920s and 1930s, there was debate about labor legislation that was for the protection of women.[73] The National Woman's Party protested that sex-based labor laws segregated women as a class. But most of the women in the lower economic class viewed those laws as helpful in protecting their health and jobs. They were often joined by men in the labor movement who for their own interests approved of laws that prevented advancement of women to higher-paying jobs. It was a tragic split among women; opponents of protective legislation believed that such laws penalized strong women; supporters of the law thought that their repeal would sacrifice the weak.[74] There was some truth to both claims. Repeal of laws that supposedly protected women would open the market to women's future advancement but at the cost of some jobs that women currently had.

The International Labor Organization founded in 1919 was for several decades a supporter of protective legislation for women. The policy had drawbacks. "Prohibiting women's work shifted the attention of social reformers to removing women from the workplace rather than attempting to improve the working conditions of all workers."[75] If, for example, exposure to polluted air is dangerous for women who are pregnant or may become pregnant, should not men be protected from the same poison? Seeing women only as child-bearers reinforced the traditional role assigned to women, and that attitude made men disappear from issues of reproduction and child care.

In 1950 the ILO shifted toward the language of equality, but that too had its drawbacks. The legislation which was aimed at enabling women to be both workers and caregivers to children and to the elderly "served to reinforce the assumption that a 'double day' was somehow appropriate for women."[76] For upper-class women who could hire help while they were at work, equality in the workplace was liberating. Other women were thrown into competition for lower-paying jobs while continuing to carry out their traditional duties on the home front.

Gradually, the International Labor Organization came to see the need for more specific laws in support of childcare. "By recognizing that both women and men may be involved with, among other things, childcare, these instruments assume neither that women are solely responsible for their tasks, nor that men have no place in them."[77] The double negative in this last sentence—women are not solely responsible, men are not without a place—is appropriately modest in its claim. United States law and practice do not reflect a strong determination to go even that far. The 1993 Family Medical Leave Act covers only about half of all workers for unpaid parental leave.

One of the ways that women tried to bridge home and workplace in the 1920s was by developing work that involved the health and development of children. Women had long been in school teaching, but married women were banned. Married women looking for careers became prominent in public health jobs after the passage of the Sheppard-Towner Act in 1921, the first federally funded health care program. The physicians at first offered no opposition to women in health care work; the women were concerned with the prevention, not the cure, of disease. By the end of the decade, however, physicians sensed a growing competition, and they changed the role of the doctor from dispenser of medicine to the expert on the body and the regulator of health. Children were thought to be in need of the scientific knowledge of the pediatrician more than the traditional wisdom of women.[78]

New ideas of sex and marriage affected life in the 1920s. The "sexual revolution" in the 1960s had its roots in the 1920s when sexual activity before marriage became common. The likelihood that a girl was a virgin at the time of marriage can best be determined by whether she was born before or after 1900.[79] A proposal in the 1920s to change marriage had interesting possibilities but was never given a chance. Ben Lindsey, a judge in the Denver juvenile court, said that there should be two kinds of marriage, one oriented toward the raising of children, the other when the aim is the companionship of the two parties.[80] This proposal for "companionate marriage" cost Lindsey his job in the clamor that followed. The need for some kind of distinction was evident then and has become more evident as increasing numbers of couples do not intend to have children. There is little reason for the state to be intervening in how they relate and separate. At the same time, government support of families—parents and children—is still scandalously inadequate.[81]

Without a reforming of stereotypes concerning marriage, there was a strong resurgence of the belief that marriage is the true destination of women. As the birth rate declined and the science of raising children took away from mother's work, the woman's role shifted toward being the perfect wife and homemaker. An entire industry grew up that was dedicated to feminine beauty. The number of beauty parlors went from 750 in 1922 to 3,500 in 1927.[82] In New York State, beautician was listed as one of the thirty recognized professions; schoolteacher was not.

The advertising industry greatly expanded around the supposed need of a woman for products to keep her husband contented. Over the protest of feminists, a new emphasis on femininity was put in place by advertisers of women's beauty products. Wifehood now included being artist, poet, philosopher, and teacher to keep her husband satisfied. This ideal dominated the scene until World War II. After its interruption in the 1940s, it was taken up anew in the 1950s and became the image of woman that was challenged in the 1960s.

Another sign of feminism's limited success in the 1920s was the spread of "home economics" in school curricula. In an earlier century, the name would have been a redundancy because *economics* referred to the home. Modern economics, however, gave little attention to the home as men studied the market. Courses in home economics, therefore, had nothing to do with the academic field of economics; they were concerned with the woman's private sphere. Home economics found its place in the school curriculum, as a federal publicist said, "because it furnishes vocational education in that occupation in which 93 percent of all American women ultimately engage."[83]

Industries dedicated to selling women "labor-saving devices," and beauty products had the support of the newly emergent sciences of psychology and sociology. Male assumptions were at the base of these sciences, and their empirical data tended to confirm the assumptions.[84] Sigmund Freud was the most famous of these theorists. His influence was limited in the United States in the 1920s, but eventually, feminist writers thought it necessary to take on the Freudian ideas that were in the atmosphere.

Freud, as Rousseau's successor, supplies women with a catalogue of outrageous comments. Unlike Rousseau, Freud does not have a dialectic that attempts a reversal in the power of men and women. From the beginning to the end of his long career, Freud was consistent in describing women as different from men, not only biologically but culturally and ethically as well. For women, "the level of what is ethically normal is different from what it is in man." Freud often simply refers to difference, but there is little doubt that the difference means inferiority in development and ethics. "They show less sense of justice than men."[85]

Freud's psychology was subject to widespread criticism. However, his separation of the sexes was widely endorsed. Emile Durkheim, one of the founders of sociology, thought that emphasizing the difference between men and women was a mark of civilization. Woman had retired from warfare and public affairs so as to consecrate her entire life to her family. "Precisely because man and woman are different, they seek each other passionately." Their differences "require each other for mutual fruition." As usually assumed in this mutual fruition, women specialized in "affective functions," and men handled the "intellectual functions."[86]

This division of virtues that Wollstonecraft had assaulted in the 1790s thus continued to occupy a respectable place in the psychological and social sciences up through the 1950s. It was embodied in Lewis Terman's IQ tests in the 1920s that tried to conceptualize measures of masculinity and femininity. It was central to the psychology of Carl Jung and his devoted followers in the United States. Talcott Parsons, the dominant voice of sociology in the middle of the century, thought that the best form for the family in industrial society is one in which the husband has the instrumental role, which includes earning the money; the wife has an expressive role that includes giving emotional support to her husband.[87] By the 1950s the men seemed to have the order of society figured out, and then suddenly the structure came crashing down.

1960s and After

The argument of this chapter is that there have been two movements by and for women that converged in the second half of the twentieth century. There is still no complete synthesis and the issue of abortion remains a chief symbol of the failure to find unity. Nevertheless, the last half century has been something other than another instance of a recurring pattern from emphasizing women's rights to a reaction of keeping the sexes (now genders) separate. Most women and most men who are sensitive to the long history of this struggle to achieve lasting improvement have been trying to find a language that recognizes the values on both sides of the historic divide. Several big changes in recent decades have made the search for success both more urgent and more likely to happen.

1960s Feminism. The reawakening of feminism in the 1960s is usually dated from Betty Friedan's 1963 book, *The Feminine Mystique.*[88] She was not alone in her criticism of the current situation of women. That fact is evident in the overwhelming response to her book, especially by women who were thankful that someone had named their problem. Simone de Beauvoir's *Second Sex* had raised the banner in 1949 but did not get much play in the United States at that time. After the war, there had been a concentrated effort to return to the "normalcy" of men at work and women at home.

To this day, some people take the 1950s to be the normal arrangement while it was in fact an unsuccessful attempt to reverse the dramatic changes brought on by the war. When sixteen million men marched off to war, it was left to the women to run the factories and most everything else. In 1942, most women said they did not wish to stay permanently in their jobs. By 1945, three-quarters of the women said they would like to continue working outside the home.[89] But when the men came back from the war, they assumed that the women would return to their "traditional role" of homemaker. The television programs of the 1950s are sometimes cited as showing the stability of family life in that era. What seems more likely is that those shows were dreams of an ideal that no longer existed if it ever did.

In the 1950s, the signs of a coming eruption were present although not many people sensed what was about to happen. Friedan had been doing studies during that decade; she and other authors sensed a discontent among middle-class women in their lovely homes in suburbia. The women were under "house arrest." There were also rumbles that the "organization man" or "the man in the gray flannel suit" was not completely satisfied with his two worlds of work and family.[90] Barbara Ehrenreich had a provocative interpretation of the Playboy phenomenon in the 1950s. She claimed it was not mainly about sex but about economics. The ads in the magazine were about the good things of the capitalist system, but the magazine was a protest by men against the burden of being sole breadwinner in the family.[91]

Betty Friedan's book brought together a flood of complaints that women had. She did not address the issue of male privilege in the home nor did she encourage men to split the housework and child care with their wives. Friedan was criticized for speaking to middle-class women whose problems were very different from women who did not have the leisure or the means to voice their complaints. Friedan was not unaware of this fact. She addressed the women that she thought could take the lead in improving the lot of all women.

One big test in the late 1960s was the welcoming of lesbians into a movement that had previously played down this issue. Some women feared that an embrace of lesbian women would generate more opposition from both women and men who believed that they were protecting the family. Inevitably there was severe criticism of public recognition of homosexuality. Protest has continued ever since, but the positive change in the public attitude toward gay and lesbian people has been astounding and has accelerated in the last two decades.

As had happened in the debate over protective labor laws, there was a divide in what a new generation of women wanted. The leaders of the movement were feminists, people who were ready to march for the political and economic rights of women. Poor women saw the problem differently; they were mainly concerned with survival and feeding their families. Many black women felt that their race was a more pressing issue of equality than was sex.[92]

Race and sex came together in a strange way during passage of the Civil Rights Act of 1964. Howard Smith, a Virginia segregationist, intending to weaken the bill and prevent its passage, added the words "discrimination on the basis of sex." His amendment passed 168-133, but it failed to stop the bill. Most of those who voted for the amendment voted against the bill itself.[93] Thus, by an ironic route with the aid of a racist-sexist coalition, Title VII of the Civil Rights bill outlawed discrimination against a woman's civil rights. The Equal Employment Opportunity Commission refused to enforce that clause because the director of the commission said it was a "fluke" that "was conceived out of wedlock."[94] The continuing failure to get equal opportunity helped to inspire the founding of the National Organization for Women in 1966; its first legal action sought application of Title VII.

Women in the United States were part of an international women's movement. By the 1970s, it was clearly a worldwide movement. In 1975, the first world conference on the status of women was held in Mexico City under sponsorship of the United Nations. There were delegates from 133 nations; 113 of the delegations were led by women. In addition there were 4,000 women representing NGOs. There was a great deal of agreement on the rhetoric of equality and the elimination of gender discrimination, but there were also some strong differences between east and west, north and south.

The United States women had to listen to criticism directed at their focus on middle-class problems.[95] Poor women, who would have loved to spend more time at home with their children, were not very sympathetic to women whose main concern was getting into the job market. By this time, the term *development* had been given a primacy in the two UN covenants of 1966; women in poorer countries took that as a way to formulate their central concern.[96]

Resolutions and declarations do not change economic and cultural realities. The United Nations tries to bring pressure for change. The process can be long and tedious. The UN can only encourage nation-states to consent, sometimes reluctantly, to laws and practices for which there is wide international support. A Commission on the Status of Women had existed from the beginning of the United Nations. Over the years, it produced a series of documents on the rights of women. In the 1960s and 1970s, it worked to make effective in practice those declarations that had been made on behalf of women. The result was the Convention on the Elimination of All Forms of Discrimination against Women, which was approved by the General Assembly in 1979 and went into effect a year later.

In the discussions that led up to this convention, there was widespread agreement. In only one area was there sustained debate. Not surprisingly, it was a clause that affirms equality of men and women in marriage. Particularly for Jews and Muslims, their religious law discriminates between men and women. They would claim that their laws pertaining to marriage and divorce do not discriminate *against* women but simply recognize that there are important differences between the roles of men and women in the family. The history of the subordination of women makes any such argument suspect, but the principle that difference is not always oppression is valid. Ten countries abstained from the vote in the General Assembly; none voted against the Convention.

One other UN document is both a sign of a continuing problem but also a sign of women taking a more vocal role on their own behalf. The World Conference in Vienna in 1993 produced a Declaration on the Elimination of Violence against Women. The declaration was recommended to the General Assembly where it was approved the following session. The widespread problem of violence finds special expression in the torture and rape of women, something that was traditionally taken to be a private matter. The UN by itself cannot stop this violence, but the success of women in bringing to public light such practices is indispensable for reducing if not eliminating violence against women. Article 4J in the declaration calls for the education of *men* and women to eliminate cultural practices that are a form of violence. The declaration appealed to the 1975 UN Convention for Protection of All Persons against Torture. Rather than emphasizing women's rights, the declaration's indisputable point is that women should be included in "all persons."

Within the United States, many feminists thought it was a logical step to finally have an Equal Rights Amendment, which would be taken off the table in Congress where it had long rested. In 1971, the amendment was approved by a large majority in the House and a few months later by a vote of 84 to 8 in the Senate. When it was then submitted to the States, with a seven-year deadline for ratification, it seemed at first that it would be a quick process. However, after the first two years when many states ratified the ERA there was a decided shift against it. After seven years, the amendment lacked three states for the needed three-fourths approval. After that, a disputed extension of the deadline did not succeed in adding the three needed states. Efforts have continued to revive interest in the amendment, but there is not widespread support for renewing the legislative battle.

The ERA had opposition from opposite directions and not enough enthusiastic support from the middle. For some people, it said too much; for other people it said too little. The political right wing professed that the whole idea was unnecessary and would degrade women. Jerry Falwell wrote that "the Equal Rights Amendment is a delusion. I believe that women deserve more than equal rights. And in families and in nations where the Bible is believed, Christian women are honored above men."[97] The political left was unenthusiastic about a restatement of equal political rights when the bigger problems were in transforming the culture. The appearance of women asking to be equal to men was seen by many women as an outdated strategy. Women were no longer asking for equality; they were ready to lead the way and men would have to adjust.

The Return of Difference. The lack of enthusiasm by many women for a statement of equal rights reflected skepticism about women becoming more similar to men. The far left and the far right could sometimes sound alike although they were looking at difference from opposite ends of the spectrum. Was there a kernel of truth in Falwell's "women deserve more than equal rights?" The paradox of asserting woman's difference in order to secure those things that should be the same for women and men reemerged. Friedan herself had second thoughts, and very soon she was calling for a "second stage" of the movement. Given that the whole history of feminism was a movement for equal rights, a shift toward emphasizing differences was difficult to fit under the banner of feminism.

Some of the emphasis on difference in the 1970s and 1980s was by opponents of women's rights. Their argument, which had not changed much since the eighteenth century, was that woman's constitution fits her for the roles of wife and mother but not for getting involved with politics and business. Those arguments in the late twentieth century were a rear-guard delaying action. Women who write books and give speeches denouncing feminism are not striking examples of stay-at-home moms. They have benefitted from what feminism gained for all women. Some of the changes in women's lives are irreversible, even for women defending traditional values.

There were prominent voices in the women's movement that were calling for an acknowledgment of the special gifts of women that should not be flattened out in sameness. Alice Rossi attracted some notice and reaction when she said in a speech that perhaps women are better suited than men for the care of infants. She later wrote that "we can envisage a society that is color-blind. But genetic assimilation of male and female is impossible and no society will be sex-blind."[98] Someone might disagree with her, but Rossi was not being disloyal to the women's movement.

Similarly, many women authors in recent decades have reminded their readers that differences between men and women do not always imply a male claim of superiority. On the contrary, these authors were arguing that most women have strengths that most men lack. The long history of women's care for children, the sick, and the aged cannot and should not be dismissed simply as oppression. Sarah Ruddick, writing on the valuable knowledge gained by mothers, or Barbara Myerhoff, writing on the strengths of women in a nursing home, were celebrating women's gifts.[99] French feminism from the early 1970s reasserted women's differences as the basis for improving society.[100]

In 1991, a book by Susan Faludi entitled *Backlash: The Undeclared War against American Women* attracted much attention.[101] For many people, the title was sufficient without reading the five hundred pages of data. The questionable part of *Backlash* is Faludi's harsh words for some women authors whom she seemed to include in the undeclared war on women. She is especially hard on Betty Friedan's *Second Stage* published in 1981.[102] She quotes Friedan that "our failure was our blind spot about the family." She dismisses Friedan's second stage as "heavy on old Victorian flourishes," which hardly seems fair to the woman who ignited the fire of modern feminism.

In the 1990 Introduction to her book, *It Changed My Life,* Friedan wrote, "I think we have gone beyond the sexual politics and confrontations with men that marked the first stage of the women's movement."[103] One could argue that Friedan's pronouncement was premature and that she had not become wiser with age. Surely, however, she had not joined a war against American women. Faludi was also not kind to other authors, such as Jean Baker Miller and Sara Ruddick, for their emphasis on the differences between men and women.[104]

One U.S. author whom Faludi did not directly criticize, Carol Gilligan, had become the most prominent voice of difference in the 1980s.[105] Faludi granted that Gilligan was not antifeminist but nonetheless is "in danger of being dragooned into the backlash's service." It is true that when *Ms Magazine* did an interview with Gilligan, it was headlined "Are Women More Moral than Men?" a question that would have received an affirmative answer in 1850.[106] Faludi writes that "difference became the new magic word uttered to defuse the feminist campaign for equality."[107] As I have pointed out throughout this chapter, the opposite of difference is sameness not equality. The term *equality* is helpful only when one specifies equal in respect to what?

Gilligan did not set out to show that women are not equal to men; she explored how women come to moral decisions and their path of moral development. She was particularly critical of Lawrence Kohlberg's theory of moral development, which placed women lower than men on his scale of one to six. Instead of arguing that women should be higher up the scale, Gilligan called into question the scale. Kohlberg's stages of moral development reflected the dominant strain of philosophical thinking about sex since the seventeenth century. Men were supposed to develop by gradually shedding all forms of dependency until they could stand alone with their solitary conscience and judgments of what is just.

Gilligan's study raised the issue of a morality that integrates justice and compassion. She implied that the moral ideal is not independence but interdependence. "Responsibility to care then includes both self and other, and the obligation not to hurt, freed from conventional restraints, is reconstituted as a universal guide to moral choice."[108]

It was fitting that Gilligan's early study was of women struggling with whether or not to have an abortion. The two parts of the women's movement collided in the 1970s after the U.S. Supreme Court decision of *Roe v. Wade* that decriminalized abortion. It is tragic that abortion became so divisive despite the fact that most of the country agrees on most of the issue. What could have united the majority is an effort to drastically reduce the need for abortion and to see that when abortion occurs that it be as safe as possible and as early as possible in the pregnancy. If 30 percent of pregnancies in the United States (40 percent in New York City) end in abortion, then clearly the country has a problem with its means of controlling birth. The labels of pro-life and pro-choice used for lobbying are not helpful to thinking about the issue or to reaching agreement on policy. As is usual in arguments about morality, how a person formulates the question is already decisive for the answer.

The question of abortion is about life; it is also about sex and control. Modern feminism might be said to have begun with the invention of the birth control pill in the late 1950s. For the first time, women could have the power to control pregnancy. The relation between a woman's role as mother and a woman's exercise of her professional talents was suddenly transformed. Kristin Luker's brilliant study of the abortion debate showed that both sides shared many values.[109] But for one side, the availability of abortion was the symbol of their freedom to compete in the work world. For the other side, the acceptance of abortion was an attack on their identity as wives and mothers. It was tragic that the two sides could not work to broaden their base of agreement even while they continued to disagree.[110]

Conclusion

The dispute over abortion highlights the competing assumptions about woman-man relations during the past two centuries. Abortion has sharpened political opposition among women, but it has also had what might be a more lasting effect: a debate by women about the identity of women. Particularly for many of the women who were marshaled to oppose the Supreme Court's decision, it was their first experience of political organizing and getting their voices heard on public issues. The feminists who had wanted to break down the wall of separation between private and public had succeeded, perhaps with mixed feelings about the results.

It is unlikely ever in the future that the difference between men and women will be expressed as public man and private woman. The women who have opposed abortion are defending the value of family life which is a legitimate concern. The United States has not yet figured out how to integrate home and job, success at work, and the care of children. It is not a woman's problem; it is a problem that can only be solved by the cooperative effort of men and women.

The long struggle for the extension of rights to women inevitably threw light on what a *human* right means. The human rights of women, just as those of men, include a right to life, a right to protection of their physical integrity, a right to develop as a human being. The identification of the "rights of man" with individual agency excluded women, but the assumption that individuals are in charge of their destiny was also not healthy for men. Human rights are about persons in relation; as a result, human rights include a passive as well as an active element. Women and men both have some learning to do.

There are differences in what rights mean for a man and a woman. The human race may never get agreement on whether some differences are based on the nature of manhood and womanhood or whether they are based on contingent events of the past. In the future, every difference may be open to change. One has to hope that the human race will have some wisdom in deciding which differences should be eliminated and which differences are worth retaining for the richness and variety of human life. There is now a realistic hope that the conversation about the future of the human race can take place between a diversity of women and a diversity of men. The consideration of issues of difference and sameness in the sexual area should take place in the context of children and a better future for people worldwide.

CHAPTER 5

Age as a Test for Human Rights

This chapter continues the theme of the previous chapter on sameness and difference. Instead of the relation between the sexes/genders of the human race, this chapter is concerned with humans as temporal beings. To live in time is to become different in some respects while remaining the same person. This change over time brings about a shift in the human individual's dependence upon fellow human beings. As long as a human life exists, neither human dependence nor human independence is total.

An implied concern of this chapter is health and sickness. A serious illness increases human dependence on the skills and kindness of others. When humans feel healthy, they tend to be oblivious of illness as a condition that affects everyone in his or her lifetime. In the later part of life, age and health concerns come closer together and sometimes fuse. Most of this chapter is about the development of healthy human beings but with full awareness that the possibility of serious illness or disability is never more than a few heartbeats away.

At the end of the chapter, I consider the reality of death, which is the destination for every human being. From all appearances, the dialectic of dependence and independence ends in the defeat of independence. The last moment is one of "giving up the ghost," and ceasing to be able to act with the independence of a human being. Human beings, if they are fortunate, can live sixty, seventy, eighty, or more years. However, from the first moment of life, they are the mortal ones. The awareness of that fact comes very early in life. It is impossible to say exactly at what age that fact becomes known, but it is probably earlier than we tend to think and before a child can articulate a concern with death.

Rousseau theorized that all of the evils in human life derive from our fear of death.[1] We build fences around our lives to ward off any perceived threat to our existence. Unfortunately, we misconceive the conflict because mortality lurks within the organism itself. It does make sense to protect ourselves against external threats that can kill us and to invoke protection from those who can help us. But it is easy to become obsessed with avoiding whatever can do us harm, not recognizing that a richly textured human life is one that requires a trust in forces beyond us, dependencies that actually support our independence.

In his book on sickness, hope, and human limits, William Lynch writes, "It is the secret fear of most people that they cannot have both dependence and independence, just it is their secret hope that they can. Fortunately they not only can but must. But such a homely truth is not much preached in our land. We are forbidden to have precisely what nature demands most. We are often forced by our culture to deny dependence, passivity, the wish and ability to receive."[2] The individual cannot give a proper place to this dependence without a social context that routinely accepts that there is no shame to needing help. We need a form of political society, Alasdair McIntyre has written, in which it is taken for granted that disability requiring dependence is something that all of us have experienced or will experience.[3]

The relation between dependence and independence is relevant to the question of human rights because of a tendency to turn our attention away from dependence. We tend to think that independence is the normal human state. Human rights become identified with independent individuals. A necessary reminder is Henry Shue's description of human life: "For everyone, healthy adulthood is bordered on each side by helplessness, and it is vulnerable to interruption, temporary or permanent, at any time."[4] A five-year-old and a ninety-five-year-old are not helpless, but they are more dependent on others than the "healthy adult." We do not usually deny that severely dependent people are part of the human race, but we tend to act as if they were beings who are less than fully human. Whether *human rights* refers to an effective set of practices can best be answered by looking at the activities and treatment of the most dependent of human beings.

The many movements for rights since the 1960s have included a "children's rights" movement. The literature of "children's liberation" contains many praiseworthy suggestions about the lives of young people; it also contains some proposals that strike most people as bizarre. I will briefly engage this literature on children's rights although my main concern is those rights that are unambiguously human rights, rights that apply to all people including children.

In one sense the thesis of this chapter is simple: Human rights apply to human beings whatever their age and health. Subsets of the human, such as children, the aged, or the dying deserve the protection of human rights. A more complex thesis of this chapter is that humans who are highly dependent, such as young children or the seriously disabled, may help to clarify what a human right is. That is, those people in the human race who think of themselves as independent, autonomous, and self-sufficient, may have something to learn from those whose dependency is obvious. The people who take care of the very young or the very old may discover important truths from those they are caring for concerning the full range of humanity.

While this chapter is about the relation between dependence and independence, it is dependence that has to receive more emphasis because of the tendency to equate human rights with agency, the ability to act for oneself and make claims for one's rights. A right is a claim made upon a community, but the claim need not be directly made by the person who is deserving of the right. A person who cannot speak, or cannot speak in a way that will be heard, needs a proxy who can voice the claim.

Child or Adult?

In modern times, there has been a sharp distinction between persons of a certain age thought to be dependent and other people who are supposed to be independent. The names for these two ages/stages of life are *child* and *adult*. We think it is obvious that these two names describe a contrast built into human nature. *Child* refers to an incomplete human being, one that needs to be taken care of by the complete or mature version of the human being. An adult is someone who has arrived and is capable of taking care of "himself."[5] Until recently the model for a complete human being was taken to be male, and the implications of that assumption still linger on. Women have finally had some success in protesting their exclusion from independent adulthood. However, most of the people called children have had little opportunity to voice their complaints about being treated as merely potential adults.

The problem that resides in the split between dependent children and independent adults cannot be solved by granting some rights at a slightly younger age. A thorough rethinking of the language of child and adult is needed. A confused and confusing language prevents the human race from coming up with better political, social, and economic arrangements. The word *child* is a very ambiguous term, a fact that is occasionally noted even by people who continue to use *child* as if it had a clear reference.

Since child and adult have been paired as opposites, *adult* is also an ambiguous term. For describing the process that goes from birth to death, we need to develop a language that reflects the continuously shifting mixture of dependence and independence in the course of a human life. I have no ideal language to propose. What I can do in this chapter is resist the language that is ready at hand. Many things said of children are simply misleading. Some language is demeaning; for example, the word *kid* usually guarantees that a young person will not be taken seriously. I will make some tentative generalizations about age while aware that there are variations across cultures, as well as exceptional individuals within any categories based on age.

The earliest stage of human life is infancy. Although it lasts only a few years, it is profoundly formative of everything that follows. The Latin *infans* means someone who cannot yet speak. The English word stays close to that meaning although we do not suddenly stop using *infant* on the day that the infant says its first word. The French use *l'enfant* much beyond this initial stage. The English word *child* includes infant; that is, childhood continues after infancy ends.

Infancy is marked by extreme but not total dependence on parents and others concerned with care of the infant. From the moment of its birth, a child is an actor, a distinct person asserting the beginning of personality.[6] Infancy is largely blocked out of human memory in part because it was so frightening. Even the well-cared-for infant has fears that are realistic. The trip from the birth canal to the end of infancy has always been perilous. In a modern country, such as the United States, the survival of nearly all infants could be guaranteed, but there is a shocking failure to use available means to care for every mother and every newborn infant. Rhetorically, there is an abundance of sentimental speech about infants, but the practical support that is needed for mothers and infants is seriously inadequate.

"Early childhood" refers to the period up to five or six years of age. It culminates in the age of reason. According to the medieval church, that was the age when one could commit sin. It is the age when the young child begins to use the rationality present since birth. Before the age of five or six, the child can act on its own and figure out how to get things done, but trial and error along with imitation are the chief tools. To create ideas that go beyond the immediate situation requires some years of both physical and mental development.

At about age five or six, the child begins to figure out the most basic rules of logic. Human development comes at a price. In this case, the opening of the mind to abstract ideas and a consciousness of oneself have the effect of closing off the young child's amazing capacity to absorb reality, most strikingly its capacity for language.

In early childhood, the infant passes from a state of nonspeaking to being a linguistic whiz who is able to sponge up the most complex language without learning any rules. Then the curtain falls, which is a sign of passing from early childhood to later childhood. The self-conscious human being tries to learn language by studying rules of grammar, a process that cannot duplicate the listening and responding of early childhood. Paradoxically, it is the realization of the complex nature of language that undermines the child's ability to absorb a language. The gains of later childhood, on the other hand, are immense. A curtain is raised on a new world of ideas, plans, and interests. The older child can now use its reason to navigate connections, develop its own independent judgment, and realize projects of its own choosing.

The age of reason does not automatically issue in reasonable individuals. Reason has to be put to use over a period of time. Aristotle pointed out that "we see that the experienced are more effective than those who have reason but lack experience."[7] That principle has not changed. Some children rapidly acquire a wide range of experience; they nevertheless remain temporal beings who need to integrate physical and mental growth. A too rapid exposure to all things human could overwhelm the developing child.

Jean Piaget referred to the "American issue" of trying to hurry up the process of development.[8] Older children should have some say in the pace of their own development. Superficially, they may seem anxious to join the company and privileges of grown-ups, but an open dialogue with them might reveal some anxiety at being pushed too fast. There is nothing wrong with acting like a child if you are seven or eight years old.

Most traditions mark the emergence of a new stage of development when a person reaches eleven to thirteen years of age. Later childhood is finished, and a new stage with no fully accurate name begins. We do have the term *adolescence* in the modern world, which is closely associated with the teenage years. A beginning of a new stage of life at age thirteen seems about right, but there is nothing especially significant about age nineteen as an endpoint for adolescence. There is a sense in which everyone is adolescent (becoming adult) from the beginning of life to long after one has ceased to be a teenager.

However this period of life is named, the word *child* should be used sparingly, if at all. The reason why people would hesitate to stop calling a fifteen-year-old a child is because of the assumption that life divides into childhood and adulthood. The fifteen-year-old does not have all the characteristics that are associated with adulthood, so therefore, he or she is called a child. We think of the fifteen-year-old as still "a dependent" and therefore not an adult. If, however, every stage of life is a mixture of dependence and independence then there are not just two stages of life, and there is no magic moment when one passes from childhood to adulthood. The use of the term *child* up to age sixteen, eighteen, or twenty-one is what makes the literature of children's rights contain some proposals for rights that are sensible and badly needed along with proposals that seem preposterous and unrealistic.

The end of childhood and the beginning of early adolescence is marked by physical changes. Both sexes experience changes in the body accompanied by emotional changes that are a source of excitement and confusion. The human race has created a huge gap between the ages when boys and girls are physically capable of producing children and the age when there is a suitable social, economic, and psychological context for taking care of children. At an earlier stage of human history, some girls became mothers by the age of twelve. Neither society nor the individual can sustain such a practice today. There is no solution for the tension that this gap causes. However, the society of grown-ups could do more to ameliorate this tension rather than exacerbate it. Institutions of society bombard older children and early adolescents with sexual stimulants and then older people claim to be shocked when the young act out their impulses.

At about the time of this physical change, the person reaches a new stage of intellectual development. The beginning of teenage adolescence is marked by a capacity for new levels of abstraction that make the manipulation of ideas more exciting and more efficient. At this age, the logic of science becomes much clearer; and the study of history is likely to be more attractive. Profound philosophical ideas that were present in early childhood but obscured in later childhood may once again become a lively interest. Piaget gave the name "formal operational" to this capacity for abstracting ideas at age eleven to thirteen in contrast to "concrete operational" abilities that start at age five or six. Piaget's study of the capacity of children and adolescents to understand logic and mathematics is an invaluable contribution for designing a school curriculum. His work, however, reveals the difference between a power to reason and the full range of human experience.

Piaget's application of his findings to the area of morality is relevant to the question of human rights and young people. His 1932 book, *The Moral Judgment of the Child*, has had a profound effect on theorizing about morality. Piaget did not claim to study human development or moral development despite his name being constantly invoked for support in these areas. Piaget concentrated on "judgment" and "the child." Thus, he traced the difference between the ages of six and twelve in a child's judgments within the area of morality. There is nothing wrong with this concentration so long as one does not equate it with moral development throughout life.

Piaget begins with an assumption that "all morality consists in a system of rules, and the essence of all morality is to be sought in the respect which the individual acquires for these rules."[9] That is a terribly cramped notion of morality, which can blind one to the development of moral attitudes and moral virtues. Some of the most important moral influences in a person's life come during infancy and early childhood. Piaget's assumption of what constitutes morality leads him to say that before the age of five a child is "pre-moral."[10] That language could be disastrous for discussing human rights and early childhood. An infant is not a responsible moral agent, but its moral life is at issue from the first moment of life. How the infant is acted upon together with how it responds is a central moral issue. Erik Erikson is more helpful here in saying that "all moral, ideological and ethical propensities depend on this early experience of mutuality."[11]

Piaget distinguished two main stages of moral judgment (within later childhood), which he called heteronymous and autonomous. In the early stage, rules are sacred commands that have to be obeyed; justice consists in following the rules. In the later stage, rules are understood to be socially adaptable; justice means giving everyone his or her fair share. Piaget thought that children would come to a form of democracy if they were not interfered with. By about the age of twelve, justice is understood to depend on a simple equality.

Piaget was struck by the response of one boy whom he interviewed. On being asked why he does not hit back when he has been struck, the boy says, "Because there is no end to revenge." Piaget comments that "the child sets forgiveness above revenge, not out of weakness." The boy's response leads Piaget to speculate that there might be a further stage of morality that would start with a language other than equality and justice.[12] Piaget's suggestion of care and compassion as a language of morality was picked up by women authors in the 1980s. This moral language is neither a stage of morality nor a morality only for women. Rather, it is Piaget's work that is limited to one stage of moral development and findings that seems to have a male bias.

Historical Snapshots

The history of children would be as difficult to write as the history of the human race because being a child is not a class of people but a universal condition of human beings. The human race may eventually devise something different, but until now every human being has been born as an infant who needs immediate and constant help to survive. What many people have sought to write in the last century has been a history of childhood, that is, the history of the *idea* and the *institution* called childhood. Implicit to writing a history of childhood is the claim that children existed for millennia previous to a moment when an idea of childhood was invented. Among authors who have written on the history of childhood, there are differences about where to draw the line, but there is a general consensus that childhood is an invention of modernity.

Histories of childhood, similar to the literature on children's rights, usually have a problem insofar as they assume that the world consists of adults and children. Childhood is thought to be the construction of a space protected by adults. Children are presumed to be inhabitants of childhood until they cross over into the independent world of adulthood. The literature on the history of childhood, like that of children's liberation, usually neglects adolescence as a transitional period. The assumption that there are only two states of life, dependence and independence, creates clarity for the thesis that childhood was invented at a recent moment in history. It also creates a current dilemma of whether to keep the wall separating childhood and adulthood or else to tear it down.

A more messy but realistic thesis would be that the human race has always had an awareness that infants and younger children need special care if they are to survive. Very often, the conditions for survival were not there. Throughout most of history, at least half of the infants died. Parents and other older people, including older children, would have been aware of the vulnerability of infants and younger children. Society took what measures were available for nourishing the young, and people made use of their scant knowledge about treating illness. Infants that did survive to be children of six and older were gradually assimilated into the work of the society.

What happened in modern times, as health care improved and the nature of work changed, is that childhood, that is, the idea of being a child, was more clearly articulated. Furthermore, the idea of being a child was extended to age twelve, sixteen, eighteen, or even later. Now adults had privileges that were held out before the child who had to toe the line if he, and recently she, was to reach the promised land of adulthood.

The best known history of childhood is *Centuries of Childhood* by Philip Ariès, a maverick historian.[13] The book influenced the nature of historiography because it was among the first histories to start with the working of society and to draw conclusions from the stuff of ordinary life, including the evolution of popular language. Ariès was inspired to study childhood from noticing that in medieval paintings, children are dressed like small adults. Piecing together a variety of data, most of it French, he arrived at the provocative thesis that childhood was an invention of the eighteenth century.[14] He noted, for example, that there was no separate (French) word for *bedroom* until the eighteenth century and speculated that until then, sex was not a secret hidden from children.[15]

The earliest history of young children's experience might possibly be found in fairy tales, a secret code of children throughout the centuries.[16] A great many of these traditional tales are stories of horrifying violence. What could be worse than visiting your grandmother and finding out that she is not your grandmother but a wolf that has eaten your grandmother and intends to eat you? Fairy tales are filled with witches, giants, evil stepmothers, and ferocious animals intent on destroying children. Such stories, it has been theorized, allow a child to externalize its fears and thus get some control of them. Given how infants and children have suffered in most of history, their fears were not without a basis.

Infants and children throughout the centuries seem to have been beaten as though there were some evil force within them that had to be driven out.[17] There are no available statistics for most of the past which is why fairy tales have to be used as an indicator of how widespread was the practice. If the full extent of the abuse of children were known, it might be revealed as the single worst scandal in human history. The practice of beating a child was not called child abuse until recent centuries.

The emergence of a literature on child abuse in the seventeenth century might suggest an increase in the practice. More likely, the contrary is true;

that is, the routine beating of children began to be recognized for the abuse that it is.[18] Child abuse has probably been in decline in modern centuries though it continues to be a widespread practice. The euphemism "corporal punishment" was coined to cover up a lot of abuse.

An important seventeenth-century book on the treatment of children was John Locke's *Some Thoughts Concerning Education*.[19] Locke introduced many humane practices into the education of infants and young children; he was very attentive to the young person's interests and desires. Most of his prescriptions still make sense today. He proposed "respect for children," something that was novel for his day.[20] As for child beating, he was generally opposed to it, believing that there were better ways for directing a child, using love and friendship or, if necessary, shame.[21] Unfortunately, he did not leave it there. He wrote, "Yet there is one, and but one fault, for which, I think, children should be beaten, and that is, obstinacy or rebellion . . . . Stubbornness and obstinate disobedience, must be master'd with force and blows: For there is no other remedy."[22]

Almost a century later, Jean-Jacque Rousseau in *Emile* seemed intent on challenging Locke's influential book. But on the matter of beating a child, Rousseau's view remained similar. The stereotype of Rousseau is that he was extremely permissive, a forerunner of progressive education. Like Locke, Rousseau was attentive to children's desires and interests, but the tutor in *Emile* was clearly in charge and entertained no challenges to his authority. When correction is needed, "punishment as punishment must never be inflicted on children, but it should always happen to them as a natural consequence of their bad action."[23] That principle seems reasonable but it includes this corollary: "If he seriously dares to strike someone, be it his lackey, be it the hangman, arrange that his blows be always returned with interest and in such a way as to destroy the drive to revert to the practice."[24]

Locke and Rousseau agreed that education begins at birth and that the first few years of life are crucial for the success of education. Both of them were against the practice of swaddling a baby instead of letting it stretch its limbs and freely move about.[25] Locke, who was a bachelor, has surprisingly detailed instruction on the toilet training of an infant.[26] The common view about Rousseau is that he wanted to let children follow their own interests. That is largely true, but he does not make the mistake of equating a *child's* interests with a theory of lifelong education. When the child is ready for rational explanations, it is ready for the end of childhood and the beginning of teenage adolescence. It is in adolescence, Rousseau says, when the hard work of education begins.[27]

A Gentler Education

Rousseau's influence on U.S. education did not occur until the 1830s when other changes in the culture created an openness for taking the child's experience as a guide. Even then, Rousseau remained only an indirect influence. Johann Pestalozzi (1746-1827), who tried to carry through on Rousseau's theory of education, was the preferred author for the "experience-centered" education that was to flourish in the United States.[28] There were efforts to incorporate Pestalozzi's insights into school curricula. Significantly, Pestalozzi's main model for how to teach is the activities of a mother. She shows the schoolteacher how teaching is to be done.[29]

Pestalozzi's influence was part of a different kind of child-rearing that was emerging in the 1830s led by Catherine Beecher's professionalization of motherhood and by advice books for mothers. A kinder and gentler attitude toward children was recommended to mothers who were supposed to be single-minded in their devotion to motherhood. A young woman could prepare for motherhood by being a school teacher and providing "loving tenderness" to pupils.[30]

Beecher thought that the men who were teachers should be working in the textile mills so that the women could be the schoolteachers.[31] She thought that one of the ugliest abuses women had to witness was turning over tender children to "coarse, hard, unfeeling men, too lazy or too stupid to follow the appropriate duties of their sex."[32] Beecher soon got her wish to see school teaching become almost exclusively a woman's job.

From the 1830s to the end of the century, children were given a prominent place in U.S. culture. Some people thought that they were given too permissive an education. Foreign visitors, such as Francis Grund and Harriet Martineau, found the country's children to be precocious, that is, noisy and disrespectful of their elders.[33] After the U.S. Civil War, there was even more emphasis on the goodness of children and the need, especially for women, to retain a childlike attitude. Beth in *Little Women* says, "Let me be a little girl as long as I can."[34]

Manuals for sexual education, such as Sylvanus Stall's *What a Young Boy (Young Girl) Ought to Know*, were very popular. The answer for what children should know about sex was not much or not much that was accurate. A boy's innocence required that he avoid all thoughts of sex, an outlook that guaranteed a Victorian obsession with sex. Sexual education was very different for boys and girls. "Whereas the masculine super-heroes achieve sexual segmentation by renunciation, heroines like Heidi simply remain in the pre-puberty state forever."[35]

Science Demands Strictness

In the early twentieth century, the science of motherhood was replaced by the science of childhood, which reversed a laissez-faire attitude toward child-rearing. The modern field of psychology emerged and with it a collection of (male) experts who dictated the proper way to raise a child. It was implied, or sometimes explicitly stated, that mothers did not know enough to be in charge of raising a child.

The leading baby doctor in the 1920s was John Watson. His 1928 book, *The Psychological Care of Infant and Child*, contains such gems as "No one knows enough to raise a child" and "It is a serious question in my mind whether there should be individual homes for children—or even whether children should know their parents. There are undoubtedly much more scientific ways of bringing up children which will probably mean finer and happier children."[36] Watson was confident that his "behaviorism," emphasizing scientific control as more important than parental love, was the key to child-rearing.

The family, however, remained outside a full application of scientific management. A better arena for the use of scientific theories and the measurement of progress was the school. Children in school were at the mercy of experts who knew how to control small children. A popular 1932 book on the sociology of education, while generally humane, has a description of a psychiatrist "who has had remarkably good success in establishing rapport with sub-adolescent delinquent boys." The psychiatrist attributed his success to a technique described this way: He first had the boy strip naked. "He sometimes had his secretary, a woman, assist in the process. He reassured the boy from time to time, 'It's all right. You're just a little boy and it's all right' . . . . He remarked that it was very difficult for a small boy to remain defiant when he hadn't any clothes."[37] The new science seems to have been mixed with some old-time humiliation of children.

The World Up For Grabs

World War II began a change in the scientific control of child-rearing. Some of the aura of science held on throughout the 1950s, but a revolution was started with Benjamin Spock's *Baby and Child Care* in 1946, which sold twenty-two million copies.[38] In some ways, Spock fit the stereotype of the male doctor telling mothers how to raise their children. However, mothers found his advice to be a practical support to their own sense of how one should treat an infant and young child. Spock would be tagged in the 1960s as the overly permissive guide to a generation of young people who had no respect for authority. His book was actually very supportive of parental authority; it was more a throwback to an earlier time than it was an invitation for children to rebel against authority.

Spock was only one strand of a gathering of forces that exploded in the 1960s. Starting with the civil rights movement, the decade gave birth to a multitude of "liberation" movements, often led by adolescents. The young could not have done it alone; they were joined by people of all ages who suddenly seemed dissatisfied with their lives. During the 1960s, one had the sense that the whole world was in turmoil led by young people with an unrealistic expectation that a better world could easily be created. The most general description of the decade is that there was skepticism about the very idea of authority. It seems unlikely that such a widespread change could have occurred earlier in history.

Among the groups who were "liberated" from authority were older children and adolescents. Their sudden newfound freedom was exciting but held some dangers for which they were not prepared. When they were released from the authority of home, school, and local policing, adolescents were sometimes overwhelmed by the availability of alcohol and other drugs as well as by a lack of guidance in sexual matters. The decade was not as disorderly as it is sometimes portrayed; it was more than a time of ridiculous clothes and loud music. At its best it unleashed protests against war, poverty, and racism. It established a world culture that holds unlimited possibilities as well as world-shaking dangers. Authority has never been the same.

The call for children and adolescents to take control of their own education was difficult to resist. The fixed curriculum disappeared and democracy was introduced into the running of schools. One of the popular books of the decade was called *Summerhill*, which describes an English school that had begun in 1910, but was almost unknown in the United States until the publication in 1960 of *Summerhill: A Radical Approach to Child Rearing*.[39] The author of the book, A. S. Neill, was the founding father of the school that claimed to be a total democracy. Each student and each staff member had a vote on any policy. Children would decide when and if they went to class. Neill professed the belief that "a child is innately wise and realistic. If left to himself without adult suggestion of any kind, he will develop as far as he is capable of developing."[40]

The Summerhill approach found enthusiastic supporters in the United States. What they often failed to realize was that Summerhill was a boarding school presided over by a patriarch. It was a school with open classrooms within a closed system. The children were free to move as they wanted—within the system. Attempts to imitate Summerhill without its conditions often ended in disaster. One experiment began with the principle that the school would have no authority until—or if—authority was needed. An account of that experiment was entitled "Summerhill, Some are Hell."[41]

It seems impossible that the attitude to infants, children, and adolescents can ever return to what it was before the 1960s even though previous generations have also believed that a new swing of the pendulum was unthinkable. It is not that we have finally found the proper balance and the right way to raise children. Older people will probably always be perplexed about the next generation and their strange ways. Technology has in some ways opened a wider gap between children and adolescents on one side and their parents, schoolteachers, and other adult guides on the other. But while communication across the generations is difficult, all ages have now been thrown together in a single world instead of living in a world of separate spaces. Children and adolescents cannot be confined in one place while the grown-ups run the world. Finding workable forms of authority that will help young people remains a major challenge.

The "end of childhood" that was written about in the 1980s has not resulted in children once again becoming little adults but rather in most people over the age of six becoming adolescent.[42] Adolescence started as a brief transition between childhood and adulthood, but adolescence sometimes seems to be swallowing both childhood and adulthood. Qualities formerly associated with teenagers, such as sexual experimentation, were increasingly found among young children and also among older adults. Popular entertainment on television and in the movies seems not to be aimed at either adults or children but at the adolescence of everyone. Wearing adolescent clothes such as jeans and t-shirt was adopted by both children and much of the adult population.

To the extent that *adolescence* means instability, emotional fragility, and instant gratification, there are obvious drawbacks in a society of forty-year-olds or sixty-year-olds acting as adolescents. Forty-year-old parents should be able to give some guidance to their teenage sons and daughters. But *adolescent* in its meaning of becoming adult can be an admission that an endpoint of maturity is never reached and that there is always the possibility of becoming a more complete human being. Teenagers will continue to not understand their parents, but parents might improve their insight into the minds of teenagers.

Human Rights for Infants, Young Children, Older Children, and Adolescents

The lengthy heading above should not be necessary in that one can simply say that human rights applies to all people of all ages. The problem is that the discussion of "children's rights" has been beset by several confusions. One problem, as I have indicated, is a lack of clarity in the meaning of *child*. A second problem is the failure to distinguish between human rights that are universal and those political, social, and economic rights that vary according to both culture and the age of a young person. While human rights should apply to all cultures and to all ages, some political and economic rights of children and adolescents may not.

The failure to make any distinctions of age in the meaning of *child* is common. Unfortunately the United Nations document, the Convention on the Rights of the Child, shares in that failure. The convention simply stipulates that for its purposes the term *child* means anyone under eighteen years old. That pronouncement does not face the problem and has the effect of undermining the provisions within the document. Some of its statements make little sense if the child is two months old; other statements are not appropriate for teenagers. A related failure of the document is the confusion of human rights with rights that vary by culture.

Like the Universal Declaration of Human Rights, the Convention on the Rights of the Child contains far too many claims for human rights. There was a UN declaration on the Rights of the Child in 1959.[43] It was shorter and more to the point than the 1990 Convention, which represented not an application of the declaration but a change of direction. The declaration emphasized protecting the child. The convention, while it does advert to the special care that (younger) children require, tries to give voice to the (older) child. In doing so, it obscures the desperate need of millions of infants and small children for protection from attack and for help that is needed to flourish. Nearly all of the declaration seems to refer to infants and younger children; in contrast, most of the convention seems to be talking about teenagers.

The Convention on the Rights of the Child garnered nearly universal support.[44] It was approved faster than any similar document in the history of the United Nations. Only two nation-states refused approval. One was Somalia because it lacked a functioning government. The other was the United States of America, which had a mixture of reasons for its reservation. One scandalous reason was that the United States wished to retain its power to execute people under eighteen years old. And the reason why President George H. W. Bush refused to sign the convention was that it did not protect the "unborn child."

Another reason why the United States would not approve the convention was a fear that it authorized too much intervention in family life. A right of self-determination by children (in the convention's meaning of *child*) could have the effect of liberating an older child or an adolescent from the parents only to result in the state becoming responsible for the welfare of the child or adolescent. A concern with family authority might be justified. But a fear of the family being undermined was exaggerated by the political right wing in the United States, which is suspicious of anything that the United Nation does. President Bill Clinton in 1995 authorized signing the convention, but he was blocked by Senator Jesse Helms in the Foreign Relations Committee who described the convention as "yet another attempt in a growing list of United Nations' ill-conceived efforts to chip away at the U.S. Constitution." [45]

Articles 5 and 18 in the convention affirm the authority of the parents. But articles 12 to 16 affirm that the child has rights to express its opinions, to freedom of thought, conscience and religion, to freedom of association, and a right to privacy. Because of the ambiguity as to which rights belong at which age there was legitimate cause for concern. There could be tension within the family if children have the right to express their views in matters affecting them, including medical decisions.[46] Still, the convention deserved a serious debate in the United States and perhaps approval with stated reservations. At least the United States would then be forced to report regularly to the Committee on the Rights of the Child on what the country is doing about the disgraceful level of poverty among its own infants and young children.

Human rights, I have argued, do not depend on the individual claiming such rights; that is, human rights are not a matter of individual agency. Children, especially infants, are a supreme test for understanding human rights as rights that apply to every human being, whatever his or her age, and whatever limitations the person has. Human rights are a support of the independence that a person has in relation to the dependence, which is also a characteristic of every human life. At the beginning of life when the infant can barely do anything for itself, it is still due some basic rights from the community. The extreme dependence of the infant is a reminder that dependence is a fact of life and that at any moment, a person of any age may find himself or herself in a position of near total dependence.

This dependence of an infant calls into question what is assumed to be the liberal position on rights, that is, the restriction of the government's power to interfere in the life of the individual. In this original sense of *liberal*, nearly everyone in the United States is liberal, devoted to protection of the individual's liberty. From Thomas Hobbes to John Rawls, there was little in political theory about the condition of infants and small children. An important change is signified by the ethicist Annette Baier who writes, "In a sense it is correct that in order for it [my right to life] to be respected, all that must be done by others is that they not kill me. But although what that means may seem clear enough when I am a reasonably tough adult, it was less clear when I was a helpless newborn, and will be less clear when I am a helpless, incapacitated old person."[47]

As Baier is suggesting here, we could say that there is one human right, the right to life, provided we understand that this right includes living as an infant and living as a dying person. It is tragic that the phrase "right to life" has become so thoroughly identified with the antiabortion movement. Whatever one's view of abortion, there is a need to affirm the right to life of infants and young children. For a five-month-old, the right to be left alone is not paramount.

One can get lost in the details of the UN document that affirms a multiplicity of rights and that stipulates that all rights apply to all children without exception. A Convention on the Rights of Children (with special attention to infancy) would have done well to concentrate on the hundreds of millions of young children who lack water, food, and protection from preventable diseases and from the violence of sexual exploitation.

The sixth article of the convention reads, "States parties recognize that every child has the inherent right to life. States parties shall ensure to the maximum extent possible the survival and development of the child." A right to life cannot be said to exist if it does not affirm both a right to survive and a right to *develop*. Thus, if one were to gather up the rights of infants and children into a single term, *life* or *development* would serve the purpose.

The use of *development* here is somewhat ironic in that a right to development has been intensely debated in recent decades but mostly by economists in reference to the development of peoples. There is almost never acknowledgment that the development of peoples depends on the development of the girl and the boy. Article 29, on implementing the convention, uses the term *development* five times without giving any special attention to its meaning.

The use of *development* to concretize a right to life is not reducible to psychology's use of the term in theories of stage development. The development of an infant has both economic and psychological elements, but a *human* right to development embraces much more. The right to live/develop is both negative and positive in the sense that it involves both intervention and protection against interventions. For development from infancy to the teenage years, the mix of intervention and nonintervention shifts. For example, Article 16 of the convention on a child's right to privacy can hardly be said to exist at six months of age, but the need for privacy begins to grow early, and it is indispensable for a seventeen-year-old. The failure to distinguish ages of "children" in the convention (and in U.S. Supreme Court rulings) leads to both lack of care for the needs of infants and lack of privacy for adolescents.

A state can be at fault in the forms of punishment it legally approves for children and adolescents. The United States finally outlawed the execution of minors in a 5-4 ruling of the Supreme Court in 2005.[48] Justice Anthony Kennedy, writing for the majority, said that executing sixteen-year-olds conflicted with "evolving standards of decency" and isolated the United States from the rest of the world. The court's decision removed dozens of juveniles from death row. "It also threw a spotlight onto state policies under which young juveniles were increasingly being tried in adult courts and sentenced to adult jails, often for non-violent crimes."[49] Sentencing a young adolescent to life imprisonment without parole surely violates "evolving standards of decency" and a right to development. Only in 2009 did the U.S. Supreme Court put restriction on the practice without banning it outright.[50]

One of the worst things that states and failed states do to children and adolescents is make them soldiers who are trained to kill. Girls as well as boys are exploited in this way.[51] The Convention on the Rights of the Child forbids the recruiting of soldiers who are under fifteen years of age, one of the few places in the convention where there is an age distinction. Numerous states violate that rule and violate the human rights of the children and adolescents involved. This violation ought to be a primary focus of the United Nations' Committee on Human Rights and it did lead to an "optional protocol," which raised the age level of soldiers to eighteen.[52]

The biggest scandal that remains is children (that is, age twelve and under) carrying AK-47s or being used as suicide bombers. Some people argue that in parts of the world a seventeen-year-old may need the choice to be armed. However, it is not believable that a child freely consents to becoming a soldier; only the desperation to survive coerces a boy or girl into an army.[53] The fact that hundreds of thousands of boys and girls are fighting in armies deserves the world's attention but does not get it.

Differences in culture affect generalizations about children. But a representative at the drafting of the convention says "there was never any serious discussion as to whether children all over the globe possess similar bio-physical features at the same chronological age."[54] That is an obvious problem for talking about the political and economic rights of children. If the convention had stuck to human rights, then it would not have had to sort out the diversity of cultural differences. An affirmation of the human rights of children should focus on what is indispensable for the life/development of infants and young children. Much of the remainder of the Convention on the Rights of the Child could have been offered as material for discussions between parents and older children together with the recognition that there are differences across cultures in the rearing of children.

Extending the Political and Economic Rights of Young People

The literature of children's liberation that emerged in the 1960s is correct that young people should generally share in whatever rights are accorded to older people. There should be a good reason for any restrictions. The reason "because I say so" is not an adequate basis of parental authority and "society says so" or "it has always been that way" are not good explanations of why a child or adolescent is denied a political or an economic right.

When a child is not big enough to exercise a particular right the restriction makes sense; six-year-olds cannot drive automobiles or heavy equipment. A more debatable case is when there is a claim that the child or adolescent lacks emotional or intellectual maturity. An age requirement may need to be imposed, but it should if possible take account of individual variations. The main issue in such debates is that the young person, including his or her opinions, should be respected. The child does not always want equality as much as an explanation of why there are differences.

At the beginning of *Escape from Childhood,* John Holt proposes that the "rights, privileges, duties and responsibilities of adult citizens be made *available* to any young person, of whatever age, who wants to make use of them."[55] He then lists ten examples, including a child's right to economic independence. His italicized word *available* somewhat softens the claim, but he leaves the decision of when to exercise rights (and duties?) entirely in the hands of the child. Like the Convention on the Rights of the Child, Holt has few distinctions within the meaning of *childhood*.

Making the right to vote *available* at six-years-old would invite children to learn about politics by participating in political activity. Most six-year-olds would presumably not be interested in exercising the right to vote but some ten- or twelve-year-olds might. Would they vote intelligently? That is not the criterion we use for older people. The main point is that people learn to be political by participating in politics. In the United States only about half the population of voters shows any interest in exercising this basic political right. Extending the franchise to children would be a way of encouraging the next generation not to be so indifferent to the exercise of this important right.

Concerning some rights, such as a right to choose one's religion, a right to direct one's education, and a right to choose one's guardians, a child may need protection from its own ignorance, lack of experience, or passing mood. That is not to say that children should be denied the right to be heard and to participate in decisions affecting their best interests. The UN Convention on the Rights of the Child says that the child has a right to freedom of expression, especially "in all matters affecting the child."[56] Interestingly, no children were consulted in the writing of the convention.

Choosing a new set of parents would be a drastic step for which no young child and few adolescents are qualified.[57] However, the idea might not be as outrageous as it sounds. In colonial times, boys, and sometimes girls, went to a new family for apprenticeship.[58] In a sense, they acquired new parents at the beginning of adolescence when conflicts over authority are often severe. Such practices as two families exchanging children for a while, or a trusted relative or neighbor acting as a substitute parent, or an adolescent having independent living space, are practices that have to be carefully worked out. Nonetheless, sometimes a child or an adolescent just needs a little distance from a parent. The key problem here is communication and the child's right to be reasonably listened to and reasonably informed.

Human Rights and the Last Stages of Life

The young and the old are sometimes allies in a conflict with the middle. The young and the old are often treated condescendingly by the (middle-aged) adults who are in charge of things. The very young should be allowed to speak for themselves as soon as they are able; the very old should be allowed to speak for themselves so long as they are able. "People say 'I know the problems of age.' They don't. Nobody's been old but the old."[59] To younger adults, the old may all seem alike, but each old person has a long history that makes him or her more unique than younger humans. The respect once demanded for old age did not always seem deserved. On the other hand, a society that treats its older population with a neglect that can border on contempt is not a healthy place for anyone to live in.

The issue of human rights for old people can be simply stated. Every individual, no matter how old, deserves the basic and universal rights of a human being. Although the category of *old* is ambiguous and has been rapidly changing, a precise agreement on who should be called old, elderly, or aged is not needed for the assertion of human rights, such as the right not to be killed and the right not to be abused, as well as the rights to receive physical subsistence, basic health care, and physical security in one's person.

One change of language in recent decades should be noticed. In the dichotomy of child and adult, everyone who was not a child was an adult. I noted above that both words, *child* and *adult*, have been undergoing change. For the meaning of adult, there are differences that one can generally ascribe to young adults, middle-aged adults, and older adults. However, older adults not long ago acquired a new name; first it was "senior citizen," and then *senior* became used as a noun as well as an adjective. The change was ostensibly for assigning benefits to the old, and older people do not object to paying less at the movie theater. It may be disconcerting, however, when buying a plane ticket to choose whether one is an adult or a senior. It is no small loss to cease being an adult. The rights that are regularly ascribed to adults can quickly disappear along with the status of adulthood. In addition, the exclusion of old people from adulthood is a reaffirmation of the stereotype that adults are people who are independent as opposed to children (and seniors) who are dependent.

Old age has become problematic because of the success in improving diet, environmental conditions, and medical practice. The success of these changes in the United States has introduced a strain on effective government programs such as Medicare and Social Security. There are simply more old people than ever before. The annals of the first Congress in 1790 (when the country's average age was sixteen) notes that "in America, there are few without families, and the ease of procuring subsistence removes all apprehension of suffering in old age."[60] At that time, the right to needed care by the old would logically be met by the grown-up sons and daughters of those who were old. Mary Wollstonecraft in the 1790s stated the obvious principle: "The parent who pays proper attention to helpless infancy has a right to require the same attention when the feebleness of age comes upon him."[61]

At some place along the way, that bond between the generations seems to have frayed. By the 1960s the majority of old people in the United States were living below the poverty line. An industry of nursing homes had sprung up and was running an exploitive business with little monitoring; the old were not being well treated. Barbara Myerhoff's film *Number Our Days* painted an indelible picture of one nursing home in Venice, California, filled with old people who had largely been abandoned by their economically successful offspring.[62] Simone de Beauvoir's 1970 book, *Coming of Age*, described the dire plight of the old. After noting that primitive people often left the old to die, she concluded that "civilized nations apply the same methods: killing alone is forbidden, unless it is disguised."[63]

In the last half century, there has been dramatic progress in the economic condition of the old. There are still pockets of poverty, but the old are generally well-off, indeed so well off as to cause resentment among many younger adults. As important as has been economic improvement is the change in the image of old age. The old have a mixture of dependence and independence in which there is greater dependence than in young adulthood. Nevertheless, the old do not have to be treated like infants; they need help to do specific things that they might no longer be able to manage on their own. Nursing homes (some of them now avoid this name) are generally much better than they were in the 1960s. It can no longer be assumed that senility is a natural stage of life. Dementia is an urgent problem, but it is a disease for which there is need of a cure.

In 1970 a group of six women met in a kitchen in Philadelphia and decided that they would change the image of old age in the country. They started organizing groups of older adults across the country. The news media found these old women cute and named them the gray panthers. As can happen with groups that are ridiculed by the news media, the women took up the name and ran with it. They were no longer seen as little old ladies sitting at home but activists for a better country. They made it clear that they were not just out for their own benefits. They argued that if getting old was imagined to be a horrible experience, then the young could not be happy in such a society. One of their victories was to get Johnny Carson to stop using a skit in which he played a batty old woman.

The leader of the group, Maggie Kuhn, said that she would stay at this work until she died. When an interviewer asked what would happen if she was taken down by illness, she replied, "Then I will make that my work."[64] Kuhn understood that older adults need to have work even if they are retired from a job. Work is the meaningful contribution that a person makes to society; one's work is part of one's identity. A job is one form of work by which one makes a living. Some people are fortunate enough to have their job be their real work; other people have to find the work which is their life's meaning when they are off the job.

The age of sixty-five acquired a talismanic meaning over a century ago, but it is no longer an appropriate age for everyone's retirement. Some jobs that are physically exhausting deserve retirement well before age sixty-five. Jobs that are mainly intellectual have no obvious cutoff point other than an individual's health. Some university professors are just hitting their stride at age sixty-five. Nevertheless, they should be required to submit a letter of resignation to take effect at a specified age, whether it is seventy, seventy-five, or eighty. Younger people are waiting in line for these desirable positions; older people could have a part-time position that would recognize that they have useful experience to share with their younger colleagues.

Whether an older person is a working professional, a healthy individual who is living alone, or a patient who is in a nursing home, the main issue is respect. That means recognition of older people as still having basic rights even when their energies are diminished. Old people need interaction with people of all ages, and especially with infants, children, and teenagers. Animals are also important companions for many older people.

Young people who visit nursing homes are often surprised to find that old people can be interesting. Of course, young people need preparation for visiting a nursing home and for getting used to the setting. For nearly everyone who is unaccustomed to a nursing home, the first reaction is likely to be shock. Nursing homes are generally better than they were, but they can still be depressing. The people working in nursing homes should not be burdened with this whole problem. There is, however, an inevitable shrinking of imagination by the people working in these settings. People who are being cared for still need intellectual stimulation. Conversation is the basic stimulant. A discussion of books or the viewing of quality movies should be available for older people who can make use of such resources.

Anything that older people can do for others is a help toward their own well-being. Erik Erikson wrote that "adult man is so constituted as to need to be needed lest he suffer the mental deformation of self-absorption, in which he becomes his own infant and pet."[65] Erikson's gender-exclusive language here is reflective of the era in which he wrote; however, his statement may in fact be truer of men than women. Women live longer than men in part because men so often feel lost when they retire. Men created a society that was unhealthy for men, one which resisted acknowledging physical weakness, illness, and reliance on others. In old age, men have to accept the dependence of interdependence. They may have to discover the value of reaching out to others by preparing a meal for friends, transporting someone for medical treatment, or playing games with a grandchild.

The Right to Live with Dignity even while Dying

One of the most contentious arguments concerning old people, and eventually everyone else, goes under the unhelpful rubric of a right to die. Up to a few decades ago, and even now in most of the world, the phrase "right to die" would be unintelligible. The phrase seems to have originated as shorthand for a "right to die with dignity." That phrase, as I have previously noted, has been used to advocate "physician-assisted suicide."

If the most basic human right is a right to live, a phrase that is as peculiar as a "right to die" suggests that the argument is misplaced. Polemics for and against a right to die, together with complex medical data and abstract theories, threaten to overwhelm the fundamental human question. Instead of talking about a right to die, a more helpful discussion would be about the implications of human dignity even while dying. A right to live with human dignity includes not having one's body entered without consent. The main question is about doing violence to oneself or others.

This question of controlling how people die cannot be answered in a few paragraphs or even a few books. The need is for a national and international conversation that has yet to take place. In the United States there have been a small number of extreme cases that have arrived at the court house. The resulting conversation has been mainly among lawyers, judges, and politicians. The national conversation should include people who are at various stages of dying, family and close friends of the dying, and health care workers who attend to the care of the dying. The last group includes not only attending physicians but also nurses and social workers.

If I had to choose a final arbiter in a difficult case, I would put my trust in a hospice nurse.

There have been in fact quiet and helpful conversations taking place during the past several decades. *Most* deaths in hospitals today are negotiated. The negotiation can take numerous forms. It can range from intense debate among interested parties in a hospital consulting room to a silent nod by the spouse of a dying patient. Anyone who thinks that there is something scandalous about such negotiating probably does not have much experience of what hospitals and hospices deal with every day. Contemporary medical machinery and drugs have complicated the simple human question of when and how we die.

In some respects, however, contemporary medicine can clarify the moral choice by providing a better picture of the actual health condition of each person, including those who have fatal diseases. Tens of thousands of people are caught in horrible situations between living humanly and dying. But it is not technology that is the culprit; it is the confusion of people who argue from a single abstract principle and whose theories are usually shadowed by the concern with their own mortality.

Dying unavoidably brings up questions of what to think about humans and human life as a whole. I noted earlier an insistence in the literature of human rights that such rights cannot be based on any one metaphysical or religious tradition. But some kind of philosophy or religion gets smuggled into court decisions on "physician-assisted suicide."[66] At both the local and federal levels in the United States, the "right to die" has usually been based on the principle of individual choice, but the courts have then limited the decision to "hastening death" for people who are terminally ill. Why the limitation?

The answer given by judges usually makes an assumption of what nature demands. Suicide by those not terminally ill would mean a "senseless loss of life ended prematurely"; the courts are concerned that "death does not come too early." A judge in one of these cases said that "obviously, the State has strong legitimate interest in deterring suicide by young people and others with a significant natural life span ahead of them."[67] Why is that obvious? Does the state or the courts have a right to decide what constitutes a "significant natural life span?" The phrase "natural death" is regularly used by lawyers and judges as if that phrase were obvious in meaning. What is "natural death" the opposite of? My point is that dying and the legal rights of individuals in relation to dying cannot be discussed without a philosophical position that religion used to supply or still does supply for some people.

There are people who are all too ready to bring to bear their particular religious beliefs on the rest of us. Similar to the preacher Paneloux in Camus's *The Plague,* they praise or at least justify suffering on religious grounds. In response to a sermon by Paneloux that God has sent the plague for a reason, the physician Rieux says, "Every country priest who visits his parishioners and has heard a man gasping for breath on his deathbed thinks as I do. He'd try to relieve human suffering before trying to point out its excellence."[68] The problem here is not religion but an interpretation of Christianity that is out of kilter with the breadth of that tradition. A bad intrusion of religion is a reason not for excluding religion from the needed discussion but rather for including a wide range of religious believers who can bring an informed attitude to the table.

The fundamental moral assumption in these discussions is that some human actions are good, others are bad. Most of the time thoughtful people, who are doing the best that they know how, get it right. There are always going to be cases that are debatable, and even after debate the best available action may remain uncertain. But when decisions are unavoidable, somebody has to decide among "the good, the bad, and the downright awful." It is human actions in all their complexity that are morally good or morally bad. When all of the weight is placed on a single principle, then other theorists are sure to point out that that principle fails to solve all problems.

It is unfortunate that in the 1960s, there was a fashionable attitude propagated under the title of "situation ethics." The term usually meant a dismissal of moral principles and of any help from tradition. The failure here was a superficial grasp of what a human situation includes. A few people at the time pointed out that even Thomas Aquinas had a situation ethic, that is, he argued that to judge the morality of any action one has to include all the elements of the situation; that would include the intention of the agent, the external and internal environment, the means that are used, the intended and the unintended results. Thomas Aquinas does not have the answer to today's medical decisions any more than do eighteenth-century writers of the Constitution. It would be rash, however, to dismiss everyone who wrote before the twentieth-century creation of our present confusing situation.

In today's world of complicated medicine, the situation of a dying person is likely to include the person who is ill, family and friends, a caregiver or more likely these days a team of professionals, and the use of medical means that can include surgery, machines, and medicines. Most of the *legal* discussion falls back upon the principle of the "autonomy" of the patient. Autonomy can seem unrealistic when the body has a variety of tubes attaching the person to machines and when he or she is only half conscious from the effect of pain and drugs. One's right to choose needs to be set within the whole situation.

Perhaps the most important of the relevant distinctions in this situation is a traditional one between killing a patient and letting a patient die. Many commentators today dismiss the distinction. But the conceptual difference between someone deliberating killing a person and someone not interfering further in the process of dying is clear. In most actual cases, the difference is clear. Admittedly, there are other situations today in which the difference between killing and "letting die" blurs. For example, if I see a child fall into a shallow pool of water and can easily save the child from drowning but do nothing, that action would be morally reprehensible; letting die in that situation would be tantamount to killing.[69] As a single abstract principle, "letting die" is not decisive; it is only one part of a complex situation.

Another traditional principle is called double effect. Nearly all human decisions have more than one effect. A person intends a result but other things also follow. Military jargon has made famous the term "collateral damage," an antiseptic phrase to cover up the fact that planes and drones kill untold numbers of people beyond the bomber's intention. "Sorry, we did not mean to kill you." The military example may unfortunately taint any invoking of a principle that is indispensable in everyday life as well as in hospitals and hospices.

A physician administers a medicine with the intention to relieve pain while also knowing that the unintended result is likely to be a shortening of life. Is it defensible to say that he or she intends the pain relief while not intending the death? The answer is it depends on all the factors in the situation. The critical questions are the patient's condition and what kind of relief is possible and helpful? What does "hastening death" mean in a particular case? If the patient's life might be shortened from seventeen weeks to sixteen weeks, a distinction of effects might be reasonably made; if the patient dies three minutes later, the distinguishing of effects is more difficult to make. In neither case, however, can this one principle stand on its own without more information about the total situation.

It is not difficult to imagine scenes of dying that nearly everyone would judge to be immoral. There are others scenes that the great majority of people would find morally defensible. Most moral decisions are based on arguing that in particular circumstances the situation is more like one than the other of the clear cases of right and wrong.[70] Morally indefensible situations, as Thomas Aquinas argued, are those in which one important factor is obviously deficient. A caregiver says his intention in administering morphine is to relieve pain, but he is an interested party in getting the patient's money. Or instead of administering a painkiller that results in a peaceful death, a distraught relative uses a shotgun to the head. A sixteen-year-old patient who is suffering terrible pain says, "I wish I could die"; on that basis, someone immediately fulfills the stated desire by whatever means are at hand.[71]

Consider other situations in which most people would grant that the action was the best that could be done in the given situation. A ninety-five-year-old man with multiple problems is very likely going to die in a few weeks; a complicated surgery would lengthen his life for perhaps a few days. The man is not mentally in a condition that allows choice. The physician in consultation with the patient's proxy decides to forego surgery and let the patient die at an earlier date but with less discomfort. Did the physician kill the patient?

Consider a situation that is common today. A patient is affected with a fatal disease and can no longer eat and drink. The person goes into a coma. These are likely to be signs that the body is preparing for death. A nutritional tube is attached to the body, but there is no improvement over months or even years. The body continues absorbing the liquid put into it, but there are no signs of specifically human activity. So long as there is any reasonable chance that a person can again participate in the human community, the best means available should be used to resist death. But at some point it makes no human sense to continue with technological means. The policy at that point should not be described as one of ceasing treatment; rather it is ceasing to use means that do not contribute to the patient's recovery or comfort.

Although the example of a nutritional tube has been one of the most debated issues in this area, most of the time the moral decision is clear. The arguments have usually been by outsiders who wield a single principle. In the great majority of legal battles over turning off the respirator or disconnecting the feeding tube, the families involved have come to a conclusion that allowing death to occur is the only thing that makes sense. In several famous cases, the family did everything possible and agonized for months or years before accepting that the time had come.[72] They were then subjected to screams of protest by self-appointed moralists or lawyers who accused them of killing their child or parent. An unintended result of dismissing the difference between killing and letting die is that in clear instances where family members have allowed death to finally occur they are accused of murder. That is no help to anybody.

The issue is not whether to extend life by artificial means. We constantly extend life by artifice and artifact. When the artificial means is supportive of a person's life, it can be a blessing. But when there are multiple signs that the person is not going to recover, and possibly that the person is no longer present, it is worse than useless to keep the organism functioning.[73] The phrase "vegetative state" is inaccurate and insulting. What is present in hospitals across the country are organisms whose life functions are now entirely dependent on machines. Those who argue that the process should go on for years or decades, might consider that they could be perpetrating torture. What could be worse than being alive for months or years with no way at all to communicate with a reality outside oneself? Some of the inhumane practices to keep someone or something alive reflect an unwillingness to accept that dying is an inevitable part of human life. At some point, one has to let go and say amen.

Respect for patients and providing them with the best care possible should be the meaning of "dying with dignity." Only within that context should the discussion take place of whether helping a person to die is sometimes an appropriate role for a physician or for a friend.[74] The Commission of Human Rights in the Council of Europe has asserted "the right not to have to suffer but to be able to die in peace and dignity." That is asking for a little too much. Suffering cannot be banished; no one can guarantee a complete absence of suffering for someone who is dying. Similarly, physicians, lawyers, or judges cannot guarantee peace to a dying person. What a society can and should mandate is that people be treated with the dignity of a human being even while they are dying.

The last half century has produced a new phenomenon in that millions of people are told that they are dying of a disease, but they have a period of months or even a few years to prepare for death. This phenomenon has led to many studies of the experience of dying, initiated by Elisabeth Kübler-Ross's *On Death and Dying*.[75] That book had some useful suggestions for interacting with the dying. Unfortunately, the author tried to create a scientific theory in imitation of "stage-development theories," and her "five stages" overshadowed the issue she raised of how to treat the dying patient with dignity.

As numerous critics pointed out, there was nothing fixed or universal about Kübler-Ross's stages of dying. One might say that what she really found was two attitudes among the dying: refusal to accept that one is dying or an accepting that death is imminent. Actually, since humans begin to die as soon as they are born, the two attitudes are always present. The denial of death can be a healthy attitude, as Kübler-Ross noted, insofar as it can spark efforts to preserve and improve one's own life and other lives. However, the acceptance of the reality of death is a realistic accompaniment to denial throughout life. Only at the very end of life should acceptance triumph. What is needed at the end is not acceptance of the fact of dying but acceptance of one's life as complete so as to include dying.

The beginning and the end of life come together though not in a closed circle. Rather, the pains of birth and infancy prepare us for a life that will always include pain, a fact that becomes more evident as a person ages and prepares to die. As commentators throughout history have said, a fear of death can prevent someone from ever really living. The old owe it to the young to be realistic about dying. "Healthy children will not fear life if their elders have integrity enough not to fear death."[76] The idea of human rights is especially challenged by how the dying are spoken about and how they are actually treated.

CHAPTER 6

Religious Traditions and Human Rights

The theme of same and different is important for understanding religious traditions and their relation to human rights. Similar to same and different in the sexual area, same and different first applies to each separate tradition and then to the relation between traditions. Similar to the area of age, the theme of same and different applies to change over time within each religious tradition. The different mixes of same and different produce unique traditions that are not necessarily in conflict with one another. However, the failure to understand uniqueness in this case has produced some of the worst conflicts in history. However bloody religious wars were in the past, they were generally localized. Today, the conflicts can have worldwide repercussions. Conversely, an understanding of the uniqueness of religious traditions could be an invaluable support for world peace and human rights.

Within Tradition and Between Traditions

Each of the major religious traditions has an intramural tension reflecting a difference of emphasis, one group insisting that the tradition is unchangeable, another group insisting on change and reform. If the tension becomes too great, the latter group intentionally or unintentionally creates a new tradition. The split does not entirely solve the problem; a tension between sameness and difference remains although now it is between traditions rather than within a tradition. Very often a new tradition fails to have staying power; traditions cannot simply be invented. In a few instances the new tradition has become one of the major religious traditions of the

197

human race. In this chapter, I select a few such developments to illustrate the importance of contemporary dialogue and the danger of severe conflict when there is no attempt at mutual understanding.

Within a religious tradition, there are forces that resist all change. Some people may be appointed or elected precisely to make sure that things remain the same. Most of the adherents of a tradition are inclined to support the sameness of the tradition over time. The stability and consistency of the tradition are what is comforting to most people. The tremendous personal support that the tradition provides in times of crises, including death, depends on a person being able to count on sameness over time. Tradition for many people means "as it was in the beginning, is now, and ever shall be, world without end."

The names for describing emphasis on sameness or difference are not neutral. Any names for these attitudes carry historical baggage. The most common language used is *conservative* and *liberal,* terms that are imports from the world of politics. Even in politics it is questionable that conservative versus liberal is now very helpful. Conservative in today's politics seems worlds apart from the 1950s meaning of the term, let alone the eighteenth-century meaning. If conservative means to conserve the past, it would seem that religious traditions are by definition conservative. If liberal means to set free, then every religious tradition is concerned with liberating the person from the shackles of ordinary life so as to find a new spiritually transformed existence. Conserve and liberate, far from being opposites, are necessary allies for any religious tradition.

There are, nevertheless, sharp differences and regular debates within religious traditions. With some misgivings, I will call the emphasis on sameness traditionalism. There are different degrees of traditionalism. Most people who emphasize sameness will acknowledge, if they are pressed, that obviously some things have to change but essential things should not. *Tradition* with a capital *T* is sometimes distinguished from traditions with a small *t*. The Tradition is thought to go back to the origin of the religion, perhaps to the words of the founder. In contrast, practices that have persisted over many years or centuries are traditions in a sense but do not have the same status as original texts and rituals.[1]

Traditionalism at its worst means an unwillingness to admit the need to interpret texts. This attitude is sometimes called being literal minded. But a genuine appreciation of the literal meaning of a text involves understanding its historical and literary context. Some people who are called traditionalist do not actually know the literal meaning of the texts which they quote.

There is an impressive and voluminous scholarship on the Jewish Bible, the Christian Bible, and the Qur'an. Scholars who spend years studying these texts—to get at their literal meaning—are sometimes accused of undermining the tradition whereas they are usually giving the tradition a firmer anchor in history.

The contrast to traditionalism within religions is reform, an emphasis that brings about difference. Reform may start from a vague feeling that there is something wrong and it needs correction. In any serious efforts at religious reform, however, the use of the intellect and scholarly knowledge are indispensable. The knowledge has to serve the reformer who is loyal to the tradition. Intellect should, as in Martin Buber's metaphor, "play first violin but not conductor."[2]

Reformers are impatient with rituals that by their nature are resistant to change. Rituals do need examination, and they may need some changing, but the change usually has to be gradual over decades or centuries.[3] Although the reformer may seem to be undermining the tradition in being critical of external forms, the aim of genuine reform is to draw upon richer strands of the tradition that may simplify the external rituals but not destroy them. The intellectually grounded reformer who opposes traditionalism may be more of a friend to tradition than is the traditionalist.

The problem for the person who advocates religious change is the standard by which to evaluate possible changes. That standard may seem obvious on the basis of scholarly inquiry into the past, but the past has to be related to the present. A Christian scholar who has a detailed knowledge of the New Testament does not by that fact know how to reform today's church.

In today's world, a reformer might look to other religious traditions for some guidance. That was almost never true in the past, and even today an ideal from a different religious tradition is of limited help. The main basis for change has to be the integrity of the tradition. Then the question is who has the widest and deepest sense of the whole tradition. The scholar is likely to assume that he or she is in the best position to represent the whole tradition. In practice, the person who is a devout practitioner may sometimes have a great insight to the tradition.

The nonreligious world offers to religious traditions a variety of standards for judgments of what is good or bad. Sometimes, the secular world offers attitudes and practices *against* which the religious tradition defines itself. Conflict with a dominant culture can be a positive factor for many religious subcultures.[4] However, if one is talking about the modern secular world, a total contradiction with the surrounding culture would not be healthy and is probably impossible.

At times, the religious group may agree with aspects of the contemporary culture, especially if the group can argue that some of the values of the secular world are echoes of religious virtues. There might be a case for arguing that dignity, justice, responsibility or care are not inventions of secular ethics but are at least in part a legacy of religious belief. A religious tradition should not be expected to conform as a whole to the standards set by the contemporary secular world. But some of those standards can be used to correct what are now perceived to be obvious biases and intolerances within the tradition, for example, biases against the rights of women.[5]

Where a religious tradition would lose its way is if it simply tried to adjust itself to current attitudes. The dialectic of same and different in a religious tradition dissolves if there is no tension at all with the world beyond it. An attempt to conform to the present would be both unsuccessful in the attempt and destructive of the values represented by the tradition.

Some religious traditions may seem determined to make no adjustments to present attitudes. But unless they are willing to withdraw to a desert or a mountaintop, a religious group has to find a way to function in the present world. It has to decide whether a piece of technology (for example, a loudspeaker for its worship service or a website for information) can be used without the culture of technology distorting the tradition. None of the religious traditions has the answer here because this is not a problem with a solution but a continuing tension to be lived with.

The outside world usually sees the internal struggle of a religious tradition as one between liberal thinkers who have cast off most but not all of their religious beliefs and the orthodox believers who stubbornly refuse to face up to a changing world. The secular embrace of those who are perceived to be liberal religious reformers can be detrimental to the cause of reform. The dialectic of same and different has to be played out within the tradition itself. The reformers who argue for change are trying to show that the tradition as a whole can bear the interpretation that they are advocating. The debate within a tradition can be a respectful disagreement; the opponent in debate can be seen not as the enemy but as one's coreligionist who is equally loyal to the tradition.

The tension between sameness and difference in a religious tradition gives each major tradition a uniqueness.[6] As usual with the distinctly human meaning of uniqueness, the traditions are not simply different from one another. They differ in the manner and degree that they are open to otherness. As is true of human beings, no religious tradition is totally unique. Each tradition rightly sees itself as highly unique; the temptation is to mistake that for total uniqueness. A totally unique tradition would have achieved universality; but at best, any historical tradition can only be a pointer toward universality. It does so not by abandoning its particularity but by digging deeper into that particularity. The lifeblood of any religious tradition is a set of stories and practices that can always be mined for a deeper meaning.

In his book *Living Religions and a World Faith*, William Ernest Hocking states that religion is based on two postulates: it must be universal and it must be particular.[7] These two postulates are usually thought to be incompatible. Hocking agrees that no existing religion successfully combines them, but each religion in its particularity can point toward universality. "No religion could present itself as the completion of other faiths until it had gone through the labor of understanding those faiths. And this labor no religion has as yet more than begun."[8] That statement by Hocking in 1938 remains true today; the labor of understanding has hardly begun. What has changed in the interim is that the major religious traditions confront one another to an unprecedented degree. The choice is no longer between understanding and indifference. The choice now is between mutual understanding and serious conflict. The entire world has a stake in each religion affirming its uniqueness in a way that leaves room for the uniqueness of other traditions.

A start toward understanding a different tradition is the willingness to admit that some of the religious terms that one has always assumed to be one's own are in fact no one's possession but are used by people with differing religious commitments. The dividing line is "between those whose religious commitment is inclusive, because they give themselves to the truth, and those whose religious commitment is exclusive because they think of the truth as something of which one takes possession."[9] Especially in religious matters, no one *possesses* the truth. Meister Eckhart, the greatest of Christian mystics, used to say that religious statements, even when true, leave out more reality than they can include.[10]

In a dialogue between secular and religious attitudes, as well as a dialogue between religious traditions, one's religious interlocutor may seem at first to be saying preposterous things. Throughout most of history that is the point when dialogue ended. Except for unusual cases when an individual scholar or a mystic crossed over to look at the world from a different vantage point, religious traditions cherished their self-containment. Between religious traditions, there was no wish on either side to be contaminated. And between a religious world and a secular world, there was a gap that could only be broached by switching sides. From the religious side, that meant conversion to the faith; from the secular side, it meant coming to one's senses.

A gradual softening has been occurring for about a century. A real conversation could hardly be said to have existed until the second half of the twentieth century. There is still a widespread attitude among secular scholars that a religious tradition can only be understood with the tools of Western enlightenment. But for serious conversation, there has to be a basic respect for one's partner in conversation. Before one can pronounce judgment on a whole way of life, one has to make an effort to understand it on its own terms. "In the case of a religion, this means that one must have some skill in how to use its language and practice its way of life before the propositional meaning of its affirmations become determined enough to be rejected."[11] One has to try to understand what it is like to be a religious believer rather than start with the question: Why do these people believe this set of falsehoods?

Between religious traditions, the gap of understanding can be just as wide and in some ways more hostile than the gap between the secular and the religious worlds. The religious believer may dismiss the secular critic simply as an unbeliever. In contrast, the relation between religious traditions involves passionate belief on both sides; what is at stake is the meaning of one's whole life and perhaps a future life as well. Men have killed for less than that; and unfortunately the conflicts between religious traditions have in fact led to some of the bloodiest wars in history.

The question before the world today is whether there are resources within the major religious traditions so that the members, without renouncing their passionate commitment to the truth as they see it, can contribute to a human tradition that is still taking shape. Before anyone can arrive at a final judgment of whether or not religious traditions can provide support for a human tradition on which to base human rights, there are multiple conversations that have to go much further than they currently have.

Even to name the participants in a dialogue of religious traditions has its problems. Fairly clear examples of a tradition are ones that are called Jewish, Christian, Muslim, or Buddhist. However, even within each of those traditions are differences that may look minor to an outsider but can seem to an insider to constitute a separate tradition. Can it be unequivocally said that there is a Christian tradition? Or is it more accurate to speak of a

Lutheran, Anglican, Orthodox, and dozens of other traditions within the scope of Christianity? Are orthodox and reform Jews separate traditions? These days even orthodox Jews have a sharp division within their ranks. Something similar applies to Shiite and Sunni Muslims or Theravada and Mahayana forms of Buddhism.

There are no agreed upon umpires to rule where one tradition stops and another begins. One can only make a fallible judgment that there are enough common bonds among people identified as Muslim or Jewish or Buddhist to say that the name refers to a tradition. What is suggested by this issue, however, is that a conversation between, for example, Christians and Jews, always has subplots of what is happening among Christians and among Jews. The serious conversation between Christians and Jews could not get going until there was conversation between Protestant and Roman Catholic Christians. And that conversation was preceded by one among differing groups of Protestants.

Religion

Before tracing the progress in dialogue between religious traditions, one should note that there is complexity not only in the term *tradition* but also in the meaning of *religion*. The term *religion*, similar to several other terms that have been examined, has two nearly opposite meanings. When that fact is not recognized, the two meanings become the source of endless confusion and sometimes heated conflict. The fact of two meanings is awkwardly recognized in the use of the phrase "organized religion." That seems to imply that the alternative is disorganized religion instead of the word *religion* applying to two different kinds of things.

Religion is a word of Latin origin. The Christian Church absorbed several of the religious terms that the Romans used, such as *devotion, piety,* and *religion*. The Christians baptized these terms by giving them new meanings. Augustine wrote a book called *On True Religion*. It is not a book claiming that Christianity is the true religion as opposed to other religions. Instead, it is about true religion that "has never ceased to exist from the origin of the human race." Since the coming of Christ, "men began to call Christian the true religion which already existed beforehand."[12] *Religion* referred to genuine practices of worship. Thus, there is a big difference between the claims that Christianity is true religion and that Christianity is *the* true religion. The claim that Christianity is true religion is compatible with a Muslim claim that Islam is true religion.

In Augustine's time, the life of the monk became the most dramatic way of following Christ and practicing religion. The monk was said to "enter religion" and henceforth to live the "religious life."[13] To this day in the Roman Catholic Church, the "religious life" means the lives of monks and nuns. For a thousand years, *religion* referred to a set of practices that every individual is obliged to perform and is found in its purest form in a monastery.

Thomas Aquinas, a member of the Order of Preachers, relied on Cicero's definition of *religion* as "offering service and ceremonial rites to the superior nature that men call divine." Thomas treats religion under the virtue of justice as the debt that humans owe to God.[14] Thomas was open to learning from Jewish and Muslim scholars, but he could not have entertained the idea that they represented alternate religions. There could only be one set of practices that were (true) religion. The Christian way was the culmination of history, and the gospel of Jesus Christ laid out the path to follow for every human being. The Christian Church was the instrument for the spread of true religion.

Toward the end of the Middle Ages, there was the beginning of a use of language that could suggest that true religion exists in other forms than were recognized in official Christendom. Marsilio Ficino published *On Christian Religion* in 1474. It is not a book about "the Christian religion" as opposed to other religions. The title refers to the Christ-oriented nature of human religiousness: "Every religion has something good in it; as long as it is directed toward God, the creator of all things, it is a true Christian religion."[15] The most daring thinker of the fifteenth century was Nicholas of Cusa. He starts from the inexactness of all human knowledge. In referring to the "one religion," he means "the unattainable truth about God . . . of which all existing belief systems are but shadowy reflections."[16]

Tragically, however, when the sixteenth-century Reformation began, the competition was for the one true religion. Martin Luther and John Calvin, as much as their Roman Catholic counterparts, assumed that only one set of practices was true Christian religion. Leaders on both sides somehow squared killing heretics with the Christian message of love. Religious warfare is likely to be the bloodiest when it is between two groups that share most of the same beliefs while each group sees the other as a corrupting force from within what is shared. A disloyal brother is treated as demonic.

The first great step in intra-Christian tolerance is signaled by a reference to "Catholic and Protestant religions" in the 1560s.[17] This usage was shortlived. By the early seventeenth century, Catholic and Protestant became variations on the Christian religion. The important implication in the reference to "Catholic and Protestant religions" was that the term *religion* was utterly changed in meaning. Instead of religion being the true worship of God, *religion* was now available as a term to describe a people or an institution. By 1622 Hugo Grotius's *On the Truth of (the) Christian Religion* no longer refers to Christian religion as true worship but rather that "*the* Christian religion *teaches* the true worship of God."[18]

As Catholic and Protestant were being folded into a single religion called Christianity, there was now a language that recognized Jews and Muslims as having a share in the term religion(s). How far to extend *religion* was a problem then and remains a subject for debate. Hindus, for example, obviously engage in practices that fit under the earlier meaning of religion, but Hinduism does not seem to be a religion. The same can be said of other traditional ways that arose in Asia and Africa. The Christian control of the term *religion* for more than a millennium remains a shadow in its uses today.

As is usually the case with radically different meanings of a word, the second meaning of religion did not entirely replace the first.[19] The second meaning is capable of encompassing the first but not vice-versa. The result is that "a religion" such as Christianity contains practices of Christian religion but much else besides that can hardly be called religious. It may scandalize some people that the Christian religion inescapably includes politics and economics as well as moral and artistic elements. Reformers are often intent on purifying their religion of any extraneous influences, but if a religion is at all successful in spreading beyond a small group, it will include more than religion. Some individuals will come to occupy offices of authority and the group is on the way to becoming an institution with a political and economic structure.

That fact about institutions does not mean reform of a religion is impossible or undesirable. But "reform" can only change the form of the organization not get rid of the form. This fact may be frustrating to radical reformers within a religion, but it is the basis of hope for other insiders and for most outsiders. Genuine reform of a religious tradition has a wide scope of possibilities for changing the relation between its religious elements and its political and economic elements. A religion, while preserving its main religious elements, could change from a force for violence to a supporter of peace, and from an obstacle in the way of human rights to being a main supporter.

Inter-religious dialogue and cooperation between religions require patience because movement is bound to be slow. Each religious tradition has its own distinctive language that has to be examined word by word. When two religions share the same term, that fact can be the basis of mutual understanding. It can also be the cause of conflict because the sharing is almost never mutual. One group takes over a word from a group that had previously exercised exclusive control. The older religion is understandably resentful of what it considers a theft of its heritage. The younger religion is either oblivious of the problem or thinks that the older religion should be grateful that its language has been extended beyond its previously limited setting.

Every religion considers itself unique, not an assemblage of pieces that can be interchanged with other religions. It conceives of itself as the bearer of an ultimate truth about human life. When conflicts arise, the tendency is to turn inward and put up stronger walls to defend its particularity. The crucial need today is to build trust between groups so that differences do not mean that one of them has to be destroyed in order for the other to flourish. A conversation about sameness and difference can lead each group to look more deeply into its own tradition to find a more universalistic reading of the whole tradition. "The aim is not only mutual understanding, but mutual self-understanding and mutual transformation."[20]

Within every religious tradition, there is acknowledgment that it is not (yet) the final truth. Of course, that aspect of the tradition does not get as much emphasis as the claim to be true religion. There is a tendency to fill in the gap between what would be a true universality and the intention of a group to be universal. By taking over all the best religious words, one group does not leave other groups space to breathe. It is not necessarily intolerant for Christians to claim that "Christ is the way" provided that they admit both that many Christians do not perfectly follow that way and that other religions might have a different language than Christians do for pointing toward the universal.

The secular meaning of "religious tolerance" is most often built on the assumption that when the outer trappings are stripped away, every religion is essentially the same. The modern project of tolerance was signified by the invention of the terms *deism* and *theism*. The two terms were at first interchangeable.[21] By the eighteenth century, deism had acquired the status of a religion. It owed its origin to a stripped down Christianity in which a supreme being gave a fillip to the universe and then withdrew to the heavens, appearing again only when the individual met his maker.

Deism was never a serious competitor to religious traditions with their profusion of details about daily practice and feelings. Deism was the first of many attempts to find an ideology that would replace traditional religion. It was based, as Nicholas Lash writes, "on the belief that nothing of unique value is embedded in tradition or history."[22] The substitutes have usually been devised by philosophical or scientific thinkers who did not have much of a feel for the actual practice of religion.

Theism went a very different route from deism. Instead of fighting traditional religions, it embraced them.[23] Whereas deism was based exclusively on reason and therefore excluded all claims to a divine revelation, *theism* became a generic term for religions that were thought to have an intelligible core. Each of the traditional religions was allowed to add its own distinctive message from god or gods on the condition that this message be kept private and not interfere in society's politics. The term *faith* took on new prominence in meaning an individual choice situated in the believer's mind next to reason. The believer and the nonbeliever could cooperate because of the agreement that reason was the guide for public policies while faith is a private affair.

The term *revelation* also acquired an importance that it had not previously had. The Latin-derived *revelation* is a translation of the Greek *apocalypse*. The idea of apocalypse/revelation was of a final judgment at the end of time. Early in its history, Christianity domesticated the idea of revelation to mean church teaching that came directly from God. But the Christian churches have never succeeded in completely controlling revelation/apocalypse as the announcement of the end of time. In theism, each of the traditional religions was allowed a claim not to *divine* revelation but to have its own revelation, a Christian revelation for Christians, a Jewish revelation for Jews, a Muslim revelation for Muslims. Thus, Christian faith was directed to a "Christian revelation," a term that did not exist before the sixteenth century.

To the extent that the religions accepted their private space with its private beliefs, they could get along with secular governments. Religions could also avoid wars among themselves. But it also meant that neither a single religion nor a group of religions could effectively support public policies. In the 1960s and 1970s, there began a worldwide movement to "deprivatize" religion.[24] Some of the world's major religions began to challenge the private and marginal role that had been assigned to religion. It is not yet clear whether the overall effect will be positive or negative for secular society.

A striking example in the United States was the resurfacing of evangelical religion, which after the Scopes trial in 1925 the (northern) news media had declared dead. At the time of Jimmy Carter's election in 1976, the news media were astounded to discover that there were tens of millions of citizens who called themselves born-again Christians. During the 1970s the Roman Catholic Church, possessing a new found confidence in its American credentials, also entered more aggressively into the political arena. The fact that human rights became an issue at the time of religion's refusal to remain private is more than a coincidence. Religion as a public factor will either be an obstacle to human rights or an important ally in the movement for human rights.

Religious Education

If religion and religions can go either way in relation to human rights, then education for an understanding of religion is an imperative. The sad fact is that in no part of the world can one find what could genuinely qualify as religious education. The term is occasionally used by some groups, but the comprehensiveness that is needed for an adequate religious education is everywhere lacking.

Religious education, like the rest of effective education, begins at birth. Parents convey an attitude to religion, especially through their own example, which infants and young children assimilate. Long before the child can exercise its own reason, it has simple but profound reactions to the universe in which it finds itself. Open-minded parents today might wish to let the child develop with a neutral attitude to religion until the child can decide on its own. But the best that the parents can do is simply be honest and not try creating an artificial world either of beliefs or no beliefs. Most young children experience the death of someone they know. When a small child asks where grandma has gone, the response should be in whatever terms make sense to the parent and that does not close off exploration of a variety of beliefs by the child at a later time.

The practice of a person's religion and the existence of a plurality of religions present an unusual challenge to the human intellect. Religion as an academic subject should be postponed at least until senior high school and the university. Consider as a parallel to religion the place of psychology in education. A child is immersed in psychology from earliest childhood, and it is important that adult teachers have some familiarity with the academic field of psychology, but we do not offer courses comparing Freud and Jung in the third grade. Concepts for understanding religion and religions are at least as complicated as those in psychology.

A comprehensive religious education would deal with both meanings of religion, that is, the practice of *religion* and the study of *religions*. A religious community is the proper setting for educating members in the particular practices and beliefs of the group. In contrast, a public or state school is the most appropriate setting for the teaching and study of religions, that is, for examining the phenomenon of religion as it exists in a variety of institutions. Unfortunately, the United States is nowhere close to sorting out the issue. A comment by one Supreme Court Justice that distinguished between "teach religion" and "teach about religion" quickly became unshakeable orthodoxy, but it simply confused the issue. Courses in state schools did not need permission to teach about religion. History, sociology, or psychology cannot avoid referring to religion and religions. But the implied equation of "teach religion" with teaching a Christian (Jew or Muslim) how to practice the Christian (Jewish or Muslim) way of life makes no sense.[25] A Christian community does not "teach religion"; it shows the Christian how to practice a Christian way of life.

It is not surprising that until recently the possibility and the need for religious education were not evident. Each religious group did its own intramural education through immersing its members in the religious practices of their particular religion. Reflection on those practices and the history of the group produced teachings or doctrine. Whether or not a particular teaching conflicted with the teaching of other groups was irrelevant or unknown. Particular teachings might be implicitly hostile to a closely related group, and when the two groups on occasion were forced to confront one another, the resulting conflict could be passionate and bloody.

From the eighteenth century onward in the West, it was assumed that religion was on the way to disappearing. With religion's disappearance, there would obviously be no need for religious education. The irony is that this assumption reached a culmination in the 1960s when it was declared that "god is dead" and that "secularity" had replaced all remnants of the sacred. Many social scientists were caught by surprise when religion erupted all over the world in the 1970s. Some of these religious groups were new, but many others were traditional groups that had been quietly waiting for the right circumstances.

The term "religious education" would not have been needed except for the recognition of the value of understanding religions different from one's own. It is not the "first language" of any religious group, but it is a needed second language for talking to other religious groups. Of course, a full-blown language could not come into existence at one moment or be produced by one religious group.

The term "religious education" was first used by Unitarians in the United States toward the end of the nineteenth century. That is not surprising in that Unitarians think of themselves as the forward edge in the unifying of all religions. Thomas Jefferson thought that the whole country would be Unitarian, but he did not reckon with the strength of evangelical Protestantism. Unitarianism, while remaining the religion of a small group, has nudged the larger religious groups toward understanding and cooperation.[26]

The term "religious education" came into use with the founding of the Religious Education Association in 1903. The founders of the organization were largely motivated by the liberal Protestantism of the day and were looking for a replacement for the Sunday school, which had carried the burden of Protestant education in the nineteenth century. However, the new organization was open to Catholics and Jews, as well as to Protestants of every denomination. The admirable ideal of the REA was to bring a religious dimension to education and an educational dimension to religion. That was to be done by professionalizing education in churches and bringing professional religious educators into the state schools.[27] More than a century after the founding of the Religious Education Association, the United States still lacks any concerted efforts at religious education in its state schools or in other public venues where widespread religious dialogue might occur.

While the United States was gaining no ground in establishing a meaning for religious education, the United Kingdom gave a legal meaning to the term "religious education" in its Education Act of 1944. Like the founders of the Religious Education Association in the United States, the forward-looking men who composed the law in England were aware that the existing range of religions in the country was narrow, but they recognized that the future of the UK might be religiously more diverse.[28] They correctly sensed that religious education should include practice and study. A religious ceremony at the beginning of the school day was much more feasible in the UK than in the United States. In the UK, both the religious ceremony and the study of religion focused on the Christian nature of the country.

The situation in the UK suddenly changed with the emigration of large numbers of Asians and Africans from countries of the former empire. If religious education were to exist in practice, it had to be open to a wide range of religions. In the 1960s, through the leadership of John Hull at the University of Birmingham, a curriculum more deserving of the name "religious education" emerged though not without controversy.[29] Since then the British have generally led the way in giving substance to the term "religious education." The men and women working in this area struggle against a good amount of ignorance and prejudice. They cannot carry the whole burden of establishing an effective religious education. In the past decade, British religious educators have joined with some of their continental colleagues to raise the issues of religious education in the Council of Europe and beyond.[30] Their resources are very limited for what is now urgently needed in the whole world.

Christian-Jewish Relations

The study of religion in general can never produce more than generalities that will not prevent misunderstandings and conflicts between actual religions. It is necessary to discuss particular religions in detail. To understand religion, one must understand religions. No one is a master of all religions, but it is a help to look at two religions for understanding each of them. For the possibility that religions might converge in a support of human rights, the relation between Christian and Jewish religions is a good starting point. These two siblings have been linked for two millennia. The third sibling, Islam, will be discussed below to complete the picture of three traditions that trace their origin to a single individual known as Abraham, Avraham, or Ibrahim.

If a visitor from another planet were to examine Jewish and Christian religions, he or she would find them very similar. They agree in their basic outlook and most of their teachings. The visitor would be puzzled at the terrible conflict that has characterized the relation between Jews and Christians throughout the centuries. Jews and Christians have badly understood each other; their misunderstandings only worsen the rest of the world's misunderstanding of both religions. Any group that claims that God spoke to them and that they hold the key to all human history are likely to be looked upon as arrogant and dangerous. The modern world looks skeptically at all exclusivisms, and it holds equality to be the highest ideal. If Jews and Christians would stop fighting each other, they could concentrate on clarifying the logic that each of them embodies, and they could cooperate in their common mission of striving for a just world.

In the last half century, there has been amazing progress in overcoming the enmity of centuries and in beginning the long road toward mutual understanding. The patient work of a few Jewish and Christian scholars has spread tolerance if not yet comprehension within their respective communities. The key moment on the Christian side was the change of attitude represented by the Second Vatican Council in the 1960s that in turn reflected a change in Protestant-Catholic relations. Many Jews were not thrilled at the way the discussion of Judaism went during the Vatican Council, but the conclusion was clear: a thorough repudiation of the "Christ killer" tradition and a recognition of Judaism as a way of salvation that does not need Christian proselytizing.[31] That was the needed beginning. Christian theology, however, is saturated with assumptions that are implicitly anti-Jewish. It will take many decades of conversations before Christians can recognize what bothers Jews about Christian theology.

Jews, for reasons of survival, have usually had a better understanding of Christianity than the understanding of Jews by Christians. Christians have assumed that they had knowledge of Judaism because they are familiar with what Christians call the Old Testament. Jews have to make a special study to acquire knowledge of the Christians' New Testament; in recent decades, some Jewish scholars have done that.[32] Most Jews are likely to have an attitude to Christianity that is based on the experience of how Christians practice their religion. The two groups find it difficult to see how similar is the logic of their belief systems: a particular group singled out by divine election to be a model for humanity by listening to and living according to divine instruction. Each has tended to see the other as narrow minded and exclusivist in contrast to the all-embracing outlook of their own group.

Emil Fackenheim, a thoughtful Jewish philosopher, could write, "Judaism is 'universalistic' for it teaches that the righteous of all nations enter the Kingdom of Heaven. Christianity is 'particularistic' for it bars from the Kingdom all unsaved non-Christians, no matter how great their righteousness."[33] The best that one can say of this accusation is that it is a simple reversal of what Christians have said of Jews. No doubt one can find Christians who think that all non-Christians go to hell. But from the earliest years of Christianity, it has been rather obvious that an all-loving God and a condemnation of the righteous do not go together. "Christ-church-sacraments" were believed necessary for those who heard the truth, but God must have other ways for those who do not have that opportunity.[34]

The "extraordinary route" to salvation was not well articulated especially when it was supposed that the Christian movement would soon spread to the whole world. It took a long while before it became clear that "light to the nations" was a better description of the church than "the ark of salvation." Any thoughtful Christian can now see that the Christian Church, on the basis of its own doctrine, is the extraordinary route. The Christian Church is necessarily a particular human institution. No church or religion is catholic or universal. Roman Catholics sometimes forget to use the adjective before *catholic*. The Christian Church in all of its branches aspires to universality while it also has to recognize that an earthly church is an imperfect reflection of a heavenly church (or "kingdom of God").[35]

It is ironic that a Jew would accuse Christianity of being particularistic because the obvious failing of the church was that in separating itself from its Jewish roots it lost its particular grounding and saw itself as universal. Without a sure particularity, the claim to universality only results in generality, that is, conceptual abstractions rather than a reality that transcends time and space. This movement away from the particular was not a one-time failing. The temptation to think that one is speaking of every human being when in fact one is only talking about an abstract humanity regularly occurs. Fortunately for the church, reforms have been possible that, as Martin Buber pointed out, always include a return to the Jewish roots of Christianity.[36] That return mainly consists in refocusing on the teachings of the Jew, Jesus of Nazareth. Today's genuine Christian-Jewish dialogue, perhaps for the first time in history, holds the possibility of a Christian reform like none previously. There are, however, no guarantees of success.

A Christian reform that would establish a particularity that points toward the universal, while it is in dialogue with other religious bodies that point to the universal, is important to the cause of human rights. The literature on human rights tends to be strongly antichurch, which may be understandable, but human rights without Christian support lose what could be a great ally. Perhaps as important, the Enlightenment as a basis of human rights is misunderstood unless there is recognition of what secular philosophy borrowed from the post-Reformation period of Christianity while it was reacting against Christianity.

In the late Middle Ages, "true Christian religion" referred not to "a religion" but to particular rituals and moral practices. When the Christian Church lost its exclusive control of the term *religion*, the pointing toward universality could have been given a boost. At the time, however, Christians and Jews (as well as Muslims), instead of presenting a united front in the cause of dignity, justice, and peace saw themselves as deadly competitors. In reaction, secular philosophy tried to leave behind religious squabbles and affirm universal principles of humanity. Secular philosophy has overtones of a religion of humanity and the literature on human rights tends to be secular sermons. Church sermons are bearable so long as they are directed to a community of people who profess the same beliefs. Secular sermons that profess not to need a community of believers can be banal and ineffective discourse.

I use as an example of the preaching of secular sermons the later writings of Richard Rorty. Rorty was both a supporter of human rights and an aggressive opponent of church doctrine as he understood it. He identified Christianity with everything that he was opposed to, such as metaphysics, natural law, and objective truth. He accurately pinpointed the Christian temptation to claim to speak in universal terms. However, in proposing that human rights should start from sympathy with the suffering, Rorty was more in league with Christian belief than he realized, but his own view of Christianity as a variation on Plato and Kant leaves out most of the story.

Rorty writes that "for Christians, sanctity is not achieved as long as obligation is felt more strongly to one child of God than to another; invidious contrasts are to be avoided on principle."[37] He is right about *invidious* contrasts but distinctions among children of God are clearly recognized in the New Testament and by Christians. The parables of Jesus are unvaryingly about particular people who need help. Nowhere in the Bible does it say to love humanity or to love individuals without noticing their age, sex, or nationality.

Jesus took the summary of his teaching from the Hebrew Bible: "Love your neighbor as yourself" is the test of any profession to love God. When he was asked, "Who is my neighbor?" Jesus responded with parables that are clear: my neighbor is whoever is in need and can be helped by my actions.[38] Dietrich Bonhoeffer pointed out that Nietzsche was actually close to the spirit of the Christian gospel in writing: "Do I advise you to love your neighbor? I advise you rather to shun your neighbor and to love who is furthest from you." Bonhoeffer comments that "my neighbor may well be the one who is furthest from me."[39]

If taken seriously, loving my neighbor can put strains on family and tribal relations. Jesus demanded the nearly impossible: "Love your enemies; do good to those who hate you." Anyone who claims to be following Jesus of Nazareth has to reckon with a demand not merely to profess love of humanity but to act in support of those humans who are suffering, especially the stranger and the enemy. The Christian message was one that called for hope and love. The first Christian communities tried to embody the message by living simply according to the gospel. The early church succeeded by a combination of social security and brilliant speculation about the universe. Poor people, widows, and children were cared for both economically and by having a meaning to their lives.[40]

The teaching of Jesus was firmly rooted in the Hebrew Bible where the test of the community is its treatment of the stranger. But to outsiders, Jewish religion may seem particularistic. The phrase "chosen people" points to the claim of difference by one small group. The belief of Jews is that God spoke to us, and we are God's partner in "mending the world." How can Jews claim to be "universalistic" in their beliefs? Here is a place where the double meaning of *uniqueness* comes into play. Uniqueness can mean either difference based on a process of increasing exclusiveness or difference based on a process of increasing openness to the other. The history of ancient Israel shows a tension between these two claims to uniqueness.

The Hebrew Bible is a strange kind of epic in which the people repeatedly fail to understand their great vocation. The community under threat turns inward and asserts that "our god" will save us. The prophets of ancient Israel (as well as their modern successors) must constantly remind the people that God is the God of the universe. One way that the prophets do so is by suddenly reversing the language of "the (chosen) people" and "the nations." At the most crucial moment when God parts the sea and allows the Jews to escape from the Egyptian soldiers who are then drowned, the angels in heaven begin to sing. But God says, "Stop your singing; do you not know that my people are dying."[41] In the prophetic tradition, prayer is first for the Jews but not as opposed to the nations. "I beseech thee that thou mayest redeem Israel. And if you willest it not, redeem the gentiles."[42]

Throughout all of history, the question for Jews has been whether to separate the community from the rest of humankind or whether to identify the Jewish community with all of God's people. Jewish life "proves" its claim by devotion to the cause of justice for all humankind. It is not a coincidence that so many leaders in the movement for political, economic, and human rights have been Jews.

The Jews did not come to belief in (one) God by reasoning about being and unity.[43] The belief came from digging deeper into the community's experience and concluding that "our God" is not our possession but the God of all. Starting with Moses, the belief moved forward and backward. Abraham was in the back story, then Noah, and finally Adam. At each step, a wider view of humanity was correlated with a more unified view of creation. The Book of Genesis is the end not the beginning of the story wherein God spoke to the other animals and said, "Let us make man in our own image." God started with one man Adam, the earthling, who already included woman.[44] The Talmud asks, "Why was only a single man created?" The answer: "to teach you that for him who destroys one man, it is regarded as if he had destroyed all men, and that for him who saves one man, it is regarded as though he had saved all men."[45]

Jewish religion at its best is thus a story of the uniqueness of each human being who potentially includes all human beings and all creation. "The divine sovereign stamps the image of the first man on each human being, and yet each human being is unique. When we are fully present to one another in dialogue our unique selves are revealed in the divine image."[46] This belief has been severely tested through the endless crises of the Jewish people. The community's struggle is to make sense of suffering, vocation, and justice. It started with Moses, who according to the Talmud, "pleaded with the Lord to reveal the final truth.' The Lord replied: 'There are no pre-existent final truths in doctrine or law. The truth is the considered judgment of the majority of authoritative interpreters in every generation.'"[47] Later, when two schools of interpretation appealed to God to settle their debate, God replied, "The opinion of these and the opinion of those are both the words of the Living God."[48] It is difficult to be a Jewish heretic.

Jews and Christians should be able to agree that the "messianic age" is still to come, and its achievement depends in part on the struggle for human justice. Both Jewish and Christian traditions are clear in their belief that every human being is created by God and therefore has a divine stamp deserving of respect. Jews and Christians subscribe to the same basis of ethics: a love of one neighbor that is rooted in the love of God. Today's world in which one can hardly avoid knowing of the needs of people all over the world makes much clearer what the love of neighbor can demand.

Although it is important to emphasize the sameness in Jewish and Christian traditions as a basis for their cooperation, it is equally important not to collapse their difference. A younger tradition always has a tendency to absorb most of the previous tradition and thereby assume a new unity. In this case, the terrible conflicts and persecutions throughout many centuries would seem to make obvious that the reality is two traditions not one. That reality not withstanding, some people at the end of the nineteenth century came up with a peculiar name for a single tradition: Judeo-Christian. The Jewish contribution is reduced to a modifying of Christian.

This adjective is nearly always used before the term *tradition*; rarely does anyone refer to Judeo-Christian religion. The invention of the term was not the result of religious interest. It was an attempt to abstract some ideas related to the success of Western countries in dominating other people and nature. The people who coined the term "Judeo-Christian tradition" did not seem to know much about either Jewish tradition or Christian tradition. A detailed knowledge of the two religions was not thought necessary for the origin of ideas about the autonomy of man and the rise of modern science.[49]

The term *Judeo-Christian* did not have a wide use until the Second World War. It had some favor on the political left for indicating a tolerant if not ecumenical outlook. Hitler produced by reaction a wider use of the term; his assault on the Jews was interpreted by some Christians as an attack on "Christian civilization."[50] Since World War II, the term *Judeo-Christian* has shifted to the right and is now often attached to the word *morality* by people who believe that the civilized world is collapsing. The objection to the term *Judeo-Christian* is that it obstructs a needed dialogue between Jews and Christians. That dialogue might lead to greater understanding of both sameness and difference in the two traditions.

Like the Jews, Christians did not speculate about a being called God. Instead, they worked out an extraordinarily complex understanding of the divine and human that cannot be subsumed under a generic term such as monotheism. They were sometimes attacked for having three gods, which can be suggested by both their rhetoric and practice. They began with their relation to a more than human Jesus and his relation to his father in heaven. They eventually devised a language of relations within God or, as some of the Greek fathers of the church said, a God whose nature is communion.[51] In inventing or refashioning terms for the Christ and for God, they produced new ways to talk about the human, especially the distinction between *person* as *who* one is and *nature* as *what* one is.

Starting with the New Testament itself, a picture was drawn by Christian thinkers that brought the length and breadth of the world into a unity. All men meet in the "Second Adam" who provides a restart for a wayward human race. All of history and the entire universe are centered on this "story of salvation." The unborn, the living and the dead are swept up into a grand unity. The humans are not at the top of the world; they are rather far down in the hierarchy of spiritual beings, but God, for whatever mysterious reasons, is lenient with them. Death was said to come into the world through sin; death it was believed was now overcome as will be shown at the last judgment.

The possibility of the Christian Church joining with Judaism and other religions to support human rights depends on its understanding that creation-revelation-redemption is a process that occurs in the present. This belief can be found within its own Christian tradition but probably will not be recognized without Jewish help.[52] It is only by attentiveness to the world about us and by respect for all forms of life that one arrives at knowledge of the creator. Creation refers to the continuous dependence of the creature on divine power. Divine creativity is expressed through "secondary causes" that have their own genuine power. This belief provided support for the rise of science and technology in the West and is fully compatible with the idea of human rights.

Muslim-Christian Relations

A second relation between particular religious traditions that can be revealing of both religions is the one between Christians and Muslims. It might be more logical to comment on the relation between Muslims and Jews because Islam and Judaism are structurally very similar. Their approaches to God have more in common than does either of them with the Christian religion. My reason for choosing Christian-Muslim relations is the threat to world peace that is implied by a conflict between these two religions. Conversely, progress in their mutual understanding would give support to human rights in every part of the world. The relation between any two of the three religions that claim to go back to Abraham always has the shadow of the third in the background.

A good reason for Christians to study Islam is to find out how Jews feel when they are placed within a Christian understanding of history. The Christian-Muslim relation reverses the Christian role; the younger sibling becomes the older one. Would Christians like to be included in a "Christeo-Muslim tradition?" A Christian is likely to be irritated by a Muslim explanation of the true meaning of the gospel or by the claim that "the Qur'an, while affirming the truth of all previous revelations, itself comprises all truth for the whole of mankind for all time."[53]

A Christian should be able to recognize this argument because it is one that Christianity has regularly employed. The claim is that whatever truths there are in other religions are included in Muslim (Christian) religion. The intention to be a universal religion is identified with actual universality. "The Qur'an is thus a universal possession and inheritance; its message is directed to the whole of mankind."[54] Any non-Muslim would be quick to point out that being directed to mankind and being a possession of mankind are not the same thing.

Islam, by its claim, is in a position to offend just about everyone who does not subscribe to the Qur'an. However, a text of the Qur'an often cited is that "there shall be no compulsion in religion" (2:257). While Muslims wish to spread the truth everywhere they claim only to be God's instrument: "The Truth is from your Lord; wherefore let him who will, believe, and let him who will, disbelieve" (18:30). Muslims have been fiercely opposed to any missionary work directed at Muslims, but they also have a better record than Christianity in not trying to impose their religion on others. For several centuries in medieval Spain, Christians and Jews lived in relative peace under Muslim rule. Although this *convivencia* has sometimes been romanticized, it still provides hope that cooperation is possible.[55]

The present conflict between Christianity and Islam is not mainly one of religious doctrines. The conflict is in large part political. Much to the surprise of Christians, Islam seemed to appear from nowhere as a political force in the world. Until the second half of the twentieth century, most Christians assumed, in the words of Alexis de Tocqueville, that "Islam will not be able to hold its power long in ages of enlightenment and democracy, while Christianity is destined to reign in such ages, as in all others."[56] The religion that was usually called Mohammedanism was thought to have disappeared in all but a few backward places. Moslems were no longer the threatening presence at the gates of Christian Europe. In the United States, *Arab* and *Moslem* were interchangeable terms, and for some people they still are.

Islam began to appear as a political/religious force in the postcolonial era in Asia, Africa, and especially the Middle East. The United States and the Soviet Union were wrestling for control of the world. For a while, Soviet communism seemed destined to lead the third world. But the quasireligious ideology of Marxism was outdone by the actual religious belief of millions of Muslims.[57] In 1969, Muammar Qaddafi achieved in Libya what he called Islamic socialism based on Islamic law, Shari'a. In the early 1970s, Western experts tended to see only nationalism and pan-Arabism in the Middle East; the experts generally missed the resurgence of Islam.

In 1979, Western countries looked on with puzzled disbelief when Iran turned to Ayatollah Khomeini, a national hero in exile, to lead the overthrow of the Shah Mohammad Reza Pahlavi. The shah's close ties to the United States made that country the most direct opponent of the Islamic revolution. Still, people in the United States were unprepared when

Iran seized U.S. hostages and goaded the United States with cries of "death to America." An ignorance of Islam by most people in the United States included most of the people in the government. It was said during this period that everyone in Washington was speed reading the Qur'an.

That situation had improved but not by much when the United States suffered its traumatic attack in 2001. Islam had finally got the attention of the United States, but unfortunately the religion was identified by many people with terrorism. For a few weeks in September 2001, it seemed that United States leaders were thinking carefully about what comes next. Then the United States decided that more might was the answer. The United States went to war not with a country but on a country or several countries for harboring terrorists. Europe took the other route by looking for a better understanding of what was moving people in the Muslim world. Its efforts at religious education, however, have been overshadowed by fear of attacks from without and fear of a growing Muslim population within Europe.[58]

The United States, as a country proud of its religious diversity and freedom, should have been better prepared than European countries for including a Muslim population and understanding Islam. From its origin in the sixteenth century, America was a dream of the promised land. The British American version of the dream was Protestant, but eventually Catholics and Jews could fit under a biblical umbrella. Other religions have had a difficult time becoming Americanized. The presence of millions of Muslims now in the United States is the greatest challenge that the nation's freedom of religion has had to meet. The test of religious education's future is whether Islam is accepted as a full partner. So far the progress has been halting. Politicians who exploit fear and ignorance are no help to finding peaceful cooperation.

Politics and religion (in its older sense) are inevitably mixed. The term *Islam* can refer both to a set of practices and to an historical-social-political institution. When Muslims say "Islam," they usually mean the first; when Christians say "Islam," they are usually looking at the second. In the United States, the relation of politics and religion is supposedly handled under the rubric of "separation of church and state." This metaphor, which was given legal standing in the 1940s, is European language that has never been very helpful in the United States and was avoided by the country's founders. It fails to address how religion, in its older sense, might be related to government in both the United States and in countries that are predominantly Muslim.[59]

In the United States, churches are excluded from having an official standing in state or federal governments, but every other influence of religion is left to ad hoc arrangements. Some of the Christian or Jewish influence on the government, especially through the idea of America, may be for the good, but it deserves an examination that it does not receive. A U.S. blindness to the pervasiveness of religion in its own country leads to criticism and misunderstanding of countries where the presence of Islam is in the open. Islam—the practice of the religion—can be a positive support of a government's stability.

Human Rights Watch in its *World Report 2012* maintains "it is important to nurture the rights-respecting elements of political Islam while standing firm against repression in its name." That statement was severely criticized by a group of women's organizations that said "you fail to call for the most basic guarantee of rights—the separation of religion from the state." In his reply to the women's groups, Kenneth Roth, Executive Director of Human Rights Watch, correctly pointed out that "there is no internationally recognized right to separate religion from the state." That is, Human Rights Watch is focused on human rights; the separation of religion and state is not a human right. The women's organizations and Human Rights Watch actually agree on the need to bring pressure on the governments of Muslim countries for the recognition of women's rights.[60]

Human Rights Watch is certainly not denying the dangers in mixing politics and religion. The helpful word *Islamist* has been coined to describe people who create a dangerous mixture of political ideology overlaid with religious justification. The word *Christianist* would describe a similar phenomenon within the Christian religious world. In much of the Muslim world, the United States is viewed as the chief Christianist country. If a U.S. president is not aware of the religious connotations of America, the military exploits of the United States in defense of America take on a Christianist character.

George W. Bush, immediately after the bombings in 2001, referred to a *crusade* against terrorism.[61] He was shocked at the criticism he received, but at least he wisely omitted the word in his subsequent address to Congress. Bush had reason to be surprised because presidents had routinely used the term *crusade* to describe U.S. wars, oblivious of the connotations of the term for Jews and Muslims.[62] *Crusade* is a word that not even most Christians today would proudly use.[63] People in the United States are surprised to find that much of the Muslim world considers the wars of the United States to be Christianist crusades. The shift from George W. Bush to Barack Obama did much to change the image of the United States, but building trust between the United States and countries that are mainly Muslim might take generations.

There is no denying that there are individuals and groups within Islam today who use texts of the Qur'an as justification for terrorist acts. What is most striking about these individuals is that they are usually homegrown in the West. They are the alienated poor in London, Amsterdam, or New York who are often in rebellion against the Muslim practice of their parents. As Olivier Roy says, their distortion of Islam "thrives on the loss of cultural identity: the young radicals are indeed perfectly 'Westernized.'"[64] Political leaders in Europe and the United States are constantly surprised that terrorist youth have had the benefits of political freedom and access to western universities. A Christian-Muslim dialogue is not going to help much without other cultural changes to protect minority rights and to lessen intolerance against strangers.

From its beginning, Islam was destined to clash with Christianity and to a lesser extent with Judaism. The problem was not that the Qur'an is hostile to either of those religions. On the contrary, "God has established for you the same religion enjoined on Noah, on Abraham, on Moses, and on Jesus" (42:13). What is implied by Islam invoking the God of Jews and Christians is that a radical reform is needed, especially in what Christianity has done to its Jewish heritage. Islam is not a reform of the Christian religion; it is an alternative to Christianity in returning to the simpler, more personal categories of Semitic religion. W. Cantwell Smith, a Christian advocate of Christian-Muslim dialogue, once asked, "If Jesus were to return today, would he more easily recognize himself in Islam or in Christianity?"[65] Christians might ponder that question. Did the centuries of struggle to get a doctrine of the Christ obscure the powerful prophetic teaching of Jesus?

Muslims have no doubt that the "divinity of Christ" misconstrues Jesus and, even worse, it corrupts the idea of one God. "The Christians say that the Messiah is the Son of God . . . How they have perverted the truth" (9:30). In Christian history, as Jesus was more closely identified with God, a multitude of other mediators came to occupy the space between God and man. Not only reverence for the mother of Jesus, whom Muslims do revere, but praying to saints and a profusion of statues and images were a distraction from the one and only Allah. Even the buildings of the Christians acquired the name church which originally referred to a gathering of the faithful. In Islam, the mosque is not a consecrated building, and there is no priestly class to mediate between the community and the Holy One.[66]

From the Christian point of view, Islam has placed the whole of mediation in a book. According to Islam, the Qur'an, which means *recitation*, is not simply a book composed by human hands; it is a text revealed by God as a reflection of a heavenly Qur'an. The great Muslim thinker, Muhammad Iqbal, writes that "as reading and reciting Koran is a dialogue with God, the true speaker of the Word, the possibilities are as infinite as is God Himself."[67]

Muslim belief in the Qur'an as the word of God makes dialogue with Christians difficult. The Muslim characterization of Christianity as a "religion of the book" is inaccurate. Jesus, the Christ, is for Christians the word of God, occupying the place that the Qur'an has for Muslims.[68] For many liberal-minded Christians, Islam is the ultimate fundamentalism that closes the mind to rational thinking. There is a paradox, however, in the fact that Islam has been the source of so much of mathematical, scientific, and philosophical thinking in the past. Many Christians are unaware or dismissive of the fact that the Christian Middle Ages depended on Muslim learning and the Arabic translations of Greek philosophy.

The acceptance of a text literally can be the basis of meditations that lead to brilliant insights and a healthy discipline of life. Jewish, Christian, and Muslim religions are all mortgaged to the past. They need to find a link between texts written in the past and the problems that face them in the present. In each religion, but especially in Christianity, there are reformers who wish to eliminate texts that seem out of date. The alternative approach is to accept the text and delve more deeply into its meaning. The modern world is impatient with this approach and tends to categorize careful attention to the text as fundamentalism.

There are no formulas that can bring Christian and Muslim beliefs together. Nevertheless, both Christian and Muslim religions profess faith in the God of all humans. The Christian should have no problem with the Qur'an's statements that "We have granted honor to the children of Adam" or "Today we have enobled the human being" (17:70). Both the New Testament and the Qur'an are concerned with kindness to the stranger and looking after the needy wayfarer (4: 37).

Encounter with the other may remind each religion that its claim to universality has to be made through a transforming of the world toward justice for all. Both religions, while not the source of human rights, can legitimately say that their religion is consistent with and supportive of human rights.[69] A cooperative effort by these religions in the direction of peace and justice is their most effective declaration of human rights.

The Abrahamic Traditions[70] and Asian Traditions

I could continue the previous pattern by considering dialogues involving Buddhist, Hindu, Taoist, Confucian, Shinto, and other traditions. In addition to the fact that such a project would require a far lengthier treatment than is possible here, there is a certain logic to considering the sameness and difference in a comparison of Semitic and Asian religions. The starkest difference would be to say that the term *religion* simply does not apply in the East. One can leave open that question by referring to *tradition*, which has less baggage than the word *religion*.

The word *religion* is in fact used of Asian traditions because there are practices that have some obvious similarity to one or more of the religions traced to Abraham. Most Christians are probably surprised to find that Buddhist and Catholic monks have long had a lively dialogue, a fact that calls into question the routinely applied categories of theism and atheism. There are, of course, deep differences between Buddhism and Christianity. So far there has not been a widespread dialogue between the Christian tradition and the much older tradition that stems from Gautama, the Buddha. The lack of knowledge on both sides is a danger, but the door has not been closed to future dialogue.

The most relevant point about Asian religions is the frequent claim by outsiders that human rights is not a part of these traditions. However, the same would have to be said about Christian, Jewish, and Muslim traditions. It is true that the term *rights* has a strong foothold in Christian history, and it was the available language for the eighteenth-century declarations. But *human rights* is twentieth-century language that is still being filled out in the twenty-first century. The cherished political rights of the West are only one test of human rights. The question is not whether the East is willing to accept a Western idea of human rights but whether a cross-cultural and inter-religious dialogue might strengthen this new idea called human rights.

In the modern era, a philosophical tradition centered in Europe developed the idea of rights. This secular tradition still needs the help of deeper strands of the three Semitic religions and the still older Confucian, Taoist, Hindu, and Buddhist traditions. Perhaps before anyone can comment on the compatibility of human rights with Eastern traditions, there is a dialogue needed about respect for human beings in their relation to other beings. The environmental movement has brought out the fact that Eastern religions may have a wisdom that was prematurely dismissed in the Western revolution that pitted "man against nature."

The dividing line between East and West is often mistakenly thought to be the concept of uniqueness. Swami Prabhavananda writes that "a Hindu learns to respect every faith and every prophet but it is impossible for him to understand any religion that claims to be unique."[71] The idea of "Christian uniqueness" is mostly a nineteenth-century development from within Christianity as historians and anthropologists began to compare the Christian religion with others. Christians asserted that a unique God gave a unique revelation to a unique community; and in the supremely unique moment of history, God sent his "only begotten Son." To many people, no real comparisons seem possible.

Unique as an assertion of possession refers to a thing; what is mine is not yours. Christianity possesses unique doctrines. But as prophets in Jewish, Christian, and Muslim religions regularly reminded people who were in positions of power, God is not a thing that is in anyone's possession. The Bible and the Qur'an are not books that are possessed but are invitations and demands requiring actions. Even the Second Vatican Council acknowledged that bishops have to listen to the word spoken now before they can address the rest of the faithful.[72] As most of Christian tradition testifies, there is no *Christian* revelation that is unique to Christian history. Christian belief is in a *divine* revelation that Christians interpret by their response. That language not only allows but invites other interpretations of the divine revealing.

Christian theology in recent decades has been more reserved in claims to possess a unique Christian revelation. However, the term *unique* has become more insistently used as a description of Jesus Christ. It almost seems that the many titles that were traditionally asserted of Jesus have become summed up in the claim that Jesus Christ is unique. The claim can be a conversation stopper in inter-religious dialogue before participants have had an opportunity to explore their differences and similarities.

The uniqueness of Jesus need not be an insuperable obstacle to dialogue. Aloysius Pieris, a leader in Christian-Buddhist understanding, writes "that Jesus is unique is obvious even to Buddhists, just as Christians would hardly question the uniqueness of Gautama. Is not each of us unique? The issue is whether Jesus' uniqueness consists of his absoluteness as conveyed by certain Christological titles."[73] What Pieris is referring to is that the uniqueness of a person is based on relations; the more unique the person, the greater the openness to include more relations. The problem with talk about the uniqueness of Jesus Christ is that the person of Jesus can disappear into the idea of Christ. The Christians do possess a unique doctrine of the Christ.

That obscuring of the person of Jesus is the problem in Christian-Hindu relations when Jesus Christ is said to be the unique divine incarnation. The

Hindu objection to Christianity is that "a Hindu would find it easy to accept Christ as a divine incarnation and to worship him unreservedly, exactly as he worships Sri Krishna or another avatar of his choice. But he cannot accept Christ as the *only* Son of God. Those who insist on regarding the life and teachings of Jesus as unique are bound to have great difficulty in understanding them. Any avatar can be far better understood in the light of other great lives and teachings."[74] It is unlikely that Christians could accept avatar as a description of Jesus, but the rest of this description of a divine incarnation is compatible with Christian belief. That is, the uniqueness of Jesus can best be understood in the light of other great lives and teachings. Christians believe that Jesus's life is a "more unique incarnation" of the divine than other great lives; that belief could be a topic of fruitful conversation between Christians and Hindus.

The main point of these examples is that any religious believer might be challenged to examine his or her beliefs when confronted by sameness and difference in another religion. As in Jewish-Christian relations and in Roman Catholic-Protestant relations, the sameness that one hopes would encourage understanding and cooperation has often set off terrible conflict. Disagreements within the same family can generate passionate feelings of disloyalty. In some ways, it is easier for a Roman Catholic to talk to a Buddhist than to a Protestant or a Jew. The gap between Christians and Buddhists is simply a fact of life not the basis of a suspicion that one's interlocutor is unable or unwilling to accept the obvious truth. Nonetheless, there is much work to be done so that an initial acceptance of difference between Abrahamic and Asian traditions is complemented by some mutual understanding of similarities.

For human rights to be accepted and to flourish, a tolerance of religious differences is indispensable. Asian traditions are generally thought to be more tolerant than Jewish, Christian, and Muslim religions. The language of tolerance developed in European struggles with the diversity of religions. Religious conflicts are not unknown in the East, but they do not match the bloody religious wars that have afflicted Europe and the Middle East. Tolerance is a Western virtue because it became necessary for halting the persecution of one religious group by another. Dutch and English reformers provided relief to Europe and beyond. [75]

An effective tolerance cannot be based on the absence of belief or the assumption that beliefs are merely an outer coating that can be scraped off. Tolerance has to be based on respect for the beliefs of other people. Tolerance also has limits. As Karl Popper insists, "If we extend unlimited tolerance even to those who are intolerant, if we are not prepared to defend a tolerant society against the onslaught of the intolerant, then the tolerant will be destroyed, and tolerance with them."[76] Who sets those limits of tolerance is a crucial political issue, and where the line is set can change over time. But groups that are intent on doing violence to other groups need to be resisted if tolerance is to endure. Tolerance is not the final virtue, but it is a precondition for mutual understanding.

Western countries might learn from the more irenic traditions of the East while Asian religions might also learn from the European struggle to find an acceptable balance of the right to express one's own religion while not offending or coercing others. Asians might feel that is not their problem, but the issue has worldwide implications today.

People do not practice a religion unless they believe that it is true. When there are no serious competitors to the religion, the truth of the religion is taken for granted. But when the intramural language of a religious group is exposed to a wider audience it can sound outrageously narrow minded. The language is mainly intended for insiders to bolster their faith. When Christian writers said that "outside the church there is no salvation," they did not aim the teaching at non-Christians but at any Christian who might falter.

In today's world, it is nearly impossible to maintain a wall between the inner language of prayer and an outer language for political interaction. The language in the Good Friday liturgy that was meant for Catholic practice became a sore point in Catholic-Jewish relations. It is not an entirely new problem but one that has now become magnified and cannot be brushed aside. As the Lutheran scholar and bishop, Krister Standahl, once put it: "How can we sing our song to Jesus without telling dirty stories about everyone else."[77]

Hinduism is often cited as the most tolerant of all religions, and it is indeed deserving of praise for its acceptance of diversity. But to the extent that *Hindu* is the name of a single religion, it asserts its own singularity. Radhakrishnan says that in Hinduism all religions are "treated generously." A few pages later, he writes, "It is said that other scriptures sink into silence when the Vedanta appears . . . . The Vedanta is not a religion, but religion itself in its most universal and deepest significance."[78] Of course he means that it is Hindus who say that the Vedanta is religion itself in its most universal significance. People who are not Hindu do not find Hindu religion to be universal.

The tendency to slide from believing that one's religion is true to asserting or implying that it is *the* truth is a common human problem, not exclusively one that is Jewish, Christian, Muslim, or Hindu. A person would not be an active participant in a religion unless he or she believed it to be the best religious choice. What makes it the best for the believer includes the choice to participate in the religion and discover its many riches. Religious language is often misunderstood by outsiders as quasi-scientific statements, each of which can be investigated for its factual truth.

When a man says to his wife, "You are the most beautiful woman in the world," he is aware that he has not surveyed the other three and a half billion women. His profession of love is not meant to denigrate any other woman nor is he likely to suddenly discover he is wrong. What he perceives as most beautiful includes his own experience as the one who perceives. Over time he may cease to feel the love he once had, but that is because the relation has changed not because his scientific evidence was incorrect. As George Bernanos wrote, "One does not lose his faith; one ceases to shape his life by it."[79]

For a Christian, the Christ way is the best religious path just as the Buddha nature is true religion for a Buddhist. The two are clearly different but are not contradictory. Contradictions arise from statements; the opposite of a true statement is a false statement. But the opposite of a profound truth can be another profound truth. An initial aim of ecumenical dialogue is to change contradictory statements to contrary statements that are acceptable to both parties.

It is natural for any religious group whose intention is universality to praise people by bringing them under the umbrella of the group's ideal. The Roman Catholic theologian Karl Rahner was often criticized for the phrase "anonymous Christian," which he used as a way out of the seeming exclusivity of Christianity.[80] Rahner said that the term was directed at the complacency of Christians, a reminder that some people who are not churchgoers may be better examples of following the way of Christ than those who profess to be Christians. The phrase, said Rahner, is a "profound admission of the fact that God is greater than man and the Church."

When Rahner was asked whether he would accept being called by a Buddhist an "anonymous Buddhist," he said he had no problem with that.[81] Calling someone an "anonymous Christian" is the highest praise that Christians can formulate within the limits of Christian theology. It implies that people who call themselves Christian because they are church members have to examine whether they are Christian in the sense of following the way of the Christ. The possible misunderstanding of language such as "anonymous Christian" is avoided by not using the inner language of Christian theology as if it were directly transferable to every religious and secular situation.

Confucian tradition holds a special place in the history of Asia as well as being a tradition that the West has long been familiar with. Unfortunately, the familiarity did not always mean a depth of understanding. Many people have a stereotype of Confucianism as a series of epigrams (perhaps learned from Charley Chan movies) or as a code of obedience. Voltaire was a great enthusiast of Confucius, but Voltaire's knowledge of Confucius was very limited. He held up Confucianism as a model of theism (belief in a supreme being) in contrast to ritualistic religions such as Buddhism.[82] Religion and morality did not become separate in the East as they did in Western enlightenment. While Confucianism is often said to be a moral rather than a religious tradition, that distinction might not be intelligible to Confucius and most of his followers. Whether or not Confucianism should be called a religion, the tradition is important for the human rights movement.

What is often the attitude of Western authors toward Asian traditions, and especially Confucianism, is that these traditions should be preserved because they are culturally important. Hahm Chaibong points out that "Confucians throughout history have espoused their philosophy because they thought it was 'true', not because it was Chinese or because it served some particularistic purpose." There has been a tendency to oppose Western liberalism's claim to universality with the particularity of Asian cultures. Confucianism is important because it defends values that are found in Western liberalism but on its own terms. And "one needs then to go a step further by showing that Confucianism also defends and preserves important values that liberalism ignores."[83]

Those values of Confucianism center on respect for the family and community in contrast to Western enlightenment's emphasis on the "autonomous individual" as the seat of values. The father as ruler of the family is not likely to find much support in Western countries today, but the world cannot get along without some form of family authority. Confucius said "only the wisest and the stupidest never change."[84] Confucian tradition did change over the centuries. What is called neo-Confucianism took on an authoritarian attitude that is not found in the earlier stratum. The contemporary Chinese government has tried to resurrect a Confucian authoritarianism for its own ends after previously denouncing the tradition.[85] Confucius saw his work as that of criticizing rulers for not following the "mandate of heaven." His work was not one of supporting the kind of political submissiveness that past or present rulers of China might prefer.[86]

The decline of ancient religious traditions would not necessarily be good news for a world that needs order, stability, and rationality. The contemporary Chinese government's invoking of neo-Confucianism results from a fear of newer religions that might be rebellious. The Falungong, for example, is a faith-healing millenarian sect that seems peaceful, but the Chinese government has brutally persecuted it.[87] In 1995, Japan, which appears to be a thoroughly secular country, experienced the effect of a utopian sect, the Aum Shinrikyo, when the group dropped deadly sarin gas in the Tokyo subway. The United States, which has the self-image of a secular country that controls religion, experiences regular outbursts of millenarian violence. The intellectual and political leaders in the United States never cease to be surprised that such things could happen in their secular country.

Conclusion

At their worst, ancient religious traditions consider their "chosenness" as proof of superiority and a license to oppress others. At their best, these traditions include the potential for reforms in the direction of dignity for all human beings. They realize that on the basis of their own doctrine, "chosen people" is a stand-in for human beings, the real chosen people. The test of genuine religion is the willingness to work for peace and justice in the world. Some religions go tragically astray in understanding that vocation, but the solution to that problem is reform within the tradition and dialogue with other religious traditions.

As I noted earlier, the topic of religion generated such disagreement that Eleanor Roosevelt ruled out religion as a major topic in the Universal Declaration of Human Rights.[88] Several delegates wanted to have explicit reference to God and religion as the basis of human rights. The Soviet Union opposed any mention of religion at all. The result was a reference in Article 18 to a right to freedom of thought, conscience, and religion, which did not face up to the conflicts inevitable in the *practice* of religion.

The United Nations has constantly had to come back to the issue of religion when dealing with conflicts in the world, most of which have a religious element. The UN most explicitly dealt with religion in a 1981 document, Declaration on the Elimination of All Forms of Intolerance and Discrimination Based on Religion or Belief. I think the length of that title is indicative of the continuing difficulty of adequately stating the question. Communist objection that atheism was not protected was met by adding the word *whatever* before belief in the Preface and Article 1.

I argued above that the long-range solution to avoiding religious conflict and finding religious support for human rights is a religious education consisting of two parts: intelligent training in the practice of one's own religion and a degree of understanding of other religions, especially those which are closest to one's own. Coercion of children to conform to a religion or academic courses that survey all the religions of the world do not measure up to the need.

The United Nations has sponsored periodic surveys, starting in 1959, of how religion is being dealt with in education. The results have not been very encouraging. A 1998 survey of seventy-seven states found that the majority religion in most states still tries to impose its views on minority groups.[89] There is still little attention to understanding the religion of people other than one's own people.[90] The United Nations deserves credit for doing such surveys. In lieu of any other organized leadership, the United Nations is for now the main prod to religious education in the world.

CHAPTER 7

Humans and Their Environment

The theme of same and different has its most striking example in the relation between the human race and all that surrounds it. Human rights are a claim upon the whole human community, but what are the implications for everyone and everything else? The literature on human rights seldom makes reference to the environmental movement, which arose at the same time as the human rights movement. On its side, environmental literature seldom refers to human rights although there are debates about who or what, if anyone, has rights.

The environmental movement has tried to engage ultimate questions and to be as comprehensive as possible. Some victories have been won, such as protecting certain species or improving air quality in many cities. Certainly, the public is aware of an environmental movement and they know of many of the environmental problems that the human race faces. Overall, however, people who study problems of water shortage, climate warming, or nuclear waste can feel like they are shouting dire warnings that people and governments blithely ignore. That situation can produce an apocalyptic outlook that issues in the warning that unless we solve this problem by the year 2xxx, the human race is finished.[1] But while apocalyptic religions can generate momentary fright, they do not produce calm, consistent, and effective action.

Perhaps it is unavoidable that the solutions for many environmental problems take a long time while human individuals wish to see rapid progress within their own lifetimes. But if movement is one step forward and two steps backward, more time is not the answer. The human race may have created such complex problems in the last two centuries that it does not know what to do about them. Governments (or a political party temporarily in power) may be reluctant to do anything that would upset their short-term benefits. Selfishness, ignorance, and inertia are undoubtedly part of the environmental problem that threatens to be cataclysmic. There are nevertheless some underlying philosophical issues that might seem to be a distraction but could contribute to a better understanding of what needs to be done.

One philosophical issue is the relation of human rights to discussions of ecology and environment. The thesis of this chapter is that a consideration of this relation would be clarifying both to the cause of human rights and to the understanding of environmental problems. The failure to address the relation between human rights and environmental concerns distorts both of these important areas.

When environmentalists do refer to human rights, they often assume a framework for the claim of human rights in which man claims to be the superior being who is entitled to rights while everything else is viewed as merely a means to human satisfaction. What I have argued in the previous chapters is that the basis of human rights is an affirmation not of isolated man but of men and women in all of their relations, human and nonhuman. Human rights require a respect for every person as a culmination of respect for every earthly being.

The environmental movement had pioneers in the late nineteenth and early twentieth centuries. But a movement sprang suddenly into view in the late 1960s. It benefited from various liberation movements immediately preceding it. However, there was a danger of simply taking over language from previous movements and extending the application of those terms (especially a variety of *isms*). Some of the assumptions embodied in these terms may have frozen environmentalism into an orthodoxy that limits appreciation of the ambiguities and paradoxes that abound in the relation of human beings to everything that surrounds them.

The environmental movement had at least its symbolic beginning with Earth Day April 22, 1970. The organizers of that day achieved wide awareness and remarkable consensus for the celebration of earth. After the battles of the 1960s over black liberation, women's liberation, and gay liberation, finally there was something that everyone could agree upon. The editors at *The New York Times* were almost breathless in describing the scene: "Conservatives were for it. Liberals were for it. Democrats, Republicans, and independents were for it. So were the ins and outs, the executive and legislative branches of government."[2] Such consensus on an issue that involved political decisions suggests that all parties did not agree on what the question is. Nobody was going to vote against the earth but conflicts about what to do on earth about earth loomed just below the surface. It was fairly clear who blacks, women, and gays were trying to be liberated from. Who was the opponent of earth's liberation?

The ready answer to who is persecuting the earth was the human race. That some human activities are destructive of the planet's resources and its natural cycles is now apparent. A philosophy that for several centuries celebrated "man's conquest of nature" has proved to be quixotic and ultimately suicidal. Unfortunately, the theoretically accurate and practically effective language for addressing the problems of human-nonhuman relations does not exist at present. But it is important to recognize where language is inadequate and particularly to avoid simply reversing language that brought on the problems.

The environmental movement of the 1970s joined an animal rights movement that long preceded it. Jeremy Bentham (1748—1832) had argued that the question of ethics should be how to alleviate pain, a question that puts human-animals and nonhuman animals in the same predicament. The first treatise on animal rights was published in 1894.[3] There was no widespread movement, however, until an essay by Peter Singer in 1973 brought the issue of "animal liberation" to center stage. Ironically, Singer's name became identified with animal rights although he was not an advocate of animal rights—or any other kind of rights. In Singer's utilitarian ethics, *rights* is not a useful category.[4]

For many people, animal rights is their primary interest in the environmental movement. The enlisting of tens of millions of pet owners gave a boost to the environmental movement. But many environmentalists whose interest is "deep ecology" see the animal rights movement as a distraction from the main question of how to reorient the human relation to life on earth. Mark Sagoff paints a picture of what he calls a bad marriage: "The environmentalist, thinking holistically, would sacrifice the individual organism to the ecological community. The animal liberationist, however, must defend all individual lives, domesticated and wild, even at the expense of normal ecosystemic processes."[5]

As a quasi-religious movement, the competing sects in the movement were insistent that they represent the true doctrine. The problem for religious movements is how to keep the particular and the universal together. People whose attention is the problem in front of them—in this case how to treat (some) animals—are impatient with dreamers who want to fix the whole world. In contrast, the people who see the big picture and the interconnection of all problems look down on mere problem solvers.

The human rights movement has a relation to both emphases within the environmental movement. The idea of rights is the obvious link to a movement to establish a legal framework for animals, at least for those animals that humans recognize as their close kin. The issue of animal suffering is a reminder that human rights are centrally concerned with protecting the most vulnerable persons in the human community. The tug of sympathy is indispensable for establishing human rights.

The environmental movement, however, has also raised profound questions about the human attitude to everything in the environment. Can the idea of human rights be sustained in a cosmic outlook? Is the idea of human rights simply part of the human pretentiousness that human life is what the universe is for? Are human rights an obstacle to resituating the human and the humans in nature?

The Human and the Natural

A central problem of language for answering these questions is the use of the terms nature and natural. Humans cannot be identified with the natural world, but they are also not separate from nature. Part of the problem is that nature is an idea in the human mind, not an actual existent. To speak of "the rights of nature" does not make sense; that would imply that nature exists in the way that a dog or a tree or a woman exists.[6] Because the abstract idea called nature is a human invention, it can be manipulated into an endless variety of meanings, giving rise to passionate debates between competing philosophies. Raymond Williams did not exaggerate in saying that nature is "perhaps the most complex word in the language" and "any full history of nature would be a history of a large part of human thought."[7]

I do not propose what *the* right way is to use the word nature. I would argue, however, that most writing on the environment seems to assume that there is some correct and obvious meaning. It is thought that people in the past got it wrong, but now we have it right. The principle I would propose is that any helpful use of the word *nature* today has to take account of a variety of meanings from the past and not simply declare such meanings wrong.[8] What that means is a constant wrestling with paradox whenever the words *human* and *nature* come close to each other. I use the term "human-nature" not as the answer for how humans participate in nature but as a reminder that we do not have an adequate language for relating *human* and *nature*. (I similarly suggest human-animal for speaking of the relation of humans to other animal natures.) It can be and has been said that "humans are within nature." It can be and has been said that "nature is within humans." Both statements can be true depending on the context.

When the term *nature* was first coined by the Greeks (there is, for example, no comparable word in the Hebrew Bible),[9] it was up to them to say what the word meant. The early philosophers seem to have used *nature* as pertaining to all living beings, including the humans. Aristotle, in his usual role of drawing together previous philosophies wrote, "Some things exist or come into existence by nature . . . the common feature that characterizes them all seems to be that they have within them a principle of movement and rest."[10] In his *Metaphysics*, Aristotle moved from a descriptive classification to saying what kind of being nature is. Aristotle could already identify six different meanings of *nature* from which he draws his own summary meaning: "Nature is the primary being of those things which have in them their own source of movement . . . Nature is the source of movement in things, which are natural because this source is inherent in them."[11] Each living thing has "a nature." It was a short step from that usage to a further abstraction that nature is "the mother of all living things." That personification of nature goes back as far as the fifth century BCE, and it served to generate a kind of religious piety toward nature.[12]

A tension developed, however, between nature(s) in general and human nature in a particular individual. Starting with the figure of Socrates, the life and the death of a human individual was seen as running up against the limits of nature. The Stoic philosophers advised that Mother Nature knows best; death, for example, is not a problem so long as you do not become attached to your wife or your child.[13] Dying is obviously natural; everything that is born will die. Nevertheless, there was a philosophical view, joined by religious strands from East and West, that did not accept that *human* death is natural, or at least that it is not exclusively natural.

This reflection on early uses of *nature* might seem irrelevant except that these issues have never been resolved and are still at the center of contemporary controversies over nature and natures. For example, there is a "natural death" movement that has become vocal in recent decades. Why fight death when it is simply natural? Books on death today often have a strong dose of Stoicism whether or not an author has read Epictetus or Marcus Aurelius. But whether many people are willing to go all the way with Mother Nature is not clear. Does acceptance of one's death as natural exclude painkilling morphine?

Christian tradition altered the philosophical meaning of nature by giving emphasis to the human individual and subordinating Mother Nature to a Father in heaven. Christian authors found support in Neoplatonic philosophy wherein both humans and other natures are located on a chain of being. These authors eventually began to think of nature not as an inflexible limit but as something that could be manipulated for human purposes. The beginnings of modern science and technology can now be traced back to the twelfth century.[14] The rediscovery of Aristotle in Europe, by way of Arab translators, helped to seal the deal. Nature was on its way to becoming an object to be controlled by new human methods.

The Language of Man and Nature

After developments in mathematics and "machine thinking," the stage was set for Francis Bacon's seventeenth-century announcement of a new project: man would conquer nature. Bacon was not a rebel against Christian tradition. He thought his views to be fully consistent with Christianity. Bacon was in fact critical of his Christian predecessors for not pursuing what he took to be the Christian calling, namely, subduing nature so that at history's end the human and the natural will once again be a unity.

The seventeenth-century language of "man and nature," was new, reductive of nature to an object for man's conquest.[15] Bacon did not imagine this relation to be a violent one; his chief metaphor for the relation between man and nature is the marriage bed. Man has to woo nature and treat "her" with respect. He should not, however, hesitate to get on top and penetrate her.[16]

When people today look back at the seventeenth century, they envision a "revolution" that pitted science and technology against Christian tradition. There was indeed a struggle against church control, most famously exemplified in the case of Galileo who actually had the support of many theologians. The main question of that era was what kind of religion was to triumph. Was the natural world to be respected for its intelligibility, or were humans to seek solutions in magical rituals? The main body of Christian writing was aligned with the new sciences in protecting the rationality of nature. On their side, "the new physicists wanted nothing so much as a philosophy of nature that harmonized with mainstream Christianity, the better to combat the socio-religious threat of magic."[17]

What has become evident in recent decades is that the compromise worked out at that time had some great weaknesses. The Christian restraint on man's wooing of nature, which Bacon could assume, was gradually eroded. Bacon did not advocate warfare between "man and nature," but the very separation implied two realities (which actually were two abstractions) in a struggle for supremacy. If man did not conquer nature, his only alternative was to submit to nature. *Nature* came to mean whatever has been conquered or will be conquered by man.

The fact that humans are themselves natural beings was almost lost sight of. Humans are neither things nor gods who create things; they are living beings that are born, grow, decline, and die. They are kindred with all the other living beings on earth. A complete opposition between the human and the natural makes no sense. What was in fact the abstraction that was opposed to nature was not human beings but "man." That abstraction had enormous power when it translated into the power of some men over other men and over all other natural beings.

The language of "man versus nature" triumphed. The accuracy of a philosophical and scientific framework that placed man on top of nature seemed to have been proved by the success of technology. However, as usually happens with a new meaning of a term, the success of the new did not eliminate previous meanings. There were many reminders from birth to death that nature does not always do human bidding. Mother Nature never died. Poets kept alive a meaning of nature as both within and without the human, a tradition which went back to Dante, Chaucer, Spenser, and Shakespeare and which continued in eighteenth-century writers, such as Rousseau, Goethe, and Pope. In this tradition, there is a human nature situated in its place within an ordered nature that is not under human control.

It was only in the nineteenth century that poets such as Shelley and Wordsworth found themselves alienated from a reality called nature. Poets were exiled from nature and yearned for it. Even as they were opposing the evils of industrialization, poets were now using the language of man and nature. Victory is complete when your opponents accept your terms for carrying on a debate.[18]

The language that originated in the seventeenth century proved to be deleterious for the Christian religion. Christian authors accepted a language of "natural religion" as part of the framework of man's rational knowledge.[19] The term "natural religion" had come into use in the sixteenth century. Interestingly, it did not then refer to what man discovers in the world beyond himself but instead what man discovers within his nature. Edward Herbert laid out the tenets of natural religion that are discoverable by every individual. Every man can establish that there is a supreme divinity that ought to be worshipped, that virtue joined to piety is the best worship, that sin is to be avoided, that rewards or punishments follow upon this life.[20] This natural religion might not satisfy the mass of men so there were additions—supernatural religion—that was an available option for a more religious person.

The term "natural religion" easily moved out from referring to innate knowledge of God to meaning a contemplation of the nonhuman world. Characteristics associated with God became identified with nonhuman nature. The Declaration of Independence was addressed to "nature and nature's God." Eventually, references to "nature or God" came to mean not one or the other but nature as interchangeable with God.[21] The addition of supernatural religion, more commonly called revealed religion, was superfluous for many people. Anyone was free to practice such revealed religion so long as it was done in private.

Environmentalism as a New Religion

The modern environmental movement can be viewed as a religious movement as well as a scientific and a philosophical movement. The movement could be a helpful regrounding of religious sentiment in something other than patriotic or nationalistic fervor. But the natural religion of the early modern era—either innate truths or truths discovered in nature—is incapable of satisfying the religious drive. Rethinking the relation of human beings to their total environment could benefit humans and nonhumans alike. The danger in any religious movement is that the prior religion is taken to be the enemy, and attacking that religion and its language creates its own orthodoxy.

In environmental literature, no enemy is more often named than the Judeo-Christian tradition. As I noted in the previous chapter, no such tradition exists, except as a nineteenth-century ideology that celebrated man's power over nature. Opposition to that ideology does not break free of the language of man and nature. Both the Jewish tradition and the Christian tradition are storehouses of religious language that could be helpful to the religious impulse of the environmental movement. They do not deserve to be dismissed, and they cannot be eliminated by citing a verse or two from the Hebrew Bible.

The religious direction of the environmental movement was set in 1967 by the publication of a modest essay entitled "The Historical Roots of our

Ecological Crisis."[22] One might suspect that the author, Lynn White Jr., got carried away in this essay and exaggerated many of his points. Making Christianity the cause of our ecological crisis created a story line that was too simple. It credited Christianity with too much power, and it neglected other elements in our history that need examination. In a brief essay, White could not be expected to provide a complete history. In subsequent essays, he tried to add some corrective detail, but most citations of the 1967 essay assume that the question has been answered.[23]

There is an irony in Lynn White Jr. being cited for the thesis that Christianity is the source of our ecological troubles. As a medieval historian, White had helped to correct a bias that presumed Christianity to be an opponent of modern science and technology. By tracing modern science and technology back to the twelfth century, White showed that Christianity was compatible with, even had some influence on, the rise of science and technology.[24] Then suddenly in 1967, Christianity, far from having resisted the rise of science and technology, was now the culprit behind the scientific outlook that caused our ecological problems.

White's essay begins with an impressive panoramic view of the relation between humans and their environment. "Ever since man became a numerous species he has affected his environment notably"(75). But "it was not until about four generations ago that Western Europe and North America arranged a marriage between science and technology . . . . The emergence in widespread practice of the Baconian creed that scientific knowledge means technological power over nature can scarcely be dated before 1850."(77). This moment, he says, "may mark the greatest event in human history since the invention of agriculture, and perhaps in nonhuman terrestrial history as well"(79). White concludes that "our ecologic crisis is the product of an emerging, entirely novel, democratic culture"(79).

A peculiar thing about this essay is that in the hundreds of times it has been quoted, there is hardly ever a reference to the first half of the essay. In fact, only three or four paragraphs are usually cited in which White draws some inaccurately formulated conclusions and makes some overdrawn contrasts. As a medieval historian, he was aware that "our science is the heir to all the sciences of the past, especially perhaps to the work of the great Islamic scientists of the Middle Ages"(80). That would seem to make Islam a key player if one were to trace the roots of modern science and technology. White strangely refers to Islam as a "Christian heresy"(85). He also refers to "Judeo-Christian teleology" (85) and "Judeo-Christian dogma" (89); both phrases have even less justification than "Judeo-Christian tradition." In the end, it is Christianity, or more precisely Western Christianity, that takes the blame.

On the basis of White's own material, the conclusion is strange that Christianity is the root of an attitude causing our ecological crisis. When the nineteenth-century founder of positivism, Auguste Comte, wished to establish a religion of humanity, at the moment when White locates the decisive marriage of science and technology (c.1850), Comte viewed Christian belief to be the main obstacle.[25] Comte's positivism had great success; Christian influence declined as the ecological problem arose. One might still argue that there is an echo of Christianity in contemporary attitudes. But to draw a straight line from a Christian interpretation of the first chapter of Genesis to the positivistic attitude of nineteenth-century science neglects the variety of attitudes in the Hebrew Bible, differences between Jewish and Christian attitudes, and the internal debates within Christian tradition.

White unfortunately began a custom of stating the "Judeo-Christian attitude to nature" by referring to the first chapter of Genesis (86). Usually a single verse, 1:28, is cited that refers to God saying to the man "have dominion over the fish of the sea and over the birds of the air and over every living thing that moves over the earth." If one is going to summarize the Bible, it would help to at least get to the second chapter of Genesis where a picture is drawn of the humans who are placed in a garden and told to "dress it and keep it"(2:16).[26] The biblical myth includes the idea of the man naming the animals (2:20) but certainly not killing them.

There is an extensive literature of Christian commentary on the book of Genesis. If one is going to find out how the Christian Church interpreted Genesis, it would make sense to consult this literature. People who attack the "Judeo-Christian tradition" seem unaware that this tradition exists. The overwhelming consensus of writers from Basil to Thomas Aquinas is that God's plan was for humans and other animals to live in harmony. According to Christian commentaries, before the fall into sin, animals would not have been used for food or clothing. Violence against other animals, just as the violence of Cain toward Abel, is a sign of sin not a matter for celebration.[27]

Almost never do critics of Judeo-Christian tradition attempt to differentiate the Jewish attitude from the Christian attitude to the environment. The Hebrew Bible, which has no word for nature, is filled with admonitions about respecting life, that is, appreciating the land and its produce and treating animals with care. The chief image of the human in the biblical exegesis of the rabbis and the ordinances of the Talmud is "guardian of the garden."[28]

There are numerous passages in the Bible and the Talmud about the responsibility to care for plants, trees, and animals. "A righteous man has regard for the life of his beast" (Prov. 12:10).[29] Even in the wartime siege of a city, "you shall not destroy its trees by wielding an axe against them" (Dt. 20:19). "The land shall not be sold in perpetuity, for the land is mine"(Lev. 25:23). One of the works that inspired the modern environmental movement was Aldo Leopold's *Sand County Almanac*. Leopold looked back to Ezekiel and Isaiah for the assertion that "the despoliation of the land is not only inexpedient but wrong."[30]

The stereotyped Christianity that White offered was sealed by claiming that Francis of Assisi represents the alternative to all of Christian tradition. He describes Francis as "clearly heretical" (91), which does not explain why Francis was canonized as a saint immediately after his death. Francis was an admirable man although people who celebrate his mystical attitude might be put off if they knew more about the asceticism he practiced or his emphasis on the crucifixion.[31] White's picture of Francis has this distortion: "Francis proposed what he thought was an alternative Christian view of nature and man's relation to it"(92). Actually, Francis did not propose any view of nature and man's relation to it. Francis never used the Latin or Italian word for *nature* in his writings; he would not have had much use for such a generality. As G. K. Chesterton wrote in his biography of Francis: "He did not call nature his mother; he called this donkey his brother and this bird his sister. He refused to see the wood for the trees."[32]

In his most misleading statement, White writes of Francis: "He tried to substitute the idea of the equality of all creatures, including man, for the idea of man's limitless rule of creation. He failed"(93). Francis could not have proposed this idea. While he believed, like every mystic of the Middle Ages, that all creatures are equally nothing without God's creative power, he also believed as did every Christian that God had created the human being with a special responsibility to be the priest of all creation. One could accuse many Christians of acting as if they possessed a limitless rule of creation, but it is absurd to suggest that that was the biblical picture or standard Christian teaching. If there is one thing Jewish, Christians, and Muslim teachings agree on, it is that humans are creatures whose power over things in creation is limited by God's rule.

Rather than an equality of all creatures, Francis saw the humans at the center of a diverse world. One of his main biographers writes that Francis accepted the biblical picture, which "asserts the belief in a divine creation, organized according to a plan that is hierarchical and unchanging, with all parts having their established positions and dependent on divine will and action. This was the most fundamental basis for Francis' conception of the natural world."[33]

White wrote that "Christianity is the most anthropocentric religion the world has seen"(86). Like most statements about anthropocentric or anthropocentricism, it is unclear what is meant. Every religion has humans at the center of religious practices; otherwise, there would be no religion without the human actors. As for what religion is directed toward, it is always toward a reality greater than the human. In Jewish, Christian, and Muslim traditions, worship is directed toward the One who has many names but is ultimately beyond the human power to name.[34] Eastern traditions and other ancient religions, whether or not they use the word *god*, are concerned with a cosmos beyond human control.

What White might have meant by the anthropocentrism of the Christian religion is its use of images of the Christ figure to represent God. Jews and Muslims see idolatry here and a constricting of imagination. Christians see their religion as one that has produced some of the world's most extraordinary visual art, based on such realities as a baby in a crib, a virgin mother, and a crucified savior. If the paradoxes of Christian belief are not understood, the failure might be described as anthropomorphism, a tendency to identify the human representation with the divine reality. While talking about an incarnation of the divine, the Christian movement also created language to carefully distinguish divine and human.

The reason for pointing out the limitations of White's essay is not to defend Christianity; it is no doubt a coconspirator in human violence, including environmental degradation. But even to make a case against Christianity one has to make some effort to understand it. Environmental language today is posited as the opposite of what is assumed to be Christian belief in the superiority of man over nature. A simple reversal would place nature superior to man. An adequate environmental language, while not abandoning the great advances of the modern West, would rediscover other ways of understanding the world from ancient and medieval Western traditions as well as from other traditions embodying human wisdom. What Lynn White Jr. said in 1967 remains true today: this work has barely begun. The time is still ripe for trying out images and language rather than settling into one *ism*.

The language of "man conquering nature" is now seen as a prescription for environmental disaster, but there is no simple cure. Feminist writers point out that "man and nature" is sexist; they are right, but the sexism is a symptom of a more encompassing problem. The language of "human and nature" is only a slight improvement over "man and nature." The abstraction *nature*, is probably unavoidable now, but it would help to start by thinking of the human relation to *natures*, other beings that share the earth with human beings, and their human natures. Insofar as human beings are born of the earth, they share in characteristics that other natural beings have. However, from the first moment of reflective self-consciousness, a human being is aware of being different from the other living and nonliving beings.

Humans and their Surroundings

How to state the sameness and difference of the human in relation to the other beings that surround them is a never-ending challenge. The human mind is not only capable of naming things; it can create abstractions that facilitate logical movements in the mind but can be the cause of what Whitehead called "misplaced concretions," a tendency to think that nature, life, or environment actually exists. Those environmentalists who are anxious to leave nothing out are especially in danger of leaving out nearly every thing, that is, the names of all the animals, the millions of individual plants, the mountains, desserts, rivers, and pebbles on the beach. Francis of Assisi might be faulted for not seeing the wood from the trees, but he was right in thinking that there is no wood without trees.

Environment was a word seldom used until the 1960s; it is now casually used as if its meaning were obvious and not in need of reflection.[35] *Environment* means surroundings; its obvious referent is to what surrounds human beings. The idea easily moves from what surrounds one person to what surrounds a community, to what surrounds the human race. The human mind can even project *environment* to settings where there are no people present, but it is still a human word rooted in the human experience of its surroundings.

On the question of where do humans stand in relation to the environment, the answer seems obvious: in the middle. The environment is what humans interact with every hour of the day. A person can either take care of his or her environment or carelessly do violence to it; a community and the human race as a whole have the same choice. A person who is careless of his or her surroundings is foolishly oblivious of the interdependence of the humans and what surrounds them.

The irony of the environmental movement is its naming of the worst sin as anthropocentrism. What men—rationalistic, individualistic, controlling men—tried to do was to remove themselves from their place at the center of the environment and imagine themselves outside and above the world of other beings. The humans' temptation is to become eccentric beings instead of beings that know their humble place at the center of earthly life.

What was in fact imagined to be separate and above was not the human being but the mind of man. The corrective is to imagine human beings—men and women in their diverse roles—at the center of the animal kingdom, at the center of living and dying organisms, and at the center of a world of wondrous things that go beyond human imagination and control. Only from the center can humans exercise their responsibility of respecting each thing.

Respect most often means simply to contemplate the beauty of each kind and each individual. *Respect* can sometimes mean using things to enhance the beauty of the world and the integrity of human life. *Respect* can also mean befriending other animals who can enter into mutual relations with humans. *Respect*, finally, can mean interventions in the nonhuman natural world to attempt healing the wounds that have been caused by human actions in the past.

Humans have not created any species, and they do not have a right to destroy any species even if in their limited vision a being seems merely to be a pest. There are few words in the language more dangerous than *pesticide*. Humans have the power to make things that can kill wholesale; they are obviously superior to other beings in their ability to kill and to interfere in the complex cycles of life. That is the underside of their superior ability to appreciate the world, care for their environment, and make things that are a novel contribution to the universe.

The functioning of the universe has an undeniable element of competition, a word whose original meaning is to work together. From its early usage, *competition* easily moved into meaning a measuring of oneself against another. Competition often produces a winner and a loser, but not always and not permanently. The present winner in one event should be mindful that the competition in the cycles of life does and must continue. Competition depends on the existence of both parties. Wiping out the competitor would rebound with bad effects on the party who is conducting a victory dance.

Rachel Carson described her revolutionary *Silent Spring* as "a book about man's war against nature."[36] She discussed with her editor entitling the book either *The War against Nature* or *The War with Nature*. The use of the metaphor of war is usually an unfortunate exaggeration. However, in this case, it is unfortunately appropriate. Carson went on to say that what she called the war against nature is "inevitably a book about man's war against himself." The literature on war and the literature on environmental ethics seldom cross paths, but wars between humans are part of a larger war that humans have carried on with other species.[37] There have always been environmental problems just as there have always been wars between humans, but in both cases, the human race has now raised the stakes. War has always been stupid, wasteful, and damaging to near and distant bystanders. Solving the problem of violence between humans is a necessary part of situating humans in their relation to other species.

Much of environmental writing argues that if only humans would recognize that they are an insignificant speck in the universe, they would stay in their place of equality with other species. The problem is that in relation to the power to destroy other species, the humans never were equal, and their power now has become enormously magnified. The attempt to downgrade the human goes in the wrong direction. Human respect for the greatness of human life is needed to restrain the human tendency to use violence against one another. If each human being were seen as uniquely important, an attitude of respect would extend to what the human being is related to, that is, to everything.

A study called environmental ethics could logically be a comprehensive study of what is good and bad about human actions. That would be a study of humans in relation to each other and in relation to the human environment of living and nonliving beings. Early in the twentieth century, people who wrote under the heading of "social ethics" thought that they were being comprehensive by concentrating on social relations rather than looking only at the individual. Now it is clear that the study of the relations between human beings is not enough. The adjective environmental could be a helpful reminder that the content of ethics cannot be restricted to relations among humans while neglecting relations with nonhumans. If that point were clear, the adjective environmental before ethics could eventually be eliminated as redundant.

No one can study the entire map of existence. Anyone who wishes to get the biggest picture possible has to be acutely aware of lacking a distinct picture of human relations. While the fabric of intrahuman relations need not be prominent in every picturing of the whole cosmos, one thing that should never be forgotten is that human beings are holding the camera. To assume otherwise is to take the position of a godlike view of the universe from above the give and take of earthly existence. Unless one is willing to introduce a divine mind, every view is an animal's view; and the human mind's eye, directly or through one of its instruments, provides the most far-reaching view. Every ethic is a human ethic; the issue is how well the humans see the world.

The term *speciesism* was coined in 1970 as a parallel and an extension of racism, feminism, ageism, and other *isms* that refer to unfair judgments by some human beings who treat others as less than human.[38] But *speciesism* is not a parallel term. If one were to try to put into practice a belief that humans are like every other species and should not try to act otherwise, the absurdity of the claim would be apparent. Any distinctly human activity would have to be eliminated, except perhaps activity to end the human species.[39] If one looks at the humans as a species, there is no *discontinuity* between a human species and other species. But the continuity includes fantastic differences of human history including the study of species.

If there were a successful attempt to rid the world of speciesism, no one would be left to say when the project had succeeded. If humans do not control the meaning of worth and value, someone or something else must. A denouncing of speciesism has to be based on a religious belief in some kind of being or life force that is of greater value than humans, but it is unclear who beyond the humans is supposed to do the evaluating.

Hierarchy

In environmental writing, the standard opposite of equality is hierarchy, a term that has few defenders these days. Even politicians, corporate executives, and military generals now profess skepticism about the values of hierarchy. In environmental writing, the fight against anthropocentricism is based on a faith in equality as the alternative to hierarchy. Paul Taylor writes, "The bio-centric outlook precludes a hierarchic view of nature. To accept that outlook and view the living world on its own terms is to commit oneself to the principle of species impartiality . . . . This impartiality applies to the human species just as it does to nonhuman species."[40]

If in contrast to Taylor's view, one acknowledges that different kinds of things on earth are not equal in all respects, there is a need to describe differences as well as sameness. The recognition of difference and sameness leads to a judgment of how to order things. The word *hierarchy* for this purpose is not an ideal word. It carries a lot of historical baggage, especially since the nineteenth century. But if only to stretch the imagination, the history of *hierarchy* is worth noting. It has a fifteen-century storyline, so it has likely been a useful description of some human experience.

Hierarchy means a sacred order. It would be understandable if the secular world rejected the idea of an order that is sacred; but almost never is sacredness the reason given for an attack on hierarchy. Instead, the objection is to the idea of an order in which each thing has its distinctive place in a scale of values.

The first fact to note about *hierarchy* is that it was coined to describe the cosmos rather than an organization. The second thing to note is that the original image of hierarchy was circular; a hierarchy was "circles inside circles." The term was inspired by Plotinus' Neoplatonic philosophy although Plotinus did not use the term.[41] In the Neoplatonism that dominated Western thinking for more than a millennium, beings emanate from the One. "In order that being be, the One must be not being but being's begetter."[42] At each level, there is an overflow of being so that the uni-verse is united around its center. "Each of our souls has a center. When we are concentrated upon this center, we are fully ourselves and 'in the Supreme'. But all other souls have centers, and one can imagine a center of centers. Through the center of our soul we contact this center of centers."[43]

Neoplatonism is strongly associated with the metaphor of a "chain of being," which is misleading unless one imagines a circular chain.[44] The food chain, for example, is not a ladder; it is a circular movement. It was only in the nineteenth century that the chain of being lost most of its meaning and was reduced to a ladder.[45] Plotinus's favorite metaphor is a chorus surrounding the One. "Each brings to the chorus something of his own; it is not enough that all lift up their voices together; each must sing choicely his own part to the music set for him."

Sharing is the principle of a world that is organized hierarchically. One of the most basic principles of medieval philosophy was that "the good is that which is diffusive of itself." Each thing overflows its being. The good can only be possessed by being given away. This principle still finds echoes in modern ethics. We ultimately judge a person's moral goodness not by their rule-keeping but by whether their actions are life-enhancing, that is, whether the good in their lives is shared with others.[46] George Eliot was undoubtedly aware of this medieval principle when she wrote of her heroine, Dorothea Brooke: "The effect of her being on those around her was incalculably diffusive: for the growing good of the world is partly dependent on unhistoric acts."[47] A hierarchy of values is a circular movement in which the good is a gift that returns to the giver.

Political Environments

The mystical and cosmic principle of hierarchy took on a new meaning in the twelfth century when it passed from Greek to Latin and was used by the Western Church to describe ecclesiastical organization. The Latin Church translated *sacred order* into *sacred orders* for distinguishing levels of the clergy.[48] Despite the fact that the image of a pyramid of power is difficult to reconcile with the Christian New Testament, the pattern of power that moves from top to bottom became the meaning of a hierarchic arrangement.

This meaning of hierarchy is one of the Church's not so helpful contributions to the modern world. The secular world had little difficulty in sacralizing the arrangement of superiors having the right to give orders and inferiors having the duty to obey. In the nineteenth century, hierarchy became almost interchangeable with bureaucracy. Since then, people have found it difficult to imagine organization as having any other form than a pyramid.

What has been happening over the last half century is an increasing skepticism about the efficiency of a bureaucratic pyramid when creative change is needed. An organization in the form of a pyramid can work reasonably well for making a standard product and for executing standard policies. Some people like to be at the top of the pyramid and give orders, but after a while, it can get lonely up there where no one will tell them what is really going on. Lieutenants do not like to bring bad news to the superior on whom he or she depends for a job.

In writing on organization, there is great enthusiasm for the topic of leadership. The qualities of a leader are endlessly discussed. Rules for leadership are formulated in catchy phrases and simple rules. In this sea of clichés, one finds people called leaders groping their way to some other image, language, and way of acting. The leaders talk of the need to listen, to get everyone involved, and to encourage creativity. The leader cannot do that while sitting atop a pyramid.

But what is the alternative? Jack Welch, former CEO of General Electric, writes, "Hierarchy is dead. The organization of the future will be virtually layerless and increasingly boundaryless."[49] Welch wisely refers to the future because his own tenure at GE was hardly a model of a layerless and boundaryless organization. It is somewhat comical to hear a president or a CEO, whose salary is a hundred or a thousand times the average salary in the company, proclaiming equality. One thing sure about the United States Marines, Harvard University, or *The New York Times* is that they are not about to go layerless and boundaryless. Bureaucracy might not be working well, but equality of everyone is not possible for any organization larger than a few people.

Can the term *hierarchy* be salvaged from its imprisonment in the image of a bureaucratic pyramid? That is very unlikely even though earlier meanings of a term do not entirely die out. But it is unwise to be contemptuous of hierarchy if one has nothing to offer in its place except equality. No fifth-century language is adequate for today's organization or to picture the heavens. But a rebellion against some of the language and images of the nineteenth century might lead one to consider earlier periods of history and their nonscientific understanding of cycles of life and the humans' dependence on their environment.

Humans, including environmentalists, get their image of the universe, their ultimate environment, from their experience of that tiny part of the world in which they interact with people and things around them. From our earliest moments, we know the difference between "to be" and "not to be." In infancy, we are aware of a universe that is immeasurably bigger than we are. It has an order that we do not begin to understand and which is first taken to be sacred and unchanging. The infant recognizes a few human beings who hold the power of life; they supply nourishment and protection against heat, cold, and falling. Mother is the primary life force while a father, if he is present, is likely to be seen as in charge of the organization. As we get older, our ideas become more sophisticated, but we never completely jettison our earliest images. It is perhaps fortunate that we do not do so because an infant's awe on beholding the universe is an attitude worth retaining.

A child's earliest sense of organization is the family in whatever form it is present. Big people give orders, little people obey. That outward pattern of authority is balanced by the day-to-day functioning of the family in which everyone knows what is to be done and the family works together. Besides giving orders, the big people take care of the little people who cannot do everything that older people can. For young children, family life at its best is one of affection, care, and a modeling of how to act. Admittedly, family life at its worst instills attitudes of fear, self-protection at any cost, and a distrust of the motives of other people. Most people probably get some of the best and some of the worst of early childhood.

When human organization goes beyond the family, as it inevitably does, there is a powerful drive to set up a father to keep wayward children in line. When Plato described his ideal society, he did so based on the principle that society is simply the "individual writ large."[50] Not surprisingly, his society included a guardian class who ruled over everyone else. The rulers are compared to watchdogs that have to control those too weak or too ignorant to rule their own lives. The human race has made some but not a lot of political progress in the centuries since Plato. His ideal society is still the model for authoritarian governments around the world. Plato dismissed the idea of democracy. The rule of the *demos*, the masses, would lead to chaos. There are endless examples of the elimination of dictators that produce only violence until another individual proclaims that he is the true voice of the people.

Here is where the earlier meaning of hierarchy would be a help. Instead of a pyramid with a ruler who claims to be benevolent, political life needs to be arranged as "circles within circles," that is, small communities within which persons are valued and between which power is experienced as shared. Larger organization has to be a gathering of small communities that move toward a center. Any number of communities can be related through a center in contrast to a pyramid whose size has a built-in limit for effective action. In any large pyramid, the ruler at the top cannot see what is going on at the bottom; those at the bottom feel like they are being treated as things rather than people.

In recent times, the attempt to change the picture has been called decentralization, a name that guarantees failure. The man (usually) at the top begins passing down power through his underlings; by the time any power gets to the bottom, it is of little value for improving lives. At the first announcement that power is going to be shared with the people, the people at the bottom are apt to take initiative. They put into practice their knowledge that human power is shared power. Their acting without proper permission leads to a conflict between the bestowers of power from on top and the people on the bottom who have discovered that they can get a lot done without asking permission. When the conflict becomes severe, the ruler on top announces that the people are not ready for power so that for everyone's sake power has to be restored to the top.

Decentralization does not work because what is lacking in a pyramid is a center. You can detop a pyramid, but you cannot decenter it. The worst disease one can have is one in which the name for the cure has been given to the disease. The real alternative to a pyramid is small communities interacting with each other around a center. The arrangement is not as utopian as it may sound.

Where political democracies are sustained they depend not on the rule of an undifferentiated mass but on innumerable groups of people who create a sense of dignity and importance in individual lives and who function to give restrained power to the center. The governing of any group should be from the center, not the top. Centeredness should be embodied in the language which is used, the personality of the governor, and the location and architecture of the government. Otherwise, there is a slipping toward the image of somebody being at the top who thinks that the world can be controlled by giving orders.

The United States of America was not founded as a democracy; there was a fear of putting government in the hands of ordinary people. However, the founding principle was that a central government would have its power delegated to it by smaller units. The weakness of the United States is that its states are not small communities. From the beginning, the states have asserted their own independence, delegating some power to a federal government. For its proper functioning, the United States needs not a federal government but a national government situated in the middle of the country. Washington, D.C. may have seemed close enough at the beginning of the country, but a central government would be better located centrally, for example, in Kansas.[51] Despite many drawbacks, the United States has managed to survive so far with enough of the elements that would make up a national grouping of small communities. However, without serious reform of the basic structure, its future is tenuous.

Philosophical Environment

Political commentary may seem irrelevant to a chapter on humans and their environment. However, a political community is not only part of the environment of human individuals and groups; it inevitably supplies much of the imagery when humans look to their physical environment and to the heavens. Some people simply project the idea of a powerful figure up above who is in charge. Even when it is clear that there is no up above in the universe, the idea does not go away. Political and scientific views are tied to philosophical assumptions about where humans stand in relation to the cosmos.

Religion, when it functions as primitive science, can reinforce the bad imagery of a god sending down a message to one group of people who have to conquer competitors. However, each of the world's long-standing religious traditions attempts to evoke awe at the grandeur of the universe and to remind the humans that they are the receivers, not the creators of existence, life, and intelligence. The Bible says that the humans are a little less than the angels. That is great praise of the human, but it is praise of human beings as a distant reflection of the divine and as receivers of goods that are to be shared with others. The constantly repeated assertion in environmental writing that Christianity (or Judeo-Christian tradition) encourages the humans to use their powers for nothing but their own selfish satisfaction misses the Bible's main storyline.

It is a central part of human life to ask questions. Some people may get to the point of only asking "how can I use this?" or "what's in it for me?" Nevertheless, human beings are capable of more diversity and depth to their questions. Their "self-interest" is not reducible to using things for a short-term benefit to the self of their immediate perception. The interests of the self are many if one does not neglect the poetic, contemplative, and caring aspects of human personhood. Plato's criticism of Protagoras was not for his saying "man is the measure of all things" but instead "man the user is the measure of all things."[52] Man, or more exactly the human being, is indeed the measure and measurer of everything unless there is some greater mind in the universe. It is true that a dog or a cat can take a measure of its owner. A nonhuman animal may have an accurate measure of its immediate environment, but as far as we can tell, it does not ask philosophical or religious questions.

The ultimate philosophical question is "Why is there something rather than nothing?" Humans are no closer to answering that question than they were when a philosopher (or a child) first asked it. The question of why can be dismissed as useless, that is, it cannot be put to use for achieving some immediate good. One could also say that a human being is useless; a human being can be put to use only if first treated like a subhuman.

Seventeenth-century authors posited a supreme being in answer to the question of why anything exists. The answer shows a failure to understand the question. Saying that there has to be a first being to explain why there are other beings is not an answer to why there is "to be." As Annie Dillard notes, "The question from agnosticism is, Who turned on the lights? The question from faith is, Whatever for?"[53]

In modern times deism/theism became the name for reasoning to a conclusion that there is a first being. In that linguistic framework, a religious person would have to be called an atheist, one who denies that a first being explains the existence of other beings. In contrast to both theism and atheism, the religious sense is an admission that humans cannot grasp why there is a universe and how the universe is ordered. One can only remain open to being surprised at the wonders of it all. A religious person today might agree with Nietzsche's judgment: "It seems to me that the religious instinct is indeed in vigorous growth—but that it rejects the theistic answer with profound distrust."[54]

A religious sense is helpful for reminding humans that they did not create the universe. Humans can have no discernible effect on their ultimate environment, but they can do serious damage to their earthly environment. A few people have speculated that possibly the earth is alive and that the humans are just (cancer?) cells; whatever short-term damage humans do will be healed by mother earth.[55] I doubt that any humans can fully accept the view that they are cells of an organism. Although humans are aware of being dependent on their environment, each person has a sense of wholeness, neither a part of the earth nor apart from the earth.

Uniquenesses of Beings

Each thing can be called unique insofar as it is itself and not another. We do not usually use the term *unique* this way because it does not add anything to a description. When people do use *unique* they are usually struggling with a paradox which they sense. They know that *unique* signifies difference but a difference that not only allows but invites comparison. For example, in Sherwin Nuland's much praised book, *How We Die*, the author's first two sentences are "Every life is different from any that has gone before it, and so is every death. The uniqueness of each of us extends even to the way we die."[56]

The paradox in Nuland's statement is that if every death is different from all others, how is it possible to write a book about "how we die"? Would it not require a description of millions upon millions of deaths? Nuland is assuming that we all die differently, but all possible ways of dying are brought together in comparing human deaths. Each uniqueness can be compared to every other uniqueness in the mixture of factors that go in to human dying.

"At the simplest organic level, any particular animal or plant has uniqueness and individuality because it lives its life and no other—that is to say, because it dies."[57] The individuality of a living thing depends upon the combination of elements in its environment. The constant process of change leads to development but eventually to a dissolution of its unique combination of elements. Every organism begins to die at the moment of its birth. Some organisms have mighty long lives that are measured in centuries; others go through the cycle of birth, growth, decline, and death in a matter of moments. Nuland says there is a natural length for a human organism. He thinks that if we could eliminate accidents and diseases that attack the organism, humans would live for about 110 years. A recent historical and statistical study suggests 130 years for a natural human life.[58] Researchers may disagree about the potential length of human life, but dying seems to be inevitable for organic life.

In trying to understand the uniqueness of the human being, it is helpful to begin with the uniqueness of each living thing. Lewis Thomas writes that "we tend to think of our selves as the only unique creature in nature, but it is not so. Uniqueness is so commonplace a property of living things that there is nothing at all unique about it."[59] Thomas plays here with the two contrasting meanings of uniqueness: the fact that each living thing differs from all others and the fact that all of them are the same in being individuals. Living beings are unique because they are in a space that nothing else occupies, but in a more important sense, they are unique because they are open to an environment from which they draw sustenance. Their uniqueness is a combination of elements that are common to the species; it is the combining that creates individual uniqueness.

As we move from plants through animals to human-animals, there is an increasing complexity in the combination of elements that constitute uniqueness.

1.) At the level of plants there may not yet be much individuality in the growth of shrubs and weeds. Nevertheless, trees can have a definite character in combining the possibilities of treeness. Ronald Reagan was criticized for supposedly saying that when you have seen one redwood tree, you have seen them all. Anyone who has ever spent contemplative time in a redwood forest knows how false that claim is. Anyone who tries to keep house plants alive in a less-than-ideal environment knows that each plant needs its own individual care. Some people talk to their plants, which is probably more therapeutic for the person than the plant, but the total environment of a living plant is at issue for its health.

2.) At the level of the smallest living organism, the combinations are so minimal that it is difficult for a human being to see the individuality of a mosquito or a cockroach. The profusion of the number of flies, roaches, mosquitoes, or bacteria indicates that the species rather than the individual can be called unique. It makes more sense for humans to concentrate on not destroying the species than trying to protect each individual. That principle is not a license for human beings to engage in any indiscriminate killing. When there is a choice between the life of an insect and a minor inconvenience for a human, there is a place for some thoughtful consideration of the insect's right to be.

3.) At the level of complex animals, the uniqueness of each one is apparent. In fact, it is difficult to avoid seeing the individuality and uniqueness of each animal. Humans nonetheless have often succeeded in blocking that perception, especially when they slaughter animals. When humans recognize that an animal has feelings, they experience a demand on the human conscience to respect those feelings. Humans do not have a license to submit sentient animals to pain. Even an animal grown for human consumption could have a good life, including having its life ended with a minimum of pain. The notion of legal rights has useful application to any animals that can suffer pain.

4.) Human uniqueness is a continuation and further development of the uniqueness in other animals. The number of different possibilities in human life is beyond human imagination. Mammals are clearly individual and unique beings that are receptive and responsive to their environment. Humans carry the process further by being open to the whole world. As Theodosius Dobzhansky put it: "All species are unique, but humans are uniquest."[60]

The uniqueness of the human is that it differs from every other animal by being similar to all of them, a recapitulation and an embodiment of the full texture of life. Human life is wondrous in its complexity and incomprehensible to itself. The biologist P. B. Medawar was fascinated by the uniqueness of the human-animal. He concluded that "the combinants are so numerous, and so generous are the ways in which they may be combined that every human being is genetically unique; the texture of human diversity is infinitely close woven."[61]

Because the meaning of *uniqueness* is often misunderstood as only meaning different by exclusion, comparisons between human-animals and other animals are thought to be a threat to human uniqueness. Stephen Toulmin refers to insights from Darwin and his successors as "resisted by those who have a major investment in the *uniqueness* of the human species, and who feel themselves threatened by any new analogies between the human species and other kinds of animals."[62] The strange fight over evolution is traceable to a misunderstanding of human uniqueness.

Toulmin is right that there are people who oppose any comparison between human-animals and nonhuman animals, but that is hardly what Christian belief requires.[63] Initially, there was not much religious opposition to Darwin's findings; he certainly did not intend to have a fight with Christian orthodoxy. The beginning of the Bible can be read as describing an evolution that culminates in the man who is called earthling. Darwin restored the continuity of all earthly creatures in opposition to the separation of man from beast in the philosophy of the early modern era.

Some of Darwin's followers claimed that evolution is proof that there is no divine power at work in the universe, a conclusion unwarranted by the evidence. In reaction, some Christians have made *evolution* an antireligious term, a use of language that makes no logical sense. Why not celebrate what was obvious to Erigena, a Christian thinker of the ninth-century: "Man is not inappropriately called 'the workshop' of all creatures, since in him the universal creature is contained. For he understands like an angel, reasons like a man, is sentient like an animal, has life like a plant and subsists in body and soul. There is no creature that he is without."[64]

It has often been assumed that unethical behavior arises from a man acting like an animal; for example, violence is often thought to be irrational behavior that overcomes reason. Human violence, however, can be highly calculative and far more destructive than the action of any other animal. It is true that other animals kill, but the killing is within boundaries; it is unusual for animals to kill their own kind.[65] Only humans can rationally create a subspecies of the human that provides a license to kill on a massive scale.

Mary Midgley says that nearly everything is wrong with the question: "What distinguishes man from animal?" It assumes that there is one element that separates them. The question should be what distinguishes the human being in its place among the animals.[66] Richard Rorty thought that what has been assumed to separate human and animal is reason. The claim of reason's superiority is what Rorty somewhat quixotically attacked with reasonable arguments.

Rorty was right that reason imagined as a separate power above animality is what gets human beings into such deep trouble.[67] The higher part of the individual is thought to be good; the lower part's unruly desires have to be controlled. People are told to get control of themselves and check their emotions. They try to follow this advice by issuing orders to the lower self, but the lower self regularly refuses to obey.

The uniquely human being does not have a higher and a lower self; it "feels" the world with its whole self. The uniquest animal extends the meaning of *world* and feels more deeply for others of its own kind. Human uniqueness includes feeling for other sentient animals for whom suffering the world includes painful suffering.

Reason should not be imagined as a power above feelings; at its best it is the transformative power of the whole self from within. Most ancient people did not locate reason in the head; they associated it with the heart where it can listen to the whole body. Reason should be a democratic governor, not an authoritarian dictator.[68] It has to listen to every cell in the body before it can decide for the good of the body and its environment. The human being differs from other animals by being like all the other animals, able to take in and respond to the whole world.

A human law to protect each thing's right to be is neither necessary nor possible. The idea of human law arose in imitation of the law and order of the heavens. Humans realized that unlike the stars in the heavens and even the animals in the field, human order is not entirely built-in. Humans could not live together without some agreements. Konrad Lorenz suggests that the first agreement may have been something like "thou shalt not put an axe into thy neighbor's head."[69] This agreement was a human application of the law of nature(s) in which humans participate according to their own nature. As G. K. Chesterton pointed out, "We talk of wild animals but man is the only wild animal. It is man that has broken out."[70] Human order is a restored order.

For human beings, there is a right way and a wrong way to act although no one has figured out a code of conduct that would fit all humans in all circumstances. The basic principle would be to treat each thing according to its nature; unfortunately, human beings do not understand all natures, not even their own. A natural law would be a summary of the laws of natures, but since those laws are unavailable, a summary tells us very little.

Nonetheless, the possibility of a natural law should encourage humans to pursue an understanding of the laws of natures.

Much of the language that we are still using in this area is left over from the seventeenth century. At that time, the conflict was between a moral and a mathematical approach to laws of nature. Mathematics is of help to human life, but a moral understanding of natures involves every art and science. What was called the laws of nature were brilliant mathematical conclusions based on empirical data. The term *natural law* was left to moralists whose views were a mixture of ancient wisdom, the experience of ordinary people, and ignorance of natures. Some of the ignorance has been cleared away, for example, about human sexuality, but a confusing polemic around the idea of natural law is still a hindrance to understanding the human relation to natures.

The argument could be made that human rights are based on natural law, but the statement runs up against insuperable opposition these days. What does have to be affirmed is that human rights are related to the nature of the human, and that human-nature is not separate from the other natures. It would not make logical sense to try to extend the idea of human rights to nonhumans. But it can make sense to see human rights as arising from the rights that each thing in the universe has and especially from rights as applied to living beings.

A right in this context is not a concept within the human's legal system but rather the respect that a human has for a world that is not of human making. In turn, when human rights have been conceived, it makes sense to see rights extending in an analogous way to other animals and to other living beings. Human rights pertain to what is most basic for all human life. Such rights are not asserted against the nonhuman world but exist in the middle of the animal world where the understanding of a human-nature is inseparable from understanding other animal natures.

The functioning of life on earth is dependent on armies of insects that human beings are barely aware of. The protection of each individual in each species is beyond imagination. It is estimated that three-fourths of living creatures are insects. When the scientist J. B. S. Haldane was asked what his years of research had taught him about God, he replied, "The creator had an inordinate fondness for beetles."[71] For humans to extend legal protection to millions of species, let alone the individuals in each species, is not realistic.

What is needed is a change of attitude on the part of humans in the way that they treat one another and the extension of a nonviolent attitude to their surroundings. They have to think in general patterns while they test their overall outlook by how they treat their most obvious kin. Those animals who can engage us as friends remind us that we have an untold number of friends who live beyond our perception. We cannot see the whole world because it is simply too big, and we do not have a view of all the animals because the bear, giraffes, and elephants in the first row block our sight.

Conclusion

Both animal rights activists and deep ecologists advocate important changes in human behavior, and they have an avalanche of data to back their proposals. But they do not help their causes by trying to bring the human animals into a position of equality with the other animals. The ecological problems are not caused because humans are too respected or because human rights are a presumption of human superiority. Violence toward the environment is an overflow of violence that humans do to themselves and to others of their own kind. Oppression, violence, and destruction are not healthy for any species.

Some human beings think that it is in their individual interest to use violence against members of their own species. The same people engage in thoughtless destruction of other animals and other elements in the environment. The protection of human rights is a defense of all who are vulnerable to human violence. Just as the "chosen people" are a stand-in for "people" as the chosen species, so the unique human species is a stand-in for all species on earth.

I think that Tom Regan overstates the case by saying that "the animal rights movement is a part of the human rights movement."[72] The rights of nonhuman animals are not a subset of human rights. And humans having rights does not translate into an equality with all other animals. Instead, humans have to be encouraged to accept their place at the center, the animal who is morally responsible. As Wendell Berry wisely puts the case: "It is only by remaining human—that is, by the acceptance and proper use of the human powers—that they can understand, respect, and preserve the animals."[73]

CHAPTER 8

The Culture and Cultures of the Humans

The theme of same and different within human life reaches a culmination in this chapter. Unfortunately, the story does not end with a neat conclusion about finding the language that would maintain the needed tension between same and different in human beings. The twentieth century went through several swings of emphasis from belief that humans are the same the world over to accepting that in actuality human life is different across nations, religions, communities, societies, and other particular human groups. In 1948, when the United Nations published its Declaration on Human Rights, its presumptuous use of *universal* as the first word of the title is indicative of an emphasis on human life as mainly or essentially the same everywhere despite obvious differences.

Manners and Morals

Ever since 1948, there has been objection to the particular morality of the West being imposed on the rest of the world. As I noted in chapter three, the two UN covenants in 1966 were not applications of the 1948 Declaration so much as a rejection of a morality supported by colonial powers. In addition, there arose a debate toward the end of the twentieth century over Asian values and whether the idea of human rights language was being imposed in Asia where it did not fit. That debate has been muted in recent years, but there is a remaining skepticism about any universal morality.[1]

One needed distinction is between the manners of a people and its morality. Manners are of their nature particular to a society. Moral

261

judgments, in contrast, are intended to be universal in scope and application. Manners and morals should be distinguished but not entirely separated. Educationally, children can and should learn manners before they learn morality. Manners can be supportive of morality, but since the language of "right and wrong" is used for referring to both manners and morals, the area is ripe for confusion.

Manners are a matter of conventions in a society; in some cases they become law; other conventional practices are simply accepted. "Everyone knows you should . . ." However, people in another part of the world (or maybe just across the river) know no such thing.

People passionately defend the manners of their society while not usually having a clear distinction between manners and morals. Societies have rituals of birth, puberty, marriage, and death that stabilize the moral order. No society can exist without a form of authority. Manners support and surround authority; a breakdown in order unleashes all sorts of conflict. Political conflicts can be a useful part of human affairs. But when conflicts lack the context of an established authority, conflicts turns violent and destructive.

Manners are reflected in such practices as dietary rules, how people dress (which is intimately connected to how people are ad-dressed), the pattern of work and rest, and the games they play and watch. Consider dress as an example of manners. How people dress is a mark distinguishing men and women, upper and lower classes, young children and grown-ups. Uniformity in dress reflects uniformity in thought and action. Soldiers and police wear uniforms to make clear who they are and what they are doing. Members of a religious group often wear a habit to identify each other and to distance themselves from the nonbelievers. Men in business and politics conform to a dress code with little thought or protest.

Most uniformity of dress goes unnoticed unless someone violates the unwritten code of behavior. A society might not require that women cover their faces, but it might exert pressure that they wear skirts. The revolution of the 1960s was partially successful in giving women more flexibility in dress. The male flirtation with the "leisure suit" now looks ridiculous, but to outside viewers, wearing a rope tied around your neck is also absurd.

The rituals and practices of a society are of their nature conservative. It is almost impossible to invent or destroy them. For their effectiveness, they do need to be changed by people who understand the history and the role of a particular practice. One usually has to join the club (or find oneself defined by membership in the club) before one can make changes in the rules. An argument over the headdress of women may seem to the outsider a silly waste of time, but a change of dress may initiate a change in the moral order of a society.

Moral judgments intend universality, but they are always embodied in the particular practices of a group, so that the morality is easily confused with manners. In the past, societies were not pressured to reflect on this question unless they were invaded by another nation's army. Today there are still military invasions, but now the invasions are in the air twenty-four hours a day. Manners of all kind are under constant threat, and although the removal of some practices may be liberating, no one knows where a general erosion of local customs will lead.

The human rights movement conflicts with some practices in Africa and Asia. But it also challenges some conventional practices in the United States and in European countries. Vulnerable populations are discriminated against in every part of the world. I have noted some of these groups in previous chapters, for example, the very young, the very old, women, religious minorities, sexual minorities, and racial minorities.

Women are obviously the largest of those groups. There are long-standing practices in many places that are abusive of women. The most notorious example is probably genital mutilation in some African countries. Various reasons are given for the practice but any cross-cultural, international, or interreligious dialogue would find the practice immoral. How to remove a practice deeply embedded in the history of a country remains debatable.[2]

In the 1960s for possibly the first time in history, one could speak of a worldwide movement. The means of communication may have been primitive compared to that of the twenty-first century, but television was finding inroads in all parts of the world even if not yet in every village and every home. Ironically, the message was one of differences, but the effect was a new unity of the world. The question then and now was not whether sameness was disappearing but what kind of sameness would survive with the renewed emphasis on difference.

I use *culture* in this chapter as a term with a somewhat promising history and a wide use in recent decades. My main interest is whether *culture* can be a helpful term for acknowledging the particularity of human life together with the convergence of numerous traditions toward a unity of the human race. A discourse of human rights is realistic only if it refers to unique human persons in their many relations within a unique human race.

A human tradition has the potential for international and cross-cultural exchanges. For people in the twenty-first century, assisted by the marvels of communication media, there is no excuse for thinking that people in another part of the world are not deserving of the right to a human life.[3] There has to be cross-cultural agreement for human rights to be effectively realized, but the movement can also go in the opposite direction. As Jürgen Habermas points out, "People seem to agree most readily across cultural boundaries in their spontaneous outrage over gross violations of human rights."[4]

A human tradition has been taking shape as the diverse traditions of the world have converged. Some traditions may simply disappear, but other long-standing traditions may retain a relative autonomy within a greater unity. Education is crucial for evolutionary change within the culture of a nation. At least some educational institutions need freedom from state control if they are to provide students with awareness of other possibilities in life and the capacity to leave a cultural group if they choose to do so.

In today's discussions of rights, the difference is often blurred between human rights and political/civil rights whose need may seem obvious to someone who is outside a cultural group. The mutilation of a woman's body or forcing a woman to marry a man who raped her go to the core meaning of human rights; but that a woman cannot get a driver's license in some Arab countries is a practice that an outsider can criticize, but human rights language is not the appropriate vehicle. There may be cultural differences in child rearing and family patterns of authority, but a child having food to eat or not being forced to carry an AK-47 are matters of human rights, not political rights. Political rights are most often a question of manners; human rights are basic moral rights.

An example of the absurdity that results from conflating human rights and political/civil rights is offered by an argument in the U.S. Congress. On a question of carrying concealed weapons, Rep. Martin Stutzman, Indiana Republican, said, "Mr. Speaker, rights do not come from the government. We are, in the words of the Declaration of Independence, endowed by our creator with certain inalienable rights."[5] This extreme view was carried even further by Newt Gingrich in a speech before the National Rifle Association. Gingrich said there was no doubt that the Second Amendment referred to an inalienable right. He criticized the NRA as too timid; during a Gingrich presidency, a human right to bear arms would be affirmed for every person on earth.

Culture

Culture and *tradition* are closely related terms; at times they are used interchangeably. Both terms refer to an existence rooted in a particular history; *tradition* usually connotes a lengthier history. Both terms are concerned with ritual practices; *culture* gives the greater emphasis to ceremonies. Both terms have a religious connection although neither word is restricted to a religious meaning today. Culture receives a better press; very often it is celebrated as something to be preserved. Tradition, in contrast, is often equated with stubborn resistance to progress.

I make use of *culture* in this chapter as a helpful but confusing idea for discussing the effects of commerce, sport, and art on the issue of human rights. Culture is a source of confusion because the term has two almost opposite meanings. In this respect, it is very similar to *religion*, which nearly reversed its meaning in the late sixteenth century. The later meaning of culture, which can be precisely traced to the second half of the nineteenth century, was overlaid on a meaning that went back many centuries. The older meaning did not disappear, and the two meanings are likely to be present in debates about culture or multiculturalism. There have been passionate debates in recent decades about the meaning of culture, but they seldom advert to a pre-nineteenth-century meaning.

Matthew Arnold has been cited numerous times for his definition of culture in *Culture and Anarchy*: "Culture is to know the best that has been said and thought in the world."[6] In that essay of 1869, Arnold was defending values which were articulated by a Bishop Wilson in 1812. Arnold sensed that the assumptions on which Europeans had built their meaning of culture were eroding. What was beginning to be called into question was the assumption that white males in countries such as England, Germany, and France had a near monopoly on the world's wisdom.[7]

Within a few years of Arnold's essay, the term *culture* underwent a near reversal of meaning. As history, archeology, and anthropology opened up new vistas on what has been thought, said, and done in the world, the term *culture* was adapted to describe the variety of human practices. In 1871, Edward Tylor's *Primitive Culture* described culture as "that complex whole which includes knowledge, beliefs, art, law, morals, custom, and any other capabilities and habits acquired by man as a member of society."[8] Edward Tylor, Franz Boas, and other anthropologists who used this meaning of *culture* may have thought it was a simple expansion of the previous meaning. However, the new meaning undercut the premise of the older meaning, namely, that there is a best that is known. Culture went from the singular to the plural. Anthropology was offering a world of many cultures, without a standard by which someone can say "that is the best" or even "this one is better than that one."

Not surprisingly, the two meanings of culture were often mixed together. Walt Whitman in 1870 was arguing for a "programme of culture" open to everyone instead of a "process of culture rapidly creating a class of supercilious infidels, who believe in nothing." Whitman was consciously or not drawing upon both meanings of culture for a rather unstable combination that he thought could find a home in the United States.[9] Friedrich Nietzsche, in his writings of the 1880s, railed against the idea of a "democratic culture." Because Nietzsche accepted the practice of using the plural *cultures*, he had to introduce the adjective *high* when he wanted to talk about *real* culture: "A high culture is a pyramid; it can stand only on a broad base, its very first prerequisite is a strongly and soundly consolidated mediocrity."[10] Nietzsche sensed that his meaning of *culture* was losing out.

Young people growing up today may have little knowledge of anthropology, but they know that people in different parts of the world have different standards of right and wrong. The emergence of cultural relativism in the late nineteenth century was a lazy and inconsistent way to approach differing codes of conduct. A method used by anthropologists was made into a moral theory.[11] The anthropologists have sometimes been at fault in overextending their findings into philosophical and ethical conclusions. Many other people, based on only a smattering of those findings, confidently declared that it was universally true that there are no universal rules.

A pronouncement that each culture has its own opinions of right and wrong and that there is nothing to do but accept that fact might be workable if the cultures in question were those of Earth and Mars. If the cultures are Muslim and Christian, Chinese and Tibetan, or Brooklyn and Manhattan, something has to be said beyond "long live the difference." "In a world where borders are disputed, peoples cross frontiers, local conflict is not containable and world war means global catastrophe, each society has an urgent concern with the existence of tension and conflicts in other societies."[12]

The earliest anthropologists thought that their study "opens to us the possibility of judging our own culture objectively . . . . Only in this way can our intellect, instructed and formed under the influence of our culture, attain a correct judgment of this same culture."[13] That claim might be true provided there is a disciplined comparison of the same and the different between cultures.

The anthropologists were strikingly successful in teaching nearly everyone to use their meaning of *culture*. Anthropologists succeeded in showing that there was more diversity in human practices than had previously been dreamt of. Moral, religious, and political assumptions were shaken up. Any group's claim to know the best way for everyone is now met with skepticism. Perhaps the anthropologists were too successful in that the popular uses of *culture* often lack any disciplined meaning with the result that *culture* can mean almost any differences.

The fracturing of culture into cultures was probably inevitable, and that development could be a positive step toward formation of a human tradition and the language of human rights. It is fortunate that a new meaning for a word does not completely eliminate the older meaning. In the case of *culture*, we need a dialectic of older and newer meanings. There is no need to give up a search for the universal in truth, beauty, and goodness even while acknowledging that universal values exist only as particularly embodied. Until the late nineteenth century and sometimes even today, a well-educated person is called cultured. Such a person of discriminating taste appreciates the finer things in life. Presupposed by that meaning of culture is a "hierarchy of values." Some music, painting, or literature is to be treasured for its high quality. Public television is dedicated to bringing culture to the masses. Some newspapers still include a section on culture for the doings of what is now perhaps ironically called high society.[14]

In 1929, Alfred North Whitehead's first sentence in *The Aims of Education* was "Culture is activity of thought and receptiveness to beauty and human feeling."[15] The sentiment is not far from Matthew Arnold's meaning, but anthropology had removed the presumptuousness of a claim to "know the best." Whitehead simply proposes "activity of thought" and "receptiveness." Implied, perhaps, is that these activities are what is humanly best, but there is no suggestion that the content of culture is exclusively or mainly composed of Western classics.

Whitehead, in commenting on the impossibility of a school curriculum being comprehensive, writes that "I have my doubts of a selection which includes Xenophon and omits Confucius, but then I have read through neither in the original."[16] Whitehead is being unduly modest here in refusing to judge because he has not completely read both Xenophon and

Confucius in their original languages. That prerequisite would surely exclude every curriculum committee in the world. There has in fact been progress in that numerous school curricula today do include Confucius both for an understanding of Chinese culture and as a contribution to (human) culture.

The idea of a human culture, similar to human tradition, is still in the making. But in this case, the two contrasting uses of *culture* already represent the particular and the universal. The fault in the older meaning of culture was not the aspiration to know the best of the human; it was the class and national biases of thinking that the best was already available in British, German, French, U.S., or other textbooks.

It is imperative to continue searching for agreements about human life across cultures, nations, religions, races, and genders. When the British Museum was founded in 1753, it was charged by Parliament with including objects "aimed at universality."[17] That is not a bad formula for how every culture has to be challenged by another culture that may more closely approach human culture.

In response to confusing conflicts, especially in North America, Australia, and Europe, multiculturalism was thought to be the answer. However, the term *multiculturalism* was a bad invention that both obscured the problem and polarized opinion on a topic that was not yet clearly conceptualized. *Multicultural* was too vaguely comprehensive while *multiculturalism* was too rigidly specific. The intention was to emphasize diversity, plurality, or manyness. But the use of a term ending in *ism* is indicative of an ideology of uniformity. The enthusiasm for multiculturalism in the United States seemed to reach a peak in the 1980s and to have declined since then.

By the time *multicultural* was coined, the manyness of culture hardly needed expression; *culture* was popularly used to describe almost any difference between human groups. Multiculturalism was an ideology that was never clear about a policy for inevitable conflicts of language, race, religion, nationality, class, gender, age, and more.[18]

Advocates of multiculturalism expressed shock and condescension that their opponents refused to accept the reality of many cultures. But their opponents were not usually monoculturalists. Everyone could see that there is a great diversity in a country such as the United States. But there were questions about which differences are the most significant and what to do about the differences. The question was not whether someone was in favor of sameness or difference but how to relate the two. Arguments about multiculturalism took place at an abstract level while nations and regions faced very particular tensions.

Multiculturalists argued that minority cultures were not sufficiently protected and that they deserved special group rights. In some cases, that was true, but just because a minority exists, it does not necessarily merit the protection of group rights.[19] There is no simple rule for how to work out tensions between minority groups and the larger culture(s). Respect for long-standing ethnic or religious practices needs to be combined with dialogue when a religious group clashes with the majority.

In addition, there are possible conflicts between the human rights of a person and the group in which the person lives (whether the group is ethnic, racial, religious, or national). When the issue is *human* rights, there should be no question that personal freedom takes precedence over traditional practices in an ethnic or religious group. However, the tendency to overextend the term *human rights* does not help. Many forms of discrimination practiced by groups may or may not deserve legislation at a national level. For any outsiders who think intervention is necessary, they have to be a sensitive to the particulars of a group's culture.

Within groups there is a need for dialogue to work out the tensions between individual and group. A much discussed idea in this context is a right to exit. If an individual's rights are violated, one obvious solution is for the individual to leave the group. In cases of gender or racial oppression, that is not an option. In an ethnic or religious group, exit is possible, but it can be very difficult because of psychological, social, and economic reasons.[20] If a person has been educated entirely within the confines of the group, exit from the group may be all but unthinkable. The problems are often acute for women.[21] Young men in some ethnic communities can also face a severe conflict between their upbringing and what the surrounding world presents.

The 1982 Canadian Charter of Rights and Freedoms provides that the charter "shall be interpreted in a manner consistent with the preservation and enhancement of the multicultural heritage of Canadians."[22] Canada has been successful in balancing its concerns for cultural diversity and individual freedom. Its idea of Canadian culture has more flexibility than either the idea of American culture in the United States or the nationalisms of Europe. Canada did protect English and French as the standard languages of the country. It had to overcome a secessionist movement within the province of Quebec. A long history of orderly government has served Canada well in difficult times; more difficult times may lie in the future.

At first glance, *multicultural* seems much more appropriate for the United States than for its northern neighbor. Has not the United States of

America from its beginning been a collection of disparate peoples, each with its own cultural contribution? In the latter part of the nineteenth century and the beginning of the twentieth century, the United States absorbed tens of millions of people. The aim, however, was not many cultures but the assimilation of the foreign-born into an American culture.

The call for multiculturalism in the United States was a well-intentioned effort to do justice to the diverse groups that make up the country. Instead of forcing groups to conform to a single culture, a multiplicity of cultures would be recognized and respected. A people's language and customs should not be disrespected or suppressed. This toleration of differences should not be for perpetuating separateness. "The important point is that the right is meant to foster a public culture which enables people to take pride in their identity as members of such groups."[23] People should be allowed and even encouraged to keep their religious and other cultural traditions, but the nation's schools should not have the task of preserving any and every group that calls itself a culture.

The United States did have several specific problems that it could not forever avoid. The most obvious was a racial problem, the remains of a scandalous history of slavery.[24] Starting in the 1940s, the country began an evolution in its racial attitudes; it still has a long way to go. *Racial* can itself cover over the specific issue of African Americans in an American culture. Immigrants from Asian countries have their own problems that need the country's attention. But as Frederick Douglass recognized in the nineteenth century, the question of white-black relations goes to the heart of what "American culture" has meant.[25] A century after Douglass, black writers were still trying to make the same point that should have long been evident to white people.[26] When a multicultural curriculum was introduced in California, resistance and protest could be found in the black communities of Oakland. Authors of the curriculum may have found that reaction puzzling, but multiculturalism was intentionally or not a way of putting black concerns into the backseat of a big bus.

A second glaring problem affecting the existence of the United States of America was its treatment of people called Indians who illogically were renamed Native Americans. (That should have entailed that all the white people would become "foreign Americans.") The Native peoples had been shamefully treated by European invaders and then by the United States government. Because so many of their ancestors were killed, the present number of Native people is a small percentage of United States people. The word *culture* is more appropriate here than in most uses within the country, but the tribal cultures had been subjected in the past to such assaults that the project of preserving or recovering the genuine culture of a tribe was problematic. But the country could at least get rid of some of the disgraceful images and language used for native peoples. The movie industry was particularly responsible for the stereotypes and lies to which Native tribes were subject.

The fact that many European nation-states might be said to have a national culture makes their problem more easily defined but more intractable than the clashes of groups with "American culture." France, Germany, Sweden, and Italy are geographically close but had distinctive cultural characteristics. Newcomers in France could not become French in the same way that the United States created Americans. Germany opened its borders to millions of Turks as "guest workers" but not until 2000 as German citizens. The cultural differences tested the limits of German policies of tolerance and welfare. Sweden absorbed many people from the former Yugoslavia and more recently from Syria. France received a wave of immigrants from Northern Africa. The Netherlands, which is rightly famous for its tolerance of differences, strained under the weight of an immigrant population that was not interested in learning Dutch and in being assimilated into Dutch cultural practices.[27]

The most common characteristic of these populations was the religion of Islam. The term *multiculturalism* hid the specific issues that each of the respective nations faced; and it failed to acknowledge the gulf between the secularized Christianity of most European nations and the surge of contemporary Islam. By the year 2011, Nicholas Sarkozy, David Cameron, and Angela Merkel, leaders of France, Great Britain, and Germany, respectively, declared the end of multiculturalism, that it "has failed, utterly failed."[28] There was special horror at a massacre in Norway, a place assumed to be the most tranquil and orderly of countries. The fact that the source of the killings was not Muslim terrorists but a Norwegian hater of Muslims did not affect the political judgment that multiculturalism has failed.

The negative reaction was understandable, but it left unclear what alternative was being affirmed. Short of closing national borders and deporting whole populations, the only alternative seems to be to pinpoint the conflicts more precisely than does the term *multiculturalism* and to concentrate on building bridges of mutual understanding. Special attention has to be given to Christian-Muslim conversation, not just among a few ecumenical experts, but nationally and in neighborhoods. Whether Europeans go to church anymore is not as important as the long history of

Europe's culture or cultures. Setbacks of violence will undoubtedly happen, but both Europe and North America have an opportunity for religious dialogue and understanding not seen since the days of medieval Spain.

Many people viewed multiculturalism as an overemphasis on difference; that tendency was countered by the emphasis of cosmopolitanism on sameness around the world. Cities with urban cultures tend in the direction of similarity. A Philadelphian may feel more at home in London than in rural Pennsylvania. The cosmopolitan is comfortable in many cities, not only Paris and New York but also Addis Ababa and Dubai. The term *cosmopolitan* has a history of more than two centuries, and the term has mostly positive connotations. Its recent meaning may be too closely allied with people who have frequent-flier miles. One dictionary of political philosophy in the 1980s defined a *cosmopolitan* as "a kind of parasite who depends on the quotidian lives of others to create the various local flavors and identities in which he dabbles."[29]

Advocates of cosmopolitanism are aware of that problem. They insist that they are not opposed to family, ethnic traditions, or patriotism. However, the biggest danger in pitting cosmopolitanism against multiculturalism is that to replace one *ism* with another is not a solution to the inbuilt human tension of sameness and difference. If we can get away from *isms*, a cosmopolitan attitude and cultural plurality do not have to be opposed; they can go together quite comfortably. Genuine participation in a way of life includes openness to the differences of other peoples' lives.[30] The universal is present in the depths of the particular. The achievement of human rights depends on the emergence of people who are rooted somewhere and at the same time have a mind open to everywhere.

Human culture is still in the making; long-standing cultural traditions cannot quickly be transcended. If in the twenty-fifth century, Earth is invaded by Mars, the earthlings will very quickly discover their human culture. For now, they have to decide whether to protect many ethnic, religious, or other elements despite the fact that these cultural factors are temporarily the source of human divisions.

Globalization

The term *globalization* is on the side of sameness. The term was invented by economists and is still controlled by economics. It could conceivably be used to describe a process that has been occurring for centuries. The ancient Greeks had already figured out that humans live on a globe that connects us all. But it is quite a different experience to travel around the globe and meet many differing cultures of the human race. The Greeks could only describe people of the non-Greek world as barbarians, people whose language was unintelligible to Greeks. The ancient Chinese thought of their empire as the center of the world. They were generally tolerant of non-Chinese who were willing to live according to Chinese standards. The Romans thought of their empire as the superior specimen of human life. Later, Christian missionaries with the help of Rome's "civilizing" process took aim at the whole world.[31] The Christian evangelizing of the world took much longer than the early Church had imagined it would, but globalizing has been a continuous process.

The naval explorations in the fifteenth century were the beginning of a new era of travel and the interconnecting of the world. Europe until then had knowledge of the East mainly through Marco Polo and a few other hardy explorers. The European search for efficient water routes led to daring attempts to find a western route to the East. The European discovery of the land that it called America was a new world for Europe Some people see a beginning to human rights with the Spanish ruling that the natives in America had souls and were worthy of evangelizing. As I noted earlier, concern for native souls did not automatically transfer to concern for their bodily welfare.

More important than the new land was the discovery of the oceans. Instead of the island of earth in the middle of water, there were now continents connected by oceans.[32] A worldwide commerce was now realistic. Goods made in one part of the world could be exchanged on the other side of the world.[33] Control of the seas became an imperative for improving a people's wealth and welfare. The religious and economic motives for foreign plantations were often difficult to sort out, but both relied upon military prowess on sea and land.

Until recently, most Europeans, Australians, and North Americans imagined this story as one of progress and success. As more accurate histories were written in the twentieth century, Europeans and their descendants elsewhere were confronted with shame for the suffering caused to native populations outside Europe. An index of the change was the lack of celebration in 1992 on the five-hundredth anniversary of Columbus's first voyage; that lack was in striking contrast to the celebrations in 1892.[34] The reversal of outlook regarding European imperialism was well-intentioned but often clumsy. The attempt of multiculturalism to create a new language filled with numerous *isms* did not effect much change. More accurate historical narratives and fairer economic policies are what justice demands.

The technological revolutions of the twentieth century greatly accelerated the pace of unification and the potential for both improvements in human life and the destruction of both human and nonhuman life. Human rights was one of the good ideas of the century largely inspired by reaction to the horrible actions of human beings. Modern forms of travel and communication make inevitable a choice between respecting people everywhere or else endless bloody conflicts between people who cannot get out of each other's way.

In the attempt to communicate with people at great distances, the radio was an immeasurable improvement over the pony express and the telegraph. The sound of a human voice is an indisputable mark that we are dealing with fellow humans. The radio remains an important tool of communication, but it has been eclipsed first by television and then by the Internet. It becomes difficult to think of a wartime enemy as subhuman when you can see him in your living room. During World War II, brave photographers worked close to the battle lines and would send home pictures for the following week's *Life* magazine. In the Vietnam War, the reporters went with the troops, and the film arrived for the evening's network news. In the first U.S.-Iraqi War, there was live television reporting from within Baghdad as the city was first being bombed.

The Internet has once again accelerated the pace of globalization beyond anyone's ability to fully grasp what is happening. A few young geniuses have jumped out in front to come up with inventions that could not have been imagined only a few decades ago. The potential for human understanding is almost unlimited. Resistance to oppressive governments has received powerful help in the instantaneous transmission of sounds and sights to every corner of the world. During the uprisings in the Arab world in 2011, the social media were credited with helping to direct the demonstrations. In June 2011, the UN special rapporteur went so far as to describe the Internet as "an indispensable tool for realizing a range of human rights."[35]

It may take several decades to find out what the Internet can actually do to bring people together and to overcome ignorance, avarice, and violence. One thing certain is that the machines alone cannot achieve success in human understanding. Since the seventeenth century, every major step in technology has been hailed as the means of human liberation. But every machine can be put to both good and bad uses. So long as there is a huge discrepancy in the power that human groups and nations bring to the use of technology, no machine will bring about human liberation.[36]

Nations look out for their own *interests*, a word that should usually be used in the plural. One interest of a nation is to generate wealth; it can also be a national interest to act as a responsible nation in the community of nations. It is not hopeless idealism to advocate ethical interests as well as economic interests. At the least, the ethical and economic interests are not incompatible. Dov Seidman writes, "When the world is bound together this tightly, everyone's values and behavior matter more than ever . . . . We've gone from connected to interconnected to ethically interdependent."[37]

A cynical attitude about the selfishness of every nation, and its people is countered by the many international organizations that help people across borders and by the international response when there are disasters. In these situations, the potential for good by television and the Internet is demonstrated. Nongovernmental organizations that know how to employ the news media on their side can sometimes be more effective in righting violations of human rights than any government can be. Human Rights Watch and Amnesty International are the best known defenders of human rights. The attitude that each of them exemplifies is defense of people without respect to nationality. Amnesty International's critical reports of the United States have caused conflict with politicians in high places.

There are many organizations that are not directly concerned with human rights but whose work is a contribution to building international awareness of problems of sickness, poverty, starvation, and homelessness. That is the work of such organizations as OXFAM, Save the Children, the Red Cross, Action Aid, and Doctors without Borders.[38] Any organization is subject to biases by reason of its origin and composition. Each of them works with restrictions, especially within nations that have authoritarian governments. Nevertheless, every act of generosity across national borders is a step toward the recognition of respect for people regardless of race, nationality, or religion.

The international response to natural disasters is now something that is expected, but it is nonetheless remarkable. Even a few decades ago, an outpouring of financial and other kinds of aid would not have been feasible. Today's media of communication can make people immediately aware of an earthquake, hurricane, tsunami, or flood anywhere in the world. Only a small number of people are likely to respond, and if the television cameras are not there to capture the scene, some big disasters can get lost in the rush of other events. Admittedly, droughts, internal wars, and endemic health problems do not attract sustained international attention. The human rights movement has a long way to go in creating a realistic awareness of what is needed and what are effective remedies for natural as well as humanly made disasters.

In recent times, there has been an insistence on not forgetting past atrocities and reliving every detail of the horror on each anniversary. It is doubtful that such obsessive memory helps anyone. The victims of a disaster are best honored by a modest public ritual in support of private memory and a letting go of hatred toward the offending group and its descendants. Obviously, healing takes time; a generation may have to pass, but at some point it is time for reconciliation.

The United States has insisted that the events of September 11, 2001 must not be forgotten.[39] No one would deny that the attacks on that occasion caused a tragic loss of life and punctured the United States's sense of invulnerability. However, after a few years, most of the world was tired of hearing United States officials speak as if the bombings were the worst thing that has ever happened. On the scale of world disasters, the events of September 11, 2001 rank nowhere near the top. A national disaster can rally a nation to pull together in aid and in mourning. It can also cause a fixation on security against future threats from outsiders. That atmosphere can lead to a disregarding of the rights of individuals from other countries and individuals who just look different.

On December 8, 1941, Franklin Roosevelt said that December 7 "is a date that will live in infamy." Fortunately he was wrong. December 7 passes each year with at most some passing reference to the attack on Pearl Harbor. For some people the atomic bombings at the end of the war more than balanced the scales of injustice. In any case, Japan and the United States succeeded in a remarkably short time to establish amicable relations. There was for a time intense economic competition that sometimes resurfaced national stereotypes, but the tension was in business, not war. When Japan suffered a terrible disaster from the tsunami in 2011, there was an outpouring of grief and aid in the United States. No one was heard to say, "Why should we help those people after what they did to Pearl Harbor?"

George Santayana is regularly quoted for having said that "those who do not remember the past are condemned to repeat it." [40] The statement is undoubtedly true, but it could use a complementary statement: "Those who cannot put aside past offenses are condemned to be blind to the present." A human tradition cannot exclude the evils of the past; they are forever part of human memory. There is no reason, however, that a terrible act in the past has to take precedence over the good that can be done in the present. Tradition is always changing, and the interpretation of the past depends on the perspective of the present. What can now be grasped is that there is a human nature that every person in every nation has a share in. What was written in the Talmud many centuries ago—that if you save one life it is as if you saved the whole world—can now come home with much greater force.[41]

The World at Play

Throughout history, humans have had to labor to produce food from the land and to make other products needed for human survival. The work of human hands remains central to every people of the world. The variety of environments encourages exchanges between different regions and their peoples. Fish from seas and rivers can be exchanged for agricultural products grown in regions where the land is fertile. Some people have been blessed with moderate temperatures; they can be productive of goods throughout the year; other people's lives are dominated by heat or cold.

Plato suggested at the beginning of the *Republic* that it was the hankering after luxuries that led to trade; otherwise, people would have been content to stay at home.[42] Whether or not he is right, it is certain that human beings have not been content to be concerned only with bare survival. The mark of human culture is excess, occasions when one puts aside the struggle to survive and devotes energy to the joyful experience of living. The world is united by the struggles of *homo laborans*; but just as universal is the energy of *homo ludens*, the human being at play.

The humans are the species of artifice, that is, makers of art. Some of those arts are put at the service of reducing the human labor that is needed to live. Technology, a nineteenth century word derived from the Greek word for art, is the realm of machines that extend the power of the human race. There are other arts that humans produce simply because they wish to express themselves and to find pleasure in life. I begin with a description of sport that is not ranked near the top of the arts; nevertheless, sport as a popular art has increasing power to cut across cultural divisions and create a sense of the whole world.

Sports

All animals love to play, that is, to run, jump, dance, sing, wrestle, and test the limits of their bodily strength with others of their kind. Humans develop their play into elaborate rituals for exploring all aspects of their lives.[43] The young in each species are the most playful; they do not feel the need to conserve their energy, or at least they do not give much forethought to running out of steam. The aim is not to be efficient but simply to let life overflow in ways that renew the organism and communicate with others. Play expresses one of the universals of human experience: the pleasure of being alive.[44] In relation to ordinary life, play is disinterested; it is an engagement in something that can be treated as serious and can teach the player how to accept failure as well as success.[45] Playing the game according to the rules has its own pleasures. But first one has to accept the nature of the game and the fact that one is not always a winner.

As the human child grows up, its play becomes more disciplined into games with rules. Play, when organized into a contest with rules and spectators, is called sport or athletics. Sports take up a big part of modern life, and their importance should not be underestimated in international relations. A sport has its origin in one place and one time. For that particular group, the sport can take on great importance. Children are initiated into the tradition of that sport and develop skills that improve over time. The immediate effect of a sport is to divide nations. Nobody but insiders can appreciate the subtleties, skill, and beauty of their sport. The particularity of each sport is a challenge to international understanding; the challenge can sometimes lead to a sharing in another's culture.

Games that are highly developed and involve full-time involvement by the players are called professional sports. A line is drawn between professional and amateur; the distinction these days is usually based on whether the players receive money for what they do. For a long while, the international Olympics tried to maintain this line, but it became ridiculous to claim that a person who trained and competed in a sport full-time with the support of a national government could be called an amateur. College football in the United States continues to keep up a charade in which the players are not recompensed for what is full-time work in many colleges.[46]

In most sports, the players begin as amateurs, and when they increase their skills, they become professionals. The dividing line should not mainly be money. Anyone can be an amateur at any sport; all it takes is a love of the game and a desire to participate. A professional is someone who has learned the discipline of the game and can discipline his or her emotions to fit the game. A professional athlete knows that eventually the game wins and the individual player has to retire from the field. Some professional sports seem particularly cruel in that old age can arrive as early as thirty years old. A sixty-year-old golfer might still be able to play a respectable game. When an attempt was made to have a "senior" baseball league, the result was embarrassing.

Some people think that applying the term *professional* to athletes is to demean the term that properly belongs to physicians, lawyers, and ministers. The marks of professional work are special knowledge in a particular area, skilled performance, and dedication to the good of humanity. Athletes qualify on the first two of those characteristics, knowledge and skill. As for dedication to humanity, most professionals do not have such a lofty attitude in the front of their minds when performing their skill. Instead of thinking about humanity, the surgeon is intent on removing the tumor; the lawyer is intent on mounting a good defense; the architect is intent on designing a particular building. Likewise, the batter is intent on getting a hit, the quarterback on throwing an accurate pass. The surgeon, lawyer, or architect may make a larger contribution to the common good, but a great athlete contributes simple joy to many lives.

Professional athletes are sometimes good examples of an older meaning of *professional*. Until the nineteenth century, the emphasis was on serving the community. Being a professional likely meant living in poverty rather than riches. A professional did not receive a salary but had to rely on donations or on grants from a rich benefactor. A life in which money is not a central concern could be liberating, but the whole system was subject to corrupting influences.

In the world of professional sports, the big money went to the owners of teams. The individual athlete was vulnerable to exploitation. A baseball player in the United States until 1970 did not have rights; the player was owned, and the owner decided what the player should receive. Since then, the baseball players have shared in the big money, a change that has threatened to overwhelm the game. The best players, however, still play the game for love of the game, whatever their salaries are.

There has always been a gender bias in sports, and the greater male interest will probably always exist. If involvement in sports were exclusively for men, then any claim to a nearly universal effect would be contradicted. However, the gender gap has closed considerably in recent decades as increasing numbers of women have become both players and spectators. The upheaval has been quietly occurring, but it has been steady over the years. In some countries, the change has been striking; in other countries, the change is barely visible yet. But like the worldwide women's movement, the direction of the change seems clear. Some particular sports have led the way; other sports have put up more resistance, or else they are sports that women might watch but in which few women would wish to participate, such as U.S. football.

In the United States, the passage of Title IX of the Educational Act of 1972, which mandated equal opportunities for men and women in school, sports has brought about a revolution for girls and young women. This change in education has gradually effected a reshaping of man-woman relations throughout society. One surprising thing about the effect of the law is that the law itself has been and continues to be widely violated.[47] Universities have been resistant to what they perceive as the financial disadvantages of balancing women's and men's sports. The government has been lax in prosecuting any school for not following the law. A law so commonly trespassed would usually have little effect. In this case, however, the existence of Title IX, even when not legally enforced, has worked wonders.

The sport that comes closest to creating world interest is soccer, which most of the world knows as football. It is a game that combines simplicity and skill in a way that almost anyone can understand. It can be played by children wherever there is an open field and an available ball. Until recently, it was a male passion, and where soccer is most prominent, there is a strong resistance to women playing the game. The United States, as is well known, is the one great exception to soccer passion; it prefers by far its own violent brand of football. Periodically, there is an uptick of interest, such as during the World Cup in 2010, but so far the effect has not been sustained. The fact that two television networks have paid one billion dollars for U. S. rights to show the World Cup in 2014 and 2018 indicates a confident belief that things are changing.

Where the United States has already made a contribution to worldwide soccer is that a national women's team has led the way internationally.[48] An absence of interest in men's soccer might paradoxically have helped women's soccer. When the U.S. women lost to Japan in the 2011 World Cup, they were consoled by the fact that they had helped the Japanese women to develop their skills. Although they were disappointed, several of the U.S. players were gracious in defeat; they said that the Japanese probably needed the win more than did the United States.

Soccer violence is not a help to international understanding. The violence is usually off the field and caused by a mixture of factors extraneous to the game. The same holds true in other sports, such as basketball, where both big victories and big defeats have set off violent demonstrations. The players themselves compete passionately but according to rules; violent outbursts are rare and usually controlled.

International sports are a great opportunity for young people to get to know people from other countries. An exchange of athletes can sometimes do more for cultural understanding than a meeting of diplomats or the signing of international treaties. Because a sport originates at one place in the world within an environment where it had support, the exporting of a sport is usually very difficult. Soccer is an exception.

The possibility of a nation gaining respect with the help of sport is exemplified by the World Cup in 2010. South Africa has had a difficult road to simply achieving a normal existence. The games in Johannesburg showed any doubters in the world that South Africa had overcome its apartheid past. It is still a country racked with economic and social problems that require patient attention. Nevertheless, it was a relief to South Africa to show to the world pictures of its beautiful country and lovely population. In a poll taken a year after the World Cup was held, 70 percent of the population thought that the staging of the event had hurt the country economically. Yet in the same poll, 78 percent of those interviewed thought that the World Cup had benefitted the country's social cohesion. Most South Africans were able to see that there are values that go beyond money.[49]

A sport that has become important for international relations is golf. The game is essentially simple: hit a small ball into a hole with the fewest number of swings. But unlike soccer's sandlot of about 120 by 80 yards, golf uses manicured lawns that can stretch between 200 and 600 yards for each of eighteen holes. That was a factor in golf being until recently a rich man's game. A set of expensive clubs were thought to be necessary equipment for hitting the ball, a country club or its equivalent was the appropriate venue for play, and gentlemen with many leisure hours at their disposal were the players. Until a few decades ago, the game was mainly of interest to men in the British Empire countries, the United States, and a few other places. Upper-class men played the professional game; retired men played gamely.

Golf is one of the sports in which women can hold their own for national and international interest. Like tennis, golf was once of interest only to a small group of women in a few countries, but both sports now command attention for tournaments around the world. A striking example of what can happen to women's sports is the success of South Korean women in golf. One woman, Se Re Park, was the inspiration for a generation of South

Korean women after she won the U.S. Open in 1998. Within a decade, South Korea was producing many of the best women golfers in the world.

The International Olympics is the most ambitious attempt to bring together athletes from all over the world for competition in dozens of sports. At the least, it is an admirable ideal even if the administration of the games has often been tainted. It does provide a showcase for small as well as big countries. For the athletes to participate in the games is a thrilling experience even if they have little chance of winning. Some nations have acted dishonorably in the pressures they used on their own athletes. The billions of dollars that the Olympic Games represent is almost guaranteed to harm the international good will that the Olympics can generate. But with all their drawbacks, the Olympic Games are a better form of national competition than a battlefield. The attacks of terrorists, such as the 1972 massacre of Israeli athletes, are a sad confirmation of the importance of the Olympics for peaceful cooperation.

The power of sports to transform international relations is modest. Sports are only a tiny part of that convergence of traditions that is necessary to make human rights effective. Athletes who achieve international stature are few in numbers, and the audience for sporting events is composed of people who might be doing something better with their time. Despite these limitations, there are few things that can compete with international sporting events' potential for reaching billions of people and conveying the need to respect the skill and humanity of people from another part of the world.

Art

The most obvious competitor to sports in transcending economic interest and finding an international audience is art. Sport itself might be thought of as art. In fact, for some people just about anything can be called art. Although what constitutes art is the topic of endless debate, there are some things that can be asserted and that find wide if not universal agreement. As a start, art is part of the world at play, what humans do beyond their mere struggle to survive. People appreciate certain activities and objects as having qualities that evoke a sense of depth and grandeur. Standards of art vary from one culture to another, but every people seems to have their own cherished works of art.

Art, similar to sport, has the problem of originating in one place and one time. That fact seems to militate against its portability. Particularity cannot be generalized. But a mark of superior art is that its particularity is precisely the way it transcends cultures and nations. The more particular is its artistic detail, the greater chance it has to point toward universality. Art supplies the logic on which human rights is based, that is, that the universal is embodied in the particular. The life of every person is the embodying of humanity and the violation of anyone's human rights is a violation of the human. Where there is a lack of appreciation of the arts, human rights are not likely to be respected.

The movement in modern times to broaden the range of what is called art is well intended although some limit has to be set. John Dewey, in his influential work *Art as Experience*, saw the problem as "that of recovering the continuity of aesthetic experience with normal processes of living."[50] If art is completely separate from "normal processes of living," it becomes the preserve of a small group of aesthetes, particularly rich people who can afford the time and money to dabble in fine things. On the other hand, art would self-destruct if it could not be distinguished from those "normal processes of living." Dewey argued for *continuity*, which includes distinction but not separation. Thus, the artistic can be realized in every area of life and not only by people classified as artists, but art also has to have qualities that evoke a profound feeling for life.

Art, like the human being, embraces both meanings of uniqueness: a particular work of art is (nearly) unique to its time, place, and other circumstances; it excludes a second. But it is also (nearly) unique in its process of inclusiveness; by bringing a great diversity of elements into harmony, it can evoke appreciation from a spectator or listener of any time and any place. Ben Shahn wrote that "the universal is the unique thing which affirms the unique qualities of all things . . . . In art, the symbol which has vast universality may be some figure drawn from the most remote and inward recesses of consciousness."[51]

This logic of unique artistic production can seem self-contradictory in our ordinary logic which moves between the individual and the general. The artist liberates our awareness by imposing a form on experience. A form for the senses is necessarily particular, but that is the only way to arrive at a glimpse of the universal. The artistic does not replace unlimited experience; instead, it upends all the general categories that we lazily use and which obscure our actually hearing one particular sound or seeing one particular tree. Samuel Beckett who pushed theater to the limits of speech said, "To find form that accommodates the mess, that is the task of the artist."[52] The artist may shock us or confuse us because the form of the art does not fit within our world. Edwin Schlossberg, who has designed museums that invite interaction between the viewer and the art, as well as between viewers of the art, says he hopes that one viewer will turn and say to another, "What does this mean?"[53]

Many of the arts struggle to maintain their integrity against the technology that creates conformity in every area of life. Attempts at being different usually only produce eccentricity. Anyone who does something strange can proclaim himself or herself an artist. But the new becomes old with startling speed. A bestselling song one year may be forgotten by the next year. It is difficult to imagine any of today's music lasting as long as Mozart's or Beethoven's. To say that is not to canonize the sixteenth, eighteenth, or any previous century. There are undoubtedly great artists who are alive today, but they have to contend with obstacles to a quiet appreciation of their work in the present and to finding a tradition that will preserve their work for appreciation by future generations.

The great twentieth-century critic Walter Benjamin thought that art had fundamentally changed in the nineteenth century, starting with the invention of photography. For Benjamin, the uniqueness of a work of art was lost when reproductions destroyed what he called the work's aura. Noting that "the uniqueness of a work of art is inseparable from its being embedded in the fabric of tradition," Benjamin compared the reactions to a statue of Venus by the Greeks who made it an object of veneration and by Christian clerics who viewed it as an ominous idol. "Both of them, however, were equally confronted with its uniqueness, that is, its aura."[54] Benjamin is probably right that a familiarity with reproductions conveys much less of the aura than could be experienced by the few people who could get to a museum in Paris or Rome. However, a possible loss of the sense of one kind of uniqueness is offset by the uniqueness of appreciation by millions of people.

Benjamin may have been unduly pessimistic about an aura of uniqueness. That quality can still be experienced when one stands before a Vermeer or a Rembrandt. Many people can identify with Henry James's description of Nick Dormer's reaction in London's National Gallery: "As he stood before them perfection of their survival often struck him as the supreme eloquence, the virtue that included all others, thanks to the language of art, the richest and most universal."[55] The survival of these fragile objects throughout the centuries is nearly miraculous. Art museums are vulnerable in wartime; their destruction can be included in crimes against humanity.

The relation between art and morality is a topic for never ending debate. At the level of general principle, it should not be difficult to see that both art and morality are united in their affirmation of human life. In practice, however, there is an inevitable tension, and occasionally head-on collision, between a work of art and a group's sense of morality. Every code of morality is concerned with social order and drawing lines that an individual must not cross. Artists typically are impatient, some very much so, with a requirement that one conform to what a society's guardians think is acceptable behavior.

Some artists are too quick to announce that art has nothing to do with morality. In the long perspective of history, art is a great contributor to moral goodness. That only happens, however, if a society does not limit art to what seems nice, pretty, and a bolstering of current morals (or manners). The artist needs a license to be different and to shake up a society's perceptions; the license does have limits, but the limit should not be that of the mayor who does not like a work of art or some group who claim to be offended. The condemnation of some movies in the 1950s now seems absurd. On the other hand, without some agreed-upon limits, the movie industry can degenerate into orgies of violence and exploitations of sex that overwhelm the genuine artistry of many movies.

Art is an important part of everyone's education in morality. Protests against a work of art are often the result of a stunted development of morality, the equating of morality with a series of prohibitions instilled when one was a child. It is quite shocking to find what Emil Durkheim says of art and morality in his book *Morality and Education*: "Art is a game. Morality, on the contrary, is life in earnest . . . . It is easy to see at a glance the distance separating art and morality; it is the very distance that separates play from work. Not therefore by learning to play that special game, art, will we learn to do our duty."[56] Durkheim may be correct that art does not teach us to "do our duty." But there might be more fruitful ways to teach morality than by equating it with doing our duty. Duty is joined to right when a young person learns a morality of responsibility. And a sense of responsibility can be well conveyed in the practice and appreciation of the play that is called art.

Examples of the Arts

The uniquely human is most strikingly exemplified in particular works of art that resonate throughout most of the world. There is no general art;

each work of art is limited by its time and place; however, someone who sees only the characteristics which stamp its origin might be blind to its possible effects. "It is true that Hebrew prophecy, Greek art, Italian opera, German poetry, and English drama belong to the world. But in every instance, they reflect their ethnic sources and environmental influences, without which they are inconceivable."[57] In modern times, especially in the last few decades, time and space may sometimes seem homogenized as movies, paintings, and music are distributed by transnational corporations. Nonetheless, the best of the arts still embody people, places, and events that are distinctive while at the same time they give intimation of the universal.

Even to list all of the world's arts is an impossible task; the most I attempt in this section is to cite some examples of how works of art embody the double meaning of uniqueness: stunning in their particularity together with an invitation to every appreciative reader, listener, or viewer. The artist need not be aware of a universalizing process. Goethe's description of poetry applies to all the arts: "It expresses something particular without thinking of the universal or pointing to it. Whoever grasps this particular in a living way will simultaneously realize the universal, too, without even becoming aware of it—or realize it only later."[58] Poetry from three hundred or three thousand years ago can still touch human hearts today.

Literature. Many of our literary forms go back to the dawn of history when poetry, storytelling, music, and dance would not have been separate forms of art. Literature has a special obstacle to its being appreciated universally, the difficulty of translation. Poetic speech as the most precise use of words suffers the most in translation. The collaboration of expert translators for any literary work is a precious gift to everyone who reads in translation. No one is so skilled in languages as not to sometimes have need of translators.

The printing press opened the world to great literature; books became available to millions of people who had previously lacked access to them. Now the Internet together with the process of digitalization has the potential to make literature available to billions of people. The usual addendum is that while technology makes possible an advance of a human tradition of great literature, the realization requires political skills and economic reforms.

One form of literary art that Plato wanted banned from his Republic was drama.[59] His countrymen had produced some of the greatest dramas in history. Plato argued that the theater was bad for both actors and audiences. It involves a kind of duplicity and can be confusing about real life that is suspended for an experiment in imagined life. Plato had cause for concern that great drama can shake the foundations of a society. The performance does not have to convey a political message to have political effect. The playwright and the actors are visitors from a realm of possibility that any authoritarian leader has to fear. Shakespeare, as much as any single individual, shaped the modern attitude toward the "solidarity that knits together the loneliness of innumerable hearts."[60]

Literature at its best is about life and especially death as the conclusion of a life. Dying is the most particular of actions for an individual and the most universal of experiences for the human race. "If the word death were absent from our vocabulary, our great works of literature would have remained unwritten."[61] The great tragic figures in Sophocles or Shakespeare are studies in the inner struggle of good and evil, which is shadowed by the individual's own mortality. The viewer does not have to master all the historical circumstances in which the drama is set. Northrop Frye wrote of Shakespeare's *Macbeth*: "If you wish to know the history of eleventh-century Scotland, look elsewhere; if you wish to know what it means to gain a kingdom and lose one's soul, look here."[62]

As in many of the arts, drama in the twentieth century took a circuitous route to the individual's soul, trying to sneak around or punch through the complex entanglements of modern life. When, for example, the dramatist did not accept the structure of the theater itself by erasing the line between the actors and the audience, the result could be either a powerful experience or else simple confusion. A play within a play had been used by Shakespeare. That possibility was explored in a variety of ways, for example, by Pirandello's *Six Characters in Search of an Author* or by Tom Stoppard's *Rosencrantz and Guildenstern are Dead*. These plays could get the audience to take a different view of what was on stage when the play within a play became the main story of the play.

In the 1950s, a number of playwrights were classified as belonging to a "theater of the absurd." The name was unfair in that the aim was not to do something absurd; no great skill is needed for irrational words and meaningless gestures. However, an attempt to uncover the absurdities that surround modern life involved showing scenes of absurdities. Finding a skillful way to penetrate a world of banal speech and deadening routine is what separates genius from merely beating against the current.[63] One playwright who stood out in the struggle to express the inexpressible was Samuel Beckett. His characters are frozen in time without wisdom from the past or hope for a future, but they doggedly go on waiting. They continue to exist "for the conversation."[64] Such a dark outlook might not seem to be a vehicle of international understanding. However, when human pretentiousness is stripped away, a nearly universal resonance can ensue.

One relatively new literary form in the modern era is the novel. The modern emphasis on the individual and the imagination has produced some brilliant works of fiction that can reveal the human condition just as well as works of philosophy can. As the process of publishing has become easier and cheaper, popular novels have widened their circulation beyond the country of their origin. The Internet makes it possible for everyone in the world to publish his or her own novel.

In recent decades, it has become more common for a novel published in Turkey or Sweden or Nigeria to become a bestseller in the United States. Popular fiction in the United States finds ready translators in Europe. Some genre, such as police procedurals are dismissed with the faint praise that they are page turners. In these days, however, almost any book reading is a good sign. Most people will never get to Proust or Joyce. There is a place for popular novels that give people a sense of place and some insight to a culture other than their own. Popular novels, along with movies and television, have made New York or Los Angeles or London familiar places around the world. The imbalance in the sources of popular culture will surely change in coming decades.

Music. The cross-cultural possibilities of music have one great advantage over literature; no translator is needed. At least translation in the sense of moving from one written language to another is unnecessary. However, transporting a form of music that is deeply embedded in the culture of one people to become integral to other cultures is a complex and unpredictable undertaking.[65] Music has its signature of time and place. Great works of music may require serious education in the nature of the music, but popular music needs no school-based education for its flourishing. Music, even more than literature, has the potential for uniting people at a profound level.

Music might be called the supreme legislator, a force that moves people and controls their movement. John Dewey, who was tone-deaf himself, could recognize that "if one can control the songs of a nation, one need not care who makes the laws." [66] The reference to the nation in Dewey's statement is a reminder that music's power can be used in the service of patriotism. Marching songs have been used both by liberating forces and by authoritarian dictators who draw upon a people's past. The Lutheran

Reformation, it has been said, sang its way across Germany; music helped to form the Germans into one people. Hitler was able for a time to exploit this tradition, but Hitler is long gone, and the great German composers are as powerful as ever.

Referring to the music of Johann Sebastian Bach, Lewis Thomas writes, "The Brandenburgs and the late quartets are not there to give us assurances that we have arrived; they carry the news that there are deep centers in our minds that we know nothing about except that they are there."[67] The great classical composers are clearly of their time, but their music can still stir the deepest feelings in a human being who is open to it. A first listening to great music may convey little understanding of it. "Reasons" in music consist of repeated listenings. Wittgenstein said that the way to understand Brahms is to listen to a Brahms's symphony, then listen and then listen again. Only after repeated listenings might one then compare Brahms to Beethoven or Haydn.[68]

Because of Europe's dominance of the world for several centuries, European standards of music accompanied the political control. Music, however, has its own ways so that in time the musical tastes brought from Europe interacted with local traditions and created new blends of music. Some folk or native music survived colonization and enslavement. A distinctive form of music grew up from oppressed people. Black people in South Africa, the United States and the Caribbean used music as a means of survival and in the process created extraordinary music. The great contribution of the United States to music has been traditions of jazz and blues, forms of music that were not invented in Hollywood. The best of music in the United States is likely to have its roots in the tradition of jazz and the Negro spiritual.

Like many of the arts, standards of music were challenged at the beginning of the twentieth century. Arnold Schoenberg's work in 1908 is usually credited with beginning what was called atonal music, an expansion of the ways music could be composed.[69] As in other arts, the dismantling of established rules could lead either to a confused mess or to works of genius. Perhaps more important than any one work by Schoenberg or John Cage, atonal music stirred imaginations for a variety of musical sounds. With the help of technology, music has embraced the world during the last century. The present quality of music reproduction is beyond what anyone could have imagined a few decades ago.

A powerful outbreak of popular music occurred in the 1960s when music became aligned with movements for justice. The many movements discussed in this book in their converging toward a human tradition were each accompanied by their own music. The Civil Rights movement in the United States is unimaginable without its music, starting with "We Shall Overcome," which became an anthem for many other peoples. Protests against the war in Vietnam found a powerful ally in folk music. Almost by himself, Elvis Presley became a white link with the black tradition and a new burst of energy in the white community. The short but powerful career of the Beatles provided not only raucous entertainment but also a new standard of musical excellence. Leonard Bernstein explained in a lecture and on television one evening how the music of the Beatles drew upon the very best musical traditions.[70]

The great success of popular music has paradoxically led to a crisis in the music industry. The Internet makes music available to everyone; with just a click, music of all kinds is there for the taking. The problem is that if the music is practically free for the listener, then where is the money to sustain the musicians and the recording industry? Presumably, a workable system will eventually emerge; there have been similar problems before but never on this (nonmusical) scale. In any case, music will not die out. In the convergence of traditions into a human tradition, music will be a central element in the human acceptance of diversity within unity.

Painting and Design. For as long as human beings have existed, they have apparently painted pictures and symbols on whatever surfaces were available. We have evidence of this fact from the discovery in 1940 at Lascaux, France, of paintings in a cave by our Paleolithic ancestors of seventeen thousand years ago. This extraordinary discovery attracted the attention of visitors from around the world. As can happen with any ancient art, an overexposure can do harm to it. Lascaux proved too popular a tourist attraction for the good of the paintings. On the other hand, the Internet makes it possible to view excellent reproductions of the caves and their treasure while sitting at one's desk.

Visual art has a special place in awakening a sense of human tradition. We do not know what ancient music sounded like; and literature connects us only to the history of writing. But from a time long before written records existed, we have artifacts that were designed by beings whom we can recognize as human. Archeology and anthropology have put us visually in the presence of our ancestors from thousands of years back. Besides the utilitarian tools needed for day to day survival, human life included knowledge of how to construct products for religious rituals, leisure, and aesthetic appreciation.

As is still true today, death was an inspiration for memorials that were a way of being connected to one's people. The burial site of Newgrange in Ireland is about five thousand years old. It was constructed with such great skill that water did not seep into it during the centuries in which it was hidden until its discovery in 1699. Most extraordinary, it was built so that the sun comes down the forty-foot entrance tunnel each winter solstice. (There is a lottery each year for fifty places within the tomb for this annual event.) Knowledge of mathematics and astronomy was needed for the design of the building. The religion of the people and their belief in an afterlife were apparently connected to the seasons of the year. Human beings continue to associate religious rituals with what most people still call the movement of the sun in the heavens.

The visual and architectural arts that have come down from past centuries and millennia are our gateway into appreciating the way peoples lived. They differed from us in so many ways, but we can still recognize humanity in its many variations and the beauty of designs that can be striking. They used whatever materials were at hand so that only the hardy products of metal and stone have survived. If one wishes to appreciate Australian aboriginal art, the place to go is the wilds of Australia where the earliest painting are done on rocks. Later works were done on bark, which is difficult to preserve. Finally, there are canvasses of aboriginal art. As the demand for the art increased, many of the artists were inclined to turn out whatever the tourist trade wanted. Instead of early paintings that enshrined a story about the people, much of the later art is neatly drawn according to the standards of the prospective buyers.

Muslim and Christian religions, while beginning from the most modest circumstances, inspired great works of art. Islam did not accept an art of human figures, but it produced other artistic beauty in poetry, architecture, and dance. Islam, like Christianity, was able to move across numerous cultures in the direction of a worldwide community that remains a Muslim ideal. The Christian meaning of church moved from describing a gathering in a home to the name of magnificent buildings. So impressive were the churches that by the time of the Protestant Reformation, they tended to overshadow the meaning of church as a community of believers.

The Protestant Reformers, in reaction, destroyed beautiful art works of statues and buildings. Both Roman Catholic and Protestant Churches became the poorer for their inability to house great art as integral to their Christian worship. Cotton Mather's description of his father, Increase, that "he put aside every art in order to convey the word of God" is sad testimony of the Puritan stripping of the altars.[71] Nietzsche's caustic comment that "if they wish me to believe in their savior, they will have to sing better hymns" is indicative of the importance of the arts and the Western Church's falling behind where once it led.[72]

The Middle Ages produced wonderful paintings, most often inspired by religious themes. The beginning of the modern era represented an expansion of themes and new techniques for capturing light and conveying three dimensions. A grand flowering of painting and sculpture reflected European dominance in the world. Other native art did not attract much attention beyond its own borders. The twentieth century's visual art, similar to what happened in other arts, was a time of experimentation and of cross-cultural enrichment. The rules of composition that had developed during centuries of European art were challenged by several schools and movements. For some people, art seemed to have become irrational splashes of paint. The movements in the early twentieth century were sometimes traced to the influence of psychoanalysis or to despair engendered by World War I. Reason, it seemed, had fled, and subterranean emotions had taken over.

In time, it became clearer where the new logic of art resided. As always there are some daring artists who receive both praise as geniuses and denunciation as charlatans. Time will usually tell. A painting by Jackson Pollock that may at first seem to be splashes of paint has a careful structure. What seems clear is that the limits of art have been expanded. Art from other cultures is likely to show up in major museums around the world, a positive step for awareness of human tradition.

Beyond incorporation of ancient art into the human tradition, modern technology has created new forms of art that ancient peoples could not have imagined. The possibilities of what can be done with film are only beginning to be explored. Even while box-office receipts control most of what is made by big movie studios, there are spectacular uses of color, sound, and movement to create what no single artist is able to do. With today's cameras, everybody in the world becomes a potential filmmaker. That may be too much of a good thing; constructing things of beauty still requires a minimum of artistic taste. Nonetheless, a true folk art, one that is rich in numerous contributions from ordinary lives is now possible. A human tradition supported by a range of arts that the world has never seen before can now be envisioned. There is no guarantee, however, that it will not be trampled upon by the dark side of the human that is driven by fear and greed.

One particular piece of architecture deserves special comment for the relation between nations and the awareness of human rights. All peoples honor the memory of their dead and construct memorials to past generations that have handed on their achievements to the living. There is little hope for humanity if the bond between the dead, the living, and the yet unborn is severed. One form of memorial, however, is especially problematic: statues or monuments to honor people who have died in war. In the past, fighting for the survival of one's people was especially honored. Young men were thought to need the discipline of soldiering to become true men. The military hero provided the example for other kinds of heroism.

Whatever defense of war might once have been conceivable, glorification of war today is a defense of the indefensible. War is the wholesale destruction of men, women, children, and the nonhuman environment. The phrase "collateral damage" is bandied about as if the devastation were merely an incidental side effect to a perfectly good undertaking. The old rhetoric of war hangs on among the politicians who send their sons (and now daughters) to kill people in another part of the world. Patriotic speeches thanking the troops are in large part self-justifications for those who do not suffer the horrors of war. After the speeches, the young person is faced with trying to adjust to ordinary life with a job and family; not surprisingly, many of them have mental as well as physical wounds. Those who come home in coffins are praised for making the "ultimate sacrifice for their country."

War memorials have been part of the coverup and the deceit of war. By glorifying the triumph of our boys over the dastard enemy, a belligerent attitude is preserved for future wars. The country has to rally behind the leader when it is claimed that war is unfortunate but necessary. Monuments of past wars are always there to remind the population that it is only by war that the country has survived and prospered. The city of Washington D.C. is a shrine to the succession of wars that have characterized United States history. The myth of America is continuously affirmed in the military rituals surrounding the war monuments.

The Lincoln Memorial has been able to generate a different attitude and to be a setting for protests against injustice. Abraham Lincoln is venerated as a Christ figure who died to save the country, a role he would find strange. The United States Civil War can not evoke the same celebration of triumph as the country's other wars. Lincoln, in his Second Inaugural Address, dared to suggest that if there is a God of justice, the country was getting what it deserved. The country still needs healing from a war in which brother killed brother. But the U.S. Civil War is less an exception among the wars than a prototype of all wars in which humans kill their brothers and sisters.

The Tomb of the Unknown Soldier was perhaps a first step toward remembering what should be the lesson of war. It was a symbol of the untold masses of people slaughtered in war. Most of the people killed in wars are anonymous; not even their names remain. Unfortunately, what could be a somber reminder of the senseless horror of war is overshadowed at the Tomb of the Unknown Soldier by military pomp and speeches about our fallen heroes.

A startling breakthrough in the United States was the construction of the Vietnam Memorial, one of the most visited sites in Washington. A young architect, Maya Lin, designed a stark slab with the names of the 58,195 soldiers of the United States who died in the war. Lin said, "I create places in which to think without trying to dictate what to think."[73] Any visitor on any day can sense that she has succeeded in providing a place of mourning and somber memories. The site is structured as a journey in which a person walks down and then ascends. "As the long polished panels reflect those that move before them, the names of the past become etched on the faces of the present and, for a moment, the living and the dead are one."[74]

It was nearly miraculous that Lin was able to build such a fitting tribute to the five hundred thousand young people who were sent to fight in a civil war that the United States did not understand. What is lacking in the Vietnam Memorial are the names of the estimated two million Vietnamese and Cambodian people who died in the war. Including those names was not possible. But the fundamental principle of war memorials for accurately remembering the dead is that all of them are my brothers and sisters. The war memorial can be a testimony against war but only if the mourning is for both sides. Instead of fostering belligerence and xenophobia, the remembrance of war could generate the determination that it should not happen again.

The United States could learn from several Japanese war memorials. The Japanese have little to remember about World War II that is glorious and uplifting. Every country finds it difficult to admit the horrors that it perpetrated during a war. The peace park in Hiroshima is admirably ecumenical in its inclusion of testimony from almost all countries, including eventually the United States. A more extraordinary remembrance of war is the monument in Okinawa where one of the bloodiest battles of World

War II was fought. In addition to the names of the Japanese soldiers killed in the battle, the names of the United States Marines who were killed are also included.

Nations can and do change. The pseudo-patriotism that has led in the past to disastrous wars has to be countered by respect for all peoples and recognition of the right to live for every individual. As I have insisted throughout this book, the world is rapidly becoming unified. We cannot wait for an invasion from Mars to create a sense of earthly kinship. As Erasmus said five centuries ago, "If men are dedicated to fighting for their country, why not make the whole earth their country?" In the future, either there will be recognition of human rights, or there is not likely to be a human race.

CONCLUSION

Here ends my brief for the defense of *human rights* as a term that has a rightful place in the twenty-first century language of international relations. It is the term around which international ethics has been built. In less than half a century, the term *human rights* has achieved sensational success. It may not match the terms Google, Facebook, or Twitter in its spread around the world, but as philosophical terms, go it is up among the all-time leaders. Like most international sensations, however, its rapid success can be its undoing. Many political leaders are ready to invoke human rights only when it suits their policies. Other political leaders dismiss accusations of their violating human rights as a plot led by nation-states that should be concerned with their own domestic problems.

Most people these days seem to accept that there are such things as human rights and they do not spend much time worrying about the origin and basis of those rights. Legal scholars, philosophers, and historians have produced an immense literature on every aspect of human rights. Some of the literature consists of sermons preached on the basis of an orthodoxy whose bible is the 1948 Universal Declaration of Human Rights. Often, that document is assumed to have ratified and extended the French and British American Declarations of the eighteenth century.

This book has challenged many points of that orthodoxy and tried to find new ways to formulate questions about human rights. While I acknowledge that the Universal Declaration of Human Rights was a great achievement for its time, I claim that it is a badly flawed document, starting with its title. The UN authors, by assuming that political rights were well known, at least in one part of the world, and that the question was whether to add economic and cultural rights to a lengthy menu of human rights, unfortunately hardened some international divisions and created a dichotomy within the meaning of human rights. By not acknowledging the newness of the category of human rights, the UN declaration conveyed an impression that is still widespread that *human rights* is simply another name for what had been called natural rights. This latter term was a badly confused idea when it was used in the eighteenth century; it is a conversation stopper in the twenty-first century.

Human rights is not a perfect term for its task. Its most obvious problem is that any right, except a right applied to nonhuman animals, can logically be called a human right. That ambiguity is one reason that *human rights* is such a popular term, but its rhetorical attractiveness threatens its clarity and effectiveness as a term that refers to the rights that belong to every human being. However, the comprehensiveness of the term *human rights* is also a strength; it refers without a strain to all genders, ages, nationalities, and cultures; it can include both political and economic matters. And *human* can include a meaning, or several meanings, of *natural* while not excluding history.

My choice of tradition to gather in all this diversity is admittedly paradoxical in that tradition is often used to refer to what is parochial and what is opposed to progress. Far from rejecting the parochial meaning of tradition, I have incorporated that into the idea of a human tradition. I have admitted that a concrete and formed human tradition is still in its infancy; its birth not by accident coincided with the advent of the term *human rights*. Instead of the West pushing its long-standing idea of rights on the rest of the world, I have portrayed the human rights movement as a worldwide conversation that might secure a true agreement among all peoples of the world about a basic moral standard. The UN declaration was among the first words spoken on human rights; the follow-up covenants in 1966, which are supposedly binding have had limited effect. But the revolution in communication since the 1960s means that the world has a much clearer choice: find common grounds for international peace and respect for all people or suffer international violence beyond all measure and precedent.

The idea of human tradition as the basis of human rights may seem to evade the problem rather than solve it. What I have tried to do is to suggest a different context and a reformulation of what a basis of human rights means. One of the twentieth century's philosophical questions that affects human rights was a controversy over foundationalism versus antifoundationalism. The metaphor of laying a foundation on which to build a house had been a favorite in much of modern philosophy and its concern for finding certitude. The metaphor seemed to assume a mathematical-logical model for human thinking. Antifoundationalism in the twentieth century was an attack on this assumption. This opposition was badly formulated. I subscribe neither to foundationalism nor to antifoundationalism. Instead, I make the claim that humans have a nature that makes possible a human tradition, but I make no claim to knowledge of an eternal and universal essence on which to base certainty.

Human beings do look for certitude but not necessarily in the form of a deduction from an abstract principle or in a construction sitting on a foundation. Wittgenstein pointed out that if one's physical contact with the surrounding world does not provide certainty, nothing else is likely to do so. My argument for the language of human rights is not based on logical deduction or abstract ideas. I have argued the case for acceptance of human rights because of a convergence of numerous factors that point to a few universal needs of human beings. I am confident that the evidence will continue to mount—provided that the human race does not destroy itself.

G. K. Chesterton wrote that philosophical certainty comes not when something proves a conclusion but when everything does. Perhaps he should have said "nearly everything." I admit that particular traditions contain frightful horrors as well as wonderfully humanizing elements. Conversation between traditions is a way to criticize and resist the horrors of human history even though there is no guarantee that such a process will be a smooth progress for the human race. But like most people, I think that one has to trust that some progress is possible.

The three chapters in the first part of this book concern history, especially linguistic history. These chapters are not intended to tell the history of human rights; instead they are to show that there was no human rights movement until the second half of the twentieth century. The chapters do pay particular attention to the origin and use of the term *natural rights*. The human rights movement has much to learn from discussions in the seventeenth and eighteenth centuries, and even from medieval canonists. However, the overall conclusion of the first part of the book is the need for a worldwide discussion that would fill out what emerged in the twentieth century as human rights.

The five chapters of the second part of the book describe human conversations that have been contributing to a human tradition. I pick out five areas to examine: gender, age, religion, environment, and culture. I do not see much need to defend what I have included, but there is an inescapable problem as to what I have not included.

Starting the discussion of the fullness of humanity with a chapter on the relation between men and women seems obvious today. Fifty years ago, the question about the rights of women was not so clear; it was then often dismissed as the complaints of a few women in rich countries who had the luxury of leisure. That view is not asserted in many places today although there remain bastions of defense for dehumanizing practices that afflict women worldwide.

In the chapter on men and women, I give brief attention to a revolution still under way: a rethinking of the relation of *heterosexual* and *homosexual*. For understanding the unity and diversity of the human race, this sexual revolution is probably more important than anyone alive can grasp. Or at least I have to admit that I cannot begin to comprehend all that is implied by gay and lesbian people no longer being blocked from public acknowledgment. I doubt that anyone fifty years ago could have imagined today's widespread acceptance of homosexuality as a fact of human life.

At the 1992 Republican National Convention, a speaker was passionately condemning homosexuality. I remember thinking that his condemnation was less important than the fact that he was admitting the reality of homosexuality into a conservative public forum, something inconceivable a few years previous. Simply by naming reality in his attack, he had already lost the game.

The chapter on age is a reminder that human rights have to include humans of every age. The middle-aged men who have dominated writing on human rights tend to think of the normal human specimen as a healthy, independent adult male. Human rights can become identified with agency, liberty, and leading an independent life. I quoted Henry Shue that "for everyone healthy adulthood is bordered on each side by helplessness, and it is vulnerable to interruption by helplessness, temporary or permanent, at any time." The main argument of my chapter, therefore, is not just that human rights should apply to all ages, but that human rights have to be conceived from the standpoint of the human condition of vulnerability and the need to care for the most vulnerable. I pointed out in the discussion of dying that the term *dignity*, which is so prominent in human rights literature, is often used in the phrase "dying with dignity" to mean suicide instead of humane care for the dying.

The chapter on religion addresses a topic that human rights literature usually avoids or else assumes is an obstacle. Anyone familiar with Christian or Muslim writing can understand why there is reluctance to allow religion into the conversation. However, religions give no sign of disappearing and to pretend that religions are not an important piece of the puzzle is not helpful. If one digs deeply into religious traditions, including Christian and Muslim, one discovers good news as well as bad for human rights. Perhaps for the first time in history, serious conversation between religious traditions is possible and in a few places actual. An advocacy of rights for every human being can fit comfortably in any of the major religious traditions. One problem with recognizing this possibility is that scholars often show a lack of patience in attending to the peculiar logic of religion within the religions.

The chapter on the humans and their environment is about human rights in context. The environmental movement is seldom mentioned in the literature of human rights, but it has helped to shape almost every human question during the last half century. Some environmentalists consider the idea of human rights to be one of the central problems of the environment; humans are not supposed to claim superiority over other species.

The language of "man conquering nature" is indeed a root cause of environmental problems. The alternative is not to claim that all species are equal but to get men, women, and children to appreciate what surrounds them and to become the responsible animals. The humans are the most unique creature on earth, and their uniqueness is an affirmation of the uniqueness of every living thing.

The last chapter on culture is a catch-all that could be a half dozen more chapters or could be a framework for the previous chapters. In the chapter, I discuss sports and arts as helps to worldwide conversation. I noted that each of the arts deserves an extensive discussion for its part in the emerging human tradition. One topic I deal with briefly in the chapter is race, which could have a chapter on its own. In the United States, talking about race in general can obscure the historic problems of African Americans. I do not see those problems as affecting the meaning of human rights; however, the achievement of human rights for all African American people remains one of the most troubling problems in the nation. The number of people in its prisons is a bad sign about the United States; the disproportion in the number of African American people in that population is a scandal and disgrace. In the wider world, race remains a major category but one I hope that will eventually fade into the background at least on matters of human rights.

I return to the opening sentence of this conclusion. Human rights are part of a language of advocacy. Every important human activity involves the question of right or wrong. In advocating an ethical position, it is important that statements are not untrue. But one's rendering of the situation is always with language that has emotional connotations. The process is one of advocating a naming of reality that is closer to the truth than any other available language. The jury for this advocacy is the human race or at least a sufficient part of the human race that can accept human rights as a universal need that should be achieved in practice for every person.

NOTES

Introduction

1   George W. Bush, Interview with Ken Auletta, "Fortress Bush," *The New Yorker, January* 14, 2004, 64.

2   Quoted in Max Rodenbeck, "Volcano of Rage," in *New York Review*, March 24, 2011, 4.

3   Jacques Maritain, "Introduction," *Human Rights: Comments and Interpretations* (New York: Wingate, 1949), 9. Maritain himself believed that he knew the source and meaning of those rights as evident in his *The Rights of Man and Natural Law* (New York: Scribner's, 1943).

4   I agree with Joseph Raz, *The Morality of Freedom* (New York: Oxford University Press, 1986), 192, that "rights have a distinctive and important role in morality. But it is also a specialized role, not a comprehensive one. They contribute their share as a distinctive type of moral consideration, not as the foundation of all moral consideration."

5   The plural *responsibilities* is nearly always unhelpful. In history and for the individual person, *responsible* begins as a verb: responsible to someone or something. That externally oriented action leads to a person internally accepting a responsibility for his or her actions. A dialectic ensues: what a person accepts "responsibility for" leads to a broadening and deepening of what he or she is "responsible to."

6   The difference is recognized by Louis Henkin, "International Human Rights," in *Human Rights*, ed. J. Roland Pennock and John Chapman (New York: New York University Press, 1981), 257-80. Despite the ambiguity in his title, Henkin notes the distinction: "The international law of human rights creates legal rights and obligations. . . . But international discourse, including international law, refers repeatedly to human rights apparently as preexisting in some other universe." (266).

7   Jeremy Bentham, *An Introduction to the Principles of Morals and Legislation* (New York: Oxford University Press, 1970), 296. Bentham introduced *international* as a modifier of jurisprudence. In a footnote, he writes, "The word *international*, it must be acknowledged, is a new one; though, it is hoped, sufficiently analogous and intelligible." He credits French Chancellor Henri-Francois Daguesseau with pointing out the need "to express in a more significant way" the meaning of "law of nations" as "law between nations." (*droit entre les gens*).

8   The Declaration of Independence says that "among these rights" are life, liberty, and the pursuit of happiness. The French Declaration presumes to name all these rights as liberty, property, security, and resistance to oppression.

9   An excellent summary of this development can be found in the first chapter of Philippe Sands, *Lawless World: America and the Making and Breaking of Global Rules- from FDR's Atlantic Charter to George W. Bush's Illegal War* (New York: Viking Books, 2005).

10 The four Geneva conventions were adopted in 1949; the United States was also a party to the 1984 Convention against Torture and Other Cruel, Inhuman or Degrading Treatment or Punishment. President George W. Bush's Legal Counsel Alberto Gonzales famously wrote in a January 2002 memo: "In my judgment, this new paradigm [post 9/11] renders obsolete Geneva's strict limitations on questioning of enemy prisoners and renders quaint some of its provisions." The memo was cited in *Newsweek*, May 24, 2004. *Newsweek* did make the memo seem worse by ending the quotation in the middle of a sentence where Gonzales specifies what he found "quaint," namely, commissary privileges, athletic uniforms and scientific instruments. Nevertheless, the first half of the statement on the questioning of prisoners was damning enough. The most comprehensive study of torture during these years, *Detainee Treatment* (Washington: Constitution Project, 2013), 3, concluded "perhaps the most notable finding of this panel is that it is indisputable that the United States engaged in the practice of torture."

11 Jeremy Bentham, "Anarchical Fallacies," in *Nonsense upon Stilts*, ed. Jeremy Waldron (New York: Methuen, 1987), 52.

12 James Nickel, *Making Sense of Rights*, rev. ed. (Malden: Blackwell, 2007), 37, says that "reflection on the idea that the holders of human rights are simply all people is too broad." He explains that "some rights are held only by adult citizens not by all persons . . . The rights of people who are very young, severely retarded, comatose or senile are justifiably limited." The alternative conclusion which one can draw is that Nickel has overextended the number

of human rights. I argue in chapter 5 that children and the very sick are chief tests of the meaning of human rights.

13   Samuel Moyn, *The Last Utopia: Human Rights in History* (Cambridge: Harvard University Press, 2010).

14   Moyn offers evidence such as in 1977 the *New York Times* used *human rights* five time as often as it had in any previous year; Amnesty International increased its membership thirty time during the 1970s; a bibliography published in 1978 listing books on rights included only one book on human rights.

15   I do not mean to dismiss important uses of *human rights* before the 1970s. For example, Martin Luther King, Jr., in his "Letter from Birmingham Jail" in 1963 notes that he was in Birmingham under the auspices of the "Christian Movement for Human Rights." In this letter and elsewhere King almost always refers to *civil rights*, which was his direct concern.

16   For example, Jonathan Israel in giving his book *Democratic Enlightenment* the subtitle of *Philosophy, Revolution and Human Rights* (New York: Oxford, 2011) seems not only to use *human rights* anachronistically but also to attribute too great an accomplishment for what he calls the radical enlightenment of the eighteenth century.

17   For example, Hannah Arendt's 1951 book, *The Origins of Totalitarianism* (New York: Harcourt, Brace, Jovanovich) uses the "rights of man," interchangeably with *human rights*. The book makes little reference to the Universal Declaration of Human Rights. A 1950 book edited by R.M. MacIver, *Great Expressions of Human Rights* (New York: Harper and Brothers) has almost no references to the UN Declaration until the last ten pages. Lectures by Leo Strauss in 1949 and published in 1953 as *Natural Right and History* (Chicago: University of Chicago Press), make no reference to the UN Declaration.

18   John Rawls, *A Theory of Justice* (Cambridge: Harvard University Press, 1971). In later writing, Rawls adopted the language of human rights as an extension of the ideas of justice and rights which he had written about from the perspective of a particular society: *The Law of Peoples* (Cambridge: Harvard University Press, 2001).

19   Ronald Dworkin, *Taking Rights Seriously* (Cambridge: Harvard University Press, 1976).

20   Michel Foucault in a 1976 lecture in *Power/Knowledge* (New York: Pantheon, 1980), 80, was one of many commentators to see the period of 1960-75 as a collapse of authority: "What has emerged in the last ten or fifteen years is a sense of the increasing vulnerability to criticism of things, institutions, practices, discourses. A certain fragility has been discovered in the very

bedrock of existence." It can be added that nothing has happened since then to disconfirm Foucault's judgment.

21 This dichotomy of the political and the economic has much older roots. As I describe in chapter 3, the split was identified by Karl Marx's early writing in his criticism of the French Declaration of the Rights of Man and of the Citizen.

22 Henry Shue, *Basic Rights*, 2nd ed. (Princeton: Princeton University Press, 1996). In writing this book at the end of the 1970s, Shue uses "basic rights" for indispensable moral rights. He very seldom uses the term *human rights*, which had not come into common use. Hugo Bedeau, "Why Do We Have the Rights We Do?" in *Social Philosophy and Policy*, 1(Spring, 1984), 59, makes the misleading assertion that "Henry Shue is the latest and most unrelenting philosopher to argue that all human beings possess what have come to be called 'welfare rights.'" Shue never argues for "welfare rights" in contrast to liberty rights; instead his basic rights undercut that dichotomy.

23 Henry Shue, *Basic Rights,* 91, in his usual acknowledgment of the limits on what he claims, writes that "security, subsistence, social participation and physical movement are almost certainly not the only basic rights." An extension of the number of such rights is developed in what Martha Nussbaum, following Amartya Sen, calls "the capabilities approach." Nussbaum identifies ten capabilities that she says are based on "the result of years of cross-cultural discussion." She may be right about her list but it surely generates debate about whether all these capabilities represent universal values. Martha Nussbaum, "In Defense of Universal Human Values," *Women and Human Development: The Capabilities Approach* (Cambridge: Cambridge University Press, 2000), 34-110. Amartya Sen, *The Idea of Justice* (Cambridge: Harvard University Press, 2009), 231-35.

24 Susan Moller Okin, "Liberty and Welfare: Some Issues in Human Rights Theory," in *Human Rights*, ed. J. Roland Pennock and John Chapman (New York: New York University Press, 1981), 235-36 offers an analysis similar to Shue of three basic needs requiring three basic rights. Her third basic right, which differs from Shue's, is a right based on "the need to be respected." I think she weakens her case in accepting the language of "liberty rights and welfare rights," which leads to questions of "priorities" among human rights.

25 Amartya Sen, *The Idea of Justice*, 373, notes that the recognition of human rights does not mean that everyone everywhere has to help prevent every violation of such rights. It is "an acknowledgment that if one is in a position to do something effective in preventing the violation of such a right, then

one does have a good reason do just that—a reason that must be taken into account in deciding what should be done."

26 Henry Shue, *Basic Rights*, especially in the Afterward (153-80) in which he replies to criticism of his treatment of duties in the first edition of the book.

27 Thomas Pogge, "Cosmopolitanism and Sovereignty," *Ethics*, 103:1(Oct., 1992), 48-75 has written very helpfully on this institutional duty. He distinguishes the *interactional* for direct personal duties and *institutional* a "shared responsibility for the justice of any practices one supports."

28 Jürgen Habermas, *The Divided West* (Malden: Polity Press, 2006), 105: "One cannot achieve justice between nations through moralization but only through the juridification of international relations."

29 Michael Ignatieff, *Human Rights as Politics and Idolatry* (Princeton: Princeton University Press, 2001), 23.

30 Ludwig Wittgenstein, *Blue and Brown Books* (New York: Harper and Row, 1964), 29: "It may seem queer to say that we may correctly use either of two forms of expression which seem to contradict each other; but such cases are very frequent." For example, some people say that "every historical event is unique" while other people think that a claim to uniqueness removes a question from history. See "Is the Holocaust Unique?" in Gabriel Moran, *Uniqueness: Problem or Paradox in Jewish and Christian Traditions* (New York: Orbis Books, 1992), 25-40.

31 A. J. Toynbee, *A Study of History* (New York: Oxford University Press, 1961), 12:11: "This word 'unique' is a negative term signifying what is mentally incomprehensible."

32 Gish Jen, *Tiger Writing: Art, Culture and the Interdependent Self* (Cambridge: Harvard University Press, 2013), 158.

33 Ellis Rifkin, *The Shaping of Jewish History* (New York: Charles Scribner's Sons, 1971); Gershom Scholem, "Revelation and Tradition as Religious Categories in Judaism," in *The Messianic Idea in Judaism* (New York: Schocken Books, 1971), 282-304.

34 The claim was made explicit in the writings of Irenaeus of Lyon in the late second century. After the Reformation, the difference between Catholic and Protestant was often put into a slogan of "scripture and tradition" versus "scripture alone." Although Luther used that latter phrase, he was careful not to reject "authentic" tradition but only the accretions of false traditions. See Eric Gritsch, *Martin: God's Court Jester* (Philadelphia: Fortress Press, 1983), 102.

35 Plato, *Phaedrus*, 275a-e.

36   H. G. Gadamer, *Truth and Method* (New York: Continuum, 1982), 241;
      T. S. Eliot makes a similar point about art in his essay "Tradition and the
      Individual Talent," *The Sacred Wood* (New York: Knopf, 1968), 41: "For
      order to persist after the supervention of novelty, the *whole* existing order
      must be, if ever so slightly, altered."

37   Leo Strauss, quoted in Michael Rosenak, *Commandment and Concern: Jewish
      Religious Education in Secular Society* (Philadelphia,: Jewish Publication
      Society, 1987), 77.

38   Samuel Beckett, *Happy Days* (New York: Grove Press, 1994); *The Unnamable*
      (New York: Grove Press, 1978; *Endgame* (New York: Grove Press, 1958), 49, 70.

39   Michael Oakeshott, "Political Education," in *Rationalism in Politics and Other
      Essays* (New York: Barnes and Noble, 1962), 128.

40   Alasdair MacIntyre, *After Virtue: A Study in Moral Theory* (Notre Dame:
      University of Notre Dame Press, 1981), 222.

41   Kwame Anthony Appiah, "Battling with Dubois," *New York Review*, Dec.
      22, 2011, 81-85.

42   Terry Nardin, "Ethical Traditions and International Affairs," in *Traditions
      of International Ethics*, ed. Terry Nardin and David Mapel (Cambridge:
      Cambridge University Press, 1992), 8.

43   Habermas, *The Divided West*, 146, discussing Immanuel Kant's advocacy of
      a world republic.

44   Aristotle, *Politics*, 1254b, 20-22; *Nicomachean Ethics*, 1143a, 8-9.

45   MacIntyre, *After Virtue*, 69.

46   Chris Brown, "Universal Rights: A Critique," in *Human Rights in Global
      Politics*, ed. Tim Dunne and Nicholas Wheeler (Cambridge: Cambridge
      University Press, 1993), 109.

47   I refer to *movements* in the general sense of any group advocating its position.
      I am neither assuming nor arguing against any technical definition of a "social
      movement."

48   That was the view of the authors of the *Universal Declaration of Human
      Rights* in placing *dignity* in the first article as the basis of rights. Mary Ann
      Glendon, *A World Made New: Eleanor Roosevelt and the Universal Declaration
      of Human Rights* (New York: Random House, 2001), 146-48.

49   Wayne Meeks, *The Origins of Christian Morality: The First Two Centuries*
      (New Haven: Yale University Press, 1995), 39.

50   R.W. Southern, *Medieval Humanism and Other Studies* (Oxford: Blackwell,
      1984), 32.

51   *Meister Eckhart: The Essential Sermons, Commentaries, Treaties and Defense*
      (New York: Paulist Press, 1981). For another example, see the fifteenth-century

work by Pico della Mirandola, *On the Dignity of Man* (Indianapolis: Hackett, 1998).

52 David Hume's essay "Of the Dignity or Meanness of Human Nature," might be taken as an exception. Hume stands out for basing ethics on sentiment and fellow feeling. However, when he asserts human dignity by a comparison to other animals, his first of many bases is "a creature whose thoughts are not limited by any narrow bounds, either of place or time." *Essays, Moral, Political and Literary,* ed. E.F. Miller, rev. ed. (New York: Oxford University Press, 1963), 83.

53 C. S. Lewis, *The Abolition of Man* (New York: Macmillan, 1947), 80.

54 Steven Pinker, "The Stupidity of Dignity," *New Republic*, March 28, 2008, 31: "Dignity is just another application of autonomy;" see also Michael Ignatieff, *Human Rights as Politics and Idolatry*, 164, who responds to criticism of his dismissal of dignity: "I now see . . . that you cannot do without the idea of dignity at all. . . . While I concede this point, I still have difficulty about dignity. . . . Dignity as agency is thus the most plural, the most open definition of the word I can think of."

55 Ira Byock, *Dying Well: Peace and Possibilities at the End of Life* (New York: Riverhead, 1997), 86.

56 Ignatieff, *Human Rights as Politics and Idolatry,* 54.

57 Gabriel Marcel, *The Existential Background of Human Dignity* (Cambridge: Harvard University Press, 1963), 134.

58 Elaine Scarry, *The Body in Pain: The Making and Unmaking of the World* (New York: Oxford University Press, 1985).

59 Avishai Margalit, *The Decent Society* (Cambridge: Harvard University Press, 1998), 262.

60 Pinker, "The Stupidity of Dignity," 30.

61 Kwame Appiah, "Response" in Ignatieff, *Human Rights as Politics and Idolatry,* 106-7: "Ordinary people almost everywhere have something like the notion of dignity." See also the author's *Cosmopolitanism: Ethics in a World of Strangers* (New York: W.W. Norton, 2007). Wole Soyinka, *Climate of Fear: The Quest for Dignity in a Dehumanized World* (New York: Random House, 2004), 98, cites a Yoruba saying, "Sooner death than indignity."

Chapter 1

1 Michael Ingnatieff, *Human Rights as Politics and Idolatry* (Princeton: Princeton University Press, 2003); William Schulz, *In Our Own Best Interests: How Defending Human Rights Benefits Us All* (Boston: Beacon Press, 2002).

2   Knud Haakonssen, *Natural Law and Moral Philosophy: From Grotius to the Scottish Enlightenment* (Cambridge: Cambridge University Press, 1996), 310-41. In today's context it is difficult to make sense of the idea that rights follow from duties. In a world of mutual relations, rights and duties are a single relation. Natural law láid down duties from which rights could be inferred.

3   Immanuel Kant, "Idea for a Universal History from a Cosmopolitan Point of View, *On History* (New York: Macmillan, 1963), 11-26. Dozens of times in the essay Kant refers to what Nature (she) intends, wills, provides, assigns, and so on. In *Critique of Practical Reason*, he calls Nature mankind's stepmother.

4   Jeremy Bentham, "Anarchical Fallacies," *Nonsense upon Stilts*, ed. Jeremy Waldron (New York: Methuen, l987), 53.

5   Bentham, "Anarchical Fallacies," 68.

6   Alasdair MacIntyre, *After Virtue: A Study of Moral Theory* (Notre Dame: University of Notre Dame, 1981), 69. The passage is left unchanged in the 3rd edition published in 2007.

7   MacIntyre, *After Virtue,* 234.

8   Jeremy Bentham in "Anarchical Fantasies," 55, concurs with this view when he asks for the source of imprescriptible rights and says: "Not by a God—they allow of none; but by their goddess, Nature."

9   Alexander Hamilton said that "the sacred rights of mankind are not to be rummaged for, among old parchments or musty records. They are written as with a sun beam, in the whole *volume* of human nature, by the Hand of Divinity itself." The contrast is unfortunate and unnecessary. Historical material would be a needed support for anyone claiming that sacred rights are written in human nature by the Hand of Divinity. Ironically, the context of this quotation is Hamilton's arguments about rights based on British tradition. *The Works of Alexander Hamilton*, ed. Harold Syrett (New York: Columbia University, 1961). I: 121-22.

10 Diane Orentlicher makes this point well in her response to Michael Ignatieff in his book, *Human Rights as Politics and Idolatry*, 141-58.

11 The phrase is especially identified with Hannah Arendt's book *The Human Condition* (Chicago: University of Chicago Press, 1958).

12 Ignatieff, *Human Rights*, 55. The italics are mine.

13 Martha Nussbaum, "In Defense of Universal Human Values," in *Women and Human Development: The Capabilities Approach* (Cambridge: Cambridge University Press, 2000), 101.

14 Kwame Appiah, *Cosmopolitanism: Ethics in a World of Strangers* (New York: Norton, 2007), 106.

15   Terry Eagleton, *The Illusions of Postmodernism* (Oxford: Blackwell, 1996), 99.

16   Plato, *Republic*, 404a.

17   The Jewish Torah has several meanings; it is often translated as *law*, which can be misleading; its earliest meaning was probably "instruction to a child" (Prov 1:8, 4:1).

18   Ignatieff, *Human Rights*, 80.

19   Ignatieff, *Human Rights*, 78.

20   On the Jewish conception of the human as a struggle between *yetzer ha-ra* and *yetzer tov*, see Robert Seltzer, *Jewish People, Jewish Thought* (Englewood Cliffs: Prentice Hall, 1980), 292.

21   James Madison, *Federalist Papers* (New York: Oxford University Press, 2008), 55.

22   Mary Midgley, *Beast and Man: The Roots of Human Nature* (Ithaca: Cornell University Press, 1978), 70: "It seems more reasonable to treat man's nature, his original constitution, as neither good nor evil, but simply the raw material for choice."

23   David Boucher, *The Limits of Ethics in International Relations: Natural Law, Natural Rights and Human Rights in Transition* (New York: Oxford University Press, 2009), 286.

24   Richard Rorty, "Human Rights, Rationality and Sentimentality," in *On Human Rights*, ed. Stephen Shute and Susan Hurley (New York: Basic Books, 1993), 115-116.

25   Schulz, *In Our Own Best Interests*, 19.

26   Schulz, *In Our Own Best Interests*, 23-24.

27   William Schulz, "Letter to the Editor," *The National Interest*, 63(Spring, 2001), 124-25.

28   Thomas Haskell, "The Curious Persistence of Rights Talk in the 'Age of Interpretation.'" *Journal of American History*, 74: 3(1987), 1004.

29   Haskell, "The Curious Persistence of Rights Talk in the 'Age of Interpretation,'" 1005.

30   Haskell, "The Curious Persistence of Rights Talk in the 'Age of Interpretation,'" 1001.

31   Robert Wilken, *The Christians as the Romans Saw Them* (New Haven: Yale University Press, 2003), 81.

32   E. R. Dodds, *Pagan and Christian in an Age of Anxiety* (Cambridge: Cambridge University Press, 1991).

33   In Origen's *Contra Celsum* (Cambridge: Cambridge University Press, 1980), 3.44, Celsus is quoted as saying that the Christian movement attracted "only

slaves, women and little children." However, Pliny is probably more accurate in describing the movement as attracting "persons of every age, social rank and both sexes" in "Letter to Trajan," *The Letters of the Younger Pliny* (New York: Kessinger, 2004), 10.96.

34   R. W. Sharples, *Stoics, Epicureans and Skeptics,* (New York: Routledge, 1996), 82.

35   Cicero, *On the Laws* (New York: Oxford University Press, 1998), 4.

36   Maurice Cranston, *What Are Human Rights?* (London: The Bodley Head Ltd, 1973), 4.

37   Avishai Margalit, *The Decent Society* (Cambridge: Harvard University Press, 1998), 11.

38   M. R. Wright, "Cicero on Self-Love and Love of Humanity in *De Finibus*," in *Cicero the Philosopher*, ed. J.G.F. Powell (New York: Oxford University Press, 1999), 188.

39   Cicero, *On the Laws*, 3:11.

40   Cicero, *The Republic* (New York: Oxford University Press, 1998), 3: 33.

41   Wright, "Cicero on Self-Love and Love of Humanity," 188-89.

42   Martha Nussbaum, "Duties of Justice, Duties of Material Aid: Cicero's Problematic Legacy," *Journal of Political Philosophy* 8:2(June, 2000), 176-206.

43   Cicero, *On Duties* (Cambridge: Cambridge University Press, 1991), 1: 57. Edmund Burke, *Reflections on the Revolution in France* (New York: Holt, Reinhart and Winston, 1959), 55, expresses a similar sentiment that "to love the little platoon we belong to in society . . . is the first link in the series of which proceed towards a love to our country and to mankind." The metaphor of link is crucial here. Does love to mankind have to go through our country? Or must the love of our "little platoon" already embody a love of all people, an attitude that is tested in how we treat the stranger?

44   Hugo Grotius, *The Law of War and Peace* (Indianapolis: Bobbs-Merrill, 1925).

45   Epictetus, *Enchiridion* (New York: Dover Books, 2004), par. 5.

46   Sharples, *Stoics, Epicureans and Skeptics*, 77.

47   Marcus Aurelius, *The Meditations of the Emperor Marcus Aurelius Antonius* (New York: Modern Library, 2002), VI: 43.

48   Terence, *The Self Tormentor* (Indianapolis: Bobbs-Merrill, 1963).

49   Marcus Aurelius, *Meditations,* Book VI, 28, 97; Book IV: 74.

50   George Ovitt, *The Restoration of Perfection* (New Brunswick: Rutgers University Press, 1986), 79-85.

51   Norman Cohn, *The Pursuit of the Millennium* (New York: Oxford University Press, 1970), 187.

52 The twentieth-century author who mediated Augustine to politicians and diplomats was Reinhold Niebuhr. What has been called realism in U.S. policies is indebted to Augustinian ideas about a dark side to human impulses. The realism has at times been a cynical view of all claims to morality. For other people (for example, Barack Obama), an acceptance of evil is a recognition that good intentions are always tainted by hubris.

53 John Rist, *Augustine: Ancient Thought Baptized* (Cambridge: Cambridge University Press, 1996), 291.

54 Peter Brown, *Augustine of Hippo* (Berkeley: University of California Press, 2000), 173.

55 Garry Wills, *St. Augustine* (New York: Viking Press, 1999), 132-35, points out that Augustine was much more concerned with greed and dishonesty than with sexual sins. He did have some fascinating ideas about how original sin affected a person's control of sexual passion. *City of God* (New York: New City Press, 2012), 14: 26.

56 Plato, *Republic*, 509.

57 Plotinus, *The Enneads* (New York: Forgotten Books, 2007).

58 Ovitt, *the Restoration of Perfection*, 63, on Augustine's Commentary on Genesis; Thomas Aquinas's solution to the problem of creation being free not necessary on God's part was to identify the necessary emanation from the One with the interior life of the Blessed Trinity; the creation of the world remains a free act of God.

59 Arthur Lovejoy, *The Great Chain of Being* (Cambridge: Harvard University Press, 1953), 86.

60 Brian Tierney, *The Idea of Natural Rights* (Grand Rapids: Eerdmans, 1997), chapter 2.

61 Gratian, *The Treatise on Laws with the Ordinary Gloss* (Washington: Catholic University of America Press, 1993).

62 Gratian, *The Treatise on Laws*, 3.

63 Charles Taylor, "Conditions of an Unforced Conscience on Human Rights," in *East Asian Challenge for Human* Rights, ed. Joanne Bauer and Daniel Bell (Cambridge: Cambridge University Press, 1999), 127.

64 Alan Ryan, "The British, the Americans and Rights," in *The Culture of Rights*, ed. Michael Lacey and Knud Haakonssen (Cambridge: Cambridge University Press, 1991), 378; Anthony Quinton in his T. S. Eliot Memorial Lecture, *The Politics of Imperfection* (London: Faber and Faber, 1978), 61, writes, "Since human nature is socially determined and thus essentially various, there can be no specific rights of men who have developed within a particular social and historical setting."

65　J. Bartlett Brebner, "Magna Carta," in *Great Expressions of Human Rights*, ed. R. M. McIver (New York: Harper Brothers, 1950), 67.

66　John Dickinson as cited in Bernard Bailyn, *The Ideological Origins of the American Revolution* (Cambridge: Harvard University Press, 1967), 78.

67　Michael Oakeshott, "Political Education," in *Rationalism in Politics and Other Essays* (New York: Barnes and Noble, 1962), 239-40.

68　M. D. Chenu, *Nature, Man and Society in the Twelfth Century* (Toronto: University of Toronto Press, 1997), 39.

69　Charles Taylor, *A Secular Age* (Cambridge: Harvard University Press, 2007), chapter 2.

70　Thomas Aquinas, *Summa Theologiae,* (New York: McGraw Hill, 1966), I. l.

71　Thomas Aquinas, *Summa Contra Gentiles* (Notre Dame: University of Notre Dame, 1976), II.3.

72　Thomas Aquinas, *Summa Theologiae*, Prologue.

73　Frederick Copleston, *Aquinas* (New York: Penguin Books, 1956), 131.

74　Thomas Aquinas, *Summa Contra Gentiles,* I: 33.

75　Josef Pieper, *The Silence of St. Thomas* (New York: St. Augustine's Press, 1999), 70.

76　Thomas Aquinas, *Summa Contra Gentiles*, III: 122.

77　Thomas Aquinas, *Summa Theologiae,* II.II. 27.1.

78　Thomas Aquinas, *Summa Theologiae,* II.II. 154.

79　Thomas Aquinas, *Summa Theologiae,* II.II, Prologue.

80　Jacques Maritain, *The Rights of Man and Natural Law* (New York: Scribner's Sons, 1943), 35.

81　Thomas Aquinas, *Summa Theologiae*, I.29.2

82　Tierney, *The Idea of Natural Rights*, chap. 5.

83　Ernst Cassirer, *The Individual and the Cosmos in Renaissance Philosophy* (Chicago: University of Chicago Press, 2010), 143.

84　Giovanni Pico della Mirandola, *On the Dignity of Man* (Indianapolis: Hackett Publishing, 1998), 4-5.

85　Richard Overton, *An Arrow against All Tyrants* (London, 1646), 4.

86　Tierney, *The Idea of Natural Rights*, chap. 9

87　Bernard Williams, *Morality: An Introduction to Ethics* (Cambridge: Cambridge University Press, 1993), 25, points out in reference to the Spanish horror at the Aztecs' practice of human sacrifice that "it would surely be absurd to regard that reaction as merely parochial or self-righteous. It rather indicated something which their conduct did not indicate, that they regarded the Indians as men rather than wild animals."

88　Bartolomè de Las Casas, *Witness: The Writings of Bartolomè de Las Casas*, ed. George Sanderlin (New York: Orbis Books, 1993); Paolo Carozza, "From

Conquest to Constitution: Retrieving a Latin American Tradition of Human Rights," *Human Rights Quarterly*, 25:2(2003), 289-96.

89   Grotius, *The Law of War and Peace*, 20.

90   Tierney, *The Idea of Natural Rights,* chap. 13.

91   Alasdair MacIntyre, *After Virtue* (Notre Dame: University of Notre Dame Press, 1984), 228-29: "It was in the seventeenth and eighteenth centuries that morality . . . came to be largely equated with altruism. . . . Altruism became at once socially necessary and yet apparently impossible and, if and when it occurs, inexplicable." The term *altruism*, however, did not get coined until the nineteenth century.

92   Grotius, *The Law of War and Peace*, 205, 213.

93   Grotius, *The Law of War and Peace*, 25.

94   Hugo Grotius, *Free Sea* (Indianapolis: Liberty Fund, 2004).

95   Charles Tilly, "Reflections on the History of European State-Making," in *The Formation of National States in Western* Europe, ed. Charles Tilly (Princeton: Princeton University Press, 1975), 42.

96   Francis Bacon, *The New Organon* (Indianapolis: Bobbs-Merrill, 1960), 23-39.

Chapter 2

1   Abraham Lincoln in an 1864 address said, "The world has never had a good definition of the word liberty, and the American people, just now, are much in want of one. We all declare for liberty but in using the same word we do not all mean the same thing." *Speeches and Writings*, ed. Don Fehrenbacher (New York: Library of America, 1989), II: 589.

2   George W. Bush, in his Second Inaugural Address of thirty minutes, used *freedom* twenty-eight times and *liberty* fifteen times. No discernible pattern of distinguishing the two words was evident.

3   Isaiah Berlin in a famous essay, "Two Concepts of Liberty," in *Four Essays on Liberty* (New York: Oxford University Press, 1969) begins by saying (121) that he will use *liberty* and *freedom* to mean the same thing. I suggest that the essay's argument might have been clearer (according to Berlin it was widely misunderstood) if he had distinguished between liberty and freedom. Instead, he adopted a distinction between "negative liberty" and "positive liberty," which required the term *liberty* to do too much. What Berlin calls "negative liberty" could have been called liberty. The more expansive meaning of *freedom* could have served for working out the contrasts and tensions of his "two liberties." Liberty is a "freedom from," but that is not the whole meaning

of freedom. I think in the essay Berlin does suggest such a distinction but not consistently.

4   Sarah Grimké, *Letters on the Equality of the Sexes* (New Haven: Yale University Press, 1988).

5   Dick Armey, *Give Us Liberty: A Tea Party Manifesto* (New York: William Morrow, 2010).

6   John Milton, *Second Defense of the People of England* (New York: Constitutional Society, 2009).

7   Noah Webster, starting with a 1787 pamphlet in support of the Constitution and culminating in his Dictionary of 1828, tried to establish a true idea of liberty in contrast to the false idea of "freedom from restraint." *Liberty* means "acting conformably to the sense of a majority of the society." Then "in such a government a man is free and safe." Thomas Gustafson, *Representative Words: Politics, Literature and the American Language 1776-1865* (Cambridge: Cambridge University Press, 2008), 311-312.

8   Besides the political meaning of *revolution* that I trace here, there are some metaphorical applications of the term. Most notable is "scientific revolution" not coined until 1939 by Alexandre Koyrė but now a routinely used phrase. In that case, the assumption in the meaning of revolution is that modern, empirical, and mathematical science was a radical but not a violent change. Steven Shapin, *The Scientific Revolution* (Chicago: University of Chicago Press, 1998).

9   Gene Sharp, *Dictatorship to Democracy: A Conceptual Framework for Liberation* (London: Serpent's Tail, 2012).

10 George Lawson, *Negotiated Revolutions: The Czech Republic, South Africa and Chile* (Burlington: Ashgate, 2005).

11 Hannah Arendt, *On Revolution* (New York: Viking Press, 1963), 35.

12 John Adams, *The Works of John Adams*, ed. Charles Francis Adams (Boston: Little, Brown and Co., 1956), X: 288.

13 Arendt, *On Revolution*, 301.

14 Pauline Maier, *American Scripture: Making the Declaration of Independence* (New York: Knopf, 1997), 20.

15 Leo Strauss, *Natural Right and History* (Chicago: University of Chicago Press, 1953), 166.

16 Thomas Hobbes, *Leviathan* (Cambridge: Cambridge University Press, 1996), 91.

17 Hobbes, *Leviathan*, chapter 13.

18 There are passages in which Hobbes seems to agree with Grotius and medieval tradition "that the sum of God's law is: Thou shalt love God above all, and thy

neighbor as thyself; and the same is true of the law of nature." *The Elements of Law: De Corpore Politico* (New York: Oxford University Press, 1994), 29. It is difficult to understand how this formula about law is related to the rest of his writing.

19   Michael Oakeshott, "Political Education," in *Rationalism in Politics and Other Essays* (New York: Barnes and Noble, 1962), 120; a contrary view is expressed by Edmund Morgan, *Inventing the People* (New York: W.W. Norton, 1988), 105. He says that most of Locke's treatise was written before the Revolution of 1689.

20   Strauss, *Natural Right and History*, 220, says Locke "cannot have recognized any law of nature in the proper sense of the term." But "the proper sense of the term" in the eighteenth century or today would be highly debatable.

21   John Locke, *The Second Treatise on Civil Government* (New York: Prometheus Books, 1986), chap. 9, par. 123, 124.

22   Jack Rakove, ed. *Declaring Rights: A Brief Documentary History* (New York: Palgrave Macmillan, 1997).

23   Adam Smith, *The Theory of Moral Sentiments; To Which is Added a Dissertation on the Origin of Language* (New York: General Books, 2010).

24   Quoted in Barry Schwartz, *The Battle for Human Nature: Science, Morality and Modern Life* (New York: W.W. Norton, 1987), 64.

25   David Hume, *An Enquiry Concerning the Principles of Morals* (New York: Oxford University Press, 1998), 3-5.

26   Jeremy Bentham, "Anarchical Fallacies," in *Nonsense upon* Stilts, ed. Jeremy Waldron (London Methuen, 1987), 49: "All men are born in subjection, and the most absolute subjection—the subjection of a helpless child to the parents on whom he depends every moment for his existence."

27   Hume, *Enquiry Concerning the Principles of Morals*, 121; John Mullan, *Sentiment and Sociability: The Language of Feeling in the Eighteenth Century* (New York: Oxford University Press, 1988).

28   David Hume, *A Treatise of Human Nature* (New York: Oxford University Press, 1967), 484.

29   Hume, *A Treatise of Human Nature*, Book III; Annette, Baier, *A Progress of Sentiments: Reflections on Hume's Treatise* (Cambridge: Harvard University Press, 1991), 174-77.

30   Annette Baier, *Moral Prejudices* (Cambridge: Harvard University Press, 1994), 10-17

31   Quoted in German Arciniegas, "The Four Americas" in *Do the Americas Have a Common History?* ed. Louis Hanke (New York: Knopf, 1964), 240.

32   Perry Miller, *Errand into the Wilderness*, (New York: Harper, 1956), 101.

33   J. Saunders Redding, *They Came in Chains* (Philadelphia: Lippincott, 1973), quoted in Howard Zinn, *A People's History of the United States* (New York: Harper and Row, 1980), 23.

34   Nick Bunker, *Making Haste from Babylon: The Mayflower Pilgrims and Their World* (New York: Knopf, 2010), 286.

35   William Bradford, *Of Plymouth Plantation 1620-1647* (New York: Knopf, 1952), 286; Roger Williams was an exception in recognizing the rights of Indians.

36   John Winthrop, "A Model of Christian Charity" in Winthrop Hudson, *Nationalism and Religion* (New York: Harper and Row, 1970), 21-24.

37   German Arciniegas, *America in Europe: History of the New World in Reverse* (San Diego: Harcourt, Brace, 1986), 118.

38   Nathan Hatch, *The Sacred Cause of Liberty: Republican Thought and the Millennium in Revolutionary New England* (New Haven: Yale University Press, 1977), 4.

39   Hobbes, *Leviathan*.

40   Bernard Bailyn, *The Origins of American Politics* (New York: Vintage Books, 1968), 40-56; Charles de Montesquieu, *The Spirit of Laws* (Berkeley: University of California Press, 1977), Book 11, chapter 6. I introduce the adjective *political* here although then as now people often refer to power *versus* liberty when they mean a particular form of power and a particular form of liberty. Then as now, people could recognize that power and liberty are not antithetical, for example, in discussions of psychological freedom; one does not have the liberty to act if one does not have the power to act. This fact at the individual level might lead one to conclude that power at the political level is neutral rather than evil.

41   Bernard Bailyn, *The Ideological Origins of the American Revolution* (Cambridge: Harvard University Press, 1967).

42   *Federalist Papers* (New York: Bantam Books, 1982), no. 10, 51-52.

43   William Johnson Everett, *God's Federal Republic: Reconstructing our Governing Symbol* (New York: Paulist Press, 1988), 81.

44   Bernard Bailyn, *Ideological Origins*, 125, citing the *New York Gazette*.

45   Bailyn, *Ideological Origins*, 86: Governor Thomas Hutchinson of Massachusetts said that "it seemed that anything with the appearance of a man" was allowed to vote.

46   Bernard Bailyn, *Pamphlets of the American Revolution 1750-76* (Cambridge: Harvard University Press, 1965), 210.

47   Bailyn, *Ideological Origins*, 127.

48 Gordon Wood, *The Radicalism of the American Revolution* (New York: Vintage Books, 1993), 165: The argument seemed at times to be about proper child rearing.

49 Thomas Paine, *Common Sense* (New York: Create Space, 2010); Winthrop Jordan, "Familial Politics and the Killing of the King, 1776," *Journal of American History*, 60: 2 (Sept., 1973), 294-308.

50 Edmund Morgan and Helen Morgan, *The Stamp Act Crisis* (New York: Collier Books, 1962); Eran Shalev, *Rome Reborn on Western Shores: Historical Imagination and the Creation of the American Republic* (Charlottesville: University of Virginia Press, 2009), 50-62.

51 Jonathan Mayhew as cited in Bailyn, *Ideological Origins*, 97.

52 Clinton Rossiter, *The First American Revolution: The American Colonies on the Eve of Independence* (New York: Harcourt Brace, 1964), 5.

53 Carl Becker, *The Declaration of Independence: A Study in the History of Political Ideas* (New York: Create Space, 2010); Garry Wills, *Inventing America: Jefferson's Declaration of Independence* (New York: Doubleday, 1978). For one of the severest criticism of Wills' book, see Ronald Hamowy, "Jefferson and the Scottish Enlightenment: A Critique of Garry Wills' *Inventing America*," *William and Mary Quarterly*, 36 (1979), 503-23; for a balance of criticisms see Ralph Luker, "Garry Wills and the New Debate over the Declaration of Independence," *The Virginia Quarterly Review*, Spring, 1980, 244-61.

54 It is surely significant that the radical movement called the Tea Party adopted its name from an event that happened before the United States existed.

55 Maier, *American Scripture*, 40; Wills, *Inventing America*, 325.

56 The idea of "self-evident truths" was attacked by critics of that time and ever since. The idea did not originate with Jefferson. Today it seems like a strange claim that a truth is evident to everyone when obviously it is not. Jefferson was drawing on a long tradition, most immediately John Locke, in which *self-evident* meant not to be argued to from more fundamental truths. For a great many reasons, a person might not grasp what is "evident in itself." The self-evident truth that all men are created equal meant for Jefferson an equality of species, that is, an equality of men insofar as they all receive a human nature. See Morton White, *The Philosophy of Human Nature* (New York: Oxford University Press, 1981), 61-96.

57 In a letter of 1825, Jefferson wrote that his purpose was "to place before mankind the common sense of the subject in terms so plain and firm as to command their assent, and to justify ourselves in the independent stand we are compelled to take." "Letter to Henry Lee, May 8, 1825," in *Writings of*

Thomas Jefferson, ed. Albert Bergh (Washington: Thomas Jefferson Memorial Association, 1907), XIII: 333.

58   Locke, *Second Treatise on Government*, no. 26.

59   I refer here particularly to the tradition reflected in Jean Jacques Burlamaqui, *Principles of Natural and Politic Law* (Indianapolis: Liberty Fund, 2006) first published in 1747.

60   Jefferson pointed out that life and liberty entailed a seeking of property but that "stable ownership is the gift of social law, and is given late in the progress of society." Thus ownership of property is not an inalienable right in contrast to life and liberty which are. "Letter to Isaac Macpherson," August 13, 1813, *Writings of Thomas Jefferson*, 13:333.

61   *New Yorker*, January 17, 2011, 72.

62   Herbert Bolton, *Wider Horizons of American History* (Notre Dame: University of Notre Dame Press, 1967), 19.

63   Lauren Dubois, *Avengers of the New World: The Story of the Haitian Revolution* (Cambridge: Harvard University Press, 2005); Mimi Sheller, *Democracy after Slavery: Black Publics and Peasant Rebels in Haiti and Jamaica* (Cambridge: Harvard University Press, 2001). The French recognition of Haiti was accompanied by draconian demands for financial compensation. Haiti did fairly well in the nineteenth century with an economy based on small farms. The U.S. occupation in the twentieth century was no help.

64   The full statement of Jefferson's is found in Maier, *American Scripture*, 239.

65   Quoted in Armitage, *The Declaration of Independence*, 77.

66   Jeremy Bentham, "Short Review of the Declaration (1776)," in Armitage, *Declaration of Independence*, 173-86.

67   Bentham, "Short Review of the Declaration (1776)," 175.

68   Frederick Douglass, "What to the Slave is the Fourth of July?" in *Autobiographies* (New York: Library of America, 1994), 434.

69   Frederick Douglass, "The Nature of Slavery," in *Autobiographies*, 427. He also used the term *human rights* in reaction to a Supreme Court ruling in 1876: *Autobiographies*, 977.

70   Arendt, *On Revolution*, 144; Edmund Morgan, *Inventing the People* (New York: W.W. Norton, 1988).

71   James Beck, *The Constitution of the United States* (London: Hodder and Stoughton, 1922).

72   Arendt, *On Revolution*, 164.

73   One person's capricious assemblies are another person's working of democracy. To what extent the U.S. Constitution was the product of wealthy men protecting their property against the majority is a passionately debated issue.

See Woody Holton, *Unruly Americans and the Origin of the Constitution* (New York: Hill and Wang, 2007).

74 Atlee Kouwenhoven, *The Beer Can by the Highway: Essays on What's American about America* (Baltimore: Johns Hopkins University Press, 1988), 54.

75 William Sullivan, *Work and Integrity: Crisis and Promise of Professionalism in America* (San Francisco: Jossey Bass, 2005), 72.

76 Arendt, *On Revolution*, 140-41.

77 James Madison, Alexander Hamilton and John Jay, *The Federalist Papers* (New York: Oxford University Press, 2008), no. 51. John Stuart Mill, *On Liberty* (New York: W.W. Norton, 1975), 5-6, gave great importance to this idea of the tyranny of the majority.

78 *Records of the Federal Convention*, ed. Max Farrand (New Haven: Yale University Press, 1911), III: 463; a delegate, Luther Martin, said the term *national* was eliminated because it might "tend to alarm." *Debates in the Several State Conventions on the Adoption of the Federal Constitution*, ed. Jonathan Elliot (Philadelphia: Lippincott, 1936), I, 362.

79 Pauline Maier, *Ratification: The People Debate the Constitution* (New York: Simon and Schuster, 2010), 335.

80 Michael Avery and Danielle McLaughlin, *The Federalist Society: How Conservatives Took the Law Back from Liberals* (Nashville: Vanderbilt University Press, 2013).

81 The right wing in the United States fervently believes in *America*, but not the *United States*. Left wing critics, who also do not distinguish between the *United States* and *America*, leave themselves vulnerable to the charge of being anti-American when they criticize the United States and its government.

82 Arciniegas, "The Four Americas," 237-38.

83 John Adams said that the country was "destined to spread over the northern part of that whole quarter of the globe"; Thomas Jefferson thought "it is impossible not to look forward" to a time when our multiplication will "cover the whole northern, if not the southern continent, with a people speaking the same language, governed in similar forms, and by similar laws." Thomas Jefferson, "Letter to James Monroe, Nov. 24, 1801" in *The Works of Thomas Jefferson*, ed. Paul Leicester Ford (New York: Knickerbocker, 1905), X: 315-319.

84 Francois Furet, *Interpreting the French Revolution* (Cambridge: Cambridge University, 181), 18.

85 Ian Buruma, *Taming the Gods: Religion and Democracy on Three Continents* (Princeton: Princeton University Press, 2010), 31. Thatcher's point was emphatically documented at the time by Simon Schama, *Citizens: A Chronicle of the French Revolution* (New York: Knopf, 1989).

86 Edmund Burke, *Reflections on the Revolution in France* (New York: Oxford University Press, 2009), 88.

87 Thomas Paine, *Rights of Man* (Buffalo: Prometheus Books, 1987); Paine's *Common Sense* had been translated into French. Paine, together with Thomas Jefferson, Benjamin Franklin, and the eight thousand French soldiers who had fought on the other side of the Atlantic, brought an American influence to France's revolution that many French writers were reluctant to admit.

88 Furet, *Interpreting the French Revolution*, 49.

89 Theodore Besterman, *Voltaire* (New York: Harcourt, Brace and World, 1969), 427.

90 For a thorough study of nature in the eighteenth century, see Basil Willey, *The Eighteenth-Century Background: Studies on the Idea of Nature in the Thought of the Period* (Boston: Beacon Press, 1962).

91 Isaac Newton expressed this view in a letter to the Anglican theologian Richard Bentley: "Sir, when I wrote my treatise about our system, I had an eye upon such principles as might work with considering men, for the belief of a Deity; and nothing can rejoice me more than to find it useful for that purpose." Cited in Margaret Wertheim, *Pythagoras's Trousers: God, Physics and the Gender War* (New York: W.W. Norton, 1997), 121.

92 Michael Buckley, *At the Origins of Modern Atheism* (New Haven: Yale University Press, 1990), 254.

93 Baron d'Holbach, *The System of Nature* (New York: CreateSpace, 2011), I:11; R.G. Collingwood, *The Idea of Nature* (New York: Oxford University Press, 1960), 104-05.

94 Denis Diderot, "Natural Law," in Lynn Hunt, *The French Revolution and Human Rights: A Brief Documentary History* (New York: St. Martin's Press, 1996), 36-37.

95 Furet, *Interpreting the French Revolution*, 31.

96 Jean-Jacques Rousseau, *Discourse on the Origin of Inequality* (New York: Simon and Schuster, 1967).

97 Furet, *Interpreting the French Revolution*, 31; Heinrich Heine, *Religion and Philosophy in Germany* (Albany: State University of New York Press, 1986). 106: "Maximilian Robespierre was merely the hand of Jean-Jacques Rousseau, the bloody hand that drew from the womb of time the body whose soul Rousseau had created."

98 Bernard Yack, *The Longing for Total Revolution: The Sources of Discontent from Rousseau to Marx and Nietzsche* (Berkeley: University of California Press, 1992), 83.

99   Christopher Hibbert, *The Days of the French Revolution* (New York: William Morrow, 1980), 60-61.

100 Arthur Young, *Travels in France during the Years 1787, 1788, 1789* (Cambridge: Cambridge University Press, 1929), 159.

101 Quoted in Elizabeth Borgwardt, *A New Deal for the World* (Cambridge: Harvard University Press, 2005), 44.

102 Jeremy Bentham's reaction in *Anarchical Fallacies*: "All men born free? Absurd and miserable nonsense"; quoted in David Boucher, *The Limits of Ethics in International Relations* (New York: Oxford University Press, 2009), 219.

103 "Preliminary to the Constitution," in Hunt, *The French Revolution and Human Rights*, 81.

104 Sherman Kent, "The Declaration of the Rights of Man and of the Citizen," in *Great Expressions of Human Rights*, ed. R.M. MacIver (New York: Harper and Brothers, 1950), 156.

105 William Doyle, *The Oxford History of the French Revolution* (New York: Oxford University Press, 2002), 288.

106 Conor Cruise O'Brien, "A Lost Chance to Save the Jews," *New York Review of Books*, April 27, 1989, 4: "The 'Age of Reason' proved to be a misnomer. . . . It was new terrestrial creeds with new Revelations and experiments who were often as arbitrary and as fanatical as the worst of the old persecuting priests and monks."

107 Doyle, *The Oxford History of the French Revolution*, 385.

108 Doyle, *The Oxford History of the French Revolution*, 119.

109 Jean Caritat Condorcet, "On the Admission of Women to the Rights of Citizenship," in Lynn Hunt, *The French Revolution and the Rights of Man*, 119.

110 Report in *La feuille du salut public* in Joan Scott, *Only Paradoxes to Offer: French Feminists and the Rights of Man* (Cambridge: Harvard University Press, 1997), 52: "Olympe de Gouges . . . wanted to be a man of state. She took up the projects of the perfidious people who want to divide France. It seems the law has punished the conspirator for having forgotten the virtues that belong to her sex."

111 Hunt, *The French Revolution and Human Rights*, 138.

112 Louis Marie Prudhomme, "On the Influence of the Revolution on Women," in Hunt, *The French Revolution and Human Rights*, 131.

113 Jean-Jacques Rousseau, *Emile or On Education* (New York: Basic Books, 1979), 358: "In what they have in common they are equal. Where they differ they are not comparable."

114 William Stuntz, *The Collapse of American Criminal Justice* (Cambridge: Harvard University Press, 2011), 77.

115 Doyle, *Oxford History of the French Revolution*, 419.

116 Doyle, *Oxford History of the French Revolution*, 399.

117 Doyle, *Oxford History of the French Revolution*, 124, 318.

118 Hibbert, *The Days of the French Revolution*, 154.

119 Hibbert, *The Days of the French Revolution*, 225.

120 Hibbert, *The Days of the French Revolution*, 229.

121 Furet, *Interpreting the French Revolution*, 47.

122 Burke, *The Revolution in France*, 96.

123 Burke, *The Revolution in France*, 16, 87.

124 H. G. Gadamer in the twentieth century defended "justified prejudice" as opposed to "blind prejudice"; see *Truth and Method* (New York: Crossroad, 1982), 247. However, *prejudice* has an almost totally negative meaning in popular discourse.

Chapter 3

1 Fiona Robinson, arguing for the limitations of rights language, writes, "The idea of rights cannot be separated from the normative principles of liberalism, including a view of the moral agent as essentially autonomous and possessing authority of his or own will, the negative libertarian view of the substance of rights, and a pluralist conception of the purpose of rights." Her description of nineteenth-century liberalism is an important reminder. However, it is not obvious why the word *right* cannot be separated from this liberalism. The term *right* pre-existed modern theories of liberalism and, in addition, liberalism itself underwent a drastic change in the twentieth century. See Fiona Robinson, "The Limits of a Rights-Based Approach to International Ethics," in *Human Rights Fifty Years On: A Reappraisal*, ed. Tony Evans (Manchester: Manchester University Press, 1998), 59.

2 Daniel Rodgers, *Atlantic Crossings: Social Politics in a Progressive Age* (Cambridge: Harvard University Press, 1998), 33-75.

3 Samuel Moyn, *The Last Utopia: Human Rights in History* (Cambridge: Harvard University Press, 2010), 36.

4 John Locke, *Second Treatise on Government* (New York: Prometheus, 1986), sec. 124. As I indicated in the previous chapter, Locke's meaning of *property* included life, liberty, and estate (sec. 123). Obviously, his meaning of *property* lost out.

5 John Stuart Mill, *On Liberty* (New York: W.W. Norton, 1975), 11.

6   Mill, *On Liberty,* 12.

7   Mill, *On Liberty,* 12, note 5; just previous to the quotation, Mill has declined to invoke the idea of natural rights, but he suggests that the idea would support his position.

8   John Stuart Mill, *Utilitarianism* (New York: Penguin Books, 1962), 319.

9   Mill, *Utilitarianism,* 310-11.

10 Mill, *Utilitarianism,* 320.

11 Karl Marx, "On the Jewish Question," in *Early Texts* (Oxford: Blackwell, 1971), 223.

12 Carroll Smith-Rosenberg, *This Violent Empire: The Birth of American National Identity* (Chapel Hill: University of North Carolina Press, 2010), 77.

13 Neil Stammers, *Human Rights and Social Revolutions* (New York: Pluto Press, 2009), 32, writes that he understands the social as "being a superordinate category and the political, economic, and cultural being a realm or demand of the social." Even if one could consistently stretch *social* to include political, economic, and cultural, any gain to clarity or effectiveness is doubtful. In addition its history and the present use of *social* show an exclusion of the important category of the ecological.

14 Marx was especially hard on German socialism for representing "the interests of Human Nature, of Man in general, who belong to no class, has no reality, who exists only in the misty realm of philosophical fantasy." Karl Marx and Friedrich Engels, *The Communist Manifesto* (New York: Pocket Books, 1964), 103.

15 Terry Eagleton, *The Illusions of Postmodernism* (Oxford: Blackwell, 1996), 113: Although the Declarations in theory were about universal freedom, they did not accord equal respect to all people (women, non-Europeans, lower peasantry). Nonetheless, "middle class society could now be challenged by those it suppressed *according to its own logic,* caught out in a performative contradiction between what it said and what it did."

16 Costas Douzinas, *The End of Human Rights: Critical Legal Thought at the Turn of the Century* (Oxford: Hart Publishing, 2000), 164.

17 Moyn, *The Last Utopia,* 49.

18 Richard Primus, *The American Language of Rights* (Cambridge: Cambridge University Press, 1999), 191.

19 Townson Hoopes and Douglas Brinkley, *FDR and the Creation of the United Nations* (New Haven: Yale University Press, 1997), 26-27.

20 Franklin Roosevelt in his State of the Union address as quoted in Elizabeth Borgwardt, *A New Deal for the World: America's Vision for Human Rights* (Cambridge: Harvard University Press, 2007), 137.

21 The 1942 Beveridge Report helped to launch the welfare state in England. It proposed a "maintenance of subsistence income" in order "to abolish physical want." The report made explicit reference to the Atlantic Charter. See Borgwardt, *A New Deal for the World*, 49.

22 Roosevelt's advisor, Sumner Wells, revised an original draft of the four freedoms by substituting for specific civil rights the more general "all human beings may live out their lives in freedom from fear." See Borgwardt, *A New Deal*, 25.

23 Borgwardt, *A New Deal*, 4, 29.

24 Borgwardt, *A New Deal*, 45.

25 Martha Minow, *Between Vengeance and* Forgiveness (Boston: Beacon Press, 1999), 31.

26 Borgwardt, *A New Deal*, 210.

27 Quoted in Telford Taylor, *The Anatomy of the Nuremberg Trials* (New York: Knopf, 1992), 167.

28 Carl von Clausewitz, *On War* (London: Wordsworth, 1997), 1:22.

29 Raphael Lemkin, *Axis Rule in Occupied Europe* (New York: Carnegie Endowment for International Peace, 1944).

30 "Crimes against Humanity" was used in a joint declaration by France, Great Britain, and Russia that condemned Turkey for the killing of Armenians. Russia's condemnation originally used "Crimes against Christianity and Civilization." See Andrew Clapham, *Human Rights: A Very Short Introduction* (New York: Oxford University Press, 2007), 34.

31 Clapham, *Human Rights*, 35.

32 See the chapter on overdramatizing genocide in Alan Wolfe, *Political Evil: What It Is and How to Combat It* (New York: Knopf, 2011).

33 The United States at the time was not alone in having few moral qualms about the bombing of Hiroshima and Nagasaki. Churchill's view was that "to avert a vast, indefinite butchery . . . at the cost of a few explosions seemed, after all our toils and perils, a miracle of deliverance." Mark Kurlansky, *Nonviolence: The History of a Dangerous Idea* (New York: Modern Library, 2008), 142.

34 Minow, *Between Vengeance and Forgiveness*, 51.

35 Geoffrey Robertson, *Crimes against Humanity: The Struggle for Global Justice* (London: Penguin Books, 2001), 240.

36 Taylor, *Anatomy of the Nuremberg Trials*, 167.

37 Stephen Schlesinger, *Act of Creation: The Founding of the United Nations* (New York: Basic Books, 2003), 38.

38 Borgwardt, *A New Deal*, 128.

39 Robert Hilderbrand, *Dumbarton Oaks: The Origins of the United Nations and the Search for Postwar Security* (Chapel Hill: University of North Carolina Press, 1990), 64-5.

40 Schlesinger, *Act of Creation*, 46.

41 The agreement is called the Act of Chapultepec after the setting of the meeting in Mexico City. See Hoopes and Brinkley, *FDR and the Creation of the United Nations*, 192-93; Jürgen Habermas, *The Divided West* (Malden: Polity, 2006), 109, says that "a reform of the United Nations, however successful, would remain ineffectual unless the nation-states in the various world regions come together to form continental regimes on the model of the European Union." The value of regional organizations should perhaps be distinguished from continental regimes that are modeled on the European Union.

42 Moyn, *The Last Utopia*, 56.

43 W.E.B. Dubois, *Writings by W.E.B. Dubois*, ed. Herbert Aptheker (New York: Kraus International Publications, 1982), 4: 2-3.

44 Habermas, *The Divided West*, 160-61, several times refers to the UN Charter's "explicit connection of the purpose of securing peace with a politics of human rights." He makes a good case that that should be the aim of the UN and over the decades the UN has tried to move in that direction. But one should not underestimate the tension between the UN charter and the Universal Declaration of Human Rights.

45 Borgwardt, *A New Deal*, 268.

46 Mary Ann Glendon, *A World Made New: Eleanor Roosevelt and the Universal Declaration of Human Rights* (New York: Random House, 2001), 208.

47 Schlesinger, *Act of Creation*, 74-77.

48 Schlesinger, *Act of Creation*, 217.

49 William Korey, *NGOs and the Universal Declaration of Human Rights: A Curious Grapevine* (New York: St. Martin's, 1998), 46.

50 Borgwardt, *A New Deal*, 191.

51 Hilderbrand, *Dumbarton Oaks*, 86-9.

52 See Karen Engle, "From Skepticism to Embrace: Human Rights and the American Anthropological Association from 1947-99," *Human Rights Quarterly*, 23:3(August, 2001), 540.

53 Even in its 1999 "Declaration on Anthropology and Human Rights," the American Anthropological Association still calls for "collective as well as individual rights." See Engle, "From Skepticism to Embrace," 552.

54 Stephen Toulmin, *Cosmopolis: The Hidden Agenda of Modernity* (Chicago: University of Chicago Press, 1990), 100, quotes Leibniz on his invention of

a universal language: "This language will be difficult to construct, but very easy to learn. It will be quickly accepted by everybody on account of its great utility and its facility, and it will serve wonderfully in communication among various peoples."

55   Mary Midgley, *Beast and Man: The Roots of Human Nature* (Ithaca: Cornell University Press, 1978), 294.

56   Jeremy Waldron, *Nonsense upon Stilts* (New York: Methuen, 1987), 179, defends the concept of human rights while not identifying the concept with any verbal formulation, for example, what is found in the Universal Declaration of Human Rights.

57   Maurice Cranston, *What Are Human Rights?* (New York: Basic Books, 1962), 1.

58   Peter Westen, "The Empty Idea of Equality," *Harvard Law Review*, 95 (1982), 537.

59   Henry Shue, *Basic* Rights, 2nd ed. (Princeton: Princeton University Press, 1996), 119.

60   Shue, *Basic Rights,* 53.

61   William Schulz, *In Our Own Best Interest* (Boston: Beacon Press, 2002), 4.

62   Glendon, *A World Made New,* 208.

63   Glendon, *World Made New,* 49.

64   Glendon, *World Made New,* 57.

65   Glendon, *World Made New,* 67.

66   Richard Rorty, "Human Rights, Rationality and Sentimentality," in *Truth and Progress* (Cambridge: Cambridge University Press, 1998), 167-85; see also Chris Brown, "Universal Rights: A Critique," in *Human Rights in Global Politics,* ed. Tim Dunne and Nicholas Wheeler (Cambridge: Cambridge University Press,1999), 103-27, 120.

67   Glendon, *World Made New,* 68.

68   Glendon, *World Made New,* 146.

69   In a similar list, the European Covenant for the Protection of Human Rights and Fundamental Freedoms uses the term *discrimination* (Article 14). The Canadian Charter of Rights and Freedoms in 1982 also guarantees "equal protection and equal benefits of the law without discrimination."

70   It is unfortunate that *discrimination* has acquired an almost wholly negative meaning. We are left with an incapacity to discriminate between differences that are good and bad, as well as between degrees of negative differences. See Richard Thompson Ford, *Rights Gone Wrong: How Law Corrupts the Struggle for Equality* (New York: Farrar, Straus and Giroux, 2011).

71   *Regents of the University of California vs. Bakke* 438 U.S. 265 (1978).

72 Rorty, "Human Rights, Rationality and Sentimentality," 185; Ruti Teitel, *Humanity's Law* (New York: Oxford University Press, 2011) uses the abstraction *humanity* to describe law that the author says is prospective about the direction for international law. However, the author's use of "humanity rights" does not seem intelligible. Human beings have rights, but humanity does not.

73 Paolo Carozza, "From Conquest to Constitution: Retrieving a Latin American tradition of the idea of human rights," *Human Rights Quarterly* 25:2(2003), 287,

74 Jeane Kirkpatrick quoted by Noam Chomsky "The Hypocrisy of It All," in *Human Rights Fifty Years On*, ed. Tony Evans (New York: St. Martin's Press, 1998), 32. Kirkpatrick did not use the phrase to refer to the Universal Declaration of Human Rights.

75 Cranston, *What are Human Rights?* 41. Jeremy Waldron in *Nonsense upon Stilts*, 180, argues against Cranston that "there is a universal human interest—recognized in all societies—in having longish periods (days and weeks rather than hours) of sustained respite from the business of getting a living." While Waldron may be right, it is still too long a stretch to assert a universal right to "periodic holidays with pay."

76 German Basic Law, Article 18 (www.bundestag.de/htdocs_e/index.html)

77 Justice Oliver Wendell Holmes, Jr. in the Supreme Court decision Schenck v. United States (1919).

78 Glendon, *World Made New*, 47; Natan Lerner, *Religion, Beliefs and Human Rights* (Maryknoll: Orbis Books, 2000), 87.

79 Muhammad Zafrilla Khan, *Islam and Human Rights* (Tilford: Islamic International Publications, 1967), 108: "In the case of a Muslim woman, permission to marry a non-Muslim, even one believing in a revealed religion other than Islam . . . has not been accorded.".

80 Charles Malik, *The Challenge of Human Rights: Charles Malik and the Universal Declaration*, ed. Habib Malik (Oxford: Center for Lebanese Studies, 2000), 117.

81 Joseph Lash, *Eleanor: The Years Alone* (New York: W.W. Norton, 1972), 81.

82 Glendon, *World Made New*, 42, attributes to Malik a "capacious notion of personhood" that had great influence on the declaration.

83 Alain Finkielkraut, *The Defeat of the Mind* (New York: Columbia University Press, 1995), 68-69.

84 Cited in Kalevi Holsti, *The State, War, and the State of War* (Cambridge: Cambridge University Press, 1996), 53.

85 Neil Stammers, *Human Rights and Social Movements* (New York: Pluto Press, 2009), 81.

86   Joseph Raz, *The Morality of Freedom* (New York: Oxford University Press, 1986), 209, favors "collective rights" for "pointing to aspects of the personal sense of identity which are inexorably bound up with the existence of communities and their culture; it recognizes the intrinsic value of some collective goods, and it frees rights discourse from its traditional association with moral individualism." I am sympathetic to his intention. I think *some* collective goods, especially those of *communities*, deserve the protection of rights. But I think *collective* is itself individualistic (a collection of individuals). In any case, groups that make a legitimate claim to rights do not have human rights.

87   For an extensive description of the Office of High Commissioner for Human Rights, see Julie Mertus, *The United Nations and Human Rights*, 2nd ed. (New York: Routledge, 2009), 8-43; also, Mary Robinson, *A Voice for Human Rights* (Philadelphia: University of Pennsylvania Press, 2005).

88   Clapham, *Human Rights,* 77.

89   Douzinas, *End of Human Rights,* 119.

90   Quoted in Clapham, *Human Rights*, 62.

91   David Scheffer, *All the Missing Souls: A Personal History of the War Crimes Tribunals* (Princeton: Princeton University Press, 2011).

92   Jonathan Power, *Like Water on Stone: The Story of Amnesty International* (New York: Penguin Books, 2001).

93   Amnesty International, *United States of America: Rights for All* (London: Amnesty International U.K., 1998). The United States was listed as one of the six worst violators of human rights: "Human Rights violations in the United States are persistent, widespread and appear to disproportionately affect people of ethnic and racial minority backgrounds."

94   In a press conference, May 31, 2005.

Chapter 4

1   It is regularly said that the Bible condemns homosexuality; the three texts regularly cited are Lev. 18:22, Lev. 20:13, and Rom. 1:26. The Bible's authors could not condemn homosexuality because they had neither the word nor the idea. The claim usually made is that sexual relations between two men is "unnatural," but the author of Leviticus did not have that word. Paul, writing in Greek, did have the word *unnatural* to describe men having sex with men; he also called long hair on men unnatural. If Paul were here today, he might be able to understand that following one's sexual orientation is not unnatural. He might still condemn some instances of men having sex with each other,

for example, in U. S. prisons, because most such activity is properly called heterosexual rape.

2   Ruth Hubbard, *The Politics of Women's Biology* (New Brunswick: Rutgers University Press, 1990), 138.

3   Jean Baker Miller, *Toward a New Psychology of Women* (Boston: Beacon Press, 1987), 56.

4   In Blackstone's influential *Commentary on the Laws of England* (1765): "By marriage the husband and wife are one person in law: that is, the very being or legal existence of the woman is suspended during the marriage."

5   Jean-Jacques Rousseau, *Emile* (New York: Basic Books, 1979), 362.

6   Shulamith Firestone, *The Dialectic of Sex: The Case for Feminist Revolution* (New York: Bantam Books, 1973).

7   Rosalind Miles, *The Women's History of the World* (Topfield, MA: Salem House, 1988), 22.

8   Aeschylus, *The Oresteia: Agamemnon; The Libation Bearers; The Eumenides* (New York: Penguin Books, 1984).

9   Aristotle, *Generation of Animals*, 775a15; 767b9.

10   Carolyn Whitbeck, "Theories of Sex Difference," *Women and Philosophy*, ed. Carol Gould and Marx Wartofsky (New York: Putnam, 1976), 55.

11   The word *parenting* is an example of a term that is sex/gender neutral. It is a very useful term so long as it does not cover over the continuing questions about different roles for mothers and fathers.

12   Elizabeth Spelman, *Inessential Woman* (Boston: Beacon Press, 1990), 47.

13   Aristotle, *Politics*, 1323a4.

14   Aristotle, *Politics*, 1254b

15   Alfred North Whitehead, *Process and Reality* (New York: Free Press, 1979), 39.

16   Plato, Republic, 454e.

17   Plato, *Symposium*, 189c-193e.

18   Whitbeck, "Theories of Sex Difference," 60-68.

19   Friedrich Nietzche was among the first to see Rousseau in that light: *Twilight of the Idols* (New York: Penguin Boos, 1968), 111.

20   Maurice Cranston, *The Solitary Self: Jean-Jacques Rousseau in Exile and Adversity* (Chicago: University of Chicago Press, 1997), 37; the phrase describing Rousseau is Lord Byron's.

21   Philip Greven, *Spare the Child: The Religious Roots of Punishment and the Psychological Impact of Physical Abuse* (New York: Vintage Books, 1992), 184-85.

22   Robert Wokler, *Rousseau: A Very Short Introduction* (New York: Oxford University Press, 2001), 102.

23   Rousseau, *Emile*, 40-41.

24   Rousseau, *Emile*, 362.

25   Cranston, *Solitary Self*, 37.

26   Rousseau, *Emile*, 358.

27   Rousseau, *Emile*, 479

28   Rousseau, *Emile*, 358.

29   The unfinished novel was called *Les Solitaires*.

30   Mary Wollstonecraft, A *Vindication of the Rights of Woman* (Cambridge: Cambridge University Press, 2010), 192.

31   Wollstonecraft, *Vindication*, 141.

32   Wollstonecraft, *Vindication*, 167.

33   Wollstonecraft, *Vindication*, 155.

34   Wollstonecraft, *Vindication*, 9. She insists (74-5) that "it is not against strong, persevering passions; but romantic wavering feeling, that I wish to guard the female heart by exercising the understanding."

35   Jane Roland Martin, *Reclaiming a Conversation* (New Haven: Yale University Press, 1987), 98.

36   Sheila Skemp, *Judith Sargent Murray: A Brief Biography and Documents* (New York: St. Martin's, 1998), 149.

37   Ann Douglas, *The Feminization of American Culture* (New York: Farrar, Straus and Giroux, 1998), 60.

38   Alexis De Tocqueville, *Democracy in America,* vol. 2 (New York: Penguin Books, 2003), part 3, chap. 12, 696-99.

39   H. Byerley Thompson, quoted in W. J. Reader, *Professional Men: The Rise of the Professional Classes in Nineteenth-Century England* (London: Weidenfeld and Nicholson, 1966), 192.

40   Hannah More, *Strictures on the Modern System of Female Education*, 1799.

41   Catherine Beecher, *Letters and Papers*, 159, quoted in Sheila Rothman, *Woman's Proper Place* (New York: Basic Books, 1980), 22.

42   Sheila Rothman, *Woman's Proper Place*, 57.

43   David Tyack, *The One Best System: A History of American Urban Education* (Cambridge: Harvard University Press, 1974), 60.

44   Barbara Ehrenreich and Deirdre English, *For Her Own Good: Two Centuries of the Experts' Advice to Women* (New York: Anchor Books, 2005), 54.

45   Tamara Hareven and Randolph Langenbach, *Amoskeag: Life and Work in an American Factory-City* (Lebanon: University Press of New England, 1995).

46   Wollstonecraft, *Vindication*, 128.

47   Vincent Harding, *There is a River: the Black Struggle for Freedom in America* (Boston: Mariner Books, 1993).

48   Nancy Cott, *The Bonds of Womanhood: "Woman's Sphere" in New England 1780-1835* (New Haven: Yale University Press, 1977), 140, 147.

49   Carroll Smith-Rosenberg, *This Violent Empire: The Birth of the American National Identity* (Charlotte: University of North Carolina Press, 2010), 136-87, documents the literary protests of women in the revolutionary and post-revolutionary era.

50   Joan Scott, *Only Paradoxes to Offer: French Feminists and the Rights of Man* (Cambridge: Harvard University Press, 1997), 42.

51   Harriet Martineau, *Society in America* (New York: AMS Press, 1966), 200.

52   John Ogden, *The Female Guide*, quoted in Cott, *The Bonds of Womanhood,* 109.

53   Quoted in Stephanie Coontz, *A Strange Stirring: The Feminine Mystique at the Dawn of the 1960s* (New York: Basic Books, 2011), 159.

54   Friedrich Engels, *The Origin of the Family: Private Property and the State* (New York: Penguin Books, 1972), 148.

55   Rothman, *Woman's Proper Place*, 27.

56   Carl Degler, *In Search of Human Nature: The Decline and Revival of Darwinism in American Social Thought* (New York: Oxford University Press, 1992), 108. He refers to Jane Stafford, one of the founders of Stanford University who ordered that the number of women admitted to the university be restricted to five hundred.

57   Barbara Harris, *Beyond her Sphere: Women and the Professions in American History* (New York: Greenwood Press, 1981), 108.

58   Reader, *Professional Men*, 181: The situation was similar in England where the census until 1911 records no women lawyers, a half dozen architects, and nineteen accountants.

59   Nancy Cott, *The Grounding of Modern Feminism* (New Haven: Yale University Press, 1987), 30.

60   Cott, *Grounding*, 205.

61   Gerda Lerner, *The Majority Finds its Past: Placing Women in History* (New York: Oxford University Press, 1979), 104; Rothman, *Woman's Proper Place*, 128.

62   Degler, *In Search of Human Nature*, 105, 294.

63   Dewey's essay was "Education and the Health of Women," *Science* 6(October, 1885) 341-42; the best known book at that time that warned against the effects of higher education on women was Edward Clarke, *Sex in Education* (New York: Nabu Press, 2010 (1873)).

64   John Dewey, "Is Co-education Dangerous for Girls?" *Ladies Home Journal*, 28(June, 1911), 42-43.

65 Martin Jay, *The Education of John Dewey* (New York: Columbia University Press, 2003), 348.

66 Alan Ryan, *John Dewey and the High Tide of American Liberalism* (New York: Norton, 1997), 167.

67 Margaret Wertheim, *Pythagoras' Trousers: God, Physics and the Gender War* (New York: Norton, 1997), 168; C. W. Bardlen, Superintendent of schools in Syracuse, said in 1908 that neither mothers nor unmarried women were suited to school teaching; it was too bad all teachers couldn't be widows. Redding Sugg, *Motherteacher* (Charlottesville: University of Virginia Press, 1978), 125.

68 James Gross, *Teachers on Trial: Values, Standards and Equity in Judging Conduct and Competence* (Ithaca: Cornell University Press, 1988), 50.

69 Ruth Cowan, *More Work for Mother: The Ironies of Household Technology from the Open Hearth to the Microwave* (New York: Basic Books, 1985), 107.

70 *Judy,* 1:1(June, 1919); cited in Cott, *Grounding,* 282.

71 Michael Oakshott, "Political Education," in *Rationalism in Politics and Other Essays* (New York: Barnes and Noble, 1962), 124.

72 Coontz, *A Strange Stirring,* 42.

73 Elizabeth Wolgast, *Equality and the Rights of Women* (Ithaca: Cornell University Press, 1980), 81: "To 'protect' women by excluding them from well-paying jobs is, by common perception, high irony."

74 Michael McGerr, *A Fierce Discontent: The Rise and Fall of the Progressive Movement in America 1870-1920* (New York: Free Press, 2003), 137; Cott, *Grounding,* 126.

75 Sandra Whitworth, *Feminism and International Relations: Toward a Political Economy of Gender in Interstate and Non-Governmental Institutions* (New York: Palgrave Macmillan, 1994), 131.

76 Whitworth, *Feminism,* 145

77 Whitworth, *Feminism,* 144.

78 Rothman, *Woman's Proper Place,* 152-53.

79 Kristin Luker, *When Sex Goes to School* (New York: W. W. Norton, 2006), 51. She refers back to findings by Lewis Terman and Alfred Kinsey.

80 Christopher Lasch, *Haven in a Heartless World: The Family Besieged* (New York: Basic Books, 1977).

81 Betrand Russell, *Marriage and Morals* (London: Liveright, 1970), 162-5. Russell thought the proposal was not radical enough. "I think that all sex relations that do not involve children should be regarded as a purely private affair, and that, if a man and a woman choose to live together without having children, that should be no one's business but their own."

82 Rothman, *Woman's Proper Place,* 186.

83 Quoted in Harvey Kantor and David Tyack, *Work, Youth and Schooling: Historical Perspectives on Vocationalism in American Education* (Stanford: Stanford University Press, 1982), 267.

84 Cott, *Grounding*, 156.

85 Sigmund Freud, "Some Practical Consequences of the Anatomical Distinction between the Sexes (1925) in *The Standard Edition of the Complete Psychological Works of Sigmund Freud,* ed. J. Strachey (London: Hogarth Press, 1961), 19:257-58.

86 Emile Durkheim, *The Division of Labor in Society* (New York: Macmillan, 1933), 56, 60.

87 Coontz, *A Strange Stirring,* 70; Talcott Parsons, *Family Socialization and Interaction Process* (New York: Free Press, 1960); for a summary of Carl Jung's influence, see Whitbeck, "Theories of Sex Difference," 62-68.

88 Betty Friedan, *The Feminine Mystique* (New York: Dell, 1964).

89 William Chafe, *Women and Equality* (New York: Oxford University Press, 1978), 94.

90 William Whyte and Joseph Nocera, *The Organization Man* (New York: Doubleday Anchor, 1957); William Sloan, *The Man in the Gray Flannel Suit* (New York: Simon and Schuster, 1955).

91 Barbara Ehrenreich, *The Hearts of Men: American Dreams and the Flight from Commitment* (New York: Anchor Books, 1987), 50. In Ehrenreich's interpretation, the pictures of scantily clad women in *Playboy* masked the economic dissatisfaction while protecting the male readers against the suspicion of their being homosexual.

92 Jo Freeman, *The Politics of Women's Liberation* (New York: David McKay, 1975), 37-43.

93 Coontz, *A Strange Stirring,* 154-55.

94 Freeman, *The Politics of Women's Liberation,* 54.

95 Betty Friedan, *It Changed My Life* (New York: Dell, 1976), 440-67.

96 Susan Moller Okin, "Women's Human Rights in the Late Twentieth Century," in *Sex Rights,* ed. Nicholas Bamforth (New York: Oxford University Press, 2005), 103-18, points out that theories of development need to be corrected for their male bias before they can be helpful to the cause of women.

97 Jerry Falwell, *Listen America* (New York: Bantam Books, 1981), 150.

98 Alice Rossi, "Gender and Parenthood," *American Sociological Review,* 49(Feb. 1984). 1-19; see also "A Biosocial Perspective on Parenting," *Daedalus,* 106(Spring, 1977), 1-31.

99 Sara Ruddick, *Maternal Thinking: Toward a Politics of Peace* (Boston, Beacon Press, 1995); Barbara Myerhoff, *Number Our Days: A Triumph of Continuity*

and Culture among Jewish Old People in an Urban Ghetto (New York: Touchstone, 1980).

100 Iris Young, *The Thinking Muse: Feminism and Modern French Philosophy* (Bloomington: Indiana University Press, 1985).

101 Susan Faludi, *Backlash: The Undeclared War against American Women* (New York: Crown, 1991); *Stiffed: The Betrayal of the American Man* (New York: Harper Perennial, 2000).

102 Faludi *Backlash,* 318.

103 Friedan, *It Changed My Life,* xvii. She describes Stage II as "the restructuring of all our institutions on a basis of real equality for women and men, the 'new yes.'"(482).

104 Faludi, *Backlash,* 325-26,

105 Carol Gilligan, *In a Different Voice: Psychological Theory and Women's Development* (Cambridge: Harvard University Press, 1982); also noteworthy at the time was Nancy Chodorow, *The Reproduction of Mothering: Psychoanalysis and the Sociology of Gender* (Berkeley: University of California Press, 1978).

106 Ms Magazine Dec, 1981, 63-66.

107 Faludi, *Backlash,* 327.

108 Carol Gilligan, "In a Different Voice: Women's Conception of Self and Morality," *Harvard Educational Review,* 47(1977), 507.

109 Kristin Luker, *Abortion and the Politics of Motherhood* (Berkeley: University of California Press, 1984), 23.

110 Luker, *Abortion,* 227: Her "modest inference" was that 20-40 percent of people in the United States were committed to one side or the other of the abortion dispute. 50-80 percent did not subscribe to either side.

Chapter 5

1 Jean-Jacques Rousseau, *Emile* (New York: Basic Books, 1979), 42.

2 William Lynch, *Images of Hope: Imagination as Healer of the Hopeless* (Notre Dame: University of Notre Dame Press, 1990), 203.

3 Alasdair MacIntrye, *Dependent, Rational Animals* (Chicago: Open Court, 1999), 130.

4 Henry Shue, *Basic Rights,* 2nd ed. (Princeton: Princeton University Press, 1996), 19.

5 John Locke, *The Second Treatise on Civil Government* (New York: Prometheus Books, 1986), chap. 6, no. 65. As I noted in chapter two, Locke gave special attention to children in his book on education, but in his political writings,

childhood is simply an imperfect stage of life that is replaced by the complete human being as adult.

6   Alison Gopnik, *The Philosophical Baby: What Children's Minds Tell Us about Truth, Love and the Meaning of Life* (New York: Farrar, Straus and Giroux, 2009).

7   Aristotle, *Metaphysics*, 981a 14 -15; David Hume, makes a similar point in *An Enquiry concerning Human Understanding* (New York: Oxford University Press, 2007), sec. IV, part1.

8   Piaget used the phrase in a 1967 lecture in New York. See David Elkind, *Children and Adolescents* (New York: Oxford University Press, 1981), 24.

9   Jean Piaget, *The Moral Judgment of the Child* (New York: Free Press, 1966), 13.

10 Jean Piaget, *The Psychology of the Child* (New York: Basic Books, 1972), 123-24.

11 Erik Erikson, *Insight and Responsibility* (New York: W.W. Norton, 1964), 231.

12 Piaget, *Moral Judgment of the Child*, 323.

13 Philippe Ariès, *Centuries of Childhood: A Social History of Family Life* (New York: Vintage Books, 1965).

14 David Stannard in *The Puritan Way of Death* (New York: Oxford University Press, 1979), 47, takes issue with Ariès's theory as it applies to the seventeenth-century British American colonies. Stannard says there is no real evidence to support the contention that there were few distinctions between child and adult.

15 Ariès, *Centuries of Childhood*, 399.

16 David Bakan, *Slaughter of the Innocents* (Boston: Beacon Press, 1972); see also Bruno Bettelheim, *The Use of Enchantment* (New York: Penguin Books, 1979).

17 John Robinson in seventeenth-century New England advised that "for the beating and keeping down of this stubbornness parents must provide carefully . . . that the children's will and willfulness be restrained and repressed." Quoted in John Demos, *A Little Commonwealth: Family Life in Plymouth Colony* (New York: Oxford University Press, 1970), 135.

18 Richard Sennett, *The Fall of Public Man* (New York: W.W. Norton, 1992).

19 John Locke, *Some Thoughts concerning Education* (New York: General Books, 2010). For a summary of Locke's writing on children, see David Archard, *Children: Rights and Childhood* (New York: Routledge, 2004), 1-15.

20 John Locke, *The Educational Writings of John Locke,* ed. James Axtell (Cambridge: Cambridge University Press, 1968), 64-65.

21 Locke, *Some Thoughts*, III: 57.

22   Locke, *Some Thoughts,* III: 78.

23   Rousseau, *Emile,* 101.

24   Rousseau, *Emile,* 97.

25   Rousseau, *Emile,* 43; James Axtell, *The School upon a Hill: Education and Society in Colonial New England* (New York: W.W. Norton, 1976), 85.

26   Locke, *Some Thoughts,* II, 24-29.

27   Rousseau, *Emile,* 166.

28   Johann Pestalozzi, *Leonard and Gertrude* (Toronto: University of Toronto Libraries, 2011).

29   Johann Pestalozzi, *How Gertrude Teaches her Children* (Ann Arbor: University of Michigan Press, 2009).

30   Bernard Wishy, *The Child and the Republic: The Dawn of Modern American Child Nurture* (Philadelphia: University of Pennsylvania Press, 1968), 72.

31   Catherine Beecher, *The Evils Suffered by American Women and American Children: The Causes and the Remedy* (New York, Harper and Brothers, 1846), 10.

32   Quoted in Joseph Kett, *Rites of Passage: Adolescence in America 1790 to the Present* (New York: Basic Books, 1978), 123.

33   Harriet Martineau, *Society in America* (New York: AMS Press, 1966 (1837))*;* Francis Grund, *The Americans, in their moral, social and political relations* (London: Longman, 1837).

34   Wishy, *The Child and the Republic, 93.*

35   John Shelton Lawrence and Robert Jewett, *The Myth of the American Superhero* (Grand Rapids: William B. Eerdmans, 2002), 116.

36   John Watson, *The Psychological Care of Infant and Child* (New York: W.W. Norton, 1928).

37   Willard Waller, *Sociology of Teaching* (New York: Russell and Russell, 1932), 12.

38   Benjamin Spock, *Dr. Spock's Baby and Child Care* (New York: Pocket Books, 1946).

39   A.S. Neill and Erich Fromm, *Summerhill: A Radical Approach to Child Rearing* (New York: Hart, 1960).

40   Quoted in Allen Graubard, *Free the Children: Radical Reform and the Free School Movement* (New York: Pantheon, 1972), 11; Neill and Fromm, *Summerhill,* 119.

41   *Alternative Newsletter,* May, 1968, 23-31.

42   The best known book in an extensive literature on the "end of childhood" is Neil Postman, *The Disappearance of Childhood* (New York: Viking Press,

1994). Like nearly all the books on the end of childhood, this book has almost nothing to say about adolescence.

43 www.unhchr.ch/html/menu3/b/25.htm

44 Lawrence LeBlanc, *The Convention on the Rights of the Child: United Nations Lawmaking on Human Rights* (Omaha: University of Nebraska Press, 1995); David Archard, *Children: Rights and Childhood* (New York: Routledge, 2004).

45 U. S. Congress, CR S—8400, June 14, 1995; www.hsda.org/docs/nche.

46 Archard, *Children: Rights and Childhood,* 64.

47 Annette Baier, *Moral Prejudices* (Cambridge: Harvard University Press, 1995), 242.

48 *Roper v. Simmons* 543 U.S. 551 (2005).

49 *New York Times Editorial,* November 9, 2009.

50 *Graham v. Florida* (2009).

51 P.W. Singer, *Children at War* (New York: Pantheon, 2005); Alcinda Honwana, *Child Soldiers in Africa* (Philadelphia: University of Pennsylvania Press, 2005).

52 The UN offered two optional protocols in 2002, one on the rights of children in armed conflicts, one forbidding child prostitution and child pornography.

53 See the remarkable record of the experience of a child soldier in Ismael Beah, *A Long Way Gone: Memoirs of a Boy Soldier* (New York: Farrar, Straus and Giroux, 2007).

54 Geraldine Van Bueren, "Opening Pandora's Box—Protecting Children against Torture, Cruel, Inhuman and Degrading Treatment and Punishment," in *Childhood Abused,* ed. Geraldine Van Bueren (Brookfield, VT: Ashgate, 1998), 59.

55 John Holt, *Escape from Childhood: The Needs and Rights of Children* (New York: Ballantine Books, 1975), 1.

56 *The Convention on the Rights of the Child,* articles 12 and 13.

57 Lawrence Houlgate, *The Child and the State* (Baltimore: Johns Hopkins University Press, 1980), 79, describes the case of an unusually mature boy named Gregory Kingsley who sought to have his mother's authority terminated over him. "Gregory's right to petition on his own behalf, and not simply through some third party, carries with the recognition that, already at age twelve, Gregory is able to make reasonable judgments about whether his mother has been carrying out her responsibilities toward him; should the court deny his petition, he deserves to have the court explain to *him*, and not just to a guardian, that he is wrong, and why."

58 Edmund Morgan, *The Puritan Family* (New York: Harper and Row, 1966), 64.

59 Bert Smith, *Aging in America* (Boston: Beacon Press, 1974), 2.

60 David Hackett Fischer, *Growing Old in America* (New York: Oxford University Press, 1978), 61.

61 Mary Wollstonecraft, *Vindication of the Rights of Woman* (Cambridge: Cambridge University Press, 2010), 153.

62 Barbara Myerhoff, *Number Our Days,* (New York: Touchstone, 1978).

63 Simone de Beauvoir, *Coming of Age* (New York: Warner Books, 1972), 87.

64 Maggie Kuhn, "Gray Panther Power," *Center Magazine*, March/April, 1975, 25.

65 Erik Erikson, *Insight and Responsibility* (New York: W.W. Norton, 1972), 134.

66 The idea of "smuggling in" philosophical assumptions is used by Steven Smith in his pointed criticism of the scientists and philosophers involved in this discussion: *The Disenchantment of Secular Discourse* (Cambridge: Harvard University Press, 2010), 42-69

67 Judge Barbara Rothstein in *State of Washington v. Glucksberg,* 1997.

68 Albert Camus, *The Plague* (New York: Vintage Books, 1948), 119.

69 There are numerous variations one can work on this example. If I see someone drowning in the ocean and I cannot swim, I cannot be obliged to rescue the person but it would be morally negligent not to try to get help.

70 Kwame Appiah, *Cosmopolitanism* (New York: W.W. Norton, 2007), 162, notes that how to help the poor of the world has no clear answer, but "on the other hand, many decisions *aren't* so hard because some of our foremost moral knowledge is about particular cases."

71 These are not just hypothetical possibilities. They or quite similar situations have happened on many occasions.

72 In one case, a boy, Jamie Butcher, became comatose at seventeen years of age. The parents did everything possible for their son. Finally on his thirty-fourth birthday, they decided to let go. They were immediately confronted with a court battle from a group called Nursing Home Action Group whose spokesperson said, "I have heard no clear reason why he should be put to death." *New York Times*, Oct. 18,1994.

73 The Catholic Church is often thought to be an obstacle to the acceptance of euthanasia. Ronald Dworkin, in *Life's Dominion* (New York: Knopf, 1993), 195, states that "the Romans Catholic church is the sternest, most vigilant, and no doubt most effective opponent of euthanasia, as it is of abortion." The statement is misleading. It is true that the Catholic Church condemns

what it calls euthanasia, meaning the intentional killing of someone. Until a few decades ago, that was the accepted meaning of the term. The users of euthanasia now often dismiss the importance of a difference between letting die and killing by simply referring to active and passive euthanasia. Catholic bishops seem unaware that in condemning euthanasia in its present meaning they are rejecting a position that the Catholic Church has had since the Middle Ages. Unlike its position on abortion that can prevent helpful compromise, the Catholic Church has long been consistent, humane, and helpful on questions regarding the dying. Before this issue had much public exposure, Pope Pius XII had written, "It is unnatural to prevent death in instances where there is no hope of recovery. When nature is calling for death, there is no question that one can remove the life-support system." "The Prolongation of Life," *The Pope Speaks* 4 (1958).

74 William May, *The Physician's Covenant* (Philadelphia: Westminster Press, 1983), 109: "A country has not earned in good conscience the moral option to kill for mercy if it has not already sustained and supported life with compassion and mercy."

75 Elisabeth Kübler-Ross, *On Death and Dying* (New York: Macmillan, 1970).

76 Erik Erikson, *Childhood and Society* (New York: Vintage Books, 1995), 269.

Chapter 6

1 Jaroslav Pelikan, *The Vindication of Tradition* (New Haven: Yale University Press, 1986).

2 Martin Buber, *Eclipse of God* (New York: Humanity Books, 1987), 39.

3 Mary Douglas, *Natural Symbols* (London: Routledge, 2003), 52: "In rejecting ritual forms of speech it is the 'external' aspect which is devalued. Probably all movements of renewal have had in common the rejection of external forms."

4 This point is well developed in relation to Evangelical religions in the United States by Christian Smith, *American Evangelicalism* (Chicago: University of Chicago, 1998), 118, 150.

5 Martha Nussbaum, "Religion and Women's Human Rights," *Sex and Social Justice* (New York: Oxford University Press, 1999), 81-117, documents violations of women's rights within religious traditions.

6 W. Cantwell Smith, *The Meaning and End of Religion* (New York: New American Library, 1964), 84.

7 William Ernest Hocking, *Living Religions and a World Faith* (New York: Macmillan, 1940), 31.

8   Hocking, *Living Religions*, 262

9   David Stendl-Rast in *Christian Faith in a Religiously Plural World*, ed. John Carman and Donald Dawe, (New York: Orbis Books, 1978), 134.

10 Frank Tobin, *Meister Eckhart: Thought and Doctrine* (Philadelphia: University of Pennsylvania Press, 1986), 86.

11 George Lindbeck, *The Nature of Doctrine: Religion and Theology in a Postliberal Age* (Louisville: Westminster John Knox, 1984), 68.

12 Augustine, *Of True Religion* (Chicago: Regnery, 1991); *Retractions* (Washington: Catholic University of America Press, 1999), I.13. 3.

13 This usage explains why Martin Luther's sharpest attacks were against *vita religiosa* and *homini religiosi*.

14 Thomas Aquinas, *Summa Theologiae* (New York: McGraw Hill, 1966), IIae, 81, 1; for Cicero, see *The Nature of the Gods* (New York: Oxford University Press, 2008), Book II.

15 Peter Harrison, *'Religion' and the Religions in the English Enlightenment* (Cambridge: Cambridge University Press, 1990), 13.

16 Harrison, *'Religion' and the Religions*, 12; H. G. Gadamer, *Truth and Method* (New York: Continuum, 2004), 396.

17 Jonathan Smith, "Religion, Religion, Religious" in *Critical Terms for Religious Studies*, ed. Mark Taylor (Chicago: University of Chicago Press, 1998), 275.

18 Smith, *The Meaning and End of Religion*, 39.

19 Immanuel Kant, writing in 1795, expresses chagrin at the phrase "difference of religion." He writes that "there may be different religious texts (Zendavesta, the Veda, the Koran, etc.) but such differences do not exist in religion, there being only one religion valid for all men." See "Peace Protests," *On History* (New York: Macmillan, 1963), 113, n.7.

20 Diana Eck, *Encountering God* (Boston, Beacon Press, 1993), 189.

21 Nicholas Lash, *The Beginning and the End of Religion* (Cambridge: Cambridge University Press, 1996), 14.

22 Lash, *Beginning and End of Religion*, 75.

23 Francis Buckley, *At the Origins of Modern Atheism* (New Haven: Yale University Press, 1990), 346: "'Natural theology' synthesized the Schoolmen and Cicero; and Christianity, in order to defend its god, transmuted itself into theism." Buckley notes that this natural theology "can be common to Christian and pagan, atheist and believer, because it is untouched by anything which either Jew or Christian would recognize as religious challenge, religious belief, religious practice or religious experience."

24 José Casanova, *Public Religions in the Modern World* (Chicago: University of Chicago Press, 1994).

25 The distinction was drawn by Justice Arthur Goldberg in *Abington School District v. Schemmp* 374 U.S.203 1963. I have summarized the legal and educational issues in "Can Religion be Taught?" in *Speaking of Teaching* (Lanham: Rowman and Littlefield, 2008), 121-141.

26 Jefferson wrote in 1822, "I trust there is not a young man now living in the United States who will not die a Unitarian." See Dickinson Adams, *Jefferson's Extracts from the Gospels* (Princeton: Princeton University Press, 1983), 409.

27 William Rainey Harper, "The Scope and Purpose of the New Organization," *Proceedings of the First Convention* (Chicago: Religious Education Association, 1903).

28 Robert Jackson, *Rethinking Religious Education and Plurality* (London: Routledge and Kegan Paul, 2004).

29 John Hull, *New Directions in Religious Education* (London: Falmer, 1982).

30 Robert Jackson, *Religious Education in Europe* (Münster: Waxman, 2007); Hans-Georg Ziebertz and Ulrich Riegel, *How Teachers in Europe Teach Religion* (Munster: LIT Publishers, 2009).

31 " Declaration of the Relationship of the Church to Non-Christian Religions," *Documents of Vatican II,* ed. Walter Abbot (New York: Guild Press, 1966), 660-68.

32 An impressive example is *The Jewish Annotated New Testament*, ed. Amy-Jill Levine and Marc Brettler (New York: Oxford University Press, 2011).

33 Emil Fackenheim, *To Mend the World: Foundations of Post-Holocaust Jewish Thought* (Bloomington: Indiana University Press, 1994), 39.

34 One of the first Christian theologians, Justin, was already formulating a Christian doctrine about the salvation of the non-Christian: "Christ is the Logos of whom every race of man are partakers, and those who, like Socrates, have lived in accordance with that Logos are Christians, even though they may have been regarded as atheists." Maurice Wiles, *Christian Faith* (Valley Forge: Trinity Press International, 1982), 28.

35 Thomas Aquinas, *Commentary on Ephesians 3:10*, lect. 3: "The true Church is the heavenly Church, which is our mother, and to which we tend; upon it our earthly church is modeled."

36 Martin Buber, *Two Types of Faith* (New York: Harper, 1961), 12.

37 Richard Rorty, *Contingency, Irony and Solidarity* (Cambridge: Cambridge University Press, 1989), 191.

38 For a study of the teachings of Jesus—by a Jew—see Pinchas Lapide, *The Sermon on the Mount* (New York: Orbis Books, 1986).

39 Dietrich Bonhoeffer, *Ethics* (New York: Collier Books, 1986), 259.

40 A. D. Nock, *Conversion* (New York: Oxford University Press, 1961), 210.

41   Meg. 10b in Avivah Gottlieb Zornberg, *The Particulars of Rapture* (New York: Doubleday, 2001), 215.

42   The prayer is that of a Hasidic Zaddik; Martin Buber, *Two Types of Faith* (New York: Harper Torch, 1961), 77.

43   William Irwin, "A Common Humanity under One God" in *Judaism and Human Rights,* ed. Milton Konvitz (New Brunswick: Rutgers University Press, 2001), 56: "Monotheism in itself may be no more than despotism in religion. The great achievement of Israel was not primarily that she asserted the oneness of the world and God, but rather the character of the God affirmed."

44   It has to be admitted that God taking Eve from Adam's rib leaves much to be desired from a feminist point of view. One might nonetheless credit the story as an attempt to find a way to express the diversity within unity of the human race.

45   *Mishnah Sanhedrin* IV, 5; Abraham Heschel, *The Insecurity of Freedom* (New York: Farrar, Straus and Giroux, 1963), 155.

46   Michael Signer in *Unanswered Questions: Theological Views of Catholic-Jewish Relations*, ed. Roger Brooks (Notre Dame: University of Notre Dame Press, 1995), 123-24.

47   *Yerushalmi Sanhedrin* 4:2; *The Essential Talmud,* ed. Adin Steinsaltz (New York: Basic Books, 1984).

48   *Erubhin*, 13b in *Our Masters Taught: Rabbinic Stories and Sayings,* ed. Jakob Petuchowski (New York: Crossroad, 1982), 41.

49   Arthur Cohen, *The Myth of the Judeo-Christian Tradition* (New York: Schocken Books, 1971), 196.

50   Mark Silk, "Notes on the Judeo-Christian Tradition in America," *American Quarterly,* 36(1984); Peter Novick, *The Holocaust in American Life* (New York: Mariner Books, 2000), 28.

51   John Zizioulas, *Being as Communion* (New York: St. Vladimir's Seminary Press, 1985), 134.

52   Franz Rosenzweig, *The Star of Redemption* (Madison: University of Wisconsin Press, 2005).

53   Muhammad Zafrulla Khan, *Islam and Human Rights* (Tilford: Islamic International Publications, 1967), 22.

54   Khan, *Islam and Human Rights*, 22; he is commenting on the Qur'an 7:59.

55   Sidney Griffith, *The Church in the Shadow of the Mosque: Christians and Muslims in the World of Islam* (Princeton: Princeton University Press, 2008). Christians and Jews were "protected peoples" who were provided with freedom to practice their religion if they paid a special tax. Another hopeful experiment was in India during the late sixteenth century when there was

some genuine dialogue initiated by Akbar and his son Jahangir between Portuguese Jesuits and Muslims. See Irfan Habib, *Akbar and his India* (New York: Oxford University Press, 2000).

56 Alexis de Tocqueville, *Democracy in America* vol. 2 (New York: Vintage Books, 1960), chap. 5.

57 Gilles Kepel, *The Revenge of God: The Resurgence of Islam, Christianity and Judaism in the Modern World* (University Park: Pennsylvania State University, 1994), 17.

58 Christopher Caldwell, *Reflections on the Revolution in Europe* (New York: Doubleday, 2009).

59 Philip Hamburger, *Separation of Church and State* (Cambridge: Harvard University Press, 2004); Daniel Dreisbach, *Thomas Jefferson and the Wall of Separation between Church and State* (New York: New York University Press, 2002).

60 "Women and Islam: An Exchange with Kenneth Ross of Human Rights Watch," *The New York Review*, March 22, 2012, 45.

61 *New York Times,* September 21, 2001.

62 Dwight Eisenhower entitled his history of the Second World War *Crusade in Europe* (New York: Avon Books, 1968).

63 Jonathan Riley-Smith, *The Crusades, Christianity and Islam* (New York: Columbia University Press, 2008).

64 Olivier Roy, *Secularism Confronts Islam* (New York: Columbia University Press, 2007), xi.

65 W. Cantwell Smith, *On Understanding Islam* (The Hague: Mouton, 1981), 259.

66 Smith, *On Understanding Islam*, 241.

67 Quoted in Annemarie Schimmel, *Deciphering the Signs of God: A Phenomenological Approach to Islam* (Albany: State University of New York Press, 1980), 163.

68 Robert Pattison, *On Literacy: The Politics of the Word from Homer to the Age of Rock* (New York: Galaxy, 1984), 71. Early Christianity was an oral religion that devalued the book. When the gospel was finally written, it was in the spoken language of the time not classical Greek.

69 The Universal Islamic Declaration of Human Rights from 1981 opens with the statement: "Islam gave to mankind an ideal code of human rights fourteen centuries ago." The claim is overstated and the twenty-three rights that follow are too many. See P.S. Ali, *Human Rights in Islam* (Lahore: Aziz Publishing, 1980); Reza Aslan, *No God but God* (New York: Random House, 2005). David Boucher, *The Limits of Ethics in International Relations: Natural Law,*

Natural Rights and Human Rights in Transition (New York: Oxford University Press, 2009), 250.

70 The phrase "Abrahamic traditions" has become a common way of grouping Jewish, Christian, and Muslim religions. There is a danger of covering over the differences too quickly. There is not a single tradition but three different traditions that lay claim to Abraham. See Jon Levenson, *Inheriting Abraham: The Legacy of the Patriarch in Judaism, Christianity, and Islam* (Princeton: Princeton University Press, 2013).

71 Swami Prabhavananda, *Religion in Practice* (New York: Vedanta Press, 1969), 108.

72 At the beginning of the document on divine revelation: *Verbum Dei*, article 1, *The Documents of Vatican II*, 111.

73 Aloysius Pieris, "The Buddha and the Christ," in *The Myth of Christian Uniqueness*, ed. John Hick and Paul Knitter (New York: Orbis Books, 1987), 171.

74 Swami Prabhavananda, in Robert Ellwood *Eastern Spirituality in America: Selected Writings* (New York: Paulist Press, 1987), 70.

75 Perez Zagorin, *How the Idea of Religious Toleration Came to the West* (Princeton: Princeton University Press, 2005).

76 Karl Popper, *The Open Society and its Enemies: The Spell of Plato* (London: Routledge, 2002), 265; Leszek Kolakowski, *Modernity on Endless Trial* (Chicago: University of Chicago Press, 1997).

77 Krister Stendahl, *Paul among Jews and Gentiles* (Philadephia: Fortress Press, 1976).

78 Radhakrishnan, *Hindu View of Life* (New York: HarperCollins, 2009), 16, 18.

79 George Bernanos, *The Diary of a Country Priest* (New York: Image Books, 1962).

80 Karl Rahner, "Christianity and Non-Christian Religions," *Theological Investigations,* vol. 5 (Baltimore: Helicon, 1966), 115-34.

81 Karl Rahner, *Theological Investigations*, vol. 16 (New York: Crossroad, 1983), 219.

82 Voltaire, *Philosophical Dictionary*, ed. Peter Gay (New York: Basic Books, 1962).

83 Hahm Chaibong, "Confucianism and Western Rights: Conflict or Harmony," *Responsive Community* 10:1(Winter, 1999-2000), 50-58.

84 Simon Leys, *The Analects of Confucius* (New York: W.W. Norton, 1997), 17:3.

85 Ian Buruma, *Taming the Gods: Religion and Democracy on Three Continents* (Princeton: Princeton University Press, 2010), 67.

86 Leyes, *The Analects of Confucius*, 13:23.

87 James Tong, *Revenge of the Forbidden City: The Suppression of the Falungong in China 1999-2005* (New York: Oxford University Press, 2009)

88 Mary Ann Glendon, *A World Made New: Eleanor Roosevelt and the Universal Declaration of Human Rights* (New York: Random House, 2002), 47.

89 Kevin Boyle and Juliet Sheen, eds., *Freedom of Religion and Belief: A World Report* (London: Routledge, 1997).

90 Natan Lerner, *Religion, Beliefs and International Human Rights* (New York: Orbis Books, 2000), 32.

Chapter 7

1 For example, James Lovelock, *The Revenge of Gaia: Earth's Climate Crisis and the Fate of Humanity* (New York: Basic Books, 2007), 189: "Our future is like that of passengers on a small pleasure boat sailing quietly above the Niagara Falls, not knowing that the engines are about to fail."

2 *New York Times*, April 23, 1970.

3 Henry Salt, *Animal Rights Considered in Relation to Social Progress* (New York: Macmillan, 1894).

4 Peter Singer, "Animal Liberation," *New York Review of Books*, April 5, 1973; *Animal Liberation* (New York: Random House, 1975).

5 Quoted in Roderick Nash, *The Rights of Nature: A History of Environmental Ethics* (Madison: University of Wisconsin Press, 1989), 152.

6 Nash, *The Rights of Nature*.

7 Raymond Williams, *Keywords: A Vocabulary of Culture and Society* (New York: Oxford University Press, 1976), 184, 186.

8 Arthur Lovejoy and George Boas, in *Primitivism and Related Ideas in Antiquity* (New York: Octagon Books, 1965), 447-56, identify sixty-six meanings of *nature* in classical times.

9 Jeffrey Macy, "Natural Law," in *Contemporary Jewish Religious Thought*, ed. Arthur Cohen and Paul Mendes-Flohr (New York: Free Press, 1987), 663-672.

10 Aristotle, *Physics*, 192b.

11 Aristotle, *Metaphysics*, 1014b.

12 R. G. Collingwood, *The Idea of Nature* (New York: Galaxy Books, 1959), 44.

13 Epictetus, *Enchiridion* (New York: Create Space, 2011).

14 Marie-Dominique Chenu, *Nature, Man and Society in the Twelfth Century* (Toronto: University of Toronto Press, 1997).

15   William Leiss, *The Domination of Nature* (Montreal: McGill University Press, 1994), 48-71; Francis Bacon, *The New Organon* (Cambridge: Cambridge University Press, 2008).

16   Francis Bacon, *The New Organon,* I, 88; Genevieve Lloyd, *The Man of Reason: Male and Female in Western Philosophy* (Minneapolis: University of Minnesota Press, 1984), 11-15.

17   Elizabeth Wertheim, *Pythagoras' Trousers: God, Physics and the Gender Wars* (New York: W.W. Norton, 1997), 83, 105.

18   For this history of English poetry, see Wendell Berry, "Poetry and Place," in *Standing by Words* (San Francisco: North Point Press, 1983), 92-199.

19   Gotthold Lessing, *Theological Writings: Selections in Translation* (London: A & C Black, 1956) 105: "The best revealed or positive religion is that which contains the fewest conventional additions to natural religion, and least hinders the good effects of natural religion."

20   Edward Herbert, *De Religione Laici* (New Haven: Yale University Press, 1944), 129, claimed that his five tenets of natural religion "have been engraved on the human mind by God . . . and acknowledged as true throughout the world, by every age."

21   Alasdair MacIntyre, *After Virtue* (Notre Dame: University of Notre Dame, 1981), 234; Ernst Bloch, *Natural Law and Human Dignity* (Cambridge: MIT Press, 1987), 58.

22   Lynn White, Jr., "The Historical Roots of Our Ecological Crisis," in *Machina Ex Deo: Essays in the Dynamics of Western Culture* (Cambridge: MIT Press, 1968), 76-92, reprinted from *Science* 71(March 10, 1967), 1203-07.

23   Lynn White, Jr., *Medieval Religion and Technology* (Berkeley: University of California Press, 1978).

24   Lynn White, Jr., *Medieval Technology and Social Change* (New York: Oxford University Press, 1962).

25   T. R. Wright, *The Religion of Humanity: The Impact of Comtean Positivism on Victorian Britain* (Cambridge: Cambridge University Press, 1986).

26   Fairly typical is Peter Singer's treatment of what he calls "the traditional Judeo-Christian view of the world" or "the dominant Western ethical tradition." Singer writes that "we all know the key passages in this tradition," and he then proceeds to quote the one passage that is always quoted (Gen. 1:24-28). From that passage he concludes, "God gave human beings dominion over the natural world, and God does not care how we treat it." His summary of the Bible, Jewish tradition, and Christian tradition is, to put it mildly, inadequate. See Peter Singer, "Ethics across the Species Boundary," in Nicholas Low, ed., *Global Ethics and the Environment* (London: Routledge, 1999), 147.

27 For commentaries on Genesis by Basil, Ambrose, Augustine, Thomas Aquinas and others, see George Ovitt, *The Restoration of Perfection: Labor and Technology in Medieval Culture* (New Brunswick: Rutgers University Press, 1986), 74-85.

28 Eric Freudenstein, "Ecology and Jewish Tradition," in *Judaism and Human Rights,* ed. Milton Konvitz (New Brunswick: Rutgers University Press, 2001), 273.

29 Samson Hirsch, "Do Not Destroy," in *Judaism and Human Rights,* 259-63.

30 Aldo Leopold, *A Sand County Almanac* (New York: Oxford University Press, 1949).

31 G. K. Chesterton, Saint Francis of Assisi (Garden City: Image Books, 1959), 12; Regis Armstrong, *Saint Francis of Assisi: Writings for a Gospel Life* (New York: Hyperion Books, 1996), 7.

32 Chesterton, *Saint Francis of Assisi,* 87.

33 Roger Sorrel, *Saint Francis of Assisi and Nature* (New York: Oxford University Press, 1988), 8.

34 Medieval theologians thought that Exodus 3:14 that says "I am who I am" was a metaphysical statement. Contemporary exegetes interpret the text in a variety of ways. Its function in context was to promise "I will be with you."

35 A book that does ask what *environment* means is Ted Nordhaus and Michael Shellenberger, *Breakthrough: From the Death of Environmentalism to the Politics of Possibility* (Boston: Houghton Mifflin, 2007), 10. The authors reject "the environment" as either including the human or excluding the human. They do not consider the most obvious meaning of environment as the surroundings that humans are related to.

36 Rachel Carson, *Silent Spring* (Boston: Houghton Mifflin, 1962).

37 L. O. Howard, when he was head of the Bureau of Entomology, spoke in 1921 about "the war of humanity against the class *Insecta.*" Edmund Russell, *War and Nature* (Cambridge: Cambridge University Press, 2001), 75.

38 Richard Ryder, an Oxford psychologist, is credited with the neologism: Peter Singer, *Rethinking Life and Death* (New York: St. Martin's, 1995), 173.

39 This policy would seem to be implied in Paul Taylor, *Respect for Nature: A Theory of Environmental Ethics* (Princeton: Princeton University Press, 1986), 115: "Given the total, absolute, and final disappearance of *Homo Sapiens,* then, not only would the Earth's Community of Life continue to exist but in all probability its well-being would be enhanced."

40 Taylor, *Respect for Nature,* 45.

41 The term was coined by Dionysius, a fifth-century Syrian monk. He is usually called Pseudo-Dionysius because writers in the Middle Ages mistakenly

took him to be a character named Dionysius in the New Testament. See Ronald Hathaway, *Hierarchy and the Definition of Order in the Letters of Pseudo-Dionysius* (The Hague: Nijhoff, 1969), 37.

42   Plotinus, *The Enneads* (London: Faber and Faber, 1969), V. 2. 1.

43   Plotinus, *Enneads*, III.6. 2. See John Rist, *Plotinus: Road to Reality* (Cambridge: Cambridge University Press, 1980), 227.

44   Arthur Lovejoy, *The Great Chain of Being* (Cambridge: Harvard University Press, 1953) is the history of Neo-Platonism's influence.

45   Wendell Berry, *Standing by Words*, 167.

46   This principle was articulated by Augustine as a mark of the spiritual. It is used by Dante in *Purgatory* XV: the love of God is increased by partnership.

47   George Eliot, *Middlemarch* (Charleston: Create Space, 2010), 667.

48   Kenan Osborne, *Orders and Ministry* (New York: Orbis Books, 2006), 118.

49   Jack Welch, *Jack: Straight from the Gut* (New York: Warner Books, 2001), 433.

50   Plato, *Republic*, 368d.

51   For a center to the country, I refer only to the contiguous forty-eight states, not all fifty; but at least that would be an improvement over the location of Washington D.C.

52   Hannah Arendt, *The Human Condition* (Chicago: University of Chicago Press, 1958), 157-58.

53   Annie Dillard, *Pilgrim at Tinker Creek* (New York: Bantam Press, 1975), 147.

54   Friedrich Nietzsche, *Beyond God and Evil* (New York: Penguin Books, 1973), 62, no. 53.

55   James Lovelock, *Gaia: A New Look at Life on Earth* (New York: Oxford University Press, 2000).

56   Sherwin Nuland, *How We Die: Reflections of Life's Final Chapter* (New York: Vintage Books, 1995), 3.

57   Alfred North Whitehead as cited in Norman Brown, *Life against Death: the Psychoanalytical Meaning of History* (New York: Vintage Books, 1959), 10-11.

58   Nuland, *How We Die*, 70; Robert Floud, Robert Fogel, Bernard Harris and Sol Chung Hong, *The Changing Body: Health, Nutrition and Development in the Western World Since 1700* (Cambridge: Cambridge University Press, 2011).

59   Lewis Thomas, *The Medusa and the Snail: More Notes of a Biology Watcher* (New York: Penguin Books, 1995), 2.

60   Theodosius Dobzhanski, quoted in Robert Sapolsky, "A Natural History of Peace," *Foreign Affairs*, 85(Jan/Feb, 2006), 104.

61 P.B. Medawar, *The Uniqueness of the Individual* (New York: Dover Publications, 1981), 185.

62 Steven Toulmin, *The Return to Cosmology: Postmodern Science and the Theology of Nature* (Berkeley: University of California Press, 1985), 165.

63 Peter Singer, in the Preface to *Practical Ethics*, 2nd ed. (Cambridge: Cambridge University Press, 1993), ix, quotes a German condemnation of the book's first edition: "The uniqueness of human life forbids any comparison—or more specifically equation—of human existence with other living beings." The statement might make sense if it just said that human uniqueness forbids equation with other living beings; but forbidding the comparison between human beings and other living beings is nonsensical. There is no way to avoid it.

64 Quoted in John Macquarrie, *In Search of Deity* (New York: Crossroad, 1985), 95. For the comparable idea in Jewish tradition, see Gershom Scholem, *Major Trends in Jewish Mysticism* (New York: Schocken Books, 1995), 269.

65 Irenaeus Eibl-Eibesfeldt, *Ethnology: The Biology of Behavior* (New York, Holt, Rinehart and Winston, 1975), 92.

66 Mary Midgley, *Beast and Man: The Roots of Human Nature* (Ithaca: Cornell University Press, 1978), 203.

67 Richard Rorty, "Human Rights, Rationality and Sentimentality," *Truth and Progress* (Cambridge: Cambridge University Press, 1998), 167-185.

68 Midgley, *Beast and Man*, 267.

69 Konrad Lorenz, *On Aggression* (New York: Harvest Books, 1974), 254.

70 G. K. Chesterton, *Orthodoxy* (Garden City: Doubleday, 1959), 144.

71 Charles Mann and Mark Plummer, *Noah's Choice: The Future of Endangered Species* (New York: Knopf, 1995), 8.

72 Tom Regan, *The Case for Animal Rights* (Berkeley: University of California Press, 1980), xiii

73 Berry, *Standing By Words*, 168.

Chapter 8

1 Joanne Bauer and Daniel Bell, eds., *The East Asian Challenge for Human Rights* (Cambridge: Cambridge University Press, 1999).

2 Efua Dorkenoo, *Female Genital Mutilation* (New York: Columbia University Press, 2013).

3 Richard Rorty's later writing on "sentimental education" offers many practical suggestions for enlarging a "culture of human rights," a culture often helped more by the arts than laws. What he positively advocates has to be separated from

his somewhat bizarre attacks on reason, knowledge, and human nature, which seem based on the premise that any introduction of those terms is Platonic or Kantian. See "Human Rights, Rationality and Sentimentality," in *Truth and Progress* (Cambridge: Cambridge University Press, 1998), 167-185.

4   Jürgen Habermas, *The Divided West* (London: Polity Press, 2006), 56.

5   *New York Times,* Nov. 17, 2011, A31.

6   Matthew Arnold, *Culture and Anarchy* (New York: Oxford University Press, 2009), 5.

7   The term *civilization* underwent a near reversal of meaning similar to the path of *culture*. Up to the twentieth century, *civilization* had an evaluative meaning; the choice was to be civilized or uncivilized. Today a plural meaning is always at least implied. Samuel Huntington wrote of *The Clash of Civilizations* (1996). Similarly the title of Niall Ferguson's, *Civilization* (2011), is in the singular but the book is about civilizations. In many of these books, the older meaning of *civilization* tends to reappear in the judgment that *Western* civilization is superior to other civilizations.

8   Edward Tylor, *Primitive Culture* (Ithaca: Cornell University Press, 2009), 1.

9   Walt Whitman, *Democratic Vistas* (Charleston: Forgotten Books, 2009), 40.

10   Friedrich Nietzsche, *The Anti-Christ* (New York: Penguin Books, 1968), 188, no. 57.

11   The movement was especially identified with William Graham Sumner although he did not invent the term. His influential 1906 textbook was *Folkways: A Study of Mores, Manners, Customs and Morals* (New York: Mentor Book, 1960).

12   Jeremy Waldron, *Nonsense upon Stilts* (New York: Methuen, 1987), 169.

13   Franz Boas, "The Aims of Ethnology," in *A Franz Boas Reader*, ed. George Stocking, Jr. (Chicago: University of Chicago Press, 1974), 71.

14   In the twentieth century, another distinction between high and (pop) low culture added to the complexity of the term. "Popular culture," though a latecomer to culture, has come to dominate the meaning. Consider Robert Levine, *Free Ride* (New York: Doubleday, 2011) which is subtitled: "*How Digital Parasites Are Destroying the Culture Business and How Culture Business Can Fight Back.*" *Culture* as a business may be worth defending, but it is a long way from *culture* as the best that the human race has known.

15   Alfred North Whitehead, *The Aims of Education* (New York: New American Library, 1955), 1.

16   Whitehead, *Aims of Education*, 47.

17   Neil MacGregor, *A History of the World in 100 Objects* (New York: Viking Books, 2011).

18 It should be acknowledged that Gary Nash, one of the most noted proponents of multiculturalism, was aware of the problem: "If multiculturalism is to get beyond a promiscuous pluralism that gives everything equal weight and adopts complete moral relativism, it must reach some agreement on what is at the core of American culture," "The Great Multicultural Debate," *Contention*, 1(1992), 11.

19 Kwame Apia, *Cosmopolitanism* (New York: Norton, 2007), 105, implies the two meanings of *culture* when he writes, "Preserving *culture*—in the sense of cultural artifacts, broadly conceived—is different from preserving *cultures.*"

20 Marie Mackey, *Multiculturalism, Religion and Women: Doing Harm by Doing Good?* (London: Palgrave Macmillan, 2009), 138.

21 Susan Moller Okin, "Mistresses of their own Destiny: Group Rights, Gender and Realistic Rights," *Ethics* 112(January, 2002), 205-30.

22 Janice Stein, "Searching for Equality," in *Uneasy Partners: Multiculturalism and Rights in Canada* (Waterloo: Wilfred Laurier University Press, 2007), 1.

23 Joseph Raz, *The Morality of Freedom* (New York: Oxford University Press, 1986), 254.

24 On the continued existence of a race problem in the United States, see Randall Kennedy, *The Persistence of the Color Line: Racial Politics and the Obama Presidency* (New York: Pantheon, 2011).

25 Frederick Douglass, "My Bondage and my Freedom," in *Autobiographies* (New York: Library of America, 1994), 406.

26 A good example is James Baldwin, *The Fire Next Time* (New York: Modern Library, 1963).

27 Ian Buruma, *Taming the Gods: Religion and Democracy on Three Continents* (Princeton: Princeton University Press, 2010), 89.

28 *New York Times*, July 24, 2011, 9; the words are those of German Prime Minister Angela Merkel.

29 Roger Scruton, *A Dictionary of Political Thought* (London: Macmillan, 1982), 100.

30 Jeremy Waldron, "What is Cosmopolitan?" *Journal of Political Philosophy* 8:2(June, 2000), 242; Bruce Ackerman, "Rooted Cosmopolitanism," *Ethics* 104(1994), 516-35.

31 Jesus did not actually say what is reported in Mt 28:16, "Go therefore and make disciples of all nations," but it accurately reflects what the early church took to be implied by Jesus's teaching.

32 Thomas Bender, *A Nation among Nations: America's Place in World History* (New York: Hill and Wang, 2006), 15-60.

33 Charles Mann, *1493: Uncovering the New World that Columbus Created* (New York: Knopf, 2011).

34 Richard Bernstein, *Dictatorship of Virtue: Multiculturalism and the Battle for America's Future.* (New York: Knopf, 1994), 39-47.

35 Vinton Cerf, "Internet Access is not a Human Right," *New York Times,* Janurary 5, 2012, A25.

36 See the interesting reflections in Malcolm Gladwell, "Small Change: Why the Revolution Will not be Tweeted," *New Yorker,* Oct. 4, 2010, 42-48.

37 Thomas Friedman, *New York Times,* July 20, 2011, A27.

38 Amartya Sen, *The Idea of Justice* (Cambridge: Harvard University Press, 2009), 364.

39 This plea to never forget a tragic event has a long history. One can find similar sentiments in the 1770s on the anniversary of the skirmish called the Boston massacre in which five people died. Joseph Warren at the second annual memorial said, "The Fatal Fifth of March, 1770, can never be forgotten—the horrors of that dreadful night are but too deeply impressed on our hearts." The quotation is from Andrew Burstein, *Sentimental Democracy: The Evolution of America's Romantic Self-Image* (New York: Hill and Wang, 1999), 68.

40 George Santayana, *Life of Reason: Introduction and Reason in Common Sense* (Charleston: Nabu Press, 2010), 284.

41 The text in Sanhedrin 37a is "Whosoever preserves a single soul . . . scripture ascribes to him as though he had preserved a complete world."

42 Plato, *Republic,* 373d.

43 Peter Kropotkin, *Mutual Aid* (Boston: Extending Horizon Books, 1955), 54.

44 Lewis Thomas, *The Fragile Species* (New York: Simon and Schuster, 1996), 34-7.

45 Johan Huizinga, *Homo Ludens* (New York: Routledge, 2008), 9.

46 Joe Nocera, "Here's How to Pay Up Now," *New York Times Magazine,* January, 1, 2012, 30-35.

47 Katie Thomas, "College Teams, Relying on Deception, Undermine Gender Equity," *New York Times,* April 26, 2011, 1

48 Andrei Markovits and Steven Hellerman, *Offside: Soccer and American Exceptionalism* (Princeton: Princeton University Press, 2001).

49 Eve Fairbanks, "Overtime in Soccer City," *New York Times Magazine,* July 24, 2011, 15. The 1995 World Cup in rugby attracted less international attention, but it was a crucial moment for racial relations in South Africa. Nelson Mandela embraced the mostly white team by donning their green and gold jersey and attending its world championship victory. Ian Thompson, "Rugby: South Africa Ascends World Stage," *New York Times,* May 26, 1995, B9.

50 John Dewey, *Art as Experience* (New York: Capricorn Books, 1958), 10.

51 Ben Shahn, *The Shape of Content* (Cambridge: Harvard University Press), 1992, 54.

52 Interview with Tom F. Driver, in Deirdre Bair, *Samuel Beckett: A Biography* (New York: Simon and Schuster, 1990), chap. 21.

53 Edwin Schlossberg, *Interactive Excellence: Defining and Developing New Standards for the Twenty-First Century* (New York: Ballantine Books, 1998), 9; for interactive museums and exhibitions, see Elizabeth Ellsworth, *Places of Learning: Media, Architecture, Pedagogy* (New York: Routledge, 2005), 131-49.

54 Walter Benjamin, *Illuminations: Essays and Reflections* (New York: Schocken Books, 1969), 223.

55 Henry James, *The Tragic Muse* (London: British Library, 2011).

56 Emil Durkheim, *Moral Education* (New York: Free Press, 1961), 273.

57 Robert Gordis, "The Vision of Micah," in *Judaism and Human Rights*, ed. Milton Konvitz (New Brunswick: Rutgers University Press, 2001), 285.

58 Johann Goethe, *Maxims and Reflections* quoted in Walter Kaufmann, *From Shakespeare to Existentialism* (New York: Anchor Books, 1959), 54.

59 Plato, *Republic*, 396.

60 Joseph Conrad, *The Nigger of Narcissus* (New York: Hard Press, 2006), Preface.

61 Arthur Koestler, quoted in Michael Kearl, *Endings: A Sociology of Death and Dying* (New York: Oxford University Press, 1989), 214.

62 Northrop Frye, *Educated Imagination* (Bloomington: Indiana University Press, 1964), 64.

63 Martin Esslin, *Theater of the Absurd*, 3rd ed. (New York: Vintage Books, 2004).

64 Samuel Beckett, *Waiting for Godot* (New York: Grove Press, 1954), 40.

65 Christopher Page, *The Christian West and its Singers: The First Thousand Years* (New Haven: Yale University Press, 2011) is an extraordinary tracing of how music evolved in a variety of places in Western Christendom to reach a unity of notation in the eleventh century.

66 John Dewey, *Freedom and Culture* (New York: Prometheus Books, 1989), 10.

67 Lewis Thomas, *Late Night Thoughts on Listening to Mahler's Ninth Symphony* (New York: Penguin Books, 1995), 162-63.

68 Ludwig Wittgenstein, "Wittgenstein Lectures 1930-33" in G.E. Moore, *Philosophical Papers* (London: Routledge, 2010), 59.

69 Bryan Simms, *The Atonal Music of Arnold Schoenberg 1908-1923* (New York: Oxford University Press, 2000).

70   Leonard Bernstein, "Unanswered Questions 1-6: Bernstein Lecture," (DVD); "Omnibus—The Historic TV Broadcasts," (DVD).

71   Cotton Mather, *Magnalia Christi Americana* (Cambridge: Harvard University Press, 1976).

72   Friedrich Nietzsche, *Thus Spoke Zarathustra* (Cambridge: Cambridge University Press, 2006), II.4.

73   Maya Lin, *Boundaries* (New York: Simon and Shuster, 2000); and "Making the Memorial," *New York Review of Books,* Nov. 2, 2000. Ellsworth, *Places of Learning,* 54.

74   "Lest We Forget," *New York Times*, November 11, 2007.

BIBLIOGRAPHY

Adams, Dickinson. *Jefferson's Extracts from the Gospels*. Princeton: Princeton University Press, 1983.

Adams, John. *The Works of John Adams*. Boston: Little, Brown and Company, 1956.

Ali, P.S. *Human Rights in Islam*. Lahore: Aziz Publishers, 1980.

Amnesty International. *United States of America: Rights for All*. London: Amnesty International UK, 1998.

Appiah, Kwame. *Cosmopolitanism: Ethics in a World of Strangers*. New York: W.W. Norton, 2007.

Archard, David. *Children, Rights and Childhood*. New York: Routledge, 2004.

Arciniegas, German. *America in Europe: History of the New World in Reverse*. San Diego: Harcourt, Brace, 1998.

Arendt, Hannah. *On Revolution*. New York: Viking, 1963.

Ariès, Philippe. *Centuries of Childhood: A Social History of Family Life*. New York: Vintage Books, 1965.

Armstrong, Regis. *Saint Francis of Assisi: Writings for a Gospel Life*. New York: Hyperion, 1996.

Arnold, Matthew. *Culture and Anarchy*. New York: Oxford University Press, 2009.

Augustine of Hippo. *Concerning the City of God*. Baltimore: Penguin Books, 1972.

—. *On True Religion*. Chicago: Regnery, 1991.

Aurelius, Marcus. *The Meditations of the Emperor Marcus Aurelius Antonius*. London: Collins, 1908.

Axtell, James. *The Educational Writings of John Locke*. Cambridge: Cambridge University Press, 1968.

Bacon, Francis. *The New Organon*. Cambridge: Cambridge University Press, 2008.

Baier, Annette. *A Progress of Sentiments*. Cambridge: Harvard University Press, 1991.

—. *Moral Prejudices*. Cambridge: Harvard University Press, 1994.

Bailyn, Bernard. *Pamphlets of the American Revolution 1750-1776*. Cambridge: Harvard University Press, 1965.

—. *The Origins of American Politics*. New York: Vintage Books, 1968.

Bakan, David. *Slaughter of the Innocents*. Boston: Beacon Press, 1972.

Bauer, Joanne and Daniel Bell, eds. *The East Asian Challenge for Human Rights*. Cambridge: Cambridge University Press, 1999.

Beah, Ismael. *A Long Way Gone: Memoirs of a Boy Soldier*. New York: Farrar, Straus and Giroux, 2007.

Beckett, Samuel. *Waiting for Godot*. New York: Grove Press, 1954.

Benjamin, Walter. *Illuminations: Essays and Reflections*. New York: Schocken, 1969.

Bentham, Jeremy. *An Introduction to the Principles of Morals and Legislation*. New York: Oxford University Press, 1970.

Berlin, Isaiah. *Four Essays on Liberty*. New York: Oxford University Press, 1969.

Berry, Wendell. *Standing by Words*. San Francisco: North Point, 1983.

Boas, Franz. *A Franz Boas Reader*. Edited by George Stocking, Jr. Chicago: University of Chicago Press, 1974. Borgwardt, Elizabeth. *A New Deal for the World: America's Vision for Human Rights*. Cambridge: Harvard University Press, 2005.

Boucher, David. *The Limits of Ethics in International Relations: Natural Law, Natural Rights and Human Rights in Transition*. New York: Oxford University Press, 2009.

Bradford, William. *Of Plymouth Plantation 1620-1647*. New York: Knopf, 1952.

Brown, Chris. "Universal Rights: A Critique," in *Human Rights in Global Politics*. Edited by Tim Dunne and Nicholas Wheeler. Cambridge: Cambridge University Press, 1999, 103-27.

Brown, Peter. *Augustine of Hippo*. Berkeley: University of California Press, 2000.

Buber, Martin. *Two Types of Faith*. New York: Harper, 1961.

Bunker, Nick. *Making Haste from Babylon: The Mayflower Pilgrims and their World*. New York: Knopf, 2010.

Burke, Edmund. *Reflections on the Revolution in France.* New York: Oxford University Press, 2009.

Carson, Rachel. *Silent Spring.* Boston: Houghton, Mifflin, 1962.

Chaibong, Hahm. "Confucianism and Western Rights," *The Responsive Community.* Winter, 1999, 50-58.

Chesterton, G.K. *Orthodoxy.* Garden City: Image Books, 1959.

—. *Saint Francis of Assisi.* Garden City: Image Books, 1959.

Cicero. *The Republic* and *The Laws.* New York: Oxford University Press, 1998.

Clapham, Andrew. *Human Rights: A Very Short Introduction.* New York: Oxford University Press, 2007.

Cohen, Arthur. *The Myth of Judeo-Christian Tradition.* New York: Schocken, 1971.

Collingwood, R.G. *The Idea of Nature.* New York: Oxford University Press, 1960.

Coontz, Stephanie. *A Strange Stirring: The Feminine Mystique at the Dawn of the 1960s.* New York: Basic Books, 2011.

Copernicus, Nicolaus. *On the Revolution of Heavenly Spheres.* New York: Prometheus, 1995.

Cott, Nancy. *The Bonds of Motherhood:"Woman's Sphere" in New England 1780-1835.* New Haven: Yale University Press, 1977.

—. *The Grounding of Modern Feminism.* New Haven: Yale University Press, 1987.

Cranston, Maurice. *What Are Human Rights?* New York: Basic Books, 1962.

—. *The Solitary Self: Jean-Jacques Rousseau in Exile and Adversity.* Chicago: University of Chicago Press, 1997.

Dewey, John. *Art as Experience.* New York: Capricorn, 1958.

Douglass, Frederick. *Autobiographies.* New York: Library of America, 1994.

Douzinas, Costas. *The End of Human Rights: Critical Legal Thought at the Turn of the Century.* Oxford: Hart Publishing, 2000.

Doyle, William. *The Oxford History of the French Revolution.* New York: Oxford University Press, 2002.

Dunne, Tim and Nicholas Wheeler, eds. *Human Rights in Global Politics.* Cambridge: Cambridge University Press, 1999.

Dworkin, Ronald. *Taking Rights Seriously.* Cambridge: Harvard University Press, 1976.

—. *Life's Dominion.* New York: Knopf, 1993.

Ehrenreich, Barbara and Deirdre English. *For Her Own Good: Two Centuries of the Experts' Advice to Women.* New York: Anchor Books, 2005.

Engels, Friedrich. *The Origin of the Family, Private Property and the State.* New York: Penguin Books, 1972.

Engle, Karen. "From Skepticism to Embrace: Human Rights and the American Anthropological Association from 1947 to 1999." *Human Rights Quarterly,* 23(August, 20001): 536-59.

Epictetus. *Enchiridion.* New York: Dover Books, 2004.

Evans, Tony, ed. *Human Rights 50 Years On.* New York: St. Martin's Press, 1998.

Faludi, Susan. *Backlash: The Undeclared War against American Women.* New York: Crown, 1991.

Finkielkraut, Alain. *The Defeat of the Mind.* New York: Columbia University Press, 1995.

Friedan, Betty. *The Feminine Mystique.* New York: Dell, 1964.

—. *It Changed My Life: Writings in the Women's Movement.* New York: Dell, 1976.

Furet, Francois. *Interpreting the French Revolution.* Cambridge: Cambridge University Press, 1982.

Gadamer, Hans. *Truth and Method.* New York: Crossroad, 1982.

Gilligan, Carol. *In a Different Voice: Psychological Theory and Women's Development.* Cambridge: Harvard University Press, 1982.

Glendon, Mary Ann. *A World Made New: Eleanor Roosevelt and the Universal Declaration of Human Rights.* New York: Random House, 2001.

Gopnik, Alison. *The Philosophical Baby: What Children's Minds Tell Us about Truth, Love and the Meaning of Life.* New York: Farrar, Straus and Giroux, 2009.

Gratian. *The Treaty on Laws with the Ordinary Gloss.* Washington: Catholic University of America Press, 1993.

Graubard, Allen. *Free the Children: Radical Reform and the Free School Movement.* New York: Pantheon, 1972.

Grotius, Hugo. *The Rights of War and Peace.* Indianapolis: Liberty Fund, 2005.

Haakonssen, Knud. *Natural Law and Moral Philosophy: From Grotius to the Scottish Enlightenment.* Cambridge: Cambridge University Press, 1996.

Habermas, Jürgen. *The Divided West.* Malden: Polity Press, 2006.

Hamburger, Philip. *Separation of Church and State*. Cambridge: Harvard University Press, 2004.

Hamilton, Alexander, James Madison and John Jay. *The Federalist Papers*. New York: Oxford University Press, 2008.

Hareven, Tamara and Rudolph Langenbach. *Amoskeag: Life and Work in an American Factory City*. Lebanon: University Press of New England, 1995.

Harrison, Peter. *"Religion" and the Religions in the English Enlightenment*. Cambridge: Cambridge University Press, 1990.

Haskell, Thomas. "The Curious Persistence of Rights Talk in the 'Age of Interpretation,'" *Journal of American History*, 74(1987): 984-1012.

Hatch, Nathan. *The Sacred Cause of Liberty: Republican Thought and the Millennium in Revolutionary New England*. New Haven: Yale University Press, 1977.

Hathaway, Ronald. *Hierarchy and the Definition of Order in the Letters of Pseudo-Dionysius*. The Hague: Nijhoff, 1969.

Herbert, Edward. *De Religione Laici*. New Haven: Yale University Press, 1944.

Hibbert, Christopher. *The Days of the French Revolution*. New York: William Morrow, 1980.

Hilderbrand, Robert. *Dumbarton Oaks: The Origin of the United Nations and the Search for Postwar Security*. Chapel Hill: University of North Carolina Press, 1990.

Hobbes, Thomas. *Leviathan*. Baltimore: Penguin Books, 1968.

—. *The Elements of Law, Natural and Politic*. New York: Oxford University Press, 1999.

Holt, John. *Escape from Childhood*. New York: Penguin Books, 1975.

Hoopes, Townsend and Douglas Brinkley. *FDR and the Creation of the United Nations*. New Haven: Yale University Press, 1997.

Hubbard, Ruth. *The Politics of Women's Biology*. New Brunswick: Rutgers University Press, 1990.

Hull, John. *New Directions in Religious Education*. London: Falmer, 1982.

Hume, David. *Essays, Moral, Political and Literary*. New York: Oxford University Press, 1963.

—. *An Enquiry Concerning Human Understanding*. New York: Oxford University Press, 2007.

Hunt, Lynn. *The French Revolution and Human Rights: A Brief Documentary History*. New York: St. Martin's Press, 1996.

—. *Inventing Human Rights: A History*. New York: W.W. Norton, 2008.

Ignatieff, Michael. *Human Rights as Politics and Idolatry*. Princeton: Princeton University Press, 2001.

Iqbal, Mohammad. *The Reconstruction of the Religious Thought in Islam*. Lahore: Institute of Islamic Culture, 1986.

Jackson, Robert. *Rethinking Religious Education and Plurality*. London: Routledge and Kegan Paul, 2004.

Jefferson, Thomas. *Writings of Thomas Jefferson*. Edited by Albert Bergh. Washington: Thomas Jefferson Memorial Association, 1907.

Jordan, Winthrop. "Familial Politics: Thomas Paine and the Killing of the King, 1776," *Journal of American History,* 60(1973): 294-308.

Kant, Immanuel. *On History*. New York: Macmillan, 1963.

Khan, Muhammad Zafrulla. *Islam and Human Rights*. Tilford: Islamic International Publications, 1967.

Konvitz, Martin, ed. *Judaism and Human Rights*. New Brunswick: Rutgers University Press, 2001.

Korey, William. *NGOs and the Universal Declaration of Human Rights: A Curious Grapevine*. New York: St. Martin's Press, 1998.

Kropotkin, Peter. *Mutual Aid*. Boston: Extending Horizons Books, 1955.

Kübler-Ross, Elisabeth. *On Death and Dying*. New York: Macmillan, 1970.

Kuhn, Maggie and Dieter Hessel. *Maggie Kuhn on Aging: A Dialogue*. Louisville: John Knox, 1977.

Lacey, Alan and Knud Haakonssen, eds. *A Culture of Rights*. Cambridge: Cambridge University Press, 1991.

Las Casas, Bartolomé de. *Witness: The Writings of Bartolomé de las Casas*. Edited by George Sanderlin. New York: Orbis Books, 1993.

Lash, Nicholas. *The Beginning and End of Religion*. Cambridge: Cambridge University Press, 1996.

Lawson, George. *Negotiated Revolutions: The Czech Republic, South Africa and Chile*. Burlington: Ashgate, 2005.

Leopold, Aldo. *A Sand County Almanac*. New York: Oxford University Press, 1949.

Lerner, Natan. *Religion, Beliefs and International Human Rights*. New York: Orbis Books, 2000.

Levenson, Jon. *Inheriting Abraham: The Legacy of the Patriarch in Judaism, Christianity and Islam*. Princeton: Princeton University Press, 2012.

Levine, Amy-Jill and Marc Brettler. *The Jewish Annotated New Testament*. New York: Oxford University Press, 2011.

Lewis, C.S. *The Abolition of Man*. New York: Harper, 2001.

Leys, Simon. *The Analects of Confucius*. New York: W.W. Norton, 1997.

Lin, Maya. *Boundaries*. New York: Simon and Schuster, 2000.

Lincoln, Abraham. *Speeches and Writings*. Edited by Don Fehrenbacher. New York: Library of America, 1989.

Locke, John. *The Second Treatise on Civil Government*. New York: Prometheus, 1986.

—. *Some Thoughts Concerning Education*. New York: General Books, 2010.

Lovelock, James. *Gaia: A New Look at Life on Earth*. New York: Oxford University Press, 2000.

Luker, Kristin. *Abortion and the Politics of Motherhood*. Berkeley: University of California Press, 1984.

Lynch, William. *Images of Hope: Imagination as Healer of the Helpless*. Notre Dame: University of Notre Dame Press, 1990.

MacIver, R.M., ed. *Great Expressions of Human Rights*. New York: Harper and Brothers, 1950.

McGerr, Michael. *A Fierce Discontent: The Rise and Fall of the Progressive Movement in America 1870-1920*. New York: Oxford University Press, 2005.

McIntyre, Alasdair. *After Virtue: A Study in Moral Theory*. Notre Dame: University of Notre Dame Press, 1984.

—. *Dependent Rational Animals: Why Human Beings Need the Virtues*. Chicago: Open Court, 1999.

Maier, Pauline. *American Scripture: Making the Declaration of Independence*. New York: Knopf, 1997.

Malik, Habib, ed. *The Challenge of Human Rights: Charles Malik and the Universal Declaration*. Oxford: Center for Lebanese Studies, 2000.

Margalit, Avishai. *The Decent Society*. Cambridge: Harvard University Press, 1998.

Maritain, Jacques. "Introduction" in UNESCO, *Human Rights: Comments and Interpretations*. Westport: Greenwood, 1949.

Martin, Jane Roland. *Reclaiming a Conversation: The Ideal of the Educated Woman*. New Haven: Yale University Press, 1987.

Marx, Karl. "On the Jewish Question," *Early Texts*. Oxford: Blackwell, 1971.

May, William. *The Physician's Covenant*. Philadelphia: Westminster/John Knox, 1983.

Medawar, P.B. *Uniqueness of the Individual*. New York: Dove Publications, 1981.

Mertus, Julie. *The United Nations and Human Rights*. New York: Routledge, 2005.

Midgley, Mary. *Beast and Man: The Roots of Human Nature*. Ithaca: Cornell University Press, 1978.

Miles, Rosalind. *The Women's History of the World*. Topsfield: Salem House, 1988.

Mill, John Stuart. *Utilitarianism*. New York: Penguin Books, 1962.

—. *On Liberty*. New York: W.W. Norton, 1975.

Miller, Jean Baker. *Toward a New Psychology of Women*. Boston: Beacon Press, 1987.

Minow, Martha. *Between Vengeance and Forgiveness*. Boston: Beacon Press, 1999.

Montesquieu, Charles de. *The Spirit of Laws*. Berkeley: University of California Press, 1977.

Moran, Gabriel. *Uniqueness: Problem or Paradox in Jewish and Christian Traditions*. New York: Orbis Books, 1992.

Morgan, Edmund. *Inventing the People*. New York: W.W. Norton, 1988.

Moyn, Samuel. *The Last Utopia: Human Rights in History*. Cambridge: Harvard University Press, 2010.

Nardin, Terry and David Mapel, eds. *Traditions of International Ethics*. Cambridge: Cambridge University Press, 1992.

Nash, Roderick. *The Rights of Nature: A History of Environmental Ethics*. Madison: University of Wisconsin Press, 1989.

Neill, A.S. and Erich Fromm. *Summerhill: A Radical Approach to Child Rearing*. Oxford: Hart, 1960.

Nickel, James. *Making Sense of Human Rights: Philosophical Reflection on the Universal Declaration of Human Rights*. Berkeley: University of California Press, 2007.

Nietzsche, Friedrich. *Beyond Good and Evil*. Edited by R.J. Hollingdale. New York: Penguin Books, 1973.

Nordhaus, Ted and Michael Shellenberger. *Breakthrough: From the Death of Environmentalism to the Politics of Possibility*. Boston: Houghton Mifflin, 2007.

Nuland, Sherwin. *How We Die: Reflections on Life's Final Chapter*. New York: Vintage Books, 1995.

Nussbaum, Martha. *Sex and Social Justice*. New York: Oxford University Press, 2000.

Oakshott, Michael. *Rationalism in Politics and Other Essays*. New York: Barnes and Noble, 1962.

Okin, Susan Moller, Joshua Cohen and Martha Nussbaum, eds. *Is Multiculturalism Bad for Women?* Princeton: Princeton University Press, 1999.

Orentlicher, Diane. "Relativism and Religion," in Michael Ignatieff, *Human Rights as Politics and Idolatry*. Princeton: Princeton University Press, 2001, 141-58.

Ovitt, George. *The Restoration of Perfection.* New Brunswick: Rutgers University Press, 1986.

Paine, Thomas. *Common Sense, the Right of Man and Other Essential Writings of Thomas Paine.* New York: Signet Books, 2003.

Pennock, J. Roland and John Chapman, eds. *Human Rights.* New York: New York University Press, 1981.

Pestalozzi, Johann. *How Gertrude Teaches Her Children.* Ann Arbor: University of Michigan Press, 2009.

Piaget, Jean. *The Moral Judgment of the Child.* New York: Free Press, 1966.

Pico della Mirandella, Giovanni. *Oration on the Dignity of Man.* Indianapolis: Hackett, 1998.

Plato, *Collected Works.* Edited by Benjamin Jowett. New York: Oxford University Press, 1953.

Plotinus. *The Enneads.* London: Faber and Faber, 1969.

Postman, Neil. *The Disappearance of Childhood.* New York: Vintage Books, 1994.

Powell, J.G.F., ed. *Cicero the Philosopher.* New York: Oxford University Press, 1999.

Power, Jonathan. *Like Water on Stone: The Story of Amnesty International.* New York: Penguin Books, 2001.

Radhakrishnan. *Hindu View of Life.* New York: Harper and Collins, 2009.

Rahner, Karl. "Christianity and Non-Christian Religions," *Theological Investigations*. Vol. 5. Baltimore Helicon, 1960, 115-34.

Rakove, Jack, ed. *Declaring Rights: A Brief Documentary History.* New York: Palgrave, 1997.

Rawls, John. *A Theory of Justice.* Cambridge: Harvard University Press, 2005.

Raz, Joseph. *The Morality of Freedom.* New York: Clarendon Press, 1986.

Reader, W.J. *Professional Men: The Rise of the Professional Classes in Nineteenth-Century England.* London: Weidenfeld and Nicholson, 1966.

Redding, J. Saunders. *They Came in Chains*. Philadelphia: Lippincott, 1973.

Regan, Tom. *The Case for Animal Rights*. Berkeley: University of California Press, 2004.

Riley-Smith, Jonathan. *The Crusades, Christianity and Islam*. New York: Columbia University Press, 2008.

Rist, John. *Plotinus: Road to Reality*. Cambridge: Cambridge University Press, 1980.

—. *Augustine: Ancient Thought Baptized*. Cambridge: Cambridge University Press, 1996.

Robinson, Mary. *A Voice for Human Rights*. Philadelphia: University of Pennsylvania Press, 2005.

Rorty, Richard. *Contingency, Irony and Solidarity*. Cambridge: Cambridge University Press, 1989.

—. "Human Rights, Rationality and Sentimentality," in *Truth and Progress*. Cambridge: Cambridge University Press, 1998, 167-85.

Rossi, Alice. "A Biosocial Perspective on Parenting," *Daedalus*, 106(1977): 1-31.

Rothman, Sheila. *Woman's Proper Place: A History of Changing Ideals and Practices 1870 to the Present*. New York: Basic Books, 1980.

Rousseau, Jean-Jacques. *The Social Contract*. New York: Washington Square, 1967.

—. *Emile*. New York: Basic Books, 1979.

Roy, Olivier. *Secularism Confronts Islam*. New York: Columbia University Press, 2009.

Ruddick, Sara. *Maternal Thinking: Toward a Politics of Peace*. Boston: Beacon Press, 1995.

Salt, Henry. *Animal Rights Considered in Relation to Social Progress*. New York: Macmillan, 1894.

Sands, Philippe. *Lawless World: America and the Making and Breaking of Global Rules from FDR's Atlantic Charter to George W. Bush's Illegal War*. New York: Viking, 2005.

Schlesinger, Stephen. *Act of Creation: The Founding of the United Nations*. New York: Basic Books, 2003.

Schlossberg, Edwin. *Interactive Excellence: Defining and Developing New Standards for the 21st Century*. New York: Ballantine Books, 1998.

Schulz, William. *In Our Own Best Interests: How Defending Human Rights Benefits Us All*. Boston: Beacon Press, 2002.

Scott, Joan. *Only Paradoxes to Offer: French Feminists and the Rights of Man.* Cambridge: Harvard University Press, 1997.

Sen, Amartya. *The Idea of Justice.* Cambridge: Harvard University Press, 2009.

Shue, Henry. *Basic Rights.* Princeton: Princeton University Press, 1996.

Shute, Sephen and Susan Hurley, eds. *On Human Rights.* New York: Basic Books, 1993.

Singer, Peter. *Practical Ethics.* Cambridge: Cambridge University Press, 1993.

—. "Ethics across the Species Boundary," in *Global Ethics and the Environment.* Edited by Nicholas Low. London: Routledge, 1999, 146-57.

Sklar, Kathryn. *Catherine Beecher: A Study in American Domesticity.* New Haven: Yale University Press, 1973.

Smith, Christian. *American Evangelicalism: Embattled and Thriving.* Chicago: University of Chicago Press, 1998.

Sorrell, Roger. *Saint Francis of Assisi and Nature.* New York: Oxford University Press, 1988.

Stammers, Neil. *Human Rights and Social Movements.* New York: Pluto Press, 2009.

Stein, Janice and others. *Uneasy Partners: Multiculturalism and Rights in Canada.* Waterloo: Wilfred Laurier University, 2007.

Taylor, Telford. *The Anatomy of the Nuremberg Trials.* New York: Knopf, 1992.

Teitel, Ruth. *Humanity's Law.* New York: Oxford University Press, 2011.

Thomas Aquinas, *Summa Theologica.* New York: McGraw Hill, 1966.

—. *Summa Contra Gentiles.* Notre Dame: University of Notre Dame Press, 1976.

Tierney, Brian. *The Idea of Natural Rights.* Grand Rapids: William B. Eerdmans, 1997.

Tocqueville, Alexis de. *Democracy in America.* New York: Penguin Books, 2003.

Tylor, Edward. *Primitive Culture.* Ithaca: Cornell University Press, 2009.

Vitoria, Francisco de. *Political Writings.* Edited by Anthony Pagden and Jeremy Lawrence. Cambridge: Cambridge University Press, 1991.

Waldron, Jeremy. *Nonsense upon Stilts.* London: Methuen, 1987.

Waller, Willard. *The Sociology of Teaching.* New York: Russell and Russell, 1932.

Washington, James Melvin, ed. *A Testament of Hope: The Essential Writings and Speeches of Martin Luther King, Jr.* San Francisco: Harper, 1991.

Watson, John. *The Psychological Care of Infant and Child.* New York: W.W. Norton, 1928.

Wertheim, Margaret. *Pythagoras' Trousers: God, Physics and the Gender War.* New York: W.W. Norton, 1997.

Whitbeck, Carolyn. "Theories of Sex Difference," in *Women and Philosophy.* Edited by Carol Gould. New York: Putnam Sons, 1976.

White, Lynn, Jr. "The Historical Roots of our Ecological Crisis," *Science* 155(March, 1967), 1203-1207.

Whitehead, Alfred North. *The Aims of Education.* New York: Free Press, 1929.

Whitman, Walt. *Democratic Vistas.* Charleston: Forgotten Books, 2009.

Whitworth, Sandra. *Feminism and International Relations: Toward a Political Economy of Gender in Interstate and Non-Governmental Institutions.* New York: Palgrave, 1994.

Williams, Raymond. *Keywords: A Vocabulary of Culture and Society.* New York: Oxford University Press, 1976.

Wills, Garry. *St. Augustine.* New York: Viking, 1999.

Wishy, Bernard. *The Child and the Republic: The Dawn of Modern American Child Nurture.* Philadelphia: University of Pennsylvania, 1968.

Wolgast, Elizabeth. *Equality and the Rights of Women.* Ithaca: Cornell University Press, 1980.

Wollstonecraft, Mary. *A Vindication of the Rights of Woman.* Cambridge: Cambridge University Press, 2010.